My Second Initiation

To my late mother Nontando Glenrose Pikoli
who taught me the correct values in life.

And my uncle Zolisa Sipoyo
who inspired me to struggle for my people.

My Second Initiation

The Memoir of Vusi Pikoli

Vusi Pikoli
&
Mandy Wiener

PICADOR AFRICA

First published in 2013 by Picador Africa
an imprint of Pan Macmillan South Africa
Private Bag X19, Northlands
Johannesburg, 2116

www.panmacmillan.co.za

ISBN 978-1-77010-345-0

ePub ISBN 978-1-77010-346-7

Editing by Sean Fraser
Proofreading by Lisa Compton
Design and typesetting by Triple M Design, Johannesburg
Cover design by K4
Front cover photograph by Lisa Skinner

Printed and bound by Ultra Litho (Pty) Ltd

The meetings, interactions and events described in this book are in the public domain in one form or another – via sources ranging from affidavits and official inquiries to media coverage and opinion pieces. Webber Wentzel and other senior counsel are gratefully acknowledged by the publisher and authors for their advisory role in this regard. Every effort has been made to ensure the factual accuracy of the contents of this book, but should any errors have occurred, the publisher and authors apologise and would welcome any information that would enable them to amend any mistakes in future editions of the book.

Contents

About this book

Mandy Wiener

As a radio news journalist, I reported on the events that led to Advocate Vusi Pikoli's suspension in 2007 and also covered the subsequent Ginwala Inquiry. I came to know Pikoli fairly well over the years and developed a professional respect for him. I have come to believe that he is deeply principled, his approach ethical and his position morally sound.

It has been said that the media had a predetermined position on its approach to reporting on Pikoli's suspension and that regardless of what President Thabo Mbeki told the nation, he would not be believed. It has also been suggested that journalists were adamant that Pikoli was suspended in order to stop the prosecution of Jackie Selebi and that government's reasons put forward at the Ginwala Inquiry were mere 'afterthoughts'.

I can speak only for myself in response to this – I endeavoured at all times to report the story in a balanced manner and to remain true to the guidelines of objective reporting. Any opinion that I may have presented was developed on the basis of evidence presented by the legal teams to the inquiry and what I deduced from the knowledge at my disposal. Perhaps if Mbeki had taken the nation into his confidence from the outset, my informed position may have been altered.

Dr Frene Ginwala made positive findings about Vusi Pikoli's character and these were, in effect, acknowledged by government in its out-of-court settlement with him. It was determined that he is a man of unquestionable integrity and I, too, believe this to be true. In all the time that I have known him, Pikoli has not given me cause to doubt his integrity.

When Pikoli approached me to write this book in 2012, I did not hesitate to take on the project. His story is profoundly important and it is one that can only better inform the South African understanding of our history and our future. It speaks to the critical principles of prosecutorial independence and constitutional democracy.

Over the intense period of writing this book, I have come to realise that Vusi Pikoli, like all of us, has his flaws. I have learned first-hand those traits that are likely to have infuriated those who sought to have him suspended. He is fiercely independent, stubbornly single-minded and has what some critics may term 'an overdeveloped sense of justice'. By his own admission, he is also far too trusting and naïve. As a result, I believe I have presented as round a picture of his character as possible.

It is important to clarify from the outset that this is not a work of objective, critical, investigative journalism. It is the story of one man as told from his perspective, with his subjective opinions and his assumptions. I am merely the storyteller, the conduit for this version of the truth. I have interrogated Pikoli and his recollection of events to the best of my abilities, and in all instances possible, I have endeavoured to corroborate his accounts. However, I have not actively sought out critical commentary or responses to his assertions.

Pikoli could have written this book himself, but as he explained to me at the start, he wanted an enquiring eye to be cast on his story. I believe that, in itself, speaks to the credibility of the man.

Preface

Mandy Wiener

Perched on a ridge south of the centre of Port Elizabeth, a stone's throw from the city's airport, is the Forest Hill Cemetery. It is from here, with the wind inevitably whipping through the grey granite tombstones and a glimpse of the Indian Ocean in the distance, that Vusi Pikoli starts each visit to his beloved hometown. It also marks the beginning of my journey into his past and his life, which has its roots in this friendly coastal city.

Before I can truly begin to know and understand Vusi's story, he insists he must first introduce me to his ancestors and his daughter, who died in 1986 while he was in exile. He tells me they must know who I am when I arrive at his family's home in the nearby township of New Brighton.

Vusi weaves between the graves, navigating around calf-high weeds and loose stones. He stops before a large dark grey slab that bears a double tombstone and an empty decorative cream vase. Engraved on the stone, in capital letters, is his surname PIKOLI and the names of his grandmother NONNIE and daughter SIYALITHATHA. They died within a year of one another and were first buried in a cemetery in Zwide near New Brighton but were later exhumed and reburied here at Forest Hill. A few rows away is his mother's grave. That tombstone carries her name, NONTANDO GLENROSE PIKOLI, and a Bible verse in a teardrop-shaped outline. There's an empty teardrop alongside it, waiting expectantly for Vusi's elderly father.

I stand silently alongside Vusi as he introduces me, aloud and in isiXhosa, to his ancestors and explains why I am here: to tell his story so that others will be better informed and will understand. It is a poignant moment and I am deeply honoured by this rare experience – a gesture that is not only important to Vusi but also one that emphasises his value system and appreciation for those who have influenced and forged him and his outlook.

'It's important for me to have a place to come and visit,' Vusi explains. 'It gives me an opportunity to talk to my grandmother, my mother and my daughter. She died when she was still young, just nine months old. She stayed with us in Lesotho for only seven days before her grandmothers came to pick her up. It's important to come here and to know this is where your loved ones are buried. I talk to them about everything. And I imagine Sandina now, as a 27-year-old had she lived, and of course her name is special to me. Sandina was named after the Sandinista revolution in Nicaragua and General Sandino. Her second name was Siyalithatha – *Siyalithatha ilizwe* – "We are now taking over" – because I was confident when she was born that we would be liberating the country.

'I was certain as far back as 1986 we would be able to honour her even though we couldn't attend her funeral. Only my message was read at the funeral when I explained her names and how hopeful I was that we would come back and liberate this country.'

And does he feel now that he has done her names justice? 'Of course we have honoured her by liberating the country. Firstly, it was our own liberation and also for the generations that will come after us.'

Squinting against the glare of the sun off the ocean, he looks thoughtfully across the windswept landscape that so often brought him stability in times of turbulence. 'When I'm here I feel at peace.'

PART ONE

Initiation, politics and exile

Reawakening the family

Vusumzi – I never thought much about that name when I was growing up, but in later years I began to appreciate just how heavy it is. *Vusa* is 'to wake somebody or something' and *umzi* is 'the family home'. My name has a multitude of meanings: to restore family values, to provide for the family, the expectations of your parents, relatives and siblings. Even the fact that I joined the struggle for national liberation at an early age can be attributed to my name.

I have named one of my sons Vusisizwe, with *isizwe* meaning 'the nation'. There is the natural progression from reawakening the family unit to the nation. His second name is Mzuvukile – when you have succeeded in your task for the family, some say '*Umzi uvukile*', 'Now the home has been revived!'

My full name is Vusumzi Patrick Anthony Pikoli, born in Port Elizabeth on 29 March 1958. I'm told I got the English names from my father's employers. He was a messenger 'boy' from quite an early age right up until he retired, working for the P.W. Harvey firm, which is still in business today. Anthony never made it onto my identity document, and as I grew older and became more politically conscious, I ditched the name Patrick. What have I got to do with the Irish? I am Xhosa, so I should have a Xhosa name.

It is the story of my surname that has really defined me. My surname has a history. It was not supposed to have been Pikoli but Ndumo.

I grew up not knowing my grandfather on my paternal side. I knew both my mother's parents and my father's mother, whose surname was Pikoli. In the African tradition, if a woman falls pregnant while she is still at home, that child takes the surname of the mother's family and even adopts that clan name. My family has always belonged to the clan of amaNgqosini. As a particularly curious youngster, I began asking questions about my grandfather's identity. When I broached the topic with my father he would not discuss this dark secret and I had a sense that he was angry with him.

Before my mother passed away, I once asked her, 'Who is my father's father?' Her response was shrouded in mystery. '*Mntanam, ayithethwa lo nto*,' meaning 'My child, do not talk about that. It is a family secret.' As a *makoti*, a bride who had married into the family, she was bound to keep the family's secrets. All she would tell me was my grandfather's name – Paps Sinandile Ndumo.

I distinctly remember when I returned from the mountain, having undergone the Xhosa cultural rite of passage to becoming a man, and entering the yard of our home there was a man there praising me in full cry, saying '*Nyana kaZalisile, Gaba-Jwarha!*' My father was so angry and I could not understand what was happening. Time passed and it was only later that I realised the man was referring to me by my real clan name *Jwarha, uMtika, Mazaleni, Mayarha, Jotelo, Soga, abantu abahle noba bephethe izikhali*. These are the names of my ancestors, who played a significant role in my clan and who are highly respected. When we have a traditional rite, we pay tribute to those ancestors who are revered. It's the African version of how Abraham, Jacob and Isaac are invoked in the Bible.

Throughout my adolescence and into adulthood, I continued to feel that I was in some way a missing link, removed from my true identity. In African tradition you derive your heritage from your father's side. Traditional rituals carried out when you are sick or marry must be done according to the father's lineage. While my father had been accepted by his mother's ancestors and was protected by them, it was difficult when it came to his children, who did not necessarily enjoy the same protection. If they continued to take that clan name, the entire heritage would be distorted. So it was important for me to know who I was.

Once I confronted my father and asked him to tell me who his father was. All he would say was that my grandfather had died in 1961 and that his name was Paps Sinandile Ndumo. I knew nothing more about him or my heritage and my lack of identity continued to nag at me.

Then, in 2008, I received a phone call from Bonile Jack, a friend I had met at school and played rugby with. Bonile told me that he had been called by the ancestors and that he had a special gift of 'throwing the bones' and interpreting the message that is delivered. He invited me to come and see him. I laughed at him, telling him that I do not believe in such things. At that time, I thought people who made these kinds of claims were liars and, having been in exile, my mind had been opened to politics and science. Despite my convictions, however, I agreed to visit him along with my wife, Girly, not really knowing the reason for the invitation.

Bonile's home is in the northern Johannesburg suburb of Bryanston, with a large yard, a pool and a tennis court. He held ceremonies there where he would sing and dance with fellow traditional healers in a small hut outside the main house. When he threw the bones, he would diagnose problems, much like a Western medical doctor with a stethoscope. Girly and I looked on as he went through the ritual in this neighbourhood favoured by the well off and business executives. It was a surreal setting.

'Your father is outside the family homestead,' Bonile read from the bones. 'I can see him, he is wandering. He does not know who he is. He is isolated.' I was taken aback. Bonile didn't know my story – in fact, few others outside my close circle of friends did. 'For you to know your father's father, you will have to go back to the Eastern Cape,' Bonile explained. It confirmed to me what I had been carrying at the back of my mind all my life.

I have long been sceptical of people who claim to have such a gift. I have since come to realise that, as in any other profession, there are crooks and imposters but there are also those who are genuine. My mother was called by the ancestors, but she refused. Recently my wife also received the calling and underwent her training. There are even politicians who are fully fledged sangomas and senior public servants who have accepted the calling but don't publicly disclose it.

Bonile's words struck me but I did not act immediately.

It was only sometime later, when I was visiting my father's home in Port Elizabeth for a traditional celebration, that I felt the urge to act. In the tradition of *ixhanti*, we place a special pole in the yard of a house and each time we slaughter an animal, the horns of the beast are placed on that pole. It is a respected holy shrine to all the family's ancestors and children are forbidden from playing around it. We give thanks to the ancestors, drink *umqombothi* – traditional beer – and invite the neighbours to celebrate with us. With all of my education, I used to think these things were meant for those who are illiterate. But not any more – cultural practices show who you are and the background that you come from.

One morning, when we woke up in my father's house, Girly turned to me and said that she had had a dream in which somebody was showing her a picture and insisting that she must see this person. I jokingly said to her that the person in the image must be my father's father. While it was initially said in jest, I immediately felt that perhaps it was more serious. I went to a neighbour, Boet Hamlet Mnci, and said to him, 'Please, Boet Hamlet, I am looking for myself.' I went to him because I had heard that one of my aunts had married into the Mnci family and I felt that perhaps he could give me answers. In the Xhosa culture, matters of this nature are kept away from the children, although all the elders in the family would know the true story. Boet Hamlet directed me to the house of Boet Zwayi, the brother who had been married to my late Aunt Buyiswa.

Boet Zwayi revealed to me that my father had only one surviving sibling, an elderly woman who lived in Grahamstown. While my father didn't want to change his surname and clan name, for me it was important for my sons to know who they are. I needed to go and see my aunt in Grahamstown, and my father didn't stop me.

Together with my wife and my elder sister, we drove the winding road from PE. All along the way, I asked myself whether I was doing the right thing. Once we reached the township, we made our way with some assistance from locals to the Xako house. We arrived to find my only surviving aunt gravely ill and on her deathbed. When I introduced myself, she jumped up and sat on the bed, removing her *doek* to reveal a mane of regal white hair.

It was as if she had been waiting a lifetime for that moment. She was vibrant and revitalised and began to tell us about our grandfather. It was a beautiful, poignant meeting.

I went back and told my father that I had met his sister and he responded emotionally. He was angry with his father for being absent in his life and he never knew he had any living siblings. I arranged for the two of them to meet and the reunion was a moving one. After that my dad said to me,

'*Vusi nyana undikhulule*, you have liberated me, you have set me free.' All his life he had called himself according to his mother's clan name but from that day onwards he was a Jwarha! It completed him. I felt that I had fulfilled my responsibility carried by my name, to reawaken my family.

Scout whistles, Jim Reeves and that jersey

As a young boy, my job was to make sure that the brass pipes outside our home were the shiniest in the neighbourhood. My mother was strict about the fact that everybody in the house had to have a task to do. I could not cook because I had older sisters and there was somebody who was paid to do the gardening. So my responsibility was to shine the brass. Every Saturday I had to shine all the pipes outside and all the brass inside. In the township there was a competition to see who would have the best-kept house. We would see who had the best-polished stoep, be it green or red, so I would polish that stoep until it gleamed. We had a well-manicured lawn with the hedges cut precisely for everyone to see. Then we would sit on the stoep and clean our shoes while listening to good jazz, the LPs spinning on the turntables inside.

My family loved music and it always featured prominently in our home life. Music was always played in our house, including choral, classical and gospel. My aunt, who was a champion dancer, lived with us and there were always records spinning on the turntables. I remember I was still at school when the famous blues singer Jim Reeves died. I cried because I used to love his music – as a boy I got emotionally attached to the singers of the times. I would sit and listen to Springbok Radio and the Afrikaans *liedjies* and those who know me can attest to the fact that I can still recount every single word of poems like 'Lui Letta' and 'Muskietejag'.

I grew up in a home that was always full of people. At times, we did not have a place to sleep in our own house because there were so many other people there, some of whom were not even relatives. As full as the house was with people, we never wanted for food. My mother baked cakes, scones and hot-cross buns, but her roast meat and potatoes were a standout. It may explain why people referred to me as *imbishimbishi*, meaning 'a plump person', when I was a chubby little boy.

My mother had a magnetism that attracted others to her. She was soft-spoken and neighbours often came to her for advice and she would mentor them. She was loved by the newlyweds and was a prominent community worker. The only time I ever knew her to be angry was when her father, a senior priest in Langa in Cape Town, died. There was a rumour that he was poisoned because of church rivalries. My grandfather had a personal assistant who would carry his suitcase containing his church garb, including his cassock. It was suspected that the personal assistant was involved in the poisoning of my grandfather because he had access to his clothes. The rumour was that his cassock was laced with poison. There was a succession race within the church and it is said that a rival, who was in a hurry to be the leader of the church, was behind the attack.

One day after my grandfather's death, his personal assistant came to my mother's home and she was so angry that she wanted to throw boiling water over him. She decided instead to use cold water and because he was sitting in her lounge, she pretended to trip – and threw the basin of water over the man. He never returned to her home again.

My mother was a writer, though she never published anything. She loved poetry and acted on stage. Professionally, she started off as a typist for a law firm and by the time she retired she was an instructor at a training centre teaching Home Economics. There were long, lonely days when she was in Durban furthering her studies. At just seven or eight years old, I kept myself busy by listening to Springbok Radio and Afrikaans *liedjies*.

Growing up, I used to think I was the last-born of four siblings, but there turned out to be many more as my father had other children. Now I find myself bringing together my hitherto unknown brothers and sisters and my children ask in bewilderment, 'Dad, who is this one now?' Much to my surprise, in 2009, one found me at the Pick n Pay in New Brighton when she introduced herself as my father's daughter. I'm still looking for two other siblings – I'm told one is in Sebokeng in the Vaal while another is somewhere in England. I'm still attempting to bring the family together as per the virtues of my name.

My relatives always predicted I would grow up to be a lawyer. I was very curious as a young boy and used to challenge everyone in debates. My aunts tell me that my arguments were very convincing and I took everyone to task. I was also a disciplinarian and a stickler for rules. When my sisters prepared bread for me, I always insisted that it be cut precisely and straight. If it wasn't straight, I refused to eat it.

I also went to school before my time. As Africans, we were supposed to enrol when we were seven years old but I was only four when I began. My mother had a friend who was a teacher and she would collect me from crèche and take me to school. At home, they had no idea that I had started school and only discovered this when I passed Sub A. Of course I was never late for class, with my neat bobby socks pulled right up, my shoes shining and navy-blue jersey with its red-and-white collar carefully folded out.

I was still at primary school when Prime Minister Hendrik Verwoerd was killed in 1966. We left classes early that day and we were told that Verwoerd had been killed by a Greek man, Tsafendas. I remember people in the township singing '*Ndakutsafenda ndikubulale*', meaning 'I will stab you and kill you'.

As youngsters, we used to engage in street battles. We divided ourselves into sections according to a cluster of adjoining streets and fight against one other. Our weapons battles escalated from mealie cobs to stones to knives to axes, and then schools would be closed and one could hear us singing this song, '*Ndakutsafenda ndikubulale*', recollecting the stabbing of Verwoerd.

I also recall as young boys secretly going to the beach in Port Elizabeth without permission from our parents. The beaches then were segregated, with different ones for whites and blacks. We would also go to the big community swimming pool in New Brighton, but I never swam and to this day still cannot swim. We would get into trouble when we got home. Our parents knew that we had been to the beach or to the pool because our skin would be so dry that it was nearly white. We came up with the plan of using

Vaseline and rubbed it all over ourselves to hide the dryness. The problem was that by the time the adults got home at five o'clock we were still so shiny that it was an outright giveaway and our secret jaunts were revealed.

I completed my higher primary-school education at Johnson Marwanqa, where I became a Boy Scout and learned many of the values that have guided me throughout my life. It was a practice introduced in black schools at the time and it was normal for kids to be recruited. As a volunteer programme, it was by no means compulsory but it was not unusual for my friends and me to be involved. One of my uncles was the Chief Scout in Cape Town and it was something that was always part of my life. I learned about how Scouts smile and whistle under all difficulties. I promised to do my best and to do my duty to God and my country. A Scout is a friend to all, a Scout is clean, thrifty and honest. We were taught to be useful members of the community, to help other people at all times. We were taught empathy, self-reliance, and that cleanliness is next to godliness.

I attended a church that started off as the black wing of the Anglican Church, though our founding priests came from the Methodist Church, and I became a server. We wore white surplices and red cassocks and walked in the procession with the priests. My mother and father were highly religious and instilled these values in me – not to lie, not to steal, to love people, to be considerate, to be an upright child who is honest and who loves the Church. As a result, I have always operated from the premise that you are a good person, unless you show yourself not to be. I have no reason not to trust another human being, because I believe that we are all created in the image of God. In fact, I have often been accused of being too trusting. I have always lived my life by these principles, taught to me as a young boy in New Brighton.

However, I can't deny that I had a terrible temper growing up and that I never ran away from a fight. When kids teased me about my stammer, when a word would not come out, I cried and they laughed. I first became aware of my stutter in Standard Three and I don't recall it ever being a problem before. There would be times when I became so frustrated and impatient that I would slap and kick children who were mocking me. In time my speech impediment improved but on occasion I still have a stammer. People rarely notice it any more, unless I become extremely angry.

Once, when I was just seven or eight years old, I stabbed a girl between her eyes with a fork when she made me angry. She had come over to our house and found me crying while I was eating a meal. She wanted to know why I was upset and I became so enraged at her question that I attacked her with my fork. She still has those scars today and that's something I am not proud of.

At St John's College in Mthatha (then Umtata) in the Transkei, where I finished my schooling, I was also known for my willingness to throw a punch. When a boy was chasing another with a knife, I stepped in. Then he charged me with his knife, so I took out my own. We were separated but I wanted to finish what had been started. Late at night in the boys' hostel, a fist-fight was arranged and the whole school came to watch. We fought and fought until my opponent finally gave up. Similarly at Fort Hare University, word quickly went round that there was a guy from Port Elizabeth who did not hesitate to use his fists. I instantly got respect and recognition.

Once, an Afrikaans teacher wanted to beat me for something I did not do and I refused to take the punishment. He stood up, walked towards me and warned, 'I am going to hit you.' We stood face to face, and I answered, 'You are not going to do that, Meneer.' My father, a strict disciplinarian, was informed about the showdown. I told him that nobody would beat me for something I did not do without me retaliating. I believed that people should accept the consequences of their actions, but also that they should not be punished for something they did not do. I have always carried this sense of justice and injustice.

My tendency to be quick to rage followed me for much of my life and I often had to keep my temper in check. While I was the director-general of justice, in 2003, I got into a punch-up with some fellows at the Menlyn shopping centre over some innocuous incident. I felt that my temper really embarrassed my wife and children, and decided that I needed to take action to be able to control it. I attended anger management counselling sessions for some time after that.

But it wasn't only my temper that I was known for as a young man. Growing up my nickname or street name was Njiva. I don't know how or when I got that moniker but it stuck with me and it even featured in my official Security Police file. Njiva is a reference to someone who is stylishly dressed. Some translate it as a jacket or a tie, or the bowtie you wear when you go to church on a Sunday. As a youngster, I always wore a tie to church. The word has different meanings to different people. Guys in the Mdantsane township say '*ukubamba injiva*', which means 'to rob a person', but that was never a translation I associated with my street name.

Not only was I slick, I also considered myself quite the charmer. I was the official love-letter writer for all my friends when they had to pen sweet words to their girls. I met my angel, my wife Girly, in 1972, when I was in Form 2 and she was in Form 1. I was in class and it was raining. I saw a girl passing by in the downpour. She was wearing her school uniform but her jersey was the wrong colour. She stood out from the crowd. There was also something about her walk, her arms swinging freely, that made her appear different from the other girls in the school. I anxiously asked a friend who was in her class who she was and I was told her name was 'Girls' and she was 'from Veeplaas'. I was adamant that I needed to talk to her. I told her then, in the schoolyard in 1972, that she would be my wife. She laughed at me.

Being politicised

A concrete bridge marks the main entrance into the township of New Brighton. It stretches across the railway tracks. That is how you know that you are entering an apartheid-era township, when you cross the railway line. Covered with faded, spray-painted slogans in varying degrees of legibility, the bridge is an unofficial testament to the rich political history of the area. Since the 1960s, political slogans have been painted onto this bridge, declaring allegiances and advocating ideologies. The officials have tried in vain to scrub them off but they have never really succeeded.

To this day, you can still see etched on the grey blocks the name of a Transkei leader. And barely visible on one side of the bridge is a reference to the Pan-Africanist Congress (PAC) and its armed wing Poqo, reminiscent of its once strong and active presence in the area. I recall that when people talked to you and the conversation became political, they would respond by saying, 'Don't talk Poqo here' – don't talk about politics. The bridge bears its own history and played its own role in the resistance.

The Eastern Cape has always been the engine of our revolution. The area is steeped in politics and has a rich history of resistance. It has produced many political leaders, including the likes of Govan Mbeki and Raymond Mhlaba who worked as organisers in this region. Here in New Brighton in the 1960s, the ANC would hold rallies mobilising people. I remember the tanks rolling down the streets and the *boers* cutting down all the trees because they felt that guerrillas would use them as camouflage from which to stage attacks on the police. They would take paraffin from our homes and anything that could be fashioned into a weapon. I was young but the memories are clear and indelible.

Driving through the streets of New Brighton today, familiar landmarks still trigger memories of our resistance against apartheid and the rich culture of politics. On a busy corner of Mendi Road, the main artery through the township, there is a petrol station teeming with taxis. The old Bantu Affairs Administration Board stood here, along with the rent office. It was one of the first buildings set alight during the 1976 riots, and Mendi Road was the epicentre of the student unrest. Just 300 metres down Mendi, neatly tucked away in a dead-end lane where I once played dixie football with my childhood friends, is the house in which I grew up – now painted an unsubtle pink. There were once two beautiful trees outside but those were cut down by the *boers*.

On the street outside my family home, I saw my first death. I was just five or six years old when I witnessed a man being stabbed to death for *i yum-yum*, a slice of peanut-buttered brown bread worth one cent at the time. The man was a notorious gangster in the township and was hated by everyone. It was such a violent death to witness and as an impressionable young boy, I was horrified by what I saw. I couldn't understand why it had to end that way. After he died, there was a party and people danced all night long. Such incidents would become commonplace in my youth because it was a regular occurrence in township life.

Crouching behind a wall at my home, I witnessed another death several years later as the 1976 unrest broke out. We had scattered after the police had opened fire on us and I was peeping out from my hiding place, keeping a lookout for the police. Nomvume Mnyazi, a former Johnson Marwanqa schoolmate who was then a student at Cowan High, who was doing her matric or Form 5 at the time, was standing behind a chimney when she was shot. I watched her fall right in front of me and looked on in anguish because I couldn't run to her immediately. Only once the police had moved out could we go to her, but by then it was already too late. We managed to arrange a car and rushed her to Livingstone Hospital, where she died. She was the first Port Elizabeth victim of the 1976 uprising.

Across from my house, in a stretch of veld where the local bottle store

– which was burnt down during the uprisings – once stood, a derelict building gathers litter. I have a vivid recollection of a friend running out of the bottle store during the 1976 unrest, carrying two bottles of brandy, shouting 'Njiva, my *laaitie*! This is freedom!' The open veld was virtually surrounded by cafés and was a popular site for political rallies organised by the ANC. The site was called Emlotheni, and leaders and trade unionists would gather here to address people. During the political lull of the 1960s and the '70s we used to play rugby, cricket and soccer in the open veld.

Alongside the veld on Limba Road, the government has established the Emlotheni Memorial Park, which was opened by former president Thabo Mbeki. The first Umkhonto we Sizwe (MK) cadres, who were sentenced to death in 1961 and hanged, were buried in Pretoria and their remains were finally moved here. Palisade fencing blocks access to the park and it's chained closed to protect it against vandalism. There was supposed to be an eternal flame signifying our struggle and freedom but unfortunately the local council has neglected it.

Vuyisile Mini, one of the giants of our struggle and a gifted poet and singer, is among those buried here. During his walk to the gallows, he sang a liberation song he had composed in defiance. '*Pasopa nansi 'ndondemnyama we Verwoerd*'. 'Look out, Verwoerd, here is the black man,' he sang courageously.

The site speaks to the history of the area. One of the only buildings that was not burnt down in 1976 is the nearby Cecil Kapi Youth Centre (formerly Ivan Peter), which served as a social meeting place for the youth in the area. And when we left for exile in 1980 we had agreed that it be renamed Majola-Kapi in honour of both Mrs J. Majola and Mr S.C. Kapi who nurtured the youth of New Brighton. This is where we learned to play table tennis and ballroom dance and where we held socials as teenagers. We also used it as an arena in which to conscientise the youth about the struggle.

My earliest memories of apartheid feature my uncle Zolisa, with whom I shared a birthday. I often heard the adults speaking about 'Uncle Zolisa' and, curious as ever, I asked them, 'Who is this Uncle Zolisa?'

My mother's brother, Zolisa Sipoyo, was serving a 20-year term on Robben Island. He was involved with the PAC and was arrested in 1963 with other Poqo activists while en route to Mthatha on a mission to kill

Kaizer Matanzima, the leader of the former Transkei homeland. As their train rolled into the Queenstown Railway Station, the Security Police were on the platform. An informer had tipped off the authorities. Uncle Zolisa had stolen my grandfather's revolver and he used it to shoot at the police, which explains why he got such a heavy sentence.

Growing up, I asked many questions about my uncle, determined to find out why he had been arrested. I missed him and when I was in high school I began to write to him. This ignited my political interest, but there were other indicators that alerted me to the racial and class imbalances in our society. I could see it all around me, with separate buses, seats and benches for whites and blacks. I could not believe it when I accidentally saw my father's wage slip. He was earning something like £20 a month at the time and it made me think twice about how a person could be expected to support a family on such a wage.

In high school my political consciousness was further awakened by the bigger boys in Form 5 who wrote the name of the ANC and slogans on the blackboards. They talked in hushed tones about movements such as the South African Students' Organisation (SASO), and spoke the names of those who had grown up in the area, such as Steve Biko and Barney Pityana, founding members of the Black Consciousness Movement.

The boys tuned in to Radio Freedom, the weak signal from Maputo thick with static, and we heard, 'This is Radio Freedom, the voice of the African National Congress.' We heard about the struggle of liberation organisations such as ZANU, ZAPU and FRELIMO. The programme started with the rattle of a machine gun and you could hear the guerrillas and the sound '*Ga-ga-ga*'. I later learned that the sound of an AK47 is very different from that recording. As teenagers, we even established a 'chess club' at Boet Baba's house in Madala Street without him knowing, which was really operating covertly as a political club. There we talked about the implementation of the M-Plan, Mandela's organisational strategy. While politics was merely a discussion point when I was in high school, it was only later, during my tenure at Fort Hare University, colloquially referred to as the 'University of Politics', that my talk was turned into action.

Politics through sport

In Port Elizabeth African townships and the northern areas (coloured townships), sport was the vehicle of political resistance – for us, sport and politics during the apartheid era were inextricably linked. It was on the rugby and cricket fields of the township that we expressed our opposition to the regime and the culture of sport runs deep in our roots. The Eastern Cape has a distinguished history of both sport and politics and produced many of the greatest black rugby and cricket players never to receive national honours.

On the township streets we played cricket using tennis balls and a tomato box as our wickets. We used just about anything as a bat. Then we graduated to the real game, but I remained an average cricketer. My strength was always rugby, playing flyhalf and centre. Under the banner of the South African Council on Sport and the South African Rugby Union (SARU), I played club rugby for Spring Rose, one of the oldest and most acclaimed rugby clubs in the country. Established in 1907, the club celebrated its centenary in 2007.

In the early 1970s, several clubs broke away from the Port Elizabeth rugby board to form the non-racial KwaZakhele Rugby Union (KWARU) and joined SARU. I represented the KWARU Colts side. Playing with us at the time were the likes of Zola Yeye, who went on to manage the Springbok team that won the World Cup, Peter Mkata, Themba Ludwaba, Mpumelelo Tshume, Duma Lamani, Gerald Majola and the Watson brothers, Cheeky,

Ronnie and Valence.

The mantra at the time was 'No normal sport in an abnormal society'. When the KWARU sides played, the entire township came to a standstill as people filled the stadium to cheer on their team. I even remember how we painstakingly planted the grass at night at the Dan Qeqe Stadium by the light of vehicle headlamps. Rugby was in our blood.

At Fort Hare we had quite the esteemed rugby team – I played with Smuts Ngonyama, Khaya Ngqula, Mkhuseli Jobodwana, Tembekile Xaso, Ntsiki Ntweni, Ntsiki Mkete, Bonile Jack, Siphiwo Mazwai and Mpumelelo 'Joe' Tshume. Former Sports Minister Makhenkesi Stofile was our manager.

Appropriately, it is through sport that I forged my friendships with those who would become my lifelong comrades, brothers-in-arms, the four men in our ANC underground unit of six who would ultimately go into exile together: Thozi, Phaki, Sizwe and me.

Thozi Majola's family association with sport in South Africa, particularly rugby and cricket, is well known. His father, Eric, was arguably one of the best flyhalves the country ever produced and an excellent cricketer too, and played both sports for the black national sides. His eldest brother Khaya (or *Meneer*, as we referred to him) was an outstanding cricketer who played a central role in the transformation of the sport in the country, while his younger brother Gerald Majola is former CEO of Cricket South Africa (CSA).

I recall playing tomato-box street cricket with Gerald and his now-adult adversary, the former president of CSA, Mtutuzeli Nyoka, as young boys. Thozi was himself a great sportsman, playing rugby, cricket and also table tennis. He was the oldest in our group by a year or two. Quite laid-back, Thozi could be both extrovert and introvert and was always able to strike up an easy friendship with those he met. He also considered himself something of a Casanova when he was younger.

Phaki Ximiya, short and sturdy, was a fiery flanker who also managed a few centuries in cricket in his youth. The Ximiya family is a prominent one in New Brighton and well respected in the community. Phaki's father and brothers were all well-known rugby and cricket players in the area. But while he was a decent cricket and rugby player, Phaki's real talent was as an outstanding ballroom dancer. Extremely patient, thoughtful and considered, Phaki always took time to ponder over situations before he got stuck in, much to my frustration. But when he did get stuck in, he didn't let go. As slow as he was with making decisions, so too was he when it came to girls.

Tall and regal, Sizwe Kondile always carried a quiet confidence about him. He was the de facto leader of our group. He was never much of a talker but rather listened to what all those around him had to say first. When he spoke, everyone listened. There were times when he walked all the way from his house to my place, just over a kilometre away, and when I started talking to him, he would say, 'No, keep quiet man. Shut up!' I would ask him why he had bothered to walk all the way to my house if he just wanted to sit in silence. And he would respond, 'No, man, I just want to be with you.' Sizwe was a strong rugby player and, like Phaki, a flanker. Along with the Majolas and Ximiyas, the Kondiles were also highly regarded in society and Sizwe's father was a black Springbok, playing for the African Springboks in the 1960s. He was a flanker and prominent in legal circles, eventually becoming the chief magistrate of Port Elizabeth and later a judge on the Natal bench.

I don't remember when or where I first met Sizwe – he was simply always around. At church, at school, in the neighbourhood, he was there. Even when he went to Amanzimtoti to do his high-school years, we spent our holidays together. He was my best friend and like my brother.

I remember this one time when Sizwe's mother was there and we were showing off about what we were going to be when we grew up. Teddy wanted to be a lawyer, Zingi was going to be involved in sport, and Sizwe – I remember him distinctly – he said that one day he was going to be the president of South Africa. It was a bit lofty. I didn't really wonder much about it except that I thought it was impossible in terms of where we were at the time. We were still young teenagers. That was the first indication for me that he was politically inclined. But another thing that struck me at the time about his sensitivity was that with all the potential the family knew he had, in terms of academics, we knew he was clever and we looked up to him, was that he also said he wanted to go and work at Ford and be a simple worker. When he said that, as immature as I was, I realised that he was sensitive to people's plight. It was being talked about him being a doctor or a lawyer in the family; and for him to say that, it was not that he was aiming low, it indicated to me his sensitivity to the plight of people.

Pat Kondile (Sizwe's cousin)

The university of politics

Being Xhosa, the natural progression for me in 1976 was to go to Fort Hare University in Alice, whose alumni include Oliver Tambo, Nelson Mandela, Robert Sobukwe, Robert Mugabe and many other luminaries. With my curious mind, I was always destined to study law, but I was also influenced by others in the legal profession while I was growing up. These included Sizwe's father, Dumile Kondile; Barney Pityana, who was doing articles with him at the time; former Eastern Cape Judge President Doc Somyalo; attorney and former SA Rugby President Silas Nkanunu; and the late Judge Patrick Maqubela. I would have legal discussions with them all, and they would never fail to pique my interest.

My parents ensured that we were all given the opportunity to study, and it was a proud moment for me when my mother dropped me at Fort Hare. My mother used to tell me that when I was born, I had a protective shield because I was a special child. In isiXhosa you were called '*umntwana wesingxobo*', meaning 'the child from the special sack'. She would tell me the story of how a white woman once told her, 'You must put money aside so that you can educate him, he is a special child.'

Fort Hare was not only a place of academia, but a place of politics too – and for me university was more about politics than my studies. I had never performed poorly at school, but at Fort Hare, I failed my second year because of my political involvement at the time. I had been too busy with student politics and my academics suffered. I had enrolled for a four-year

B.Proc degree in 1976. Sizwe came a year later after dropping out of medical school and signed up for a three-year B.Juris. Thozi was with me at Fort Hare, while Phaki was still finishing school in New Brighton.

I had always been aware of the politics around me while growing up and especially during my high-school years but I had never been politically active as such. Thozi, who was older than me, was more involved and used to fill us in on what was going on:

> *In 1973 I was part of the SCM – the Student Christian Movement – at school. We had an invitation for a leadership course that was run by Steve Biko and the Black Consciousness Movement [BCM] people in Port Elizabeth. So we went. We were picked up by a kombi from our school on a Friday – I think it was a long weekend – the place was called Waverley Hills, a farm area between Port Elizabeth and Uitenhage. That's where I met Steve Biko for the first time. He was giving the lectures, but in the middle of that the Special Branch came. They blocked the place and they started searching it. Then Steve Biko was taken away. Barney Pityana was taken away. But we remained. The other guys continued with the lectures. Then on Monday, when we went back to school, the Special Branch was there to collect all of us that attended. Now we were questioned. What was it that was there? I can tell you, those guys at Waverley were speaking above our heads, we didn't understand a thing that they were telling us. But we knew we had taken notes, hidden them, and they had told us that now we must be careful. Even our own school, our principal was actually demoted. That's how I got involved with BCM and politics. Now they started giving us tasks, like talking to other students. I started talking to Vusi and my friends. I started explaining about BCM. I was more BCM-orientated then. But I think the thing that sparked everything was the '76 uprising.*

As I became more immersed in politics at Fort Hare, I began to question the status quo more than ever before. Why are black people being oppressed like that? Why are we being killed like this? Why are we starving? Why are we being ravaged by disease? Why are we being denied education?

When Soweto exploded in 1976, I was on holiday during my first year at university. When we went back to Alice, we met students from Soweto who had witnessed the violence and had seen their brothers being killed and sisters being shot at. They told us that kids were dying in Soweto and asked what we were going to do about it. We couldn't continue with schooling as if we had not been affected. The Students Representative Council (SRC) called a mass meeting at the Great Hall at the university.

The hall was packed and filled with expectation. Many of the older students were more political and belonged to underground ANC cells and to SASO and the BCM. The SRC president took the stand and told us that Soweto was on fire. Someone stood up and said, 'We must do something – we can't just sit here.' It was exciting and Thozi and I marvelled at the high level of the English that was being spoken.

One said, 'Why don't we set up a day and pray for those who are dying?' Another asked, 'Why don't we collect money for the families of the children dying in Soweto?' Mbuyiselo Ralawe had been working underground. He took the microphone and said in response to the often-repeated statement from speakers that 'we must do something' without saying what this 'something' is: 'Something means one thing and that is rioting.'

That is what set Fort Hare alight in 1976. And our 1976 SRC president, Memani Gaba, said: 'You claim to be the replicas of the rioting masses in Soweto and yet you enjoy the luxuries and comforts of Fort Hare.' This was not a revolutionary address but meant to discourage us from taking any form of action.

We ran down to the campus, smashed windows, started fires and broke down the university. Thozi and I tried to burn a tractor, using diesel, as he recounts:

> *We were going towards the admin building to go and burn it but the police were very heavy. They blocked us. We saw this tractor grader and we said, 'Let's destroy this.' The only part of that thing we could pour diesel in was the seat, because the rest was just steel. So we took diesel from it, we poured it on the seat, and we burned it. But the seat didn't light. We just wanted to destroy something but we were chased away.*

It was the first time I tasted tear gas. We had only seen it on the few black-and-white television sets around at the time The street-smart guys from Soweto knew what they were doing so they quickly got water and we covered our noses and mouths with wet handkerchiefs as we threw stones at the cops. It was an adventure and we were venting our anger at the system and the university represented that system. At the time, black universities such as Fort Hare were headed by Afrikaner male rectors and young white lecturers. We felt that we were being used as an experiment for these young graduates to gain experience before going to teach at white universities – Bantu education was well and truly entrenched at Fort Hare and it was another terrain of struggle against apartheid. Black graduates were being restricted to a certain quota and we, as students, felt that we were being held back from succeeding and entering the job market.

The response from the authorities was to shut down the university and expel everyone. Officials arranged special trains to take us home and they divided us up into provinces to travel on different lines and at different times. Armed police went to all the rooms to make sure that everyone was in the hall. The Cape Town and the Port Elizabeth guys took the same trains as far as Cookhouse, and along the way there was a big punch-up about who was smarter, the Cape Town guys or the PE guys.

When we arrived home, we had to explain to our parents that we had been expelled. My parents had not considered that I would be involved in politics in any way and I told them that I had participated in the burning and damaging of property. They were concerned and tried to get people to talk to me about it. They were worried about the money that they were spending on my studies and my father called on me to make a choice. He said if I wanted politics, then I should continue with political activism, but if I wanted school, then I should be a student. I, however, wanted both.

I had come back to New Brighton from Fort Hare to find that pupils in the township were ready to follow the lead of those in Soweto. Phaki was in matric at Cowan High School at the time and was in the thick of things:

> *The first shot happened in Soweto in Johannesburg and then we followed in August to a big extent. There was no serious schooling in PE from August until December 1977. PE used to be a very friendly area, but with the eruption of the 1976 uprisings, the situation changed. The police used to be a terror for us. You would hear that Land Rover at a distance and*

it would disappear. In my class we were having discussions following up on what had happened in Soweto. What was different for us was that we were at school. Why were we going to school when others were involved in the struggle? Whilst we were engaged in this discussion at Cowan, I was not aware that other classrooms were having the same discussions. It started at Newell High one morning and then they came to us, singing. Whilst the principal was talking to us, we jumped through the windows and doors, to join Newell. The principal rushed to close the school gates but some of us were already with Newell moving away. When I turned back, the principal had succeeded in blocking the majority of the students. I asked these chaps to wait and I went to my class and said, 'Guys, I'm going with or without you to join those guys.' I walked out past the principal's office and I'm told that apparently we were in single file. The principal lost control and the whole school followed. We joined Newell and then we moved with them singing. We got to Ferguson and that's where we were stopped by the police. We were told to sit down and we were surrounded by the vans and officers with nice new batons. It was terrible. On that day I got to know how close it is between being a hero and a villain. We started moving towards the vans and other guys started running away. I had an opportunity to follow the other guys. I was about to go for the fence, but something just said I must look back. I saw girls with fists up, defiantly going towards that van. I couldn't take the fence and I turned back.

During that time in Soweto there were so many children who were killed. My schoolmate, Nomvume Mnyazi, was the first but there were others. One night I was standing on a street corner in Mendi Road chatting to my friends. It was late and I said, 'Guys, I'll see you tomorrow morning.' The following morning I heard that one of those guys, Ngxeki, an excellent footballer, had been shot dead. The police had come past, seen a group of black guys at night, and opened fire without provocation.

The police were rampant at the time. You could hear the distinctive, easily identified sound of the Land Rover tyre. You could hear it coming as it turned into the street. That sound stayed with me for years.

There was mayhem in the townships, and people were dropping like flies. Young white police recruits were unleashed as if this was a dress rehearsal for border duty in Namibia. We never flinched but faced the enemy with a steely resolve to overcome apartheid no matter what. We were prepared to die for our liberation.

Going to the mountain

Sizwe and I went to the mountain together and became men together. Going to the mountain is the process of graduating from being a boy to being a man. You are circumcised and are taught how to be a responsible person in life because you are no longer a child. You learn to look after your parents, take care of weaker siblings, earn respect and respect your elders. And yet, even though you are a man, in the eyes of your mother you are never an adult.

Age mates who are also friends usually go to the bush at the same time and, in December 1976, my friends and I all expected to go together. However, because of the student unrest at Fort Hare University at the time and the fact that I had been expelled, I had to write exams in January 1977. Thozi and Phaki went ahead to the mountain in December, and Sizwe and I went together once we had finished our exams. Sizwe waited for me because we wanted to go together.

On the last day of my exams, Sizwe came through to Alice and we travelled to the nearby village of Ngcothoyi. We wanted to experience initiation in the proper, rural way and also chose that village because my mother's sister was married to the chief there. The elders in my family, including my father and paternal uncles, accompanied us.

That night we celebrated amid a chorus of praise singing and dancing. Those friends who weren't coming with us arrived to bid us farewell from boyhood. A goat was slaughtered and, as required by tradition, Sizwe and I had to eat the foreleg of the animal. I felt my emotions oscillate from anxiety to excitement and later to the fear of the unknown. I knew that I was entering a new phase in my life, that with manhood came respect and the authority to attend to the problems of my family and my community. But I also had a sense of foreboding as I knew that the next four weeks would be painful and difficult, both literally and figuratively.

At dawn the following morning, we ran to a nearby river, took off our blankets and jumped into the flowing water. Together with the male elders and Ingcibi, a so-called traditional surgeon whom we could not identify at the time, we made our way to the site of our grass huts where the circumcision would be performed and where we would spend the next month. Our hut was beautiful and was personalised, made just for us. In a clearing between thorny trees and thick shrubbery was this oasis, a haven of serenity where an orchestra of insects and birds entertained us. The air was crisp and clean.

We, boys on the cusp of manhood, sat outside our grass-and-reed hut. Ingcibi just emerged unannounced from amongst the men who were there, slapped me on my thighs and in an instant, with a masterful stroke of his short, sharp spear (called *umdlanga*), it was done. He started with me because I was *u Sosuthu* (Sizwe was joining me, therefore I was the one to be circumcised first). These were the days before any real concerns about disease or viruses and the surgeon used the same blade on Sizwe. There were no painkillers, only wild herbs and traditional ointments. For the duration of our stay, Ikhankata, a so-called traditional nurse, would treat the wound on a daily basis and this was the moment in the day we hated most.

For the first seven days, we ate no meat at all and for a Xhosa boy that can never be good. We could not eat any salt and instead would be given *iinkobe*, a type of corn-and-pumpkin dish. The water we drank was cloudy in an attempt to ensure that we passed as little water as possible in order to not disturb the wound.

Sizwe and I were *ooqabane* – meaning each one smears the other's back. As per custom, we had to paint our entire bodies with the white mask *ifutha* but we could not do that on our own. He had do it for me and I for him. I was his mirror and he acted as mine. The process strengthens the bond you share with each other because you share pain together, and in the wilderness you face danger together. Those who are superstitious about witchcraft believe that this is the reason you take turns to sleep while the other is on guard duty, ensuring that no evil spirits came to attack us. You stare down the enemy together – he covered my back and I covered his. He looked this side, while I looked that side. We were prepared to die for each other. That's what we learned in the bush, that's what comradeship means. You do not go to the mountain with just anybody – you choose to go with your best and trusted friend.

During those weeks we whiled away the time by chatting and talking nonsense. When the pain became unbearable we could comfort one another, although we would be careful not to talk about women for obvious reasons – we could not afford to be aroused because that would set us back!

The day we finally left was a day of celebration. We had successfully weathered the storm and come through at the other end. From our hut, which had become our home, we went down to the river again to wash. We had not cleaned ourselves for four weeks and had been wearing nothing more than a blanket that we had fashioned into a skirt and shirt. Our hair, which we had cut when we first went into the bush, had grown and was shorn off again. From the river, we returned to our hut, where an elderly, prosperous and wise man was appointed to anoint us. In our case it was Chief S.M. Burns-Ncamashe, who was a historian, an isiXhosa writer and poet, and a well-respected academic. The idea is that we would follow in the footsteps of that person. It is an honour to anoint boys in the bush and it is an honour that has been bestowed on me several times in my adult life.

All the materials we had used during our stay were clumped together in the hut – our bedding, clothing and utensils – and, in a symbolic act that showed that we were leaving our boyhood behind us, we burnt them all. Similar to the biblical story of Lot and the pillar of salt, we were not allowed to look back and see it all burn. We were leaving the past and looking forward towards our future, towards a life of adulthood.

As we made our way towards the village, we could hear the beating of drums in celebration. As Africans, we beat drums, sing and dance in times of joy and this was such a moment. We arrived in the village to find the women, our mothers and sisters, celebrating us as we took our rightful place in society. We stood naked, with only our pouches to cover the essentials, before our sisters as they smeared red clay on our bodies. An ox, goat and several sheep were slaughtered and we feasted on meat and traditional beer.

Sizwe and I had become men.

The process had not been an easy one, but it prepared me for the hardships, in various shapes and forms, I would face later. Later in life I would go to the mountain a second time, through a second initiation, and I was prepared for it, knowing full well that life was going to be tough.

The death of Steve Biko

We returned to Fort Hare University in early 1977, but I had yet to become a member of any formal political organisation. We were still a loose formation of students who were politically conscious.

Then Stephen Bantu Biko was killed.

I was on campus at the time and word spread like wildfire that the *boers* had killed Biko. We were angry and wanted to organise a memorial service on campus but the rector, De Wet, refused. We told him we were going ahead with or without his permission. He warned us that we were breaking the law in terms of the Riotous Assemblies Act but we defied him anyway. We arranged for the memorial service to be held on the sports field near the Students' Centre. A group of around 1 000 turned up and we were joined by some of the lecturers, including Makhenkesi Stofile.

It was a clear, beautiful Eastern Cape day and there was a mood of defiance in the air. The atmosphere was celebratory – we celebrate our heroes when they die, not mourn them. I was nevertheless filled with anger at Biko's death because he had died in detention, in solitary confinement, with no explanation. Minister Jimmy Kruger had gone on record saying that Biko's death had 'left him cold' and I was furious. Biko was tortured at the Sanlam building in Strand Street in Port Elizabeth, my hometown.

The service was about to begin when we saw police vans making their way towards us. We stood our ground and didn't run away because we refused to be intimidated. The university stadium was still under construction and the police vans kicked up dirt and dust but we continued to stand our ground. One of the lecturers, a hippie whose name was Mr Soul, ran away in his bellbottoms and platform shoes, leaving his wife behind, but the police quickly caught him. They arrested all the male students, leaving the female students and the other lecturers behind.

We were formally charged at the Alice Magistrate's Court but because there were so many of us they had to convert garages into courtrooms. When the orderly said, 'Silence in court!', we responded, 'Silence in the garage!' and burst out laughing. We were given a further charge of contempt of court so we responded with 'Contempt of garage!'

Some students were taken to Fort Beaufort, King William's Town or East London, while others remained in the police cells in Alice. I was in the group that was taken to Fort Glamorgan near East London, *kwaNongqongqo*, for my first taste of prison.

Many political prisoners were being held there at the time and it was the domain of a feared Security Branch officer, a Captain Schoeman, who was tiny but vicious. We remained there for about a week, but our spirits were high and we were often told we were making too much noise in the cells. We were in communal cells and they didn't want us to sing, but we defied them by singing freedom songs. We had to walk in formation and were counted in the mornings and afternoons. When we really angered the prison warders we would be punished by being deprived of food for the whole day, skipping all three meals, '*die drie maaltye*'. We were given what looked like *amasi*, sour milk, but without the rich cream. In fact, it was more like *intloya*, the dregs left behind in a bottle. This was ironically called Phuzamandla.

This was my first prison experience, and it was not a pleasant place to be. But we were a group of friends together, which made it more bearable. We were held in a big communal cell, dingy and dark, and all we had were thin, grey blankets to keep us warm. For me, the experience was far easier to bear having been to the mountain just a few months prior. We were upbeat and would tease the wardens by telling them we would get out of jail and rule them one day. It was our own way of hitting back at them.

Pume Canca, who had been arrested with us, was doing his BA Law. His father was an attorney in Idutywa and had heard that we had been arrested, so he came to check what was happening. He paid bail for all of us

– a total of R16 000. There were about 800 of us so that amounts to around R20 bail each.

While we were in prison, we were seen as heroes by the girls on campus. They would say to the others who hadn't been arrested, 'Real men are in prison, what are you doing here?' Makhenkesi Stofile's son was born on the day that we were taken into custody and he was named Sikhulule, meaning 'release' or 'liberate us'.

We were released just before Biko's funeral and demanded that the university provide us with buses to travel to King William's Town. The officials relented and provided transport. Thousands of people travelled from across the country, through heavy police barricades and roadblocks, to be at the Ginsberg Cemetery. Many wore African shirts emblazoned with Black Power salutes and slogans and, with a strong police presence, the event was more reminiscent of a political rally than a funeral. We listened to impassioned speakers, and mourners punched the air with their fists in the Black Power salute.

A fist, the symbol of the Black Consciousness Movement, had been carved into Biko's coffin, which was carried by a donkey cart. Many of us had never met Biko, but he was our hero. There was anger, but there was also optimism and a certainty that in the end we shall triumph. We felt like setting fire to the whole town. We were greatly inspired and returned to the university with large posters carrying the image of Biko with his cuffs breaking through chains, telling us that one day we shall be free.

Throughout 1978 and 1979 we demonstrated and complained about Bantu Education and made demands from the university authorities, refusing to go to the dining hall and boycotting classes. After my spell in detention, I decided to start taking politics seriously. Biko's death was a watershed event and this mobilised me and others. We became more organised. In celebration of the centenary of the Battle of Isandlwana, the ANC declared 1979 the Year of the Spear, and it was the first time that I personally felt the presence of the ANC beginning to mobilise through underground structures. There were ANC cells on campus and BCM cells were still operating, but I still didn't belong to either of these organisations. At that time, because of the underground nature of the organisation, we never went out looking to join the ANC. People would be recruited, of course, but I was never approached. The mass participation I was involved in, the open defiance by the bulk of the students, sufficed for me and I never took a conscious decision not to join either organisation.

The following year, 1980, also proved a watershed year and the ANC declared it the Year of the Freedom Charter. I was in my fourth and final year of my B.Proc degree.

Meanwhile, in Port Elizabeth we were working with the Congress of South African Students (COSAS) and the Port Elizabeth Students Representative Council (PE SRC) led by one firebrand Sipho Pityana – whose standpoint was that 'They were not violent but only violent when provoked' – in trying to establish PEYMO, the Port Elizabeth Youth Movement. We started drafting a constitution, but while most of us were in favour of the non-racial Freedom Charter, others were supporting Black Consciousness. It was clear that we weren't ready to form one organisation and had to suspend our attempts. After we had left for exile, the local movement became PEYCO, the Port Elizabeth Youth Congress, and Mkhuseli Jack was appointed president.

On campus, however, we became skilful at organising ourselves and we knew that every time we started a boycott, classes would be suspended for two or three days and we would be sent home. You would go and see your parents and they would ask, 'Why are you here?' You explained and they wouldn't accept your story.

Sizwe was arrested in 1980, when the police used tear gas against us while we were boycotting classes and on our way to Lovedale. We went back to the campus and were furious when we saw a woman coming from class. I was so angry she had betrayed the cause that I threw a brick at her and narrowly missed her head. I wanted to hurt her because I considered her a sell-out and felt let down. At the time, I would have felt justified in causing her pain because we regarded the likes of her as sell-outs and dissenters but now, looking back and being a democrat, I believe that she had every right to do as she chose.

I also became known for leading the students in shouting slogans during the protests. There were moments of low morale and of silence, but when I shouted the entire student body echoed the lines of Ingoapele Madingoane's protest poem, repeating after me:

FREEDOM IS THE LAW OF NATURE – JUSTICE IS DEEPLY ROOTED IN THE UNIVERSAL ORDER OF THINGS – WHEN THE WHITE MEN CAME – OUR HOMES PRISONS BECAME – WHEN THE WHITE MEN CAME – OUR MOTHERS GIRLS BECAME – WHEN THE WHITE MEN CAME – OUR FATHERS BOYS BECAME – WHEN THE WHITE MAN CAME!

Even after I left, that slogan continued to be shouted at Fort Hare.

We set up an ad hoc committee with regional and special committees so that there would be a structure in place when we were expelled. The idea was that when we were kicked out, the chairpersons of those committees would continue calling meetings of students in those provinces so that we continued communicating and taking joint decisions. I was elected chairperson of the Eastern Cape.

We held these secret meetings on campus to discuss strategy and tactics. At one such meeting, Mpumi Gaba stood up and said, 'Comrades! You are wasting time, I am leaving you, we will meet in the bush', and he never came back to class again.

When we were expelled for a second time, we resolved that it was important for us to hold a meeting with our parents so that we could get their support. We held a preliminary meeting of students at St Stephen's Hall in New Brighton, one of the popular sites of political events in the township, to plan for the parents' meeting a few days later – and it was that meeting that led to my detention under Section 22 of the General Law Amendment Act.

As I was addressing the packed hall, somebody indicated that there was a white guy at the door who wanted to see me. I adjourned the meeting and went out to see the men, who were well-known security officers. Among them was a Captain Du Plessis.

Du Plessis wanted to know what the meeting was about. I told him and gave him my name and my address and explained that I was chairing the gathering. He wanted to know about our agenda and told me that I was 'cheeky'. He asked what I was studying and when I told him I was to be a lawyer, he said he would see to it that I would never practise in Port Elizabeth. The captain insisted that if we were going to have another meeting – the one with our parents – we would have to apply to 'Sanlam', the head office of the police's Special Branch in Port Elizabeth, for a permit. I told him I would not be applying for any permit. Why should we need a permit to talk to our parents?

The police left and I continued with the meeting.

That Saturday our parents came to the Roman Catholic church hall in large numbers and we explained to them why we had called them together. Early the next morning, at around 2 a.m., while I was sleeping at home, we were woken by loud bangs at the door and torches shining through the windows. The Special Branch had come to arrest me.

But, wow, did my mother fight them! She asked for their names, wrote them down and told them, 'I want my son back here in one piece!' My father, who was usually the more militant one, kept quiet and left it to my mother to deal with the officers. I was thrown into the back of a police van, where I discovered others who had been taken in that night, among them Archie Sobukwe, Tango Lamani, Duma Lamani and Andile Tyibilika.

The cops drove us to the Sanlam building, their headquarters where Biko had been brutally beaten and assaulted. There was a moment of fear, but there was also defiance, that we were doing the right thing by fighting for our liberation. At Sanlam, we were separated, placed in rooms and interrogated individually.

What were we doing? What was the boycott of classes about? Was I a member of a banned organisation? Was I sent by the ANC?

I stated that we were students fighting against Bantu Education. We wanted free and equal education and that's what our struggle was all about. I was not manhandled, not even slapped. I was ready for that because I knew people were being tortured and beaten up. A black Special Branch officer complained, 'We go to sleep very late because of you guys.' I was furious and told him to get away. I was still fit then and, because I was a rugby player, I was confident that I could deal with him in seconds. I told him that I would beat him up, that by the time his superiors came I would have dealt with him, but he just walked out.

We were then moved to St Alban's Prison outside Port Elizabeth and were made to write out a sentence that included every letter of the alphabet, for the purposes of identifying and tracing our handwriting later. For 14 days we were held in isolation in single cells. We only talked when they brought us food and it was difficult simply to sit and be quiet and think about life.

I thought about how I wanted to be free, but there had been others before us, starting with Nelson Mandela, on Robben Island. My uncle was still in prison at the time and I thought about him, how much he had sacrificed and what he was going through on Robben Island. I started thinking about my purpose in life. I questioned whether I was doing the right thing. My parents continued to hope that I would finish my studies and start practising law so that I could help improve their situation. But at the end of the day I felt that what I was doing meant that I was fighting for them too. Our lawyer, Silas Nkanunu – or Boet Sy, as we referred to him – began making a noise about our case and after 14 days in detention they finally opened the doors.

On the day we were released, in June 1980, MK cadres placed limpet mines at the SASOL plant in Secunda and blew it up. It was at that point I realised that we were in fact small fish and the Special Branch had arrested us simply because it seemed that the country was on fire and they had been unable to close in on the 'real terrorists'. I saw SASOL's blazing fuel tanks as fires of freedom, and they led me to fantasise about being a fully trained MK guerrilla and carrying an AK47 and placing limpet mines. It was time to go beyond student activism and to get serious about the struggle.

Into exile

As I jogged through the streets of Port Elizabeth in June and July 1980, I would look at the industrial factories and lose myself in dreams of returning one day to blow them up. I envisaged how we would go into exile, get our training, come back as fully prepared cadres of Umkhonto we Sizwe and carry out a carefully planned sabotage campaign.

Around August 1980, my friends and I began to have serious discussions amongst ourselves. We felt we needed to participate more meaningfully in the struggle, and yet there was still some reluctance and hesitation. We realised that we needed to hook up with the ANC so that we could be trained, and thought about making contact with those who were already in exile. But first we felt that we should formalise the process and establish a proper a unit. Phaki explains how that came about:

> *I'm sitting with my brother-in-law Thembi Mbiyabo, my brother Phumi and Gomi [Nangamso Nzube] and they're drinking. Normally when they are drinking they speak about politics, how hateful the boers are and what they can do about it, but when they are sober they forget about that. I'm sitting quietly and they're trying to draw me into this discussion. I say, 'No chaps, there's no point in discussing it with you. You're militant now because you're drunk. When you're sober you won't be saying those things.' The following morning Thembi and Gomi rocked up at my place and challenged me; 'Yesterday, you said that when we are drunk we say*

these things but when we're sober ... we are sober now. What can be done?' they asked. That's when that unit got formed up.

I approached Vusi to say there is this discussion about making contact with people outside to see what we can do. At first, when I raised 'going outside', leaving the country, he said, 'What, and leave my mother alone?' You would think that his mother was not staying with his father and his elder brother and his sisters. He was always close to his mother. He dismissed me. Then Thozi agreed. It didn't take long for him to agree. I went to Vusi again and raised the matter; he had time to think over it but this time around he was agreeable. Vusi then brought Sizwe into the group. We got together, Thembi, Vusi, Sizwe, Thozi, Gomi and me, and the unit became full.

We were all in agreement that we would choose the ANC over other organisations. We were from a non-racial fold in terms of sport and felt that non-racialism was the ideology to which we subscribed. The ANC best suited this ideal. We also felt that the Freedom Charter was ideologically in line with what we felt at the time and it would be a natural progression from Black Consciousness.

We knew that a political activist, whom we regarded as our elder brother and friend, Thozamile Botha, and his wife, Sis Fez, had gone to Lesotho and decided that he would be our contact person there to take us to the ANC. We had no intention of phoning ahead – instead, we would simply rock up in Maseru. It wasn't well planned, but our hearts were telling us to go. The problem was that Sizwe, Phaki and I didn't have passports, but Phaki was able to make a plan at the last minute, so Sizwe and I stayed behind and Phaki was able to go with Boet Thembi Mbiyabo and Gomi Nzube and Thozi. Phaki used Ntsiki Ntweni's passport:

I got somebody else's passport, you know mos: 'They're all the same, they all look alike.' Yo! At the border I got a fright. All the other passports were being processed and this chap took mine to the back and I thought, 'Ai, what am I thinking using somebody else's face? I didn't even change the face.' But he came back and we were able to go through. You can imagine the relief. We met Thozamile and through him we were able to make contact with people like Chris Hani. They were very excited. We thought

> *to ourselves, 'We are getting guns' but we were given pamphlets and told to calm down, this is where you start.*

Phaki, Thozi, Thembi and Gomi returned from Maseru and there was all this literature including copies of the Freedom Charter and *Sechaba* magazines camouflaged as wildlife brochures and hidden in the door panels of the car. We split into three groups of two and assigned each team a spot at which to distribute the pamphlets, at the same time on the same day. Sizwe and I went to a busy marketplace in Korsten, and Phaki and Gomi went to the bus terminus in town. For some reason, Thozi and Thembi did not manage to distribute their pile and we immediately sensed a security risk – should the police find the pamphlets they would realise that there were ANC people active in the area. We told them they simply *had* to hand them out – where and how was their responsibility.

The following day, there was a student meeting at the Rio Cinema in New Brighton, and it was there, as Thozi remembers, that they recruited a young boy to distribute the papers:

> *There was a meeting at Rio Hall. Our aim was to deliver the pamphlets there. When we got there the place was surrounded by police. I said to Boet Thembi, 'Let's get some of the leaders and we hand the pamphlets to them because we will be arrested immediately.' I actually went inside the hall and went to the toilet. Then I called one of the leaders and said, 'Look, I've got this with me and I can't stay here. When you go, just throw them anywhere so that people can pick them up.' There were a lot of pamphlets. It was a letter from Madiba called 'Between the anvil and hammer'. I said to those boys that when they were asked who brought them, 'Never say you saw me. I was never here.' I remember I was wearing a blue overall and I went to change it after that. I wore my tracksuit and then I went to watch rugby and I said at the rugby match, 'Nothing happened.'*

What we did not anticipate was that Sipho Majombozi, who was a friend and was also at Fort Hare at the time, as well as a member of our 'chess club', would take the pamphlet, stand up on the stage and read it out to the entire audience. By this point, we were worried that sooner or later the pamphlets would be associated with us.

Later that night, Phaki and I were holding a meeting with the youth at the Ivan Peter Youth Club e Hoza when Sizwe and Thozi came flying in, insisting that they needed to speak to us urgently. 'Things are bad,' they told us. Boet Thembi had been arrested. They were sitting with him at home, watching cricket on TV, when the Security Police came in and asked for Thembile Mbiyabo. As Thozi recounts, he and Sizwe left, walked a distance away and watched as Thembi was taken away by the Security Police:

> *We were going to plan another distribution of pamphlets because we still had a lot and they were in Thembi's place. Then there was a knock. The dog started barking. Thembi had a big Alsatian. So he opened the door and without looking back, he was just standing with the door open, he said, 'It's them guys – they are here.' So it was. They came in and I counted them. There were 18 of them, Special Branch. Eighteen. And you know our houses in New Brighton, they are a bit small. They filled up the house. Now I was thinking, 'What are we going to do?' They filled up the house, and on TV it was Australia playing cricket. So I just concentrated on the cricket game but I was counting them. There were 15 whites and three black guys. Then this Security Branch policeman, Roelofse, he went and stood in front of the TV and he said, 'Sorry to disturb you, guys, we can see you are keen to watch the game. We have got work to do in this house.' He asked us our names and I was the first one – I don't remember the name I gave him but I never gave him my real name. I just gave a name and Sizwe did the same. And then he asked us, 'Can you stand outside?' and I say that's the biggest mistake they made. When we went outside, we ran immediately. We went out slowly, got out of the gate. Now we were looking for Vusi and Phaki. Fortunately we knew where they were.*

That was the catalyst that sent us into exile.

We went to the Majolas' house to think about what to do. Khaya wasn't there but his chocolate brown Firenza was – and so were the keys, so we took the car. We went to our homes, grabbed whatever we could, including a few items of clothing, and disappeared quietly. We decided to go and check what was happening at Thembi's house. Thembi was married to Phaki's sister so, much to his horror, we sent him into the house. Phaki's sister was sobbing and confirmed that the Security Branch had indeed taken Thembi. She also told him that Gomi had been told about the arrest. We debated about going to Gomi's house and decided against it because he had already received the message and was told that he shouldn't sleep at home as the police may be hunting for him.

Our next stop was the home of Phaki's older brother, Boet Winky, who was a pharmacist. We explained to him that we were in trouble, but didn't tell him where we were going, largely because we had no clear plan about what we were doing. There was just blind panic. The only thing that was clear was that we couldn't go home – and, in fact, we never did go back to our homes. Boet Winky gave us a few hundred rand.

But the real terror set in as we were driving Khaya's chocolate-brown Firenza from Winky's place up Maqanda Street, past the stadium back from KwaZakhele to New Brighton. At the end of Maqanda Street is a stop street where we could turn either left or right. It was around 10 p.m. and we could see the lights of several cars in the distance. They were driving slowly and appeared to be moving in convoy. In the townships we knew that three or four vehicles crawling along in a cavalcade probably meant the Security Police.

Everyone in the car started screaming at Thozi, telling him which way to turn. He shouted back at us to keep quiet, indicated left and then promptly turned right.

In New Brighton some lanes lead off the main roads into hidden culde-sacs, each surrounded by about eight houses. We found our way into one of these lanes off Sangotsha Street and dumped the car facing the entrance. On foot, we made our way to the home of Silas Nkanunu, our lawyer. There we told him that we were an ANC cell and that Thembi had been picked up. Boet Sy told us not to panic and suggested that we should go home and sleep – but we knew that was not an option. We gave him the keys to the Firenza and went to sleep at Thozi's aunt's house nearby.

Thozi picks up the story:

> *We went to my aunt's house in another street, but it was very close to where we left the car. Then my aunt, she was a very strong lady, she started with Phaki. Phaki was actually shaking. She said, 'Hey, no June–July here in my house, you decided to get yourself involved in this, so you stay with it. Myself, I am going to try and cover you as much as I can, but no-*

> *body must be scared.' June–July is winter. In winter a person shivers. After that, my brother Khaya came. I couldn't recognise his face it was so swollen. They had beaten him. When he went to collect the car that morning, they were sitting on top of the car. Now he had to tell them where he got the key and how he knew the car was there. I said, 'Boetie, don't look for me any more because the next time they do this to you, you will tell them where I was. Please, don't look for me. Otherwise you will get everybody in trouble now. Don't even try and look for us.'*

We later heard that Gomi had also been arrested that night, while we were on the run. When the police came, he opened the door for them and they said they were looking for Gomi Nzube. 'Gomi' is how he was known in the township but his real name was Nangamso. He showed them his brown *dompas* and in it his name was given as Nangamso. The Security Police were about to leave when his father woke up, saw the police and asked, 'Gomi, what do these people want?'

As unintentional as it was, it was a giveaway. Gomi was arrested and, together with Thembi, was charged for being in possession of banned literature belonging to a banned organisation. They spent three years on Robben Island.

Phaki, Thozi, Sizwe and I knew that we couldn't stay in one place for very long and that we needed to move around. Naturally, my parents worried and eventually they contacted Thozi's folks. But once they got word that we were safe, they were relieved and pleased that wherever we were, we were together. We spent the next day hiding at the guardhouse at the public swimming pool, Edamini, as we called it. A hunchbacked friend of ours was guarding the pool and we felt we could stay there temporarily. But then one of Thozi's cousins got wind that we were holed up there and wanted to see for himself. He arrived worried and excited and said, '*Ndifuna ukunibona ngeliso lenyama ukuba niyaphila*' – meaning 'I want to see with my naked eye that you guys are still safe'. Because he was a talker and so excitable, we knew that he would blab, so we told him to get lost.

That day Girly went to my house looking for me, not knowing what had happened the previous night. She had been doing her B.Com at Fort Hare and was active in politics there, but I had not confided in her that I was active in the ANC underground. It would have been too dangerous and I didn't want to place her safety at risk. When Girly got to my house, my grandmother was worried and said to her, '*Mntanam, akalalanga aph' ekhaya*' – 'My child, he did not sleep here at home last night. Where is he? Tell me, I won't tell them. Was he with you?'

Girly and Mthozami Xiphu, one of our friends, found out where we were and fetched us in her parents' car. Girly took us to her home where we spent the night in an outside flat usually used by her younger brother. Her mother never knew we were there. From there we moved to a friend's house in Zwide township where we spent the day behind drawn curtains, refusing to let his girlfriend leave the house because we worried that she would tell people where we were.

Then, moving in the dead of night, we went to the home of Toto Tsotsobe, and our final hideout was at Danny Jordaan's home in the coloured area of Bethelsdorp. At the time Danny was playing club cricket with us and we all played for United Cricket Club.

Over this period of three days, our instinct focused on survival and avoiding arrest. This was our reality – we faced imminent arrest and, possibly, a heavy jail term. We knew that there was no turning back. We never felt fear or that we should give ourselves up. We also didn't have time to think twice about the situation in which we found ourselves. And yet, although there was anxiety about the dangers we faced, we were also excited by the fact that we were living out our political aspirations.

While the four of us were running around, senior members of our community stepped in. Knowing that we were in trouble they began making plans for us to get out of town. These elders included Boet Sy and the legendary sports administrator, struggle stalwart and father of KWARU rugby Dan Qeqe, after whom the rugby stadium was named. Dan Qeqe's brother had a farm in King William's Town and they arranged that we would hide out on that farm until we could find out what was happening with Thembi and Gomi's case. Danny's younger brother Andrew drove us to King William's Town, with Boet Winky travelling ahead to check if there were any roadblocks.

When we got to Zwelitsha, Dan's brother got cold feet and didn't want to keep us there. It was midnight, we had nowhere to go and we were running out of money. All we had with us were the few items of clothing we had grabbed on the night Thembi and Gomi were arrested. Out of options, we told Andrew to drop us at the bus terminus in East London. We slept in a bus shelter and took the first bus to Mdantsane township in the morning. It was the anniversary of Steve Biko's death and there was a funeral of a notorious black policeman, Ncoko, who had been killed by MK, so the place was buzzing with police. As a result, we made our way to the home of my uncle who had a shop in Mdantsane, but hadn't realised that it was also popular with the cops. We stayed at his place until we arranged transport to take us to Mthatha, and then from Mthatha we travelled on to Matatiele in a Volkswagen Beetle. The driver realised the urgency and that little Beetle went flying along with six of us crammed inside.

We arrived at a house in Matatiele not knowing who it belonged to and it was only much later that we discovered it was the home of the chairperson of the ANC in the Eastern Cape, Dr James Njongwe, who had been banished to Matatiele but was originally from Port Elizabeth. There we found the militant Mrs Njongwe, who was excited to meet us. Our parents would have panicked and been afraid for us, but this old woman did not see us as children. She was excited about seeing these young, politically conscious young men in her house. Two of her sons were already in exile and were trained MK guerrillas. One of them, Boy (whose MK name was Thabiso or 'Silver Assassin'), was our first instructor in military and combat work, while his younger brother Bryce (his MK name), a gallant fighter, was later killed inside the country in mortal combat with enemy forces. Mrs Njongwa immediately organised for someone to take us across the border to Lesotho.

We had to wait until late at night for a van that had been arranged for us. We didn't know where we were going because the van was travelling up a mountain, and at one point we were told to get out of the vehicle and to continue on foot. We didn't know the guide either, but we went forward on blind faith and trust that those who were helping us were comrades. In pitch darkness and freezing cold, we walked on, stumbling over the rocky mountainside. We weren't properly equipped for the journey because we had never anticipated leaving the country and we were not properly dressed for winter in Lesotho. Although we were all very afraid and anxious, we were excited too.

I had always wanted to go into exile to fight, to join Umkhonto we Sizwe, but to be honest, when we did actually leave, it was more by accident than as a result of a deliberate decision on our part. It was the circumstances that drove us to leave the country. We knew that ultimately we would end up in exile but the timing was unexpected. I've never regretted how circumstances impacted on that destiny because fate often leads people in a particular direction. A series of events in my life had led to this, from the type of people I had met to the activities I had become involved in, and one was bound to believe that this outcome was in the stars. It was meant to happen.

Of course, apartheid was an evil system that had to be fought on all fronts. We could not live as third-class citizens and accept that the apartheid government would rule forever. It was founded and set up on injustice. That is why I didn't feel any obligation to obey unjust laws. They were wrong and had to be fought.

What makes you a human being is not your colour, it's your character, what is inside you, whether you are black or white. It is you as an individual, depending on your conscience, to do what is right, to distinguish between right and wrong, what is to be fought, what is to be accepted. This is what drove us.

We accepted that we might never see our parents, friends, relatives and girlfriends again, but we were prepared for that. I also hadn't finished my law degree – I was in my final year – but at the time our slogan was 'Freedom Now, Education Tomorrow'. There was excitement and a sense of adventure. We wanted to do something real about our liberation.

I knew that there was a risk that I might die but I was also prepared to kill. We had reached a point where the oppression suffered by a black person in South Africa had become intolerable. We had to either accept being slaves or we had to fight the slave masters and free ourselves from the yoke of oppression; there was no sentiment about it but rather a determination to free ourselves. Of course there was fear, that was natural, but it was about transcending that fear in pursuit of our ideals of true freedom. When Mandela made his speech from the dock at the Rivonia trial, he described it as an ideal for which he was prepared to die if needs be and I felt the same way.

After we had walked for some time, the guide told us to stop. We turned around and looked back and in the distance we could see lights flickering. 'Those lights,' he told us, 'are South Africa.' We had crossed the border and

I felt freedom wash over me. We were in an independent African state. As I looked back, I said goodbye to South Africa but vowed to return triumphant one day, knowing that our mission was to liberate the country.

Life in exile

We arrived in Lesotho eager to start our military training so that we could act on our naïve notion of 'blowing up Port Elizabeth'. We were keen to get to the camps as soon as possible. Listening to Radio Freedom as teenagers contributed to the picture we had of freedom fighters and that inspired us. We had a romantic view of what the life of a freedom fighter was like and what the camps would offer us. People fighting in Angola and Zimbabwe may have been referred to as 'terrorists' but we saw them as heroes who were an inspiration to us. We would hear those freedom songs and the sound of the machine guns and that sound meant being free, fighting the oppressor and liberating ourselves.

As head of the ANC and MK in Lesotho at the time, Comrade Chris Hani came to see us. Militant, brave, fearless, likeable and generous, he was a father figure who remembered every soldier by name and made us feel at home. At first I thought we were getting some kind of special treatment but that was simply the way Comrade Chris was. He said, 'No, guys. You will not start with military training. You have an important task. You must strengthen the underground machinery of the ANC in the Eastern Cape.'

We wanted military training but that was not the ANC's plan for us. We were to remain in Lesotho, we were told, and to continue the work our unit was doing. It was our job to help establish a powerful underground machinery in the Eastern Cape. The region was seen as strong in terms of mass mobilisation, strikes and demonstrations, but weak in underground structures that could be used to receive operatives and hide weapons. Our job was to build those cells and continue with our schooling. Comrade Chris did, however, agree that we should go on a crash course in Lesotho to learn how to handle firearms, offensive and defensive grenades, Makarov pistols, light machine guns and AK47s, as well as the 'She' and Scorpion, whose very soft trigger mechanism I remember well.

My first experience of pulling a trigger was actually a misfire. We had been through all the training without actually shooting a bullet or visiting a shooting range. It was all theory – how to assemble and dismantle a weapon – but none of the ammunition was live.

At times we carried out guard duties at Comrade Chris's house. We used to call it 'Moscow'. The hours midnight to 4 a.m. were known as the 'Break my Heart' hours, because it was freezing and we would be very sleepy during those hours and had to fight off drowsiness. One night while standing duty outside Chris's house, I heard dogs barking and prepared myself for any eventuality. There was a distinct possibility of an attack and the threat was real – Chris was a marked military man. I cocked the AK; my finger was itching to use it. And then, with my finger on the trigger, I unintentionally fired. Comrade Chris had been asleep and came out, crouching with his AK in hand, because he thought he was under attack. I was so embarrassed and had to apologise. In the camps, if that were to happen, the entire camp would have been awake and in their positions within seconds.

While in Lesotho, we also underwent intelligence and counter-intelligence training, as well as a course in military and combat work (MCW), and were thus well prepared to go on missions back into the home country. But first we had to create our 'legends'. We had to declare ourselves refugees through the United Nations High Commissioner for Refugees and the Lesotho government and had our fingerprints registered by the local police. I would find out decades later, when I actually saw my South African Security Police file, that those fingerprints found their way back to the South African Police, which suggests that there was cooperation taking place at the time. We had to have a legitimate reason to be in Lesotho – we were refugees and students.

The year 1980 marked a turning point for the ANC. Most significantly, there was a qualitative change in the type of comrade who was going into exile. After 1976, some of the youth who hadn't even finished matric were leaving the country in large numbers, but towards 1980 there was a new crop of middle-class, educated, university students who were choosing to join the struggle. Our leaving had an impact on others in Port Elizabeth, who were saying, 'But these guys didn't really have to leave.' I was doing my fourth and final year of B.Proc, Sizwe had finished his B.Juris and was doing his LLB, and Phaki and Thozi were both still studying. There were other guys from Fort Hare who were also coming over and we linked up with them in Lesotho to continue the struggle.

Our unit was given a house in Maseru and we had to wait until the following year, 1981, to enrol at Roma University. We were involved in political discussions and conducted political lessons for those new recruits from South Africa. In between, we had to continue with our work of making contact with people at home. We made use of the students at Roma who were not refugees, who travelled between the two countries.

We also decided that, as a unit, we should consider going back into South Africa on missions to strengthen underground systems there. Phaki came to us and asked, 'Chaps, why are we not trying to go and assist as we are being challenged to?' We discussed approaching Chris about the matter but then it emerged that Sizwe had already been talking to Chris about it for some time. So it was decided that he would be the first to go into the country. He was the natural leader of the group and it made sense that he would be sent on the first mission. Sizwe was always the calm one, not easily rattled and not excitable, and his strength of character established him as the clear leader – although Thozi may disagree with that view. So it was that Sizwe went back to South Africa on a recruitment drive, to meet with those we trusted in the country to form underground cells. The mission was successful and so he went again. Phaki was the next to infiltrate. In the meantime, we had enrolled at Roma and began our studies there in 1981, except for Thozi, who had by that time left for Tanzania.

Sizwe's disappearance

Sizwe disappeared in June 1981.

He had just come back from one of his missions.

A few days before, we were walking together through the streets of Lithabaneng township on the outskirts of Maseru, chatting about life. Sizwe turned to me and said, 'There are three important women in my life: my mother, my sister Lindiwe and my girlfriend.' I asked him which girlfriend and he told me it was Nowi Tshiki. He explained that he was having a problem with Nowi because she was supposed to visit him but had had to postpone. Sizwe was upset by it, but I told him he needn't be so uptight because she would come when she could. He was not impressed.

And then he asked me a strange question.

'Do you know whether, as a movement, we have walkie-talkies?'

I didn't know but suggested we ask the senior comrades who knew these things. I asked him why he wanted to know but he didn't say. I felt so strange and to this day I can't figure out that conversation. Part of me thought that perhaps he had been arrested on his last trip and they sent him back to Lesotho and he was worried about the safety of his family at home. Maybe he wanted to remain in touch with the ANC when he was in the country. I have always tried to convince myself that Sizwe could not have meant anything untoward, but the questions have never gone away.

Late the following night Sizwe arrived at our house and knocked on the window looking for a cigarette. Only Thozi and I were there because Phaki was on a mission inside the country and Sizwe was staying at the home of another comrade who was on a visit to Lusaka. He had walked to our place, which was quite a distance away. I'm not sure what he was busy with at the time, because we operated on a need-to-know basis and there were things that we would be asked to do that did not involve the others and would not be discussed. It was a security arrangement. We didn't ask him where he was coming from or where he was going. Thozi had temporarily stopped smoking so we had no cigarettes.

Sizwe said, 'I'm leaving if you don't have a cigarette. I'm going to look for a cigarette.' We ignored him. It was late and we went back to sleep. Thozi remembers that night vividly:

> *He walked that distance to come and ask for a cigarette and I'll always remember that when he got to us, he said, 'Jissus, I knew you had stopped smoking.' And that's the last we saw him. He left us, he went to Ngoako Ramatlhodi's place where Ngoako and Tito Mboweni were staying and he sat with them for a long time. They had arguments, discussions – normal discussions that we have about the situation at home – but they were not aware that he was from an operation. They were not part of our unit. I mean, we worked together, but on missions inside of the country we were broken up into different units, so they were not aware of the circumstances that Sizwe had just returned from the country, but they discussed a lot with him until 2 a.m. He was on foot … From there he went back to where he was staying and there was no transport in Lesotho that time. Then in the morning, that's when we heard he had been to Chris's place and borrowed a car to go and make a call. And Chris gave him money to put fuel in the car. One person who saw him at the garage, he said he saw him putting petrol in the car and then he had to go and make a call. And that's where he was arrested … he went to the Holiday Inn and that's where they captured him.*

That was the last time that we saw him.

Chris Hani arrived at our house the following afternoon. Thozi and I were sitting around doing political reading and Chris wanted to know if we had seen Sizwe. He explained that in the morning Sizwe had come to his place to tell him that he was having a problem with his girlfriend. Chris told him to go and phone her and talk through the issues and gave him his car. He was driving a yellow Datsun Stanza SSS at the time. That was around eight o'clock in the morning and by three o'clock Sizwe still hadn't returned. Chris thought that Sizwe might be with us but we told him that we had last seen him the previous night. We started to panic.

It was unlike Sizwe to disappear without a trace or at least somebody not knowing where he was. He had Chris's car and he knew that Chris was a busy person. Chris asked us to look for him and gave us a car, and sent Comrade Socks Sokupa to accompany us. We went everywhere Sizwe could've gone and even considered that he may have committed suicide.

Sizwe was a private person and I was probably the one who had the best understanding of him. We were very close, and I was always completely open and honest with him. I held no secrets back, but he on the other hand was quiet and measured and didn't give much away. If he was going to share anything with anyone, it was going to be with me but no one truly ever knew Sizwe. What he shared with me about Nowi he never told anyone else about and we spoke freely about women and love. If we were going to be grouped into teams for tasks, Sizwe and I would always be paired together. I felt that he was my brother. He could have gone with Phaki and Thozi to the bush for his initiation but he chose to wait for me. That spoke volumes.

We couldn't work out what might have happened to him. At no point did we think of the possibility of abduction at all. We drove around and thought, if he was going to commit suicide, the likely place would be Modimo Nthuse (God help me), a winding and treacherous road where you could drive off and kill yourself. We went to the 'Arrival Centre' where Sis Mandisa Williams stayed. She was working for the International Red Cross and was like an elder sister to us. We would go there when times were tough, so we went to ask her if she'd seen Sizwe, but he wasn't there.

So we went back to Comrade Chris and told him we couldn't find the man. Comrade Chris said we needed to notify Sizwe's family. First, I called Nowi, Sizwe's girlfriend, to find out whether they had actually spoken that day. She confirmed that they had, but that the call had ended very strangely. Sizwe had hung up midway through the conversation, while she was still talking. She kept saying 'Hello? Hello? Hello?' but there had been no response from Sizwe.

By eight o'clock that evening Sizwe had been gone for 12 hours. I couldn't bring myself to call Sizwe's father so instead I phoned Boet Sy and explained that we had no idea what had happened to Sizwe, that he had disappeared without a trace.

Vusi and Sizwe went together. They were big buddies because they played rugby together, sport and so forth. We didn't know the inner part of it all as they did certain things behind our backs.

It was partially an element of respect and also a security matter in the sense that whatever you did, you tried not to expose your parents. We received a report that Sizwe was abducted by the Security Police. Sizwe's father, an attorney, was my friend and I was acting as an intermediary. The commander in charge in Lesotho was Chris Hani. There was an active campaign amongst the parents to try to find Sizwe. When the police stole him, captured him, abducted him into South Africa, oh there were rumours of him being there and there and at one time there were rumours that he was being held in Humansdorp. We tried all means to verify that and get to Humansdorp but I think the Security Police must have got wind that information is leaking somewhere and they removed him and that was the end of it.

Molly Blackburn was involved. It was not successful. We asked her to help locate where this boy is detained because we knew he was detained by the Security Police, in their hands, but we did not know where. We just wanted to locate him. It had happened before. People just disappeared completely so it was important to trace, follow up and establish where that person is detained so that the Security Police know that it's known that so-and-so is being detained at such a place. The Security Police were generally hostile in all the matters that I was involved with. In those days, anybody who was detained by the Security Police, his life was at risk. Anything could happen, they could disappear.

Silas Nkanunu (lawyer)

Spies and speculation

Our lives changed when Sizwe disappeared.

We didn't know what had happened. We started hearing stories that he had been seen inside the country, that he had been seen in Joburg. There were also stories flying around that he was actually a sell-out. An internal operative who came to Lesotho for debriefings said his brother saw Sizwe in Sandton in the company of some white guys. People were beginning to say, he's an *impimpi*, an informer, he must have gone to South Africa with Chris's car, all sorts of strange talk. Loose talk.

And, as a result, we – the three of us who were left – felt that we were also being looked at with suspicion. The careless talk hurt me. There was no way Sizwe could have sold out. *Ai, ai, ai,* I was hurt. I felt like I had lost a brother. Thozi, Phaki, Sizwe and I had come a long way together and I felt that I knew Sizwe intimately. I simply couldn't comprehend that he had become a traitor.

These things were never said directly to us. Nobody ever came to us and said, 'Look, guys, we don't trust you any more because Sizwe has sold out.' But we heard stories and people talking.

My response was always that unless somebody came forward with clear information about what had happened, we don't know if he is in South Africa or how he left or what happened to the car. Chris never said anything but he also found it strange. He really believed in us and had confidence in the unit. The fact that he had given Sizwe a car showed the level of confidence he had in us. Thozi had a particularly difficult experience:

> *It was a June 16 celebration. Chris's wife came and then she said, 'Now, call Thozi.' We were two Thozi's, there was Thozamile Botha and there was myself. So I went to her. She was at the door. Ai, the way that woman insulted me and insulted all of us! That we were sent by the Special Branch here. We were here to steal ANC cars. That we are all spies, we were sent by a surrogate government. And in front of people. I left the hall immediately, I said, 'That woman insulted me!' I went back home and Chris came. He found me still crying and then Chris was very angry with Limpho. It was that time I was doing guard duties at Chris's house and I said, 'I am not going to that house any more, I will never go to that house.' I said, 'But if that woman doesn't want me in her house, how am I going to sit there in that house? I can't go there.' But Chris took me in his car, we went back and I did my duty, but I said, 'I do not want to see this woman in front of me.' You know, I was one of her confidants. Limpho's personal car was never driven by anybody except me. I was the only one who would drive her car.*
>
> *I don't know whether [Sizwe] was a spy or not a spy up to now. Now if somebody can tell me did he really see Sizwe with the Security Police, was anyone arrested because of information Sizwe gave out that endangered us during that time? You can't get anything. There's nothing that you can hear that Sizwe gave this information. So really, to me, I don't want to say because Sizwe was my friend – he was not a spy, but I still want to get facts about what really happened.*

We were all shattered by the accusations. Phaki remembers how difficult that time was:

> *It's not nice when you see some of your comrades are talking behind your back. There is mistrust. And you have to pretend as if you don't see. We couldn't accept songs about Sizwe that said he had sold out. There was nothing that could back up that Sizwe had probably sold out. Each time you sat down and thought about it, Sizwe had just simply disappeared and no one could tell us what had happened. People were jumping to conclusions that Sizwe had turned against the movement. When they tried*

to sing the songs about Sizwe being a sell-out we refused to join in. There was also a finger coming in our direction.

A long time after Sizwe disappeared, in 1986, I was coming back from inside the country and was taken by our ANC security chaps and questioned. Nobody was telling me exactly what was going on. They kept on saying I should write a report. I would write a report and then be made to write the report again. And then they'd interrogate me on those aspects that were not very clear in the report. Then I could see, no man, I'm being suspected of being an informer or something.

And then I was asked, 'Did you meet with Sizwe?' because they were being told that Sizwe had been seen inside the country.

'No, I didn't meet Sizwe.'

'For how long have you been working with Sizwe against us?'

It was terrible and you're trying to explain yourself. You don't know what has happened to Sizwe. You still don't think that Sizwe sold out but these people are convinced that Sizwe is on the other side.

I was at Roma when Sizwe's mother came to Lesotho to try to find answers. It was around three months after he had vanished. She also didn't know what had happened and I didn't go and see her. I didn't have the courage to look her in the eye. It was a difficult time – she knew that Sizwe and I were close, and the ANC leadership was sceptical and suspicious of her motives in Maseru and why she had arrived in town. It was a tough situation, emotionally, for all of us and I felt that I didn't have the strength to sit with her and not be able to account for her son. I was with Sizwe until more or less the last hours before he disappeared and I was weak. I was not strong enough to face her. It's like you go on a mission and one of you dies while the other survives – any mother would ask, 'Why my son and not you?' I was worried that seeing me would make her grief even more difficult to bear. Phaki went to see her in Maseru, but the reception was hostile because some of the leadership in Maseru believed that Sizwe had sold out and they wanted to know why she would want to collect his clothes if she didn't know where he was. That was a weak moment in my life – when I was not able to look Sizwe's mother in the eye. She was the mother of my best friend, but I didn't go and see her.

Captain Du Plessis arrived with his colleagues. He said, 'When you are investigating a terrorist, this is how you go about it, you have got to get the truth.' He then showed us the way you retrieve information from a terrorist. Sizwe was tied at the knees. He said I must handcuff him from the back. We then made him lie on the floor and we put a sack on him – we refer to it as 'the prisoner's bag'. We put this over his head and you have to put this on very tightly so that he can't breathe and then at the same time there was a small machine. This machine has a crank handle with two wires. When you use this crank handle it's very painful to the victim. That is how information was retrieved from a prisoner. Every time we saw that he [was] suffocating we took the bag off his head and then he'd be asked questions. This machine, when used, is very, very painful, you will give us any information that we want from you because of the pain. It shocks you. There's a handle and the second person takes the two wires, puts it on your body wherever they choose to. If you wind this machine to be more powerful you splash water on the victim and then the victim will give us the information because of the pain. The captain showed us how to use the machine. He said that we should not beat him up because he does not want a 'Steve Biko' case again.

Abridged TRC testimony of policeman Ginotry Danster about Sizwe's torture and interrogation at the Jeffrey's Bay Police Station (18 February 1998)

The Maseru raids

In the early hours of 9 December 1982, their path lit by a full moon, 100 South African soldiers crept into Maseru, the capital of Lesotho. They had clandestinely crossed the border and were in search of a cluster of homes on the outskirts of the city where members of the ANC were thought to be living. The commandos picked their way through the suburbs and met no resistance from the kingdom's minuscule 2 000-man paramilitary defence force. At around one o'clock the South Africans opened fire on over a dozen homes pointed out by informants. Within an hour their mission was accomplished and they crept back across the border.

At dawn, the chief of the South African Defence Force (SADF) General Constand Viljoen, briefed the media about Operation Blanket, which he described as a pre-emptive strike against ANC militants in the mountainous kingdom of Lesotho. He claimed that the ANC was planning attacks in South Africa against political leaders in the homelands of Transkei and Ciskei. To buttress his point, he displayed Communist-bloc issued rocket launchers, rifles and grenades. The ANC denied the South African claims and denounced the invasion as a 'cold-blooded massacre', saying those killed were political refugees and not terrorists. Forty-two people were slaughtered, 30 of them members of the ANC. The others were Lesotho residents, including five women and two children.

I was on campus in Roma when we heard the news that the *boers* had invaded Maseru. It was about 6 a.m., around the time General Viljoen was preparing to conduct his briefing. We dropped everything and rushed through to Maseru, which was around 40 minutes away.

Between 1982 and 1985, Girly and I were stationed at Roma, where I was studying and doing underground work for the ANC. I had to begin my degree again from my second year and, although I wanted to go for military training, the ANC wanted me to carry on and do an LLB. I was the chairperson of the ANC Youth and Students in Lesotho and was the chair of our unit at Roma. Along with me there at the time were Ngoako Ramatlhodi and Tito Mboweni. Phaki, Thozamile Botha, Jomo Kambule, Shakes Mkhonto, Loyiso Mpumlwana and Hlubi Radebe were also there. We concentrated on mobilising students from the Cape who were in Lesotho.

We arrived in Maseru hours after the raid had taken place and began going to the known houses of comrades. Others who were already there pointed out which houses had been the targets of the attack.

Comrade Mavimbela's house had been raided. Comrades who had just come from Robben Island had been there to meet with the ANC to be debriefed and were waiting to meet their wives after finally being released from prison. At some houses the *boers* killed all the comrades and then set the buildings on fire.

One image I have never been able to erase is of Comrade David – I never knew his surname because in exile these things were not relevant. He had been shot in the back of the head and the exit wound was a large hole in his forehead. When I got there, parts of his brain were still oozing out because of the heat of the day. Our political instructor, Comrade Gene Gugushe, had attended the South African Communist Party (SACP) 'party' school in Moscow to learn Marxism and Leninism. On the night of the raid when the SADF commandos attacked the flat where he was staying, he returned fire with a Makarov pistol but he was clearly under-armed, essentially defenceless against the firepower of the *boers*. He simply couldn't defend himself, but he was one of the heroes of the raid as he fought back despite being overwhelmed.

The *boers* had also been to Comrade Mathabatha Sexwale's house. Booker T (which is what we called him) had an AK and he had also fought back. He had come out fighting and the *boers* ran but Kananelo (Kay) Sexwale, who was only a young girl at the time, was wounded. Dr Norman

Ngciphe, a comrade with whom I had attended St John's College, was also killed. One comrade, Trinity Zokwe, who was a well-known soccer star in Mthatha, escaped from the house naked and ran for his life. They chased him but the bullets hit the road behind him. The smell of gunpowder hung in the air, which was thick with the stink of death. The attacks had taken place at private residences in outlying suburbs and every home told a different story, each reflecting the modus operandi of the unit that had attacked that particular site. In some houses women were killed, in others they were spared. In some instances the buildings were burnt down, whilst in other cases the occupants were gunned down and left for dead. In those residences where there were weapons the comrades fought back, but where people were not armed they were massacred. But the SADF didn't operate consistently.

Twelve locals were killed simply because they had been staying in houses previously occupied by ANC people. We did not stay in one house for long – no more than three to six months at a time – and that's how some locals were caught in the crossfire. One of the guys who was part of that raid, who was pointing out the houses to the *boers*, once actually stayed with us in my house in Maseru before he defected and I met him later on in life in Lusaka as an ANC prisoner.

A trail of death and destruction was left behind in Maseru. Fear had seeped in across the city and civilians were terrified. The locals felt vulnerable but in some cases it also served to strengthen the bond between them and the ANC, whereas in other instances it led to further fear of association.

We had to carry the bodies to the mortuary. It was hot in Maseru and the cold room was not working, so the bodies started decomposing and the smell of death lingered so that we could smell death wherever we went. The night before the funeral we dug 30 graves with shovels, so that we could bury our comrades. In a war situation, soldiers are not allowed to grieve. You externalise your grief in the form of defiance and this is what we had anticipated. There were no games being played – these were war games and war games kill. So I didn't grieve; instead I turned my emotion into anger. These were our comrades we were digging graves for but we refused to feel sombre or allow ourselves to be defeated by low morale. Instead, it had the opposite effect and strengthened our resolve. This was a real war and we had been attacked in our homes and we were planning to fight back. That led to some comrades changing their life plans – some chose to go home and hand themselves over, whilst others chose to give up their studies and go for military training in Angola.

We had to take the coffins from the mortuary. It was difficult for comrades in Lusaka to come to the funeral because they would have to fly over South Africa, but Oliver Tambo did turn up unexpectedly. He only interacted with the leadership of the ANC and officials in Lesotho and I was just part of the regular rank and file, so I was not able to speak to him. It was nevertheless a highlight for me to see him in the flesh for the first time ever. He was a heroic figure, one we had read about in magazines and listened to on the radio. Seeing my leader in person motivated and excited me even further. And, of course, there was euphoria in the stadium as some South Africans who had travelled to Maseru for the funeral to bury their relatives were able to see the ANC leader-in-exile with their own eyes. He was the driving force behind the ANC, and had been guiding it in all its years in exile. We used to refer to Lesotho as the 'Belly of the Monster' because it was the only country where the ANC had a presence and yet remained completely surrounded by South Africa. The fact that O.R. was willing to travel over South Africa from Maputo and risk his safety further entrenched his position as a hero of our struggle, who was genuinely concerned with the welfare and plight of his soldiers.

In 1985, when the *boers* raided Maseru yet again, we also lost many comrades but it was only one house that was targeted. It was a house they knew fairly well – and they also knew that comrades were going to be infiltrating South Africa from here the following day. One of the guys I was with at St John's College as well as Fort Hare was also killed. His name was Zola Dubeni, but we called him Brezhnev. Nomkhosi Mini, the daughter of Vuyisile Mini, was also killed, as well as Themba Sgananda, a fit and able comrade from Cape Town. Comrade Juluka (Leon Meyer), a coloured comrade from East London, was killed along with his white girlfriend, Jacqui, but their child, who was only a year old, survived. Comrade Morris Seabelo, a new commander of political and military structures, also died. In total, six comrades. During my time in Maseru I had worked with those who were killed and I came to know them all well.

While many of my comrades were murdered in the Maseru raids, their deaths only served to strengthen my resolve. It confirmed to me that what we were doing was correct and just, and further encouraged me to fight for liberation until the bitter end. The emotion that we felt as we dug the graves of our comrades and the inspiration we all drew from seeing O.R. Tambo served to make us more resolute. We did not feel defeated – we felt and knew that we were at war.

Marriage and children

I had proposed marriage as far back as 1972 but Girly and I only wed on 13 February 1982. I was 14 when we first met and I proposed in jest when I told her then that she was going to be my wife. At 24, I felt that I was old enough to start a family and we loved each other and didn't need to wait any longer. Girly was also pregnant so the time felt right. In the months after I went into exile she would come and visit in Lesotho but decided to move permanently after our marriage in early 1982.

We were a perfect fit and our relationship was solid. As Girly recalls, she made the decision to come over and join me in exile:

> *At that time, Vusi and I had become so close. It had stopped being a girl and boy kind of relationship and we were in a much more strong woman and man relationship, which we were quite serious about. My mother kept on asking, 'So what are you going to do now?' She was quite sympathetic in the sense that she would give me money and would let me go on a train to visit. But I knew after the very first visit that I was going to have to part with home.*
>
> *I knew I was going to have to leave and follow Vusi, not because he had left but because I really believed now. I had matured and I made this decision quite consciously, because of what I had been exposed to in terms of politics. I understood the actions I was taking, absolutely, and I thought I was now prepared to do this.*

> *But nothing prepares you for exile. People hide its impact and at that time they were trying to attract as many people as possible to join the struggle. It was talked about in hush-hush tones and they painted this glorified picture. The big thing they mentioned was the opportunities for you to develop and to go out there and be this and that. So I saw it as an opportunity to be able to achieve an education.*

Girly and I were made for one another. Over the years I had had a number of girlfriends, but I remained her only boyfriend. She was always loyal to me but, I have to confess, I had a roving eye. It was the culture of the time and, growing up, it was expected that a young man would have more than one girlfriend or he would be disrespected by his peers and called *isishumane* – a derogatory term. But Girly always had a special place in my heart.

The marriage officer was Father Michael Lapsley, the social justice activist and Anglican priest who would later lose both hands and the sight in one eye as a result of a letter-bomb explosion in Harare in 1990. Before we were married, Mike counselled us about the institution of marriage, what it meant, what the implications were, and that getting married meant that our lives would change forever. I recall saying to him, 'Comrade Mike, you have never been married. What do you know about marriage if you were never married?' Mike was a good comrade and laughed at my insubordination.

Girly and I quarrelled so much the night before the wedding that we nearly called it off. I can't tell you why we were quarrelling, but I suppose it was because of the nerves, tension and anxiety. Girly's uncle came from South Africa, as did my sister Nonkululeko and Boet Silas Nkanunu. There were no best men or bridesmaids, it was just the two of us – or three, rather, because Girly was heavily pregnant at the time. I wore a blue three-piece suit that came from home and Girly wore a sari-style dress in a similar colour. I felt that I had the best catch and was damn excited that I was marrying the love of my life. I wanted to shout it from the rooftops, and all the quarrelling from the night before was forgotten. That was the best day of my life.

We hadn't planned a party but our comrades, unbeknown to us, organised a big bash and we ended up having the party of our lives at Father Mike's place. So many of our friends were there and it was lovely simply because it was totally unplanned.

A couple of months later, in May, our daughter Zukiswa was born. When Girly started having labour pains, we immediately went to Father Mike because he had a van. We drove to St Joseph's Hospital, not far from the campus in Roma. We were both very excited and as we rushed to the hospital, I sat in the back of the van with Tito Mboweni, a very young man at the time, and Comrade Shakes.

When we arrived at the hospital, Tito – equally concerned about Girly – went running in with her and Mike. I, however, dragged my feet. The closer we got to the labour ward, the more I was overcome by fear and anxiety. So it was that the doctors thought that Tito was the father and that he wanted to witness the birth. They asked him, 'Are you the father? You can go in!' But Tito said 'No, no, no!' Of course, I didn't go in – I was just too scared! Fortunately, I have since been able to witness and experience the birth of my last two sons, and what an experience in terms of bonding with both the mother and the newborn that was. Naturally, I regretted not having been there when my daughters and my eldest son were born.

Zukiswa was my first child with Girly but I did already have a son, who was born in 1977, when I was a 19-year-old student at Fort Hare. It was a December romance. It was a moment of temporary infidelity, of weakness, of male ego and indiscretion all connected with being young. The mother, from Fort Beaufort, had been visiting Sizwe's family for the holidays because her aunt had married Sizwe's father after he divorced Sizwe's mother. The young woman was in town and she was lonely and Sizwe asked me to take her out.

Then I heard from Sizwe that the young woman was pregnant and I said, 'Wow!' I expected that her family would seek payment for damages as per the African tradition but her parents never brought the case to my home. She came from a strict family and they didn't want to hear anything about it. Three years later I left the country and I only saw her again in 1996, when the young man graduated from boyhood to manhood after his initiation and, as his family, we took him gifts. I told Girly about my son while we were in exile and she accepted him and treats him like any other son.

When I saw Zukiswa for the first time, it was as though I was looking at a picture of myself. She had a special place in my heart. There had been an air of expectation around her birth – I had not been a hands-on parent before and I was nervous about what she would be like as a child and how she would impact on our ambitions.

Sandina, my second daughter, was born in 1986. It was the height of the State of Emergency in South Africa and the *boers* were eager to push the ANC out of southern Africa up into the continent. However, the Political and Military Command (PMC) in Lesotho instructed us that all trained comrades should infiltrate South Africa rather than move further up into the continent.

Even though I was in my final year, I was ready to give up my LLB. I had also been to Angola so I was more confident about handling weapons and I volunteered to go inside the country. The previous year there had been a coup in Lesotho and then there was the second raid on Maseru.

The ANC was under pressure to leave and the South African Police had a list of names of those of us who were at Roma University. Our names were all there so some of us decided to go inside the country and infiltrate.

At home in South Africa, the Total Onslaught campaign was in full swing – a grand strategy by the apartheid government to try to isolate the ANC and its military wing by driving it out of the frontier states by depriving us of military bases. We felt that the execution of the struggle would be difficult and we needed to be based inside the country in order to start preparing for the people's war.

Girly was far into her pregnancy at the time and so, because of the threat of deportation and rumours of another raid by the South African Defence Force, and also because Girly would be unable to fly out in her state, we decided that she should be induced. The decision may sound harsh when we consider it now, but that was the reality we faced. We had hard choices to make – of course I was anxious about my wife and there was always the threat of the *boers* coming into Maseru at any time and there was pressure from the Lesotho government. There was pressure all around us. Friends of ours, the couple Dr Lungelwa Martin and Dr Vuyo Letele, were both medical doctors and gynaecologists, so Girly spent a week with them in Mohalieshoek where they were practising. They induced her and our little girl was born.

It was a difficult time for us, as Girly remembers well:

Every now and again we were told we had to disappear and sleep else-

where. I remember there was a period when we slept outside the graveyard – myself, Vusi and Phaki. It was May and winter in Maseru is extremely cold compared to South Africa. We spent something like three weeks at the graveyard. All we could take was a small blanket because the neighbours must not notice that we were moving out, because we didn't know who was in the neighbourhood. So we just had to dress warmly and move out when it was night.

Look, having children in exile was not the best of things to do, but when you are young, you are always bold and courageous. She was born around the time of the second raid on 27 January 1986. I was doing the final year of my BA and we were about to write December exams at the time. There were lots of funny movements around and they were quite noticeable. There were these high-riding motorcycles with white guys driving aggressively and everybody said all was not right.

My second daughter's birth happened in the third week. I was lucky: I was taken in by Professor Bill and Aunt May McClain who were always supportive towards us as South African students. We decided that the best thing to do was an induction. One of the comrades who had a car drove me to Mohalieshoek and I gave birth there. There was something about this girl. Immediately when she popped out, her eyes were open. She didn't cry, she didn't yell, she looked at me and it was like the stars coming out of her eyes. It touched me in a way that shook me inside.

Even the doctors said, 'Ha, this one, her eyes are open, she is not talking, she is not crying. She is just happy to be here.'

There was something about her eyes – like she had small sparks coming out of them. I thought I would go to the grave with that feeling, almost of being electrocuted by her. And to this day, I think it was just an angel with us for a moment, come to grace our lives for a short while.

According to tradition, when the first child is born, the parents send the name from home. My mother gave our first daughter the name Zukiswa, which is derived from Girly's real name Nozuko. 'Uzuko' is 'glory' and 'Zukiswa' is 'to be glorified'. Girly also gave her the name Lifakazi (inheritance) after her own father, Lifa. With the birth of our second child, it was my turn to name her.

I gave our second daughter two names. The first was Sandina, derived from the Sandinista Revolution of Nicaragua. I admired the Revolution of Nicaragua and General Sandino, so I gave her that name. Her second name was Siyalithatha, from *Siyalithatha ilizwe* – 'We are now taking over', because I was confident that one day we would be liberating the country.

We spent only seven days with the baby and then our parents came to take her away. My mother and Girly's mother came to fetch her. Life was uncertain then. There were deportations and raids and we felt that she would be safer at home. Zukiswa had already been sent back to Port Elizabeth. It was so difficult for us, but we thought it was in her best interests.

He [Sizwe Kondile] gave us information regarding training in Lesotho, who was active in Lesotho, several infiltrations that he had knowledge of, that he received training in the handling of weapons himself, as well as political training, that he also came in in order to do recruitment and to find safe places. He also pointed out several places to us where the freedom fighters – after they had infiltrated the RSA from Lesotho, where they had got out of taxis, where they were being transported to. And he also pointed out where trained terrorists found themselves, which we followed up. The position in which Kondile was was perfect in the sense that, firstly he was a confidant of Mr Chris Hani, he lived with him, he was intelligent and I was of the opinion that he could fill that void for us because with the correct briefing he could join in and we could possibly have known when people were infiltrating, where they were infiltrating and with what purpose they were infiltrating. He was prepared to co-operate. The only way in which we would be able to use him and to get the information from him again was to make use of a principal agent who at that stage already had several informers in Lesotho and the Transkei and he would have to communicate with him. This person had access to Lesotho, as well as ANC circles. The information that I tried to obtain was information that we needed very urgently and therefore it was essential for me to have him transferred as soon as possible, so that I could obtain the information from him. That's why I had to inform him as to how it was going to work and who would make contact with him.

It was round about the end of July, the beginning of August, but it's only speculation. I went to his cell. At that stage he was showering in the cell complex. I sat down on his bed to wait for him until he had finished showering. When I sat down on the bed I heard some paper. I took out those papers thinking that those were reports he was compiling for me. I started reading through those notes and received a note apparently directed to the ANC. It was in his own handwriting. If I can remember correctly, it was to inform the ANC, it was directed to a person to inform the ANC that firstly, he had been arrested, and secondly that he pretended to be an informer. That at this stage he had provided no information which would harm any ANC member. That was what it was all about, shortly. I realised I had made a mistake, that he was not loyal and that he had misled me. I think the normal reaction of a security policeman [was], for example, in the first place, because I trusted him, I was shocked, I was terribly disappointed. I realised that this whole network was in danger because of this. I didn't say anything, I did not take those notes. At that stage I honestly want to tell you I did not know what to do. I didn't know what the next step had to be, and I wanted to seek assistance. I arranged that he would get a barracks room at the Jeffrey's Bay Police Station and that he should be guarded by Raath with the specific instructions that he absolutely had to make provision or see to it that nobody visits him and nothing could get out of that barracks room.

I approached General Nick van Rensburg to assist me in this regard. I told him in detail, if I remember correctly, Van Rensburg was aware of the fact that I regarded this as a breakthrough to recruit Kondile. I am honest today to say that I was proud of that. This whole thing exploded in my face and he was the only person at this stage who could give assistance to me. He had more experience than I had.

Van Rensburg then proposed that we go to Colonel Erasmus, now General Erasmus, he was Divisional Commander of the Eastern Cape Security Branch. There I sketched this whole dilemma for him and we considered various alternatives. There were not many. Firstly, because we couldn't detain him for a longer period. If we should do that we had to release him at one or other stage or charge him. And then this information and the identification, in other words of the information network, would become known. By eliminating this – the agent – it would lead to making known of other sources and this was also sketched to Erasmus. Erasmus asked at that stage that all the problem areas regarding Kondile had to be put in writing, I did just that. I gave it to him and he wanted to consider all the various options.

We decided that there was no other alternative [but to kill him] and we contemplated and asked where? How? Firstly we did not have the experience in this regard. We did not have the place to do it and if I can remember correctly [Van Rensburg] told or suggested to Erasmus that he was in contact with Dirk Coetzee from Vlakplaas and that Dirk had the necessary infrastructure to solve or address these problems. He agreed to this and said we had to make the necessary contact and that we had to get a team together to do this. At that stage it was decided that Mr Kondile had to be killed and that Dirk Coetzee's and Vlakplaas' assistance should be obtained. Kondile's vehicle, when he was arrested and detained in Bloemfontein, was left behind there in Bloemfontein, not at a police station, as far as I can remember, but at a safe place. I made contact with the Security Branch in Bloemfontein and asked that this vehicle should be handed over to us again. I can't remember today with whom I had made contact in Bloemfontein. I can't remember whether we met him at the Security Branch or at the police station or where, but what I can remember is that we did find the vehicle there and Sergeant Raath was the driver of the vehicle and he followed us in this vehicle to Komatipoort.

Abridged TRC testimony of Captain Hermanus Barend du Plessis
(9 February 1998)

Going inside

The Caledon River was full and angry that morning. It was moving in a hurry and the current was strong following several days of heavy rain. A Basotho man, shining his shoes outside his hut when we passed, had followed us to the river's edge and suddenly issued a warning: 'No one has crossed that river for the past three days. If you're thinking of going across, I would advise against it.' It jolted us. Phaki could barely keep his head above water and I couldn't swim at all.

My name was Thozamile Feni, at least, that was the name in my passport, and I was on a mission to infiltrate South Africa as an underground combatant. Phaki was with me and we were determined that the operation would not be aborted.

The day before, Phaki and I, together with Girly and a friend, Nonkumbulo Tshombe, checked into a hotel not far from the river near the Ficksburg border. We were acting as two ordinary couples who were staying for the night. I couldn't sleep at all – my stomach was uneasy, there was anxiety, fear and excitement and we got up at 5 a.m. eager to get on our way.

An ANC unit had prepared false documentation for us, and I was given the MK underground name Steve Mpilo when I was at training camp in Angola. I was over the moon when I was finally sent to 'the camps'. I had heard stories about comrades who had died in training, but that did not discourage me at all. I left alone and flew to Lusaka and made my way to

Luanda. I couldn't hide my excitement at what lay ahead and the prospect of real military training. Phaki had already been and he had told me all sorts of elaborate stories about his experiences. I knew that Angola has a very hot climate, but I was still overwhelmed by the heat as soon as the plane entered Angolan airspace. I was taken by truck to the Pango camp and along the way the trained MK soldiers escorting me cocked their weapons in certain areas along the route where Unita ambushes were commonplace. This fuelled my excitement – as well as a fear that we could face an ambush at any time.

At the end of a long gravel road, the truck stopped at a sentry post and we made our way into the camp. With people living in tents and dugouts, it met all my romanticised expectations. Pango was a camp preparing special units and those who were there were experienced soldiers, identified for specific tasks. I was assigned a section and spent three months in training during which I fired many weapons for the first time. I was most excited about firing an RPG-7, a Soviet rocket we had sung about in South Africa and now I was doing it in reality. I quickly adapted to the environment and loved my time in Angola. It was a realisation of a lifelong dream for me and it had prepared me for my mission back into South Africa.

To further prepare to go back inside the country, I shaved off my long hair and gave myself a 'chiskop'. I also wore glasses and new clothes that no one could identify me by. We knew that some of the Roma students were also being used by the regime and we could be spotted.

Phaki and I left Girly and Nonkumbulo at the hotel and walked in the direction of the river, passing the Basotho man polishing his shoes as we went. The plan was for our driver, Soci Tshangisa, to make his way across the border, our bags in his boot, and pick us up on the other side.

Phaki and I were contemplating our next move when the Basotho man offered to show us another way. Of course, we had to consider whether we could trust him or not. As a cover, we told him that we were students and that our passports had expired so we needed to get across to renew them. We asked him about his alternative route and he said, 'Through the border post.' I told him he must be crazy.

But our options were limited so we had very little choice but to follow him towards the border post. Once there, however, we didn't join the queue. Instead, we went across a bridge through to the no-man's-land between the two countries. There is nothing I hate more than not being in control of a situation, and at that point I didn't know what this man was doing or where he was taking us. He told us to wait and I had no idea why.

As it turns out, a truck was making its way past us and he was waiting for it to get to the perfect spot so that it would obscure the view from the South African side. There was a hole in the fence next to us and, as that truck moved past, we slipped through to the other side.

We had walked about a kilometre, and the border was still visible, when two young boys approached us. They had seen that we hadn't gone through the border post and began threatening us. 'Hey, this way you are using, you must give us money if you do not want us to report you to the police,' they warned us. I was damn angry.

I felt that Phaki and I could deal with these boys. Silence them. I was prepared to kill them if necessary. Phaki wanted to pay them off, but I refused. The money was for the operation and we couldn't waste it. I was furious, as Phaki recalls:

> *Vusi is a friendly guy. He's very playful and he's easy to make friends with, but he is also very easy to fight with. Vusi doesn't back off. He doesn't know the meaning of backing off. That's where people like Thabo Mbeki made a mistake! Vusi immediately said, 'These bastards!' He wanted to sort them out and I said no, not where we were. The environment was not right. We were not far from the border but Vusi was clear he was not going to give these boys money and I knew that we had no choice. We had to give these boys money. We debated it. I said leave it, let me handle it. And I had to buy them. I don't know how much I gave them. They were happy and they moved away. Fighting with those boys, we don't know what it could have attracted. Vusi doesn't want to think you think you're clever. He'll sort you out.*

We waited on the South African side of the border where we had arranged for Tshangisa to collect us. As we stood there, a police van trundled past. Then it passed a second time and still we were waiting for Tshangisa. By now we were nervous, so we decided to walk back towards the border post in the hope that we would not appear suspicious. We reached a shop and went inside, so that we could look out the window towards the bridge. We could see Tshangisa's car parked on the side of the road and he was talking with some white guys. Anxious, we peered through the window and watched as he got into his car, drove out behind two other cars and was followed by another vehicle. He was being escorted by the police and was being taken away. Our plan was falling apart.

We later learned that Tshangisa had been arrested and was kept in custody in the Free State. He was quizzed about the clothes he had in his car and used the story that he sold clothes to students in Roma for a living, which also explained why he had cash on him. Some of the police didn't believe him. He was a well-known activist in the Eastern Cape border area (East London–King William's Town) and the police in the Free State had been told about that.

Immediately, Phaki and I had to rethink our plan. We weren't sure how long it would take Tshangisa to crack and whether the police would find out that we were in the country. Chances were that they would mount roadblocks going south because they would know we were heading to the border region and they would stop cars going to Bloemfontein. We therefore decided to go north and to take public transport. We jumped into a taxi to Welkom.

Then, as we were passing some mines, we were pulled over by the traffic cops. I was sitting at the back of the taxi and it occurred to me that I should check my identity document just in case. Lord behold! The document was a disaster: it had been used by Thozamile T. Feni, a known activist in the border region of the Eastern Cape who had only recently arrived in Lesotho from South Africa, and – even worse – the date of birth was listed as 1940. I was born in 1958, 18 years later, and that would be a clear giveaway.

I had been so excited that I hadn't bothered to check it beforehand, and now I was convinced I was being sold out. I asked Phaki for a pen and I tried desperately to add a tail to the *0* to make the date look like 1949. To my relief, the traffic cops were only interested in the car and the driver and they didn't check the rest of us. I resolved that as soon as I was settled in the country, I would arrange a new identity document – which I did through some underground connection in the Ciskei government.

But that trip proved messy. For one, comrades were negligent in preparing the documentation. I wasn't sure whether it was because so many people were being sent inside that those who were left to deal with the arrangements were failing in their task, but it was clear that sloppiness and complacency had crept in. Phaki agreed that things had not been planned as they should have been:

> *A commander would usually take you across the river, and hand you over to somebody on the other side so that that person could account for what happened to you. There always needed to be somebody in the chain who knew your whereabouts. You should never be left there on your own.*

Along the way to the Eastern Cape, we had several more potentially disastrous moments. We didn't realise it at the time, but as we were getting onto a taxi in the township of Thabong, a woman who knew us from Port Elizabeth saw us but we didn't see her. It was only around 2008 that she told me, 'I'm sure it was you and Phaki that I saw that day.'

Then, on a bus to King William's Town, we were stopped once again and a black guy climbed on. He looked at everybody, trying to see if he could identify any ANC guerrillas. He must have been an *askari* but he didn't notice us. The bus also stopped outside the SADF headquarters in Queenstown at one stage. In Alice, our former Fort Hare rugby team manager, Makhenkesi Stofile, gave us a place to sleep and some money to continue on our journey. He was housing another comrade at the time, Mzwakhe Ndlela, who was on his own mission into the country. Mzwakhe and I trained in the same military camp in Angola and had become close friends. He was a fitness fanatic and a very committed comrade. He was on a different mission and we were not supposed to have encountered each other.

Finally, however, we made it to Port Elizabeth and decided that we would walk the long stretch from town to New Brighton to ensure nobody would see us. We knew that Zola Yeye worked in the library so we sought refuge there. The library belonged to the Bantu Affairs Administration Board and had been previously burnt down, so police officers had been stationed outside – completely unaware that they were guarding ANC guerrillas playing table tennis inside the building.

I stayed in South Africa for about three months, organising underground structures and setting up networks, all the time trying to avoid being detected. We had one close shave when Phaki's brother Winky took us to stay at a house in New Brighton that was housing known activists. I was worried and warned Phaki that we shouldn't stay there long. The place could be raided at any time.

That night Stone Sizani, another activist, arrived, but I was still uneasy. That night we slept in Zola Yeye's car in his parents' yard. We agreed that anything was better than staying in that house because the police could come kicking down the doors at any minute. And that's exactly what happened. That very night, the house was raided. Stone was found there and he was detained. We were very lucky.

We moved from place to place and stayed wherever we could. We slept during the day and worked at night, going out to give contacts tasks to carry out. One of our hideaways was in some flats at the back of a shop near the single men's quarters in Kwazakhele owned by Boet Feya, Fezile Sobikwa:

> *It was expected of us that if they come back inside here we must shelter them. It's not about whether I know him or I don't know him. The ANC brought them to me and I would still do it even today. You know, when it's summer, people forget how cold winter was. The oppression that was here, it's a miracle that we're still laughing. When they left here, that was when the brunt of oppression was coming to kill people. They were actually killing people and there were riots in this township. The struggle was very, very tense then. The government was intensifying because they were killing our people and that's why some of them were sent to go out of New Brighton. We were supporting them to go into exile. We couldn't all sit here and hope that one day God is going to send a messiah. We couldn't. Others had to go overseas. We also were busy intensifying, with our limited resources, the struggle. They would arrive at the door and you don't care, you don't want to know, what is he here to do. There is no appointment. They come and you close the door, that's all. And I don't want to know what it is they've come to do because if I'm arrested then I must just know he is here, not what he was going to do. Even if I was hit by the forces I wouldn't have been able to explain anything that is detrimental to the ANC. I didn't worry when they came. It had to happen. It had to happen. Some houses needed to be secured here for that to happen. Yes, there were others like them that I sheltered. I could also have been shot or arrested or whatever in pursuit of them. They wouldn't have arrested*

them – they would have made sure that they shot them.

While I was operating inside the country, I saw my mother and I asked her to bring my baby to me. I knew this was a security breach but I had to see my baby girl. Zukiswa was about four years old at the time, so I didn't want to risk seeing her because she definitely would have spoken about seeing me without realising it. My mother and older brother brought Sandina to me at Girly's parents' home.

Imagine how I felt! I had only seen my baby for seven days before she was spirited out of the country. I was so grateful to have the opportunity to spend time with her, not knowing it would be the last chance I would ever have.

I slept at the time in the house of Colonel Nick van Rensburg whilst operating in that area and on our way back from Jeffrey's Bay Police Station he said that at a time they would have to make a plan with this man that I've just seen because during interrogation he dived through a window with his hands handcuffed behind his back in an effort to get away from his interrogators and sustained brain injuries. It wasn't a question of seeing a man with plasters and stitches all over him. To me he looked quite normal, but apparently by the people that knew him well his behaviour became peculiar. He told me that they called in a doctor friend, who warned them that there was some blood on the brain as a result of him falling on his head, and if they want to avoid a second Biko case they'll have to do something about it. It then became obvious to me that he was illegally detained, because he was held in a white single quarters, which was in those days abnormal, absolutely abnormal. We then discussed that at a time they will, of their convenience, he will let me know, and we will meet up at Komatipoort. His car, the Datsun Stanza, will be taken through to Swaziland to give the impression that after his release he went into Swaziland and went to the ANC. They pretended to release him at Bloemfontein, where he was originally arrested and held by, at the time Warrant Officer Hendrik Prinsloo, who is now Colonel Hendrik Prinsloo, still with Police Headquarters in the Security Section, and that is where his car, the Datsun Stanza of the late Chris Hani, was officially held, and his belongings. Because he was then connected also in the Port Elizabeth area he was passed over to them for interrogation too. So they then released him, and abducted him on the road and brought him with the Datsun Stanza back to Jeffrey's Bay Police Station.

Abridged TRC testimony of former Vlakplaas commander Dirk Coetzee (Durban, 5 November 1996)

Losing a child

In October 1986, the phone rang in a communal house used by comrades in the Avenues in Harare, Zimbabwe. Girly and I weren't there at the time, but Stix Sifingo took a message from my parents and arranged a time for them to call again. When the phone rang a second time, it was my uncle.

The voice on the other end of the long line was hollow. My uncle was calling to tell me that my baby Sandina had died. He also told me that I should take the news like a man. I had been ready for some kind of tragedy but thought it would be about my father or my mother – I did not conceive it would be about one of my daughters, who were both at home in Port Elizabeth. Uncle told me that she had been sick for some time with measles.

I was shattered. 'It can't be!'

My comrades already knew but were afraid to tell me. I had left Girly at our flat and now had to go to break the news to her. I had no idea how I would do it. I was grateful that I had at least had an opportunity to see Sandina when I was inside the country, but Girly had only spent a few days with her after her birth in Lesotho:

> *I just crumbled and I was shaking all the time. It took me years to get over, but actually, it never goes away, it just stays in the distance. The experience brought Vusi and me closer together. Something bonded and*

> *our relationship was qualitatively stronger. Because in exile, really, there's hardly any family support. Most of the relationships crumbled under those conditions. It was sad that we couldn't bury the child. She had been staying with my mother-in-law, who had brought up our firstborn. She's a lady I have always had admiration for. She was very motherly, very loving and I saw the care she gave to my own kids. I had no issues about what could have happened. I made peace that she did all she could.*

Comrades came to our place to try to comfort us. In Port Elizabeth, my father was devastated – in fact, he had a nervous breakdown when Sandina died.

We had to communicate with our family at home about the funeral and the service. Of course, neither Girly nor I were at the funeral and Sandina was laid to rest without us. I sent a letter that was read out in our absence. The police, however, thought that I would attend and they were there in large numbers waiting to arrest me.

It was all part of the struggle – you get killed or you kill somebody, and you do not get to bury your loved ones. Those were the things we accepted when we left the country. We knew that life would never be the same – nothing was ever going to be normal again and there would be times like these. But I never thought that I would lose a child.

We thought that we were doing the right thing for her. It was always the intention that she would join us later, when she was older, but at the time we were left with no other option but to make sure that she went home. Obviously, we had this sense of guilt. Would she have died if we had kept her with us? What if Girly had taken her to Lusaka? All these questions were bound to come up, and we had to accept reality.

We could not, however, push the blame on to anybody. What disturbed us most was that we were not able to bury her ourselves. Girly and I talked about Sandina daily, and she was in our prayers every night. Girly felt that she was a special child. When she gave birth to her, she felt that there was something about her that was different from any other child that she has had. She was a special child, but one who was never meant to live. You can't fill the void by having another child but each one that we have has his or her own special features and characteristics.

Sandina's death definitely had a profound effect on me, on us. We felt strongly that every minute with her counted, and after her death we were more convinced than ever that we should never take anything for granted. We treasured the time we had spent with her and I felt privileged that I had the chance to be with her when I was illegally in South Africa.

I have seen what other people have gone through and it is clear that we are not the only ones. Many others lost their loved ones and could not bury them. And so I accepted it, but it was harder for Girly and it took time for her to come to terms with the loss of Sandina. But we had to move on.

Life in Zimbabwe

After being forced out of Lesotho in 1986, Girly and I made our home in Zimbabwe after being redeployed there. I had missed out on my second semester of my LLB studies because I had gone into South Africa on a mission and arrangements were made for Roma University students to write their examinations in Harare. I had been busy with underground work and had spent some time in Lusaka so I was not interested in writing the exams and didn't believe I was sufficiently prepared. I hadn't attended any classes and had no notes, but both Girly and the ANC insisted that I write. Even comrades were sent to convince me. Ngoako Ramatlhodi, who was in my class with me at the time, gave me his notes to study so that I could write my LLB exams. They proved extremely useful and the hints he had highlighted were particularly helpful. I wrote and passed, much to my amazement.

I was then persuaded by my wife and some comrades in the ANC to enrol for a master's degree. I felt that it would be a waste of time, but Girly was insistent. I needed a legitimate reason to remain in Zimbabwe and being a student was the obvious choice, so I signed up for a two-year LLM at the University of Zimbabwe under the tutelage of constitutional law Professor Shadrack Gutto and the late Kempton Makhamure. Meanwhile, I continued with my political work as a member of the Regional Political Committee of the ANC.

While in Zimbabwe, Girly gave birth to two boys: Phumlani in 1988 and Lisolomzi a year later, in 1989. It was her turn to name the children and Girly gave our first son three names: Phumlani (meaning 'you can rest') Vusisizwe ('revive or restore the nation') Mzuvukile (from my name, meaning 'the family has been awakened'). Our second son has only one name, Lisolomzi, which translates as 'the eye of the family'. Growing up, he was so disappointed that he only had one name that he gave himself a second one – Junior. My eldest son had been named by his maternal grandparents and was given the name Mphumzi, 'the one who is reliable and allows others to rest whilst he is working for their benefit'.

Life in exile with children was not always easy, particularly for Girly:

> *I remember this particular day when I had had my last-born and we were in Harare. The ANC policy was that you had to suckle a child until it was three months old. I have always struggled, from my first-born, with being able to suckle a child for a long time. I raised this matter formally with the lady who was handling social work issues to request formula milk given my predicament. The treasury office declined. My child was living on glucose in the meantime.*
>
> *I woke up one day and I said to Vusi, 'You know what? I am going to go and fetch my money!' I told him, 'You stay with the child.' There was a bottle of glucose because that's all I had to feed the child.*
>
> *At the office two comrades were responsible for treasury work. As I was explaining my predicament, a reply from them was, 'No, no, no, comrade, three months. Three months. Don't come be silly here, just get out.' The more I tried to explain, the more ridicule they expressed. I reminded them that they were male and not female. Ai, it became so ugly! I then issued a demand that they hand over the money immediately, or else ... At this point they manhandled me out of their office. I spotted the cash box and I used it to hit one of them repeatedly; they were behind a counter so they could not get out.*
>
> *They screamed very loudly and managed to attract the attention of Uncle Stanley Mabizela (my mother's younger brother) who was the ANC chief representative in Zimbabwe at that time. He came to the office wanting to know the problem, and I explained my predicament and the response of those comrades. He instructed them to give me the money whilst he was in their office.*

> *I went home with the formula and I did not tell my husband how I had managed to get the milk. Uncle Stan visited our place that evening and wanted to know if I had hit the comrades. I denied knowledge of that and Vusi was just as shocked. I told them that was news to me, as I was too small to be able to hit those male comrades. I must confess they were not convinced by my response.*
>
> *Exile wasn't a bed of roses. Whilst I have many good memories and occasionally I still feel nostalgic, it could be so ugly at times, even though we were amongst comrades. We have to tell these stories and not bottle them up.*

In 1989, when Lisolomzi was a few months old and Phumlani just over a year, we smuggled the boys out of the country via Botswana. My sister and her husband, who was from what was then Bophuthatswana, came to pick them up. Girly and I took a bus to Gaborone with them but along the way Lisolomzi's milk powder was confiscated by the authorities because they were concerned about foot-and-mouth disease. He couldn't have been more than three months old at the time and Girly couldn't breastfeed, so he starved for the entire journey and cried non-stop. Our daughter Zukiswa, who had started school in Zimbabwe, was also with us. At the hotel where we spent the night, we were awoken in the early hours by a fire alarm and a bomb scare. All together, our little family stood outside in the rain in the middle of the night, while the police scoured the place for the non-existent bomb.

The following morning my sister arrived and we encountered yet another problem: smuggling the boys into South Africa with no passports. But she succeeded nevertheless. Unfortunately, though, the two boys were on Girly's passport and when we returned to Zimbabwe, the authorities there wanted to know what had happened to the children. They didn't believe us when we told them that they had gone to South Africa and eventually the ANC had to be pulled in to assist.

Given what had happened to Sandina, it was difficult to send our children back to South Africa again but we realised that it was part and parcel of the struggle. We were confident in our belief that our parents had taken good care of her and there had been no negligence on their part. We knew that these were the risks inherent in any struggle for liberation but of course we also missed the children.

It might sound somewhat cold now, but at the time our focus was completely on the struggle. We felt that we needed to be involved, but at the same time we still had to try to live a normal family life. And we created a fiction in our heads that the lives we were living were indeed normal. In hindsight, I don't feel we could have done what we did better or differently. We felt that they had a better chance of survival at home. My actions may have been detrimental to my children but I am proud of how they ultimately turned out.

To illustrate the kind of threats we faced, there was a time when the house we stayed in in Zimbabwe was targeted for attack by the South African Defence Force. Comrade Kingsley Mamabolo came to warn us that the *boers* were in Harare and that we should find somewhere else to sleep. But he had been too afraid to come into the house and had flashed his lights at our gate in an attempt to wake us and warn us.

There were seven of us inside the house – and only one AK47. We had no grenades and no other weapons with which to defend ourselves. We decided to leave one comrade behind with the AK and the rest of us found somewhere safe. And the *boers* did attack several sites, including our ANC office in Angwa Street in Harare. At the time Harare was still what we called a 'forward area', which meant that it was used for underground political and military operations – and that also meant that the *boers* could attack at any time.

It is for reasons such as these that we felt it would be safer to have our children at home. All sorts of calculations were taking place in our minds all of the time and, at the end of the day, we felt that we couldn't focus on the struggle and still do all our duties if the children were around and we were in constant fear of their safety as well as our own. So, while we still wanted to have children, we simply couldn't expose them to unnecessary risk and danger.

As part of my work as the chairperson of the ANC Youth in Harare, we put together a number of conferences and hosted Afrikaner students who came to visit us. One particular tour organised by the Institute for a Democratic Alternative in South Africa (IDASA) produced one of the more memorable incidents.

We liked to show the Afrikaner students the banned movie *Cry Freedom* and then have a discussion with them about their thoughts on it. Some would say, 'We knew things were bad in South Africa, but we didn't know they were this bad!' while others would respond by saying it was all merely ANC propaganda.

On one such trip was Carel Boshoff Jnr, whose father was the founder of the Afrikaner enclave Orania, while his grandfather was apartheid architect H.F. Verwoerd. Carel was extremely conservative and right wing and we specifically targeted him for a special discussion. The group was staying at the Holiday Inn in Harare and we sat late into the night with Carel, trying to explain the evils of apartheid, why the future belonged to us and how there was an opportunity for us as the youth to work together to build South Africa.

It was a good discussion and we left well after midnight, hopeful that we had converted him to our way of thinking. Before we departed, Carel said to us, 'I am not going to say I am convinced with what you are saying' but it was the first time he had heard the other side of the story. He had been led to believe that Afrikaners are superior to any other person, including white English-speaking South Africans, but we had had an opportunity to present him with an alternative.

The following morning we went to the hotel to say goodbye to the delegation. One of them came to us to ask what we had done to Carel. We were confused and asked why. That morning when Carel had gone to breakfast, his eyes were red, his hair wasn't brushed and he looked a mess. We were hopeful that Carel hadn't slept because he was pondering the alternatives to apartheid, but were disappointed to hear that after we had left, Carel hadn't slept because he felt he had opened himself to terrorists and was convinced that we were going to come back to his room to kill him. He was so afraid that he sat on his bed all night waiting for the ANC terrorists to murder him in his hotel room. After such a wonderful discussion, we had been convinced we had got through to him – but the opposite was true.

Shifting sands

Towards the end of the 1980s, we could see the political sands shifting in South Africa and we were beginning to think that liberation was imminent. There had been P.W. Botha's Rubicon speech, which he did not carry through, and then there was the release of Govan Mbeki and the Harare Declaration in 1989 that set us talking.

O.R. Tambo addressed us at the ANC Youth Conference in 1987 held at the Solomon Mahlangu Freedom College in Tanzania saying, 'Comrades, we might find ourselves at the negotiating table sooner than we expect.' Then came the release of Walter Sisulu and all the other leaders, with the exception of Nelson Mandela.

Then, on 2 February 1990, then State President F.W. de Klerk stood up in parliament and made a speech that changed our lives. Girly and I had gathered with comrades at the home of Jaya and Premmy Appalraju, who had a big house in Harare. There were many other comrades who later became ministers and senior government officials. We had gathered knowing that there was going to be a big announcement, but we had no idea what it would be.

We stood together in front of the TV and watched as De Klerk, in his Afrikaans drawl, unbanned the ANC and other liberation movements and announced the release of Nelson Mandela from prison. We all started laughing and shouting and hugging one another. There was so much jubilation in that room – it was as if everyone's birthdays had come at once.

At the same time, however, we were also sceptical about suspending the Armed Struggle. I was amongst those who were uncomfortable about the idea and thought that it was possible that we were being sold out by our leaders.

We believed that liberation meant marching on the streets of Pretoria with our AK47s. That had been drummed into us for years and we were working towards the people's war. In the camps, we had spoken about the armed seizure of power and not of a negotiated settlement. However, our language had begun to soften with the Harare Declaration and the unfolding of negotiated guidelines.

Ironically, when De Klerk made that speech and we heard people talking about unbanning the ANC, we temporarily forgot that we actually wanted to fight. We were so overwhelmed with excitement.

During this period I was asked to sit on a committee that was looking at the extent of the ANC's assets in light of the fact that we would all be going home to South Africa. The party had many houses and cars in Zimbabwe so our treasurer-general, Comrade Thomas Nkobi, asked me to be part of the group that would audit the assets with the assistance of a team of lawyers.

Controversially, I resigned and left the committee midway through its work, simply because I felt that one or two of the people I was working with on the Committee were not honest. There were properties I knew about that were not being declared and I started asking about the other ANC assets that weren't being recorded. I knew for a fact that there were farms, houses, cars and other assets that hadn't been disclosed and I'm sure some individual members of the ANC benefited at that time – not only in Zimbabwe but in Tanzania, Angola and other places.

I went to Thomas Nkobi and Penuell Maduna – as the comrades who had appointed me to that committee – and told them I could not sign off on the audit because it was evident that it was not proper. They asked me not to leave the committee, but I explained that unless there were people who were straightforward with me, I could not in good conscience remain.

As a result, I went to Lusaka to work in another department. There was talk that the ANC wanted to make me deputy chief representative in Zambia or in Japan but I was not interested. Little did I know that my troubles were only starting.

Girly and I lived in Lusaka for a short while where I worked in the legal department. Girly was then in the first group of women who came back to South Africa, along with Baleka Mbete, Nosiviwe Mapisa-Nqakula and others. I was asked to go and study again – this time to do a practical course on legislative drafting in London. It was a three-month course at the Royal Institute of Public Administration at Regents College. So while Girly went home, I went to the cold of London.

I have run away from only one fight in my life.

As a young township man with the street name 'Njiva', I loved clothes – English clothes, American clothes, any type of clothes. At the time, I had a stylish 'London Fog'-branded lumber jacket and took it with me to London.

In a traditional Irish pub somewhere in the city, Bongo Qina and I were sitting having a pint, watching all the beautiful English and Irish women. Bongo decided to be friendly with one of them and tried to chat her up. What he hadn't realised was that her boyfriend was around. Of course, a fight ensued and they started punching one another. I went to intervene and suddenly there was chaos. There was one other black guy in the pub playing pool with some of his white friends but the fight immediately turned into a black/white issue and they chased him out of the bar. As we retreated we were throwing punches wildly – and then we made a run for it.

I was so disappointed when I realised that I had left my London Fog jacket behind, and the following morning I actually went back to the scene of the fight, but of course nobody knew anything about my beautiful jacket.

While I wasn't exactly moving in political circles in London, there was an awareness at the college where I was studying about what was going on in South Africa. There were students there from around the world and they were fascinated by what was going on at the southern tip of Africa. Our lecturers showed a special interest in us and we entered into long, informal discussions about what the future held for the country.

I knew that there was euphoria about people returning to South Africa and I was watching all this from afar in England. I too harboured my own desires of returning to my home in the Eastern Cape and my family, but I still had a mission to accomplish – even if it was in wet, wintery London.

Returning home

In November 1990 I returned to Lusaka and began to make plans to go home to South Africa.

There was organised chaos at the time because senior leaders of the ANC were coming in and going out of the country after De Klerk's announcement in February 1990. At first just three leaders returned home to test the waters: Jacob Zuma, who was in charge of intelligence; the head of the legal department, Penuell Maduna; and Gibson Njenje, who was a senior intelligence officer. Shortly thereafter, however, everybody went crazy about going back to South Africa. Exile is not home, even for those who were entirely committed to the fight for liberation. Some comrades had been out of the country for over 30 years and the prospect of returning home was enticing. As a result, the departments were being run by junior guys like ourselves.

The leaders would return to tell us about how wonderful it was at home. But comrades started asking, 'What's happening to the rest of us?' People were impatient and wanted to go home. Then some people began to leave on their own accord, without a controlled process, and some were being sent back to Lusaka to ensure that departments continued to run. Meetings were called and people got frustrated and rowdy, sitting day in and day out drinking Zambian beer. Things were getting out of control.

Some of the comrades began to insult the leaders, saying, 'Look! They enjoy being in Cape Town and Johannesburg but they have forgotten about us.' Comrades were told to register and be cleared in South Africa before they could leave. There were promises of houses being built for us, as well as all sorts of other promises made to MK soldiers – few of which were ever fulfilled. Trained cadres were also told that they would hold senior military positions in the new defence force, but the reality was very different. Those comrades had a right to be frustrated with the process because they were not being regularly informed about the situation. For example, Thozi was the last person to leave Uganda because he had soldiers to look after there, but stocks were running low, there was no food and he struggled to maintain people's morale. Those of us who were working in departments did not face the same frustrations because we had something to do every day and we had to ensure that the offices kept on running.

The organisation was also facing a problem of funding. It was clear that although the ANC was looking after all of us while we were in exile, it could not continue to do so in South Africa. Scandinavian countries had been propping up the party and most of the funding had come from donations that were drying up with Mandela's release and the unbanning of the party. We were used to receiving handouts from the ANC, and all of a sudden there was this vacuum.

While in exile we weren't working in conventional jobs and we weren't getting paid so the ANC gave us a monthly allowance. They provided food and we received second-hand clothes from the Scandinavian countries. These would arrive in large bales and we would go to the stores and grab whatever we could, regardless of the size. Many comrades sold the clothes to the locals in whatever country we were in.

When we returned home, those with malicious intentions stepped into the financial void left by the ANC. It was the first time that someone such as Glenn Agliotti was able to hook up with the likes of Jackie Selebi, who was the head of the Repatriation Committee.

Some of us had to find paying jobs and yet continue to work for the ANC. Those who worked at Shell House, the ANC's headquarters, were paid R2 000 a month, but those of us who could find employment on our own were encouraged to do so. As in any struggle or liberation movement, there are always the elite that come in the form of those who are educated and are working in departments that could organise jobs for themselves and not depend on the process of repatriation.

Then, in 1991, at the age of 33, I found my first formal employment. It was during a meeting in Lusaka between our Economics Committee, headed by Max Sisulu, and an insurance company that I was offered my first job. I was interviewed by Munich Re.Insurance in Johannesburg in December 1990 and started work as an assistant manager in January the following year. The salary at the time was R4 000, which seemed like so much money. I could not believe my good fortune and I was very excited to share the news with Girly. My colleagues in the ANC were earning half that, and there was even a housing subsidy and a company car thrown in. Other Fort Hare graduates, as well as some Robben Island prisoners, had found employment there too because it was a progressive company. In 1990 the ANC had been given offices in the Munich building before moving to Shell House, and the party later bought that same building, which is now known as Luthuli House.

I was quickly promoted to legal advisor at Munich, but I continued doing work for the ANC, researching electoral law and systems in preparation for the transition to democracy. Together with Sandile Nogxina, I travelled to Namibia to observe their system, and we produced a booklet on electoral laws for the ANC. The party also asked me to lead a delegation to Zimbabwe and Canada to look at parliamentary systems there.

It was a tense few years as we watched the shift towards liberation, with the country regularly teetering on the brink of civil war. There were the talks at Codesa and ongoing negotiations, and we waited with great anticipation to see what would happen and whether the dream for which we had sacrificed much of our lives would eventually become a reality.

It was towards the end of October, beginning November, that I got instructions from Brigadier Skoon to meet up with Colonel Nick van Rensburg at Komatipoort with Major Archie Flemington and his men. I knew that the operation involved that we had to get rid of the man that I'd seen in Jeffrey's Bay, and I asked him to arrange with the forensic laboratory, specific with General Lothar Neethling, for knock-out drops for me to be picked up. I continued, myself and Paul van Dyk from Pretoria, down to Komatipoort, where we met up with Major Archie Flemington and two of his junior men, sergeants or warrant officers – I can't remember the names unfortunately – and went to a piece of ground about 10 kilometres outside Komatipoort on the border gate road, on the farms where they join up, Avonstont and Constanopoulos [*sic*]. Whilst we were there we turned left off towards the mountain. It's very close to the Mozambican border, and at the point where the old wagon route went over the mountain. Three cement slabs is still left there up until this day, which I was able to detect a few months ago, and in line towards the road, from the mountain to the road – it's a very short distance, I would guess about one kilometre, if not less – it was an open veld with a few trees around, quite a distance from the main road. Colonel Nick van Rensburg arrived with a Cortina vehicle with Captain Herman du Plessis, with the Sergeant Jan, and with Sizwe Kondile in a balaclava and handcuffed. They took the balaclava off when he got out of the car. I supplied the knock-out drops. I can't remember which of his men administered it and in what drink, whether it was a beer or a cool drink in that specific instance. The drops have the effect that if you put in four drops for a not too big person it was supposed to knock him down as if he had been administered chloroform or anaesthetic. If you would administer more, so it was told to me by the general, then he would eventually fall into such a deep sleep that he would die. Now, drops were administered to Sizwe Kondile in a drink whilst we were sitting around drinking ourselves, opening beer and whatever other drinks and alcohol and after about 20 minutes to half an hour Mr Kondile started swaying, he was sitting down and uneasy. He looked quite normal again to me when he arrived, as I said, not like someone with serious brain injuries that I could pick up. He eventually fell over backwards and lay on his back, and at a stage either Colonel Nick van Rensburg or Major Flemington said, 'Well, chaps, let's get on with the job.' In the meantime the two junior officers of Major Archie Flemington, with a Land Cruiser bakkie, brought dense bushveld wood, big logs of it, with tyres, and one of Major Archie Flemington's men, a sergeant or a warrant – a slender-built tallish man, light hair, took a [Makarov] pistol with a silencer on, and whilst he was lying, Mr Kondile was lying on his back, shot him on top of the head. There was a short jerk and that was it. The four junior non-commissioned officers, Paul van Dyk, Jan – Sergeant Jan from Colonel Nick van Rensburg's branch – and the two Ermelo men, each grabbed a hand and a foot, put it onto the pyre of tyre and wood, poured petrol on it, and set it alight. Now, of course the burning of a body to ashes takes about seven hours. And whilst that happened we were drinking and even having a braai next to the fire. Now, that I don't say to show our braveness, I just tell it to the Commission to show the callousness of it and to what extremes we have gone to in those days. And a body takes about seven hours to burn to ashes completely, and the chunks of meat, especially the buttocks and the upper part of the legs, had to be turned frequently during the night to make sure that everything burned to ashes. And the next morning, after raking through the rubble to make sure that there was no big pieces of meat or bone left at all, we departed and we all went our own way.

Abridged TRC testimony of former Vlakplaas commander Dirk Coetzee (Durban, 5 November 1996)

Comrade Chris

Girly and I had just come back from buying groceries for the house, the boot of our car laden with produce, as we pulled into the driveway of our first house that we had bought in Primrose Hill in Germiston. I parked the car just as the news jingle began to play.

Chris Hani had been shot.

We ran inside the house and immediately began phoning everyone we could think of, trying to confirm the news. 'Hey! What's happening? Is this true?'

We didn't have cellphones then so we had to use the landline. We were a close community of comrades so the news spread quickly. We were shocked, angry, devastated. I thought about going to Chris's home in Dawn Park but I didn't know what I would do there and there would be so many people. Chris was dead. He was gone.

I was angry, my wife was angry. Chris had been a father figure to me in Lesotho, as he was to so many other young cadres. We were suspicious of the suspension of the Armed Struggle and felt that these guys would kill off the ANC leadership one by one. Some said, 'This is crap. The *boers* are not to be trusted. They are not serious about talks, they have their own plans.' This is why we felt that MK should not be disbanded. It was the same across the country and I remember that in Port Elizabeth the ANC supporters wanted to set the whole town on fire. That very nearly sabotaged the peace talks.

We were not yet free, De Klerk was still running the government and the struggle was not yet over. We didn't have the universal franchise and the things we had been fighting for had not yet been realised after the unbanning of the ANC. If there had been a military instruction by the commanders to fight, I would have had no hesitation in picking up arms.

But the leadership of Nelson Mandela came through and saved us from descending into chaos. He stood up that evening and told the nation that Chris Hani had been killed by right-wing Afrikaners, but that it was a white South African woman who had led police to arrest them. If Mandela had been hot-headed, there would have been chaos and more people on both sides would have died.

We had to take instruction from our commander-in-chief. We were still 'hot', fresh from exile, and if Mandela had said MK should be mobilised, I would have been there. I realised that he was being pragmatic about it and that is why I believe he saved the country.

It was while I was leading a delegation in Toronto, Canada, in March 1994 that news broke about Shell House being attacked. Girly was working for what was known as the Women's Section of the ANC at the time but by March 1994 they had already moved out of the Lisbon Bank building in Sauer Street, and they were also at Shell House.

ANC security guards killed 19 Inkatha Freedom Party (IFP) members who were planning on targeting the party's headquarters. We heard on the radio and on television that IFP members had surrounded Shell House. I was extremely worried about Girly, but also about the fact that the IFP was descending on the ANC's headquarters. Girly could have been killed and we did not trust the South African Police because they had often collaborated with the IFP – as they did in Boipatong, for example. I wanted to be there in South Africa to defend my organisation. So it was that when I returned from Canada I told Munich Re.Insurance that I had to leave. I didn't know what I would be doing, but I believed I had to play a role in the new government.

I was the commander of the South African Police death squad. I was in the heart of the whore. My men and I had to murder political and security opponents of the police and the government.

Captain Dirk Coetzee, November 1989 (from In the Heart of the Whore *by Jacques Pauw)*

Democracy dawns

Girly and I woke up early on the morning of 27 April 1994 and, together, we drove the streets of Johannesburg. It was beautiful, watching the long queues of people waiting for their opportunity to vote. We were so excited and we wanted to soak up the atmosphere so we drove and drove, just the two of us in the car.

There had been so much tension at the time and so many attempts to disrupt the elections: the right-wing bombing campaigns; the Afrikaner Weerstandsbeweging (AWB) storming into the World Trade Centre; the IFP refusing to participate in the polls. We hadn't been sure whether Election Day would ever come and whether it would be peaceful.

There was much anxiety and the night before we could hardly sleep. I was 36 years old and this was the culmination of everything we had been fighting for – to be able to elect a government of our own choice, to have free and fair elections and to let the people of the country decide. It was something we had been denied all those years and for the first time we felt that we were in charge of our own destinies. There was relief; it felt like our dignity was being restored.

We voted at a school in Cyrildene and the feeling was just so overwhelming. We stood in a snaking queue and as we inched closer, we didn't care how long it took. There was so much friendliness, with white compatriots sharing jokes and talking with us about how wonderful it all was.

I was emotional that day as I thought about all the comrades who had died in the course of the struggle. I thought about my baby, Sandina, and of course, I thought about Sizwe, who wasn't there to see this day. It was what he had died for. I imagined Sizwe smiling broadly and I could hear his laughter, 'We've made it, sonny!'

I also thought about some of the other comrades we had lost. Comrade Zakes Matakane was killed in combat inside the country. He used to say, 'Let us talk about the armed seizure of power.' And then there was Comrade Mzwandile, Comrade Roll Call, Comrades Pieces, Zola, Nomkhosi, Siphiwe Mazwai, Comrade Maputo and many others. We had lost so many comrades but at that moment I felt that they had not died in vain. Their spirits were there on that day.

Comrades gathered at our new home in Malvern to hear the results being announced. We were so sure we were going to win by an overwhelmingly large margin, and we were, I must say, a little disappointed with the result when it came in. We did not get the two-thirds majority we were hoping for, but in hindsight it would not have been good for a nascent democracy.

But nothing could take away from the feeling of us winning. Everything we had sacrificed while we were in exile was worth it. We also thought we understood the enormity of the task that lay ahead. It was time for reconstruction, to build a new society in our country. It is easier to destroy than to build and we had been trained to dismantle apartheid, to destroy. We were prepared to kill and, collectively, as the ANC, we had killed people for our liberation. We now had to say, let us come together as South Africans and build a new nation and a future for our children.

PART TWO

Working as the NDPP

Stepping into government

After the elections, Girly went to Cape Town as a member of parliament for the new ANC-led government. I remained in Johannesburg at our home in Malvern with our children, who had been enrolled in school by then.

I did a short stint with the Independent Electoral Commission during the winding-down period in the wake of the elections. Then, in August 1994, four months after we had won our freedom at the polls, I received a call from Justice Minister Dullah Omar asking me to take the step into government. He wanted me to work with him as one of his two special advisors in Cape Town.

The concept at the time was that special advisors would play a kind of bridging role. The public service was dominated by apartheid-era civil servants and the new cabinet ministers had to be advised by trusted cadres of the ruling party because the directors-general (DGs) came mainly from the erstwhile apartheid government. ANC ministers were, of course, new to government and the old regime directors-general remained in their posts as part of the sunset clauses agreed to during negotiations for a democratic country. There were white civil servants at the top who were retained and they needed people as a buffer between the directors-general and the ministers.

The other appointee was Enver Daniels, the current chief state law advisor. My own experience was of being involved in consultative conferences, looking at the legal system, and liaising with the Law Society, law lecturers and others in the profession, so my new appointment was something of a continuation of that process.

Our specific task was to restructure the department of justice. There were 11 departments countrywide and we had to amalgamate those into one department. We also had to look at the rationalisation of laws, because each of the homelands was governed by its own systems and we had to consider issues of compatibility and contradictions that existed in the legislation. Along with that, we had to bring together the old directors-general in the old TBVC states, as the Transkei, Bophuthatswana, Venda and Ciskei were known then.

Bringing together 11 departments was an enormous task and the challenge was to establish a new culture even while the old civil servants considered us with suspicion. We had no experience or knowledge of government, but we knew everything about the national liberation struggle – and now we had to adapt and learn from them. We all had to learn to do things differently in accordance with the new Constitution to which we owed allegiance. In that sense we were all learning, but old civil servants seemed to handle it better because many of the old processes and systems remained the same post-liberation. Fortunately, I had been involved with drafting the terms of the ANC constitutional guidelines and the new Constitution did not differ much from what we had discussed and drafted in Lusaka.

The first priority was earning the trust and confidence of the old bureaucrats. Fortunately, I fitted in comfortably and established a good relationship with the director-general of the department of justice at the time, Advocate Jasper Noeth, and also developed lifelong relationships with Danie Schmidt and Blendyn Williams, which I value to this day.

One had to be extremely diplomatic and tactical about introducing change, doing so in a non-threatening way, and then convincing people that change is good and that they will also benefit from it.

Of course, there were also expectations, especially in the Bantustans, where many people felt that they remained oppressed despite having served the apartheid regime, and felt that it was time for the black man to oppress the white man. The 1994 government was seen by some as a 'black government', and the message was that 'the whites must be shown and taught a lesson'. There were also expectations of high salaries and, as a result, there were strikes in the former Bantustans, which I had to personally address. I seemed to be fighting fires all over the place.

Introducing new policies in the department was also a serious challenge for us. Conferences were held with law academics and we floated the possibility of introducing a new four-year LLB, the new requirements for the legal profession, abolishing Afrikaans and Latin, the move away from the judicare system to the public defender system of legal aid and assessing its effectiveness, and we also discussed the transformation of the prosecution services and gave consideration to establishing a single prosecution service headed by one person.

At the time, while Dullah Omar was justice minister, attorneys-general (AGs) were still in office and there was not yet a single national prosecuting policy. This meant that, for example, the AG in the Free State could decide not to prosecute certain minor offences if he or she saw fit, because there was no national policy governing decisions on prosecution. The idea was to introduce a national policy to be applied throughout the country and to have one person in charge of prosecutions.

Of course, at the time there was much suspicion. As the apartheid government neared its demise, it decided to look at the independence of prosecutors. This was a political ploy that was born of the fear that the new government that was coming in to power would see prosecutors being dictated to by politicians and that would lead to all kinds of trouble for them. In 1992, the apartheid government introduced the Attorney-General's Act, which sought to bestow independence of some kind on prosecutors. When this was discussed as a policy, they felt that having a 'Super AG', or a national director, would translate into someone who could be influenced into taking political decisions. While prosecutors were still part of the department of justice, the provincial AGs enjoyed a level of independence.

I have always believed in the independence of prosecutors and continue to value it as an essential doctrine in a democratic, constitutional state. If we do not have independent prosecutors who refuse to take instructions from political principals, then you will have a partial and unfair application of the law. These were the kind of matters I was grappling with as special advisor to the minister during those early years.

During my tenure as DG, I also had to deal with the fairly contentious issue of allegations brought to me by the head of the Master's Office, Mike

Tshishonga, and the fallout that followed. Tshishonga, the former head of the department of justice in Venda, was appointed to head the Master's Office in 2001. He came to see me one day about complaints from staff members in his office about liquidator Enver Motala and his proximity to Minister Penuell Maduna. They were concerned that Motala was being given the bulk of the work because he was favoured by the minister. The Master's Office was in a chaotic state at the time and was responsible for billions of rands – and it was all a mess. In the end, Tshishonga didn't come out with clear allegations of corruption. I explained to him if there was any real proof, he should lodge a formal complaint with me, which he failed to do.

I then received a call late one night from Minister Maduna instructing me to remove Tshishonga from his post. Maduna did not care where I moved him, he just wanted him to be moved. Of course, I wanted to know why but Maduna couldn't really explain. In the end I did not dismiss Tshishonga, but I did feel that I should move him from that office. I made a suggestion that we should create the post of chief operations officer in my office and I offered it to him, assuring him that he would report to me and not to Maduna.

Later, without my knowledge, Tshishonga took documents from the office and leaked them to the press and the office of the public protector. The documents were related to the work that Motala was doing and Tshishonga made allegations to the media that the minister was corrupt. Judge Pillay of the Labour Court would later find that Tshishonga had made a 'protected disclosure' to the media. Maduna also called Tshishonga a 'dunderhead' and Tshishonga sued him in response.

I felt that these were very serious allegations to be made by a deputy DG and that he had undermined my authority as the director-general so I charged him for taking out documents belonging to the department without my authorisation. Tshishonga's defence was based on the Protected Disclosures Act, but we lost the internal case. I left that office while the matter was still ongoing but Tshishonga eventually moved on too.

In retrospect, I feel that it was a moment of weakness that I failed to defend Tshishonga against Maduna. I don't believe that I protected Maduna from any allegations of corruption, but I do feel that I shouldn't have acted against Tshishonga in the way that I did. I could have done more to side with Tshishonga, but instead chose to do what the minister wanted.

That experience, unbeknown to me at the time, actually prepared me for what was to come as that, too, would be a request from the justice minister, albeit a different one, that would mark my career as national director of public prosecutions (NDPP).

The Truth and Reconciliation Commission

In 1995, Minister of Justice Dullah Omar asked me to lead a delegation to Chile to look at the Chilean National Commission on Truth and Reconciliation that had been set up there.

The Comisión Nacional de Verdad y Reconciliación, or the Rettig Commission, had been established in 1990 by newly elected Chilean President Patricio Aylwin to investigate human rights abuses carried out during the military dictatorship of the regime under General Augusto Pinochet. It was mandated to document human rights abuses resulting in death or disappearance during the years of military rule, but significantly, torture and other abuses that did not result in death were left outside the scope of the commission's mandate. The commission had released its report in February 1991.

In the early 1990s in South Africa, many people – myself included – felt that we should avoid military tribunals such as those held at Nuremberg by the Allied forces to prosecute prominent members of Hitler's Third Reich. I felt that there would be little point in reopening old wounds just as we were coming back from a war situation. This was also the position pursued by Kader Asmal during our discussions when we were still in exile. We had to find a way of dealing with unlawful excesses and the model pursued by Chile emerged as the likely option to follow.

While in Chile, we met with NGOs, the government and other role players to listen to and to learn from their experiences. Some of the families we met were not happy with the process as they felt that it had favoured the perpetrators rather than the victims.

President Mandela advocated reconciliation, and while Chile's approach was more one of amnesty, we had to find a way to incorporate the reconciliatory aspect. Our model had to look at the victims as well as the perpetrators and the concept of reparations. On our return from Chile, we submitted a report to the minister and made recommendations. Thereafter we began drafting the legislation for the Truth and Reconciliation Act and the framework around which it would operate.

It was not a perfect solution to the problem and there are still families of victims represented by various NGOs in South Africa who are not happy with the TRC, simply because the process tended to favour the perpetrators. This is the same position as in Chile, where there are still NGOs calling for justice. Two years later, I was appointed DG of the justice department and over those years, the department was responsible for the TRC process, giving support to the Commission and dealing with the task of reparations and compensating victims.

Although the TRC was an independent commission established in terms of an Act of parliament, with its own CEO, we gave administrative support. The process had to be seen to be beyond the influence of both government and the ANC.

While I played an official role in the TRC, I also had a personal investment in the process. I had spent years in exile as a freedom fighter against the apartheid government and my best friend, Sizwe Kondile, had been kidnapped and killed by the regime. In April 1996, I personally appeared before the TRC sitting in East London.

Majestic and imposing, East London's maroon-and-white city hall rules over the otherwise unremarkable town centre from its throne on Oxford Street. A Victorian Renaissance-style building built in 1897, its tall clock tower stands as a tribute to commemorate the diamond jubilee of Queen Victoria. The structure is an undeniable reminder of the English colonial history of the region.

On the morning of 17 April 1996, fighting my trepidation, I made my way towards the city hall where the first sitting of the TRC was taking place. Elsewhere in the world, a partial solar eclipse was casting a shadow over

Earth, an appropriate illustration of my mood. I walked past the proud statue of a soldier on horseback, a memorial to those who died in the Boer War, through the vestibule towards the marble staircase.

Just a day before, some of the most poignant and indelible moments of the TRC had played out inside this remarkable hall. Archbishop Desmond Tutu had laid down his head on the table before him and wept uncontrollably, overcome with emotion. He had been listening to wheelchair-bound victim Singqokwana Malgas testify about his brutal torture and harassment at the hands of the Security Police when he was moved to tears. Earlier in the day, the wife of one of the Cradock Four victims, Nomonde Calata, had pierced the silence in the room with a wrenching wail, forcing the Commission to break for a moment, the effects of which could only be quelled by Tutu's singing of the freedom hymn that was generally regarded as our national anthem at the time, '*Senzeni na?*'

The purpose of the TRC was to uncover the truth, heal wounds, bring closure and find a reconciliatory path forward by facilitating restorative justice. I was anxious about the process because it would mean ripping open crudely healed wounds, but I was also hopeful that the ever-elusive truth would present itself.

For nearly a decade, we had not known what had happened to Sizwe and rumours of his defection and treachery had persisted. It was only when Dirk Coetzee, the head of Vlakplaas – a paramilitary hit squad that included former, turned, ANC combatants (contemptuously referred to as *askaris*) – had broken his silence to investigative journalist Jacques Pauw that we first learned about Sizwe's torture and murder. In fact, Sizwe's family would only hear details about his death from an article in the *New Nation* newspaper on 9 February 1990. Several reports also featured in the liberal Afrikaans newspaper *Vrye Weekblad* as Pauw revealed the extent of the state-sanctioned apartheid hit squads.

Coetzee had been taken to Lusaka, defected to the ANC, and then appeared before the farcical Harms Commission in London, set up to investigate alleged murder and unlawful acts of the security forces. I had heard some of the details from my friend Sandile Nogxina, with whom I was working in the legal department in Lusaka at the time. Nogxina had also been close to Sizwe as we were all friends at Fort Hare. He told me that he had met Coetzee in Lusaka and had spoken to him about Sizwe's case.

My friend Phaki also came face to face with Dirk Coetzee while they were both in Lusaka, shortly after the story had broken in South African newspapers. Coetzee had just been taken into the fold of the ANC. Phaki relates:

> *I find myself in this workshop in Lusaka where Dirk was and he came to join us. He was hiding out there with the ANC at the time. I was told that this is Dirk Coetzee and people were calling him Comrade. It was disgusting. I couldn't accept that. I couldn't also show it because the other comrades have accepted that the guy is amongst us. I just sat there but really feeling terrible. I didn't feel like going up to him and asking him why he had killed my friend. What I felt like was giving him a punch. Today I'm curious about that history, but at the time I was thinking more of fighting than thinking about history and trying to record what happened. I was still seeing somebody on the other side and I wasn't sure if he was playing games with the movement. But guys were accepting him. Dirk could have helped. He could have come forward to tell the story fully. A person like Dirk, he had 1989 and he had 1996 at the TRC. Unlike maybe the other guys, Dirk had a chance to come out fully. He had come to be accepted within our ranks even if some of us were not accepting him fully. He had become an ANC person. So when he is not coming out truthfully on everything, it leaves you with the impression that he is still hiding the other guys. It all seemed too buddy-buddy.*

I was also keenly aware that Sizwe's mother, Charity, would be there and I would finally have to see her, 15 years after she had come to Maseru. She would be first to give evidence to the investigations committee probing the gross violation of human rights. Four Eastern Cape security policemen, who had all been stationed in Port Elizabeth at the time of Sizwe's death, had applied for amnesty for his murder: Nicolaas Janse van Rensburg, Johannes Gottfried Raath, Gerrit Nicholas Erasmus and Hermanus Barend du Plessis, the man who had threatened and confronted me while I was a student activist in PE. The four men would testify on their own behalf, while Coetzee and another policeman, Ginotry Danster, testified on behalf of the family who were opposing the application.

I watched as Dr Alex Boraine invited Charity Kondile to appear before the committee. 'The story that you have given to the Commission and the Commission staff is a very stark and terrifying one and we are very sympathetic to the need for courage and strength in trying to tell this story which has caused you so much pain,' Boraine explained to her. Evidence leader Advocate Dumisa Ntsebeza guided her through her testimony while Sizwe's son, Bantu, listened from the audience.

Charity testified about how she had come to learn that her son was missing and how she 'spat venom' at the police commissioner's failure to address concerns expressed in letters about the unlawful detention of political prisoners. She spoke about the deep disappointment she experienced during her visit to Maseru when it appeared that all in the ANC had turned against her son. Sizwe's mother also directly addressed the harrowing details of the brutality of her son's murder:

> *Dirk Coetzee goes on further to say that when he died, they put his body on a pile of wood with a tyre near the Komatipoort River at night, where it took them nine hours to burn his body. Dirk Coetzee further states that twice they were burning his body, the flesh was smelling good, and they were having beers at that time. So it was like a braai to them. As a mother I feel that, no matter whether it was politics, fighting for his land, I don't think he deserved all that treatment, I feel it was grossly inhuman, I feel if they could have killed him and gave us the body or left it in the veld there. I feel that this was tantamount to cannibalism, or even Satanism.*

Charity told the Commission that, after almost a decade of accusations and confusion sown by the police, she was able to speak with a high-ranking ANC official about the revelations that had exonerated her son:

> *I got hold of the late Mr Chris Hani's telephone number and I telephoned the SACP offices in Johannesburg. I was answered on the first day by Mr Charles Nqakula. On the second day Mr Chris Hani himself was there. Chris was very friendly on that day, he even said, 'Mrs Kondile, we have finally established that your son has been kidnapped, we are very sorry about everything.' That was just about a month before he died and Mr Hani said to me, 'Mrs Kondile, if there should be a memorial service for*

Sizwe, I shall be very happy to come down and speak on behalf of the ANC.' Those were our parting words.

Hani was killed and the memorial never took place. Charity finished her testimony with a request to the Commission:

I would ask the Commission to assist us to bring the perpetrators of this brutal murder before the court, so that these perpetrators could be charged and punished for what they did and the manner in which my son was murdered. And I further ask the Commission to see what it can do to pacify the Kondile family for the loss of a beloved son, deprivation and the loss of a father and provider to Bantu, because I feel Sizwe would have provided for Bantu. Information of Sizwe's character and loss of his belongings, damage to the Kondile family's dignity and trauma with the whole family, especially his siblings, his father, his closest friend, Bantu and myself. And I'd further add that it's a request from my mother-in-law that I should have expressed to the Commission that the Kondile family would be the last people to turn traitors, because even the state president himself, President Mandela, and the late Mr Oliver Tambo were once sheltered under her roof in Port Elizabeth.

I was called to testify next. I recounted my shared history with Sizwe, how we went into exile, the news of his disappearance and the pain of the confusion that followed. Advocate Ntsebeza asked me about the relief I felt at learning that Sizwe had indeed not been a spy. I commented:

In the course of our liberation discussions we always believed that death is not really an issue because death is an integral part of a liberation struggle when you've got two opposing forces. But what induces a sense of shock and revulsion is the method and manner of how people were killed. It came as a big relief when we read in the New Nation in 1990 that at least there is a person who seems to know exactly what has happened to Sizwe and this being in the person of Dirk Coetzee.

Because of my role in drawing up the legislation around the TRC and my position in the ministry of justice, I also gave testimony about the purpose of the Commission and the thinking behind it. Ntsebeza asked if I would sanction the findings of the committee in the case of my own friend. I assured him I would:

> *Our interim constitution being the supreme law of the land enjoins us to promote national unity and reconciliation in our country as a mechanism of ensuring that. It further tells us that those people who committed atrocities in the conflict of the past, who come forward to make a full disclosure and their act or mission having been associated with its political objective, then those people shall be granted amnesty. My own understanding of that tells me that it is not automatic that a person by virtue of having applied for amnesty, that person shall be granted amnesty.*

I felt that we had to move forward and accept Sizwe's death as a casualty of the struggle. It could have been me or anybody else and we can't afford to live in the past.

Sizwe's mother and I spoke that day, but unfortunately a point of conflict had emerged. She was unhappy about Bantu receiving the R30 000 reparation from the TRC. As DG of justice, I was in charge of facilitating those payments and we had a falling-out over the matter. Sadly, she felt that I had abandoned my friend by not advocating that she (Sizwe's mother) receive the money. My position was that the payment should go to Bantu and he should decide whether or not to share it. I knew that he had outstanding school fees to pay at the time and that it was the sole responsibility of Carol (Bantu's mother) to finance Bantu's studies.

Over a week in February 1998 in Cape Town, the four police officers applying for amnesty for their role in Sizwe's death testified before the TRC. Each day, Sizwe's mother and son sat in the audience listening to the gruesome details. Dirk Coetzee, in short-sleeved checked shirts and with his ubiquitous, awkward grin, was also there. All four officers testified, their grey hair neatly combed over and large teardrop-style era-appropriate glasses resting on the bridges of their noses and tucked under black headphones. Fundamental contradictions emerged between the versions given to the TRC by the former Vlakplaas commander and the four officers.

In a lilac shirt and paisley tie, Hermanus 'Doep' du Plessis was the first to give evidence, sitting in front of a banner that read, 'Truth. The road to reconciliation.' He recounted how Sizwe was arrested in July 1981 while in Bloemfontein and he was alerted about his detention because Sizwe may have had information of interest about the Eastern Cape.

Du Plessis had been the one in charge of Sizwe's interrogation and testified about how he had successfully recruited him to become an informant. However, he had discovered a note in Sizwe's cell that revealed that he had tried to make contact with the ANC and that he had only pretended to be an informer. Du Plessis explained how Sizwe had become a threat because they had already told him the name of their principal agent in their intelligence network in Lesotho. As a result, the police took a decision that Sizwe had to be eliminated.

Nick van Rensburg told the Commission that he called Dirk Coetzee and asked him to assist. The Security Police had faked Sizwe's release from the Jeffrey's Bay police cells and later abducted him and took him to Komatipoort. Van Rensburg testified that Coetzee had suggested that if they did not want the body to be found then they should burn it and throw the remains into the river. As Van Rensburg officiously related the events and imitated Sizwe's swaying as a result of the drops given to him, Coetzee listened through his headphones in the audience and Sizwe's mother breathed deeply, looked skyward and wiped her nose with a handkerchief.

The men denied the suggestion from Coetzee that there had been a picnic atmosphere and that they had eaten meat and drunk alcohol as Sizwe's body burnt on a pyre of wood and tyres. Van Rensburg explained that they had braaied meat and ate before Sizwe was shot, not during the event.

Gerrit Erasmus, then the divisional commander of the Eastern Cape, gave the order to execute Sizwe despite never having met him. 'There were no rules in this game that we were busy with from the side of the opposition. There weren't normal procedures and acts that were of any use any more, that's what I am trying to tell you,' Erasmus testified when the chairperson pushed him on the 'awesome power' he had to pass sentence of death on a man.

Coetzee took the stand again, and stayed true to the story that he told repeatedly to journalists, the Harms Commission and in his original evidence before the TRC. He insisted that Sizwe was killed because he had been tortured, had dove through a window, and had landed on his head and sustained injuries. The Security Police did not want another Steve Biko case, which would have huge political implications. Coetzee also contradicted the officers on who had pulled the trigger. The four claimed it was a Sergeant Roy Otto from Vlakplaas who had since committed suicide, while Coetzee remembered it being 'one of Major Archie Flemington's men', a slender-built, tallish sergeant with light hair. There was also disagreement on when the shooting had taken place. Coetzee said he recalled it taking place in November while the officers argued it was July 1981. The men also denied an accusation by policeman Ginotry Danster that Sizwe had been tortured.

On 23 February 1999, the TRC released a statement granting all four men amnesty.

I cannot say with certainty that the process of the TRC brought me personal closure. At the time, I still had many questions that I wanted to ask the policemen responsible for murdering Sizwe. I particularly wanted to come face to face with Du Plessis, who had been Sizwe's 'handler'. One of the remaining mysteries to me is what happened between Maseru and Bloemfontein. As far as we knew, Sizwe had been kidnapped in Lesotho, leaving a public phone hanging with his girlfriend on the other end shouting his name. The police generals' stories only start in Bloemfontein. Down the line, I would, in fact, get the opportunity to meet Du Plessis and pose various questions to him.

I think the TRC achieved limited success. It did serve as a platform for the survivors and for relatives of victims to at least talk about what had happened to their loved ones, and for someone to listen – even if nothing could be done about it. That in itself was therapeutic. And it was also a cathartic experience for the perpetrators because apartheid dehumanised us, especially those of us who were involved in the actual conflict. People had an opportunity to talk about what they had done, to show remorse and to repent.

Where we failed was with the reparations and compensation to victims and relatives. It should not have been a question of money as such, because there can be no monetary value placed on human life or on torture or suffering. Perhaps the government could have done more, and still could do more, to find other ways of recognising the human suffering.

An ideal way to do this is through scholarships or bursaries for the children of victims. In the case of Bantu, Sizwe's son, his father's friends were the ones who ran around trying to help him find a job. Bantu is not the only one. Collectively, the families of victims could have been better looked after with scholarships and access to health facilities and counselling. There is a sense that justice has not been done and that those responsible are not remorseful. In addition, there was a failure to pay proper tribute to all of those who sacrificed their lives during the struggle for national liberation. This is particularly true in rural areas, such as in KwaZulu, where there were clashes between the IFP and UDF, and in the Eastern Cape with UDF/AZAPO clashes. The memorial at Freedom Park in Pretoria should be duplicated in other areas across the country so that at least we know that everybody who died in the struggle is honoured.

To this day I worry that Sizwe's spirit is still wandering. According to my beliefs and customs, it is important to be able to go to the exact spot where he died and bring his spirit back, even if all we can find is a minute finger bone. Attempts have been made by Madeleine Fullard and the Missing Persons Task Team at the NPA to find the exact location of the murder and any potential remains that may still exist. Dirk Coetzee did try to assist with pointing out a site in Komatipoort, but it was not accurate. Madeleine had wanted Coetzee to accompany her to another site they were investigating, but Coetzee died in March 2013 before he could be of any further help.

I feel cheated that I did not confront Dirk Coetzee face to face. It is a real pity that he has taken some of his secrets to the grave with him, which is no consolation to the victims and their families who have many lingering questions.

Komati River is where Sizwe's flesh was reduced to ashes. There were other officers there and I urge them to come forward. What they have done is known – but now they need to assist Sizwe's family and friends to close this tragic chapter.

Where is Nicolaas Janse van Rensburg? Where is Hermanus Barend du Plessis? Where is Johannes Gottfried Raath? Where is Gerrit Nicholas Erasmus? These are the men who applied for and were granted amnesty. They are the men, including Coetzee, who were having a 'braai and drinking liquor' at the time of Sizwe's death. He paid the ultimate price, branded a traitor by his own comrades, and yet was killed by Coetzee and his death squad. Coetzee was later embraced by the same comrades. What a twist of fate, how ironic, what a travesty of justice.

As a commander of the notorious Vlakplaas, Coetzee killed many more struggle activists whose whereabouts might never be known because he went to the grave with some of the apartheid-era secrets. Some of those who commanded Coetzee are still alive, and some of them went to the TRC to tell lies to save their skins. Others never even went to the TRC, which still makes them liable to prosecution should they be uncovered. I believe it is this fear that keeps them from telling the truth; their motto is probably 'Why reveal it if it is not known?'

The TRC only did half the job. It gave us half-truths and half-reconciliation, quarter-reparations but full amnesty. At the very least, there should have been full disclosure and yet there were many murderers who got away with murder – literally. The lingering question I still have is, how sustainable and genuine is reconciliation without truth and justice? The South African story is yet to be told.

I suppose it is in the nature of all wars for national liberation that the first fatal casualty is always the truth. As a gesture of goodwill and reconciliation and a sincere yearning for post-war reconstruction of our society, the democratic government established the TRC to try to heal the wounds of our divided past. The truth is that in 2013 we still have the Boeremag in our midst. How many Dirk Coetzees are still roaming free?

Sizwe's wandering spirit still needs to be laid to rest.

There are many such wandering and restless spirits. We need to lay those freedom fighters to rest in the African way. I will only rest the day we can retrieve Sizwe's remains, even if it is just a fragment of a bone. That alone would be enough for me.

One day all will be well, Tshonyane.

A call out of the blue

I walked out of the gym on a weekday afternoon in January 2005 and scrolled through the missed calls on my cellphone. At the top of the list was *The Presidency*. I immediately returned the call and the voice on the other end said, 'I will put you through to the president.'

It wasn't entirely unusual for President Thabo Mbeki to phone me as I was DG of justice at the time and we would have informal sessions as DGs of the cluster. I had a relatively good relationship with President Mbeki at the time, developed during the post-democratic years. We had never interacted while in exile, although I had heard much about him. I remember people talking about him as a brilliant mind who was writing speeches for O.R. and that he was being groomed to take over from Tambo one day.

'Comrade Vusi, where are you?' the president enquired. I told him I was in Pretoria and he asked if I could come and see him. We arranged a meeting for the following day.

It was not my first visit to the official residence at Mahlamba Ndlopfu, but despite this, the palatial setting, sprawling gardens and impressively high ceilings left me awestruck. My first visit had been when the justice cluster had asked me to seek an audience with the president. There had been personal tension between National Police Commissioner Jackie Selebi and Bulelani Ngcuka, the national director of public prosecutions (NDPP). The cluster had asked that I, together with National Intelligence Agency (NIA)

DG Vusi Mavimbela and Correctional Services Commissioner Linda Mti, ask the president to intervene.

I took a seat in the waiting room and considered why I had been summoned to see the president. I knew I had not been called to enjoy a drink and that there must be a pressing matter. Finally, I was ushered into his office, where Deputy Minister of Foreign Affairs Aziz Pahad was waiting alongside Mbeki. We exchanged pleasantries and small talk before the president got down to business.

'Vusi, you know about this matter that we do not have an NDPP,' he said. I confirmed that I did. Bulelani Ngcuka had resigned in July of the previous year after having been at the centre of a political storm in which he had investigated the then Deputy President Jacob Zuma for fraud and corruption after Zuma was implicated in the Arms Deal investigation. Ngcuka later declined to prosecute Zuma for fraud and corruption, at the same time saying that there was a prima facie case that was unwinnable. Ngcuka had developed a reputation as a graft buster, spearheading a very public fight against corruption. Ngcuka was pushed into a corner following allegations that he had been an apartheid-era spy, although the Hefer Commission of Inquiry did exonerate him. While it was never stated publicly, Ngcuka had effectively been forced to resign. There was too much political pressure, too much tension between him and Selebi – and many lies were told over that period.

In December 2004, Justice Minister Brigitte Mabandla told me she was anxious about the fact that there was no head of the NPA and that it was working on her nerves. Despite this, I still hadn't expected the president to offer me the job, but he did.

'Kgalema [Motlanthe, the deputy president] and I have decided that you should go to the NPA and be the NDPP,' he told me, adding that the minister had agreed.

'Do I have a say in the matter?' I asked the president. He assured me I did but they had already made the decision for me. It was something to which I needed to give some thought. At the time, Girly was the deputy DG at the NIA and I felt that there may be a conflict of interest and an overlapping of fields. In fact, she wasn't terribly excited about the prospect of my becoming NDPP because it would also mean that she would have to resign. I told my children, but they simply saw it as a promotion and didn't appreciate the implications of the job.

But it was my mother who was most reluctant. She had seen what had happened to Ngcuka before me and was concerned that the same fate might befall me.

'Oh really, *mntwanam*?' she said, meaning 'Oh really, my child?' '*Kutheni ufuna ukuthatha umsebenzi kaBulelani nje*?' – 'Why are you taking Bulelani's job?' she asked in her soft-spoken manner. I explained that Bulelani was no longer there, but she was very worried about what had happened to him.

While I knew that Ngcuka had been forced to resign, I didn't think too much about it. I knew that somebody had to do the job of NDPP and that I had been asked to do so. I did not consider the potential for controversy – only what was expected of me. I accepted the job because the mandate is defined in the legislation. All I had to do was to carry out my responsibilities in terms of the NPA Act and the Constitution.

A week after my meeting with the president at Mahlamba Ndlopfu, on the evening of Friday 21 January 2005, government spokesperson Joel Netshitenzhe issued a statement on the outcomes of a cabinet meeting and *lekgotla*. In a paragraph at the end of the three-page release was an announcement about my appointment:

> *The President wishes to announce that he has appointed Advocate Vusumzi P. Pikoli as the National Director of Public Prosecutions with effect from 1 February 2005. The President and government are confident that Adv. Pikoli will undertake the tasks delegated to this critical component of our justice system with distinction.*

It didn't take long for my phone to start ringing with interview requests from the media and messages of congratulations. I had not been one of the publicised front-runners for the job – journalists had tipped the acting NDPP Silas Ramaite for the position as well as my old friend and former Limpopo Premier Ngoako Ramatlhodi.

In an interview with the South African Press Association, I stated: 'The biggest issue is building public confidence in the criminal justice system, to have prosecutions at the centre, ensuring effective prosecutions.' I also paid tribute to Ngcuka and responded to past public criticism of the office by saying 'one has got to make sure that there's better cooperation amongst all law-enforcement agencies to make sure we focus on the one thing that really matters, which is to fight crime'. However, I chose not to comment on pending cases that had been left by Ngcuka.

To the *Saturday Star*, I played down my reaction at getting the job: 'I'm not sure if "excited" is the right word; it's not going to be an easy job but somebody has to do it and the president has chosen me. I've got no axe to grind with anybody and will work within the dictates of the job.' I gave an assurance that the law would be applied fairly and equally to all citizens, rich or poor, and to politicians as well.

Opposition parties also waded in with their reaction to my appointment, issuing press releases to the media. The move was also welcomed by the official opposition, the Democratic Alliance, and the party's justice spokeswoman Sheila Camerer lauded it as a good appointment, 'most importantly because he is not a high-profile ANC politician'. She said that my record at the justice department was 'patchy', but noted that I had made 'laudable attempts to sort out its appalling finances and roll back the endemic corruption' at the department. The sentiment amongst some opposition politicians was that I was 'too soft for the job'. Camerer questioned whether I was tough enough for the job, stating: 'You need to be ruthless and tough in that job, and I believe that his approach is not up-front in-your-face style.' Former ANC member and founder of the United Democratic Movement Bantu Holomisa also called me too soft and 'too much of a gentleman'.

On 1 February 2005, I drove through the boomed gates of the VGM building, the NPA's official headquarters hidden away in suburban Silverton. Its official title is the Victoria and Griffiths Mxenge Building, named after anti-apartheid activist lawyers who were killed by the regime in the 1980s. In the cavernous auditorium, which had been the SABC's Pretoria bureau in a previous incarnation, I was introduced to the staff of the NPA.

Justice Minister Brigitte Mabandla and her deputy Johnny de Lange accompanied me. All the national deputy directors of public prosecutions were there. I had interacted with the NPA through my position as DG of justice so I did know a number of people in the room. I had met Dr Ramaite several years previously when he was interviewed for the position of deputy attorney-general of the then Transvaal Provincial Division

(TPD) and I had also interviewed Leonard McCarthy for the job of senior state advocate. Willie Hofmeyr I knew from the days of the TRC and as a member of the Portfolio Committee on Justice. Even prior to that, I had heard much about Willie and how he had been detained during apartheid and undertaken a hunger strike while in prison.

Mabandla made the formal introduction to the institution's employees, telling them that she expected the best from me. 'I am expecting that in the next five years there should be a further qualitative improvement in delivery and in levels of excellence in the services that you provide,' she told prosecutors before addressing me directly. 'Advocate Pikoli, good wishes and I know you will deliver.'

I took the podium and quipped that I was surprised to see such a large turnout at the meeting. I assured staff that I would work closely with the country's law-enforcement agencies and pledged to treat accused persons with dignity and sensitivity. 'We shall serve with integrity. I think it is what is required of this institution and this we shall do together. In our work, we shall be guided by the Constitution and the law.'

One of my primary concerns was what was perceived to be an exodus of staff from the elite investigating unit, the Directorate of Special Operations (DSO), colloquially referred to as the Scorpions. With many concerned about the potential dissolution of the unit, I told staff that the immediate challenge was to build confidence in the NPA, but that I could do little to stop those of them who wanted to leave the organisation. Deputy Minister De Lange echoed this sentiment, stating that the unit should continue to do its work in terms of the law until such time as a decision was taken about the future of the Scorpions.

Once the formalities had been finalised, I got down to the business of assembling my team, as well as dealing with my inbox and the pile of matters mounting on my desk. Walking the corridors of the VGM building, the walls adorned with images of prodigious legal minds such as Godfrey Pitje, Bram Fischer and Ismail Mahomed, the enormity of my task was undeniable. Still I did not entertain any thought of potential controversy lurking ahead or any ominous matter I would have to overcome. All I thought about was doing what was expected of me.

The first person I seconded on to my staff was Kalyani Pillay, with whom I had worked at the justice department, where she was my advisor. She had been a state attorney and had experience in the field. I had recalled seeing her CV when she applied for the position of head of the state attorney's office in Johannesburg in 1995 – at the time she had her own legal practice in Pietermaritzburg and was a young attorney and we were looking to entice more junior, black women to the public service. Pillay would effectively become my most trusted right hand at the department of justice and the NPA.

I also had to familiarise myself with the office and set up individual meetings with the heads of the divisions, specifically my four deputies: Silas Ramaite, Willie Hofmeyr, Leonard McCarthy and Jan Henning. In a series of one-on-one meetings, I tried to get an understanding of what they were busy with, to gauge whether there was anything that required urgent attention and to take the temperature of the organisation.

Contrary to popular belief, the NDPP is concerned with general prosecutions in the country and not only high-profile, much-publicised matters. Under Ngcuka, the perception had been created that the NDPP only busied himself with cases that grabbed media attention. There are criminal trials playing out in courts across the country every day and the work of the NDPP is to make sure that all of those cases are run properly and smoothly. I had to look at the backlog of cases and matters piling up at lower courts too.

Of course, there were several highly publicised, controversial matters awaiting my attention and it quickly became clear that I was walking into what was being described as a 'pressure-cooker job' by some media. The previous year ANC Chief Whip Tony Yengeni had been convicted of defrauding parliament by accepting a discount on a luxury car during the tendering process for the multibillion-rand Arms Deal while he was a member of a parliamentary committee exercising oversight of the deal. When I came into office he was appealing the court's decision. A corruption probe into former Limpopo Premier Ngoako Ramatlhodi was also on our radar screens and had the potential to cause political waves.

In the very week that I walked into my new office, a far-reaching corruption trial implicating the deputy president of the country and of the ruling party was resuming in the Durban High Court. Jacob Zuma's financial advisor Schabir Shaik was facing accusations of corrupting Zuma in relation to the Arms Deal. If Shaik was to be convicted, I knew that I would have to decide whether or not to charge the deputy president. The tentacles of the Arms Deal reached deep and far and the multifaceted investigation into those who had been implicated was also ongoing.

My immediate litmus test was the so-called Travelgate affair. A group of MPs, mostly from the ANC, had allegedly colluded with travel agents to submit false claims and inflate the price of airplane tickets to cover the costs of luxury car rentals and hotel accommodation. There had been media reports that the NPA was considering plea-bargain deals with the ANC lawmakers that would see them returning to the back benches with little more than a slap on the wrist. *Business Day* newspaper wrote in an editorial: 'Pikoli cannot and should not allow such a travesty of justice to tarnish the start of his tenure.'

My inbox contained a minefield of cases with political implications and potential pitfalls. Yet it was the very existence of the investigating unit behind nearly all of these cases that would in reality provide me with my first real hurdle. Just 13 days after I took office as NDPP, President Thabo Mbeki announced a commission to investigate the possibility of incorporating the Scorpions into the South African Police Service.

The Scorpions' sting

As DG of the justice department, I was never a fan of the Scorpions' 'Hollywood' style of operations. It was a reputation that earned the elite unit much criticism – the flashy image of over-branded high-performance cars, sirens blaring for the cameras and open invitations to journalists to attend operations. I am not a colourful person and for me it was always a question of making an arrest, not of having a reporter there to take photos and capture the moment. During my term as NDPP, we never invited any journalists. There would, of course, be leaks, but to this day I do not know how word got out.

Bulelani Ngcuka had a very different style to me – he was engaging, robust and not media shy. He also had a justice minister in Penuell Maduna who liked to talk and meet with the press. Steve Tshwete, the minister of safety and security, was equally boisterous, so when the Scorpions were operating with Maduna and Tshwete, the unit was something of a media darling. Organised crime syndicates were being busted, major arrests were being made, confidence in the justice system was sky-high, the ministers formed a formidable team and the public loved it. The Scorpions had a catchy slogan that I really did like: 'Loved by the people, Feared by criminals, Respected by peers.' People would see a black Scorpions car with the red logo in the streets and would get excited.

That was not my style – glamour and glitter do not appeal to me – but the approach proved effective as the public loved to see crime-busters in action. Everyone applauded when images of Willie Hofmeyr's Assets Forfeiture Unit carrying out big-screen TVs from people's houses were flashed all over the news. They didn't complain when small-time crooks were being arrested. They loved that the new kid on the block was cracking down on syndicates. But then politicians started to feel the heat and many of them realised, 'Aah, now this is beginning to involve us.' They had never complained before, but suddenly they became very vocal about the Scorpions' style of operations, that they were picking and choosing only the cases they believed would earn good press coverage and that members were being trained by international agencies. That is when I began to appreciate the value of what Ngcuka had been doing.

On Sunday 13 February 2005, following his annual state of the nation address, President Thabo Mbeki told an SABC interviewer that he would be appointing a commission to investigate the feasibility of incorporating the Scorpions into the police. Judge Sisi Khampepe would later be appointed to chair the commission.

I had been in the job of NDPP for 13 days when that announcement came. The issue had, however, been brewing for some time and Minister Mabandla had even alluded to it when she introduced me to staff at the VGM building on my first day of work. 'It's not even about moving, it's about alignment,' the minister had said of the Scorpions' future at the time.

The Directorate of Special Operations (DSO) had been called to life by Mbeki in parliament in June 1999, when he said that the country needed new ways and means of fighting crime. I was acting DG of justice at the time and when I heard the president announcing this new unit, I knew nothing about it. He told the country that he would leave the matter in the hands of the security cluster ministers, which meant that we as DGs were given the task of coming up with a new model. Although Mbeki announced that he had been working with the ministers on this matter, we felt that it came from nowhere. No minister came to us to say, 'You have heard the statement of the president, and this is what we want.' It was the bureaucrats who came up with the model of the Scorpions.

So, as DGs of the security cluster, we sat down to grapple with the issue. We couldn't rely on any policies and had to approach organised crime as a dynamic and constantly changing entity. All the departments were represented, from the police, NIA and the South African Secret Service (SASS) to the justice, home affairs and foreign affairs departments.

Our first presentation to the ministers was shot down, particularly by Joe Matthews, then deputy minister of safety and security. He said, 'Guys, we want a completely new thing and what you've done is just rearrange the furniture in the room.'

I also remember that there was a fight between Maduna and Tshwete about where the new unit would be housed, but ultimately the justice minister won the day and it was decided that the DSO would be located within the NPA. Tshwete argued that the function of fighting crime should sit with the police, but what won it for Maduna was the idea of not rearranging the furniture. It had to be a new structure with new ideas and also be independent.

We decided on a *troika* principle: the unit should focus on intelligence-driven, and prosecution-led investigations, and would be tasked with tackling top-level crimes with the specific aim of securing convictions. This system would see prosecutors, investigators and intelligence operatives working closely under a single command.

The major issue that then arose was if the unit was to be intelligence driven that meant either it should have intelligence capacity to collect information or it should make use of existing intelligence structures. At that time, there were political killings in KwaZulu-Natal, and People Against Gangsterism and Drugs (PAGAD) was in full force in the Western Cape, with bombs exploding everywhere. We knew that for the structure to work, investigations had to be done properly. At first the unit worked closely with the NIA, but then we asked what the role of the investigators would be if they were not going to be gathering information.

During the process of hammering out the legislation and negotiating how the unit would look and act, I had a falling-out with Minister Maduna. Ngcuka, as NDPP, had assumed control over the process, playing a prominent role in recruiting police members and guys from the NIA and that irritated the minister. At a meeting at the offices of NIA, we were told, 'Look guys, Bulelani is outmanoeuvring you here.'

It was quite clear from 2000 already, while the unit was being conceptualised and legislation drafted, that there were existing tensions and fractious opinions. As justice DG, I was sceptical about this unit having intelligence capacity because there were National Intelligence Acts that already established intelligence structures and the unit couldn't be set up outside of the law. There was no provision to establish yet another intelligence agency but at the same time it was absurd to think the unit would be effective without that capability. It had to be done within the law.

In the meantime, Ngcuka was all hyped up and in a hurry. He was spending money without accountability and wasn't following proper procurement procedures. He would say that they needed this and that and, as long as there was money in the budget, he would spend it. I, on the other hand, as DG, had to make sure everything was properly resourced and this led to a clash in 2001.

Although I tried explaining that things had to be done according to the book, Ngcuka felt that I was trying to sabotage him. He said, 'This is what the president wants,' and I responded, 'Yes, it could be what the president wants but that does not mean that we must not follow the law in getting there.' He was in a hurry and I had to slow him down a bit. That was the only real problem we had during our time working together.

When the announcement about the Khampepe Commission was made, I had to work with my team to prepare our submissions on behalf of the NPA and the DSO. We had to address the known criticisms of the unit. We had to defend its mandate and location, and respond to suggestions that cases were being cherry-picked, that we were fudging our high conviction rate and that the unit was doing the bidding of certain politicians. The Scorpions had been at the centre of a storm of criticism after Ngcuka had levelled allegations of corruption against Zuma and we were still dealing with the fallout.

My honest thinking at the time was that President Mbeki was trying to please those who didn't like the Scorpions. I don't think he ever wanted the DSO to be relocated elsewhere or to be given another mandate. He wanted to have an objective judgment on the matter and having that judicial sanction would stop the debate from continuing.

Personal politics led to the establishment of the Khampepe Commission. Bulelani Ngcuka and Police Commissioner George Fivaz enjoyed a good rapport, but when Jackie Selebi took over from Fivaz, there was no appreciation of that close working relationship. When Selebi came on the scene, he did not hide his dislike for the Scorpions. Ngcuka was able to second some of the best detectives to the Scorpions and had taken some of the good guys from NIA; he was also recruiting from universities because he needed capable graduates to deal with complex economic crimes. This added to the perception that the unit was elite and that the members received special training and were better salaried.

Further tension was also caused by the fact that the Scorpions were being trained by the FBI and by Scotland Yard, even though it was a publicly known fact and was never a secret. In addition, an agreement had been reached by former Ministers Dullah Omar and Joe Nhlanhla to have representatives from the NPA, SAPS and intelligence trained by Kroll International, a corporate investigations and risk-consulting firm based in New York. Critics felt that the Scorpions were dabbling in foreign intelligence matters and this wasn't well received.

I also did not agree with the argument that the mandate of the Scorpions was the normal police mandate. They were not going to be involved in 'standard' murder cases – their arena had to be complex commercial crime and high-end crimes, including corruption. They were not going to operate like the normal police service – and this is where the bitter rivalry came in.

The mandate of the Khampepe Commission was not to examine the Scorpions' existence, but rather to determine the unit's optimal placement. Khampepe was tasked with examining the rationale behind the establishment of the directorate, its mandate and relationship with other security and intelligence agencies, how to strengthen integrated efforts against organised crime and the options regarding the appropriate location of the directorate.

Interested parties were invited to make submissions in May 2005 by way of affidavit and it was then decided that public hearings should be held.

My turn came on 11 October 2005 when I had to appear publicly before Judge Khampepe and her commission. We had engaged the services of Senior Counsel Marumo Moerane, who prepared lengthy submissions. Advocate Moerane led me through my evidence for around two hours while I responded to the criticisms of the Scorpions. 'I regret that issues of this nature have found their way into this commission,' I submitted, stating that issues of national security should not be brought into the public domain.

I insisted that the DSO was not a threat to national security and accusations that it was a law unto itself were entirely incorrect. 'The DSO can only have authority conferred on it by law. I don't see a way in which anyone can say the DSO is a law unto itself when legislation makes it clear the minister of justice exercises final responsibility for the NPA.' I explained that the NPA had a legal obligation to submit an annual report to parliament which also included the DSO activities.

'The minister can call upon the national director to explain the reasons for any matter seized by the NPA, including a decision to prosecute or not prosecute,' I submitted.

I further explained that the DSO should not be regarded as an intelligence structure as this was not its function. 'The law allows the DSO to gather, keep and analyse information. The same law authorises the DSO to institute criminal proceedings and the same law gives the DSO power to investigate,' I elaborated.

It was also important that I address the conflict between the Scorpions and other agencies. 'I did not inherit a perfect organisation,' I told Khampepe, 'but I inherited an effective organisation whose work speaks for itself. Like any other organisation there will be problems but it's going overboard to say these problems make the institution dysfunctional. The criminal justice system is a chain and it is imperative for law-enforcement agencies to work together and make sure that chain operates effectively. Our approach is cooperation and not confrontation.'

Under cross-examination, Advocate George Bizos (on behalf of the NIA) quizzed me about vetting for security clearance and threats to national security, outside consultants being employed to assist investigations and leaks to the media. I admitted to Khampepe that I was not satisfied that there were adequate systems in place to detect leaks when they occurred and that we couldn't rule out the possibility that outside consultants might be members of a dangerous organisation, but I made it abundantly clear that I was willing to work closely with the NIA on these matters.

Concerns around vetting and security clearance were a major point of conflict. Because of the nature of the work Scorpions members were doing, they had to be properly cleared as they would have access to classified information such as cabinet minutes or secret documents. You had to be sure that the individuals did not pose a threat to the security of the state.

That was one of the first issues that I attended to when I came into the office of NDPP. I made an arrangement with Billy Masetlha, NIA director, to fast-track the vetting of DSO members. The NIA went so far as to give us a covert office to work out of and we had a relationship of close cooperation – then all of a sudden there was an about-turn and the NIA and Masetlha became hostile, accusing the Scorpions of posing a threat and working with foreign intelligence agencies and compromising national security.

I was annoyed, particularly because I had personally approached Masetlha after a Scorpions member came to me to raise an alarm about a senior manager at the DSO. This manager had been seen entering foreign embassies and no one seemed to know why. I told Masetlha that I had this information and I gave him the name of the individual and an undertaking to work with him on the investigation. Masetlha never reported back to me on what had happened with the matter, but at the commission he accused the DSO of working with foreign intelligence agencies. Yet I had given them an opportunity to carry out counter-intelligence activities within the DSO to ensure we didn't have the wrong people working for us.

Leonard McCarthy, head of the Scorpions, explained to Khampepe that he had proposed that guidelines be drafted for the agencies to work together. However, the police had stalled these efforts. 'When the president suggested the commission, officials stepped back from the guideline process to await the outcome of the commission,' McCarthy explained. The process had been under way since 2001 and he had even extended an olive branch to the SAPS by acknowledging them as the main law-enforcement agency in the country, but that had failed. McCarthy also gave multiple examples of how the DSO and SAPS were working effectively on the ground and relocating the Scorpions would prove to be a nightmare.

The public hearings concluded in October 2005 and, although it took a considerable amount of time for Khampepe to release her findings, the report was finally signed in early February 2006. I had wanted the outcome to be made known promptly and publicly as the commission had caused a lot of anxiety amongst the affected staff and they wanted certainty on the way forward. Judge Khampepe finally handed over her report to President Mbeki at the Union Buildings in May 2006. The report then went before the National Security Council, consisting of all the security cluster ministers and the cabinet.

In late June, following a cabinet meeting, the findings were publicly announced at a press conference in Muldersdrift. Presidency DG Frank Chikane told the gathering that the DSO would remain within the NPA, but that political oversight would move to the minister of safety and security. This effectively meant that the Scorpions would have two bosses – prosecutors in the unit would continue to receive instructions from and be accountable to me as NDPP, but the oversight and responsibility of the law-enforcement component would fall under the minister in charge of the police. Cabinet also approved a recommendation that a coordinating committee be established to deal with the operational issues and look at individual cases to ensure no duplication. The DSO would continue to deal with high-level priority crimes as originally conceptualised.

The outcome was largely favourable for me in terms of how to streamline the reporting lines but I was not entirely sure how it would work in practice. Following the outcomes, President Mbeki called the DGs of the security cluster to a meeting in Cape Town to check what was happening and whether we were all satisfied with the outcome. He gave us a tongue-lashing and told us that he wanted to see Khampepe's recommendations implemented. However, the committee was never set up and the events of politics overtook his wishes.

Despite the commission's recommendations being released in 2006, the full content of the 144-page report was not officially released for another two years – only in May 2008 was it gazetted. The timing was interesting because by then I had been suspended, the Ginwala Inquiry was under way and legislation to have the DSO disbanded had been approved by cabinet. Supporters of the Scorpions had hoped that the report would provide fresh ammunition but it proved quite the opposite, with Khampepe critical of the Scorpions and of me.

She found that the Scorpions had illegally gathered intelligence, ignored its own vetting laws and compromised state security. She also identified an urgent need for the unit to stop publicising investigations:

> *The improper media sensation associated with the investigation and/or arrest of some individuals resultant from the leaks in the DSO may open a practice that is inconsistent with the right to a fair trial guaranteed under Section 35 of the Constitution. There was, in my view, no plausible*

> *reason furnished for this conduct on the part of the DSO, which conduct is to be frowned upon. I find the conduct to be reprehensible, unprofessional and corroding public confidence in the law enforcement agencies. I am convinced that the DSO will, in conducting itself within the parameters of the law, still continue to enjoy the public confidence that is shown towards its work and the efficiency with which it constantly strives for in the execution of its mandate. I believe that the public confidence will not be eroded but will be enhanced when the DSO does its work within professional ethics and in harmony with the fundamental rights guaranteed in the Constitution and the Bill of Rights.*

The issue of vetting was highly criticised by Khampepe, who found it disturbing that some Scorpions members hadn't been properly cleared. She also suggested that I be strongly reprimanded for the failure and that there should be an urgent reconciliation of the numbers of investigators who were appointed who didn't comply with the requirements of the law:

> *The NDPP should in the circumstances be strongly admonished for his failure to adhere and monitor further adherence to this prescript. I further recommend that urgent appropriate reconciliation be undertaken by the NDPP to establish those special investigators whose appointments do not comply with the provisions of the Act and that the NDPP take remedial action in regard thereto.*

Perhaps her strongest rebuke was related to what she called the rivalry between the Scorpions and the police – and she held Selebi and me responsible for the tensions:

> *It may be necessary for a reprimand by the president and/or parliament as a mark of displeasure. The institutional tensions that are explained by the personalities that head these institutions are regrettable in the extreme.*

This was balanced against numerous favourable findings that supported the DSO. Ultimately, Khampepe concluded that the Scorpions should not be moved into the SAPS:

> *After careful consideration of the evidence as well as the arguments submitted by various stakeholders, I am persuaded that no compelling argument has been made to point to the DSO's establishment as unconstitutional. For reasons that are in the body of the report, it is my considered conclusion that the location of the DSO within the NPA is constitutional and jurisprudentially sound.*

Despite the recommendation of a judge and these crystal-clear findings, the Scorpions no longer exist today. The ANC conference at Polokwane in 2007 resolved that the unit should be dissolved and two pieces of legislation were subsequently passed to ensure that this happened. The ANC chose to use Khampepe's report selectively to motivate for the dissolution of the unit – they didn't want the Scorpions, finish and *klaar*.

The laws were successfully challenged in the Constitutional Court by Johannesburg businessman Hugh Glenister and the Court ruled that the legislation was constitutionally invalid because it did not provide enough protection against political influence. The Directorate for Priority Crime Investigation, also known as the Hawks, has been established and is positioned within the SAPS. While some of the Scorpions investigators relocated to the police, most quit and were lost to the private sector.

One result of this, in my opinion, is that the country's levels of corruption have increased and our ratings in terms of the Transparency International Index on corruption are going down annually. Nobody wants to tackle what we call grand corruption or political corruption. We focus on small cases, charges are being withdrawn and cases are being dropped. Politically influenced matters such as those involving Northern Cape ANC Chair John Block and even ANC President Jacob Zuma have been affected.

As a result, we are losing the respect we used to have in terms of being seen to be serious in the fight against corruption. The whole world was coming to South Africa to learn from the experience of the Scorpions, we were hosting delegations, the United Nations was proud of the unit. And we lost all of that.

We know the cost of corruption to the economy and that is money that does not find its way to the poor. Most of those investigators are in the private sector now. Leonard McCarthy has gone to the World Bank, prosecutor Anton Steynberg to the International Criminal Court and many others to consultancies and forensic audit firms.

In my view it was clearly a political decision to disband the unit, aimed at protecting corrupt politicians. The Scorpions started out as the darlings of the public but when the unit was doing its work too well, it became the villain in the eyes of some people – and I would say those people are few.

If I had come into office as NDPP in 2005 and announced that I was withdrawing charges against Ramatlhodi, not prosecuting Zuma, dropping charges against the Travelgate MPs, and would not oppose the appeal by Tony Yengeni, then I'm sure the Scorpions would still be alive today. But the unit would not be very effective. It would have been alive in name only and nobody would have feared the Scorpions' sting.

Prosecuting Zuma

I closed the door to my office in the VGM building and turned on the television. I wanted to be alone. I knew it would be a long judgment and I didn't want to be influenced by anyone. They would make comments and remarks and I felt that if I watched it by myself I would have the space to reflect on the ruling so that when I met my team I would have developed my own thoughts on the matter.

It was 2 June 2005 and Judge Hilary Squires was delivering his verdict in the case against Jacob Zuma's financial advisor Schabir Shaik. I had been NDPP for four months.

Judge Squires took hours to finalise his 165-page ruling and I sat in my office watching the live broadcast until it was complete. Shaik was found guilty on two counts of corruption and one count of fraud and was sentenced to 15 years in prison. Squires found that Shaik had tried to solicit a bribe for Zuma from arms-manufacturing company Thomson CSF.

When Judge Squires convicted Shaik, I didn't celebrate, pump my fist or pop bottles of champagne. As a prosecutor, I was pleased because I knew that my team involved in the case had been through hell. Witnesses had to be put in the Witness Protection Programme. How safe is your own life as a prosecutor if that step is taken?

Securing that conviction was vindication that they had been on the right track all along and I felt that my guys had done the job in spite of all the hardships they endured. My predecessor, Bulelani Ngcuka, had also been through hell. The Hefer Commission was a direct consequence of the case against Shaik and would never have taken place were it not for that prosecution. Doubts about the Scorpions arose specifically because of this trial and it was also the source of complaints about the unit's Hollywood style. The trial had been emotionally draining.

What many don't realise is that when people go through complex matters, it takes a toll on prosecutors as well as their families. You cannot separate a prosecutor from his or her family – they feel the pain and they feel the joy and, when things get tough, they suffer the ridicule, the insults and the hurt.

So when Judge Squires drew proceedings to a close, I was relieved. But I was all too aware of the implications and what would follow.

When I walked into the office of the NDPP, I knew I would have to deal with burning issues, but I didn't think too much about it until judgment had been delivered. I knew that the Shaik charge sheet mentioned Zuma so many times that anybody reading it would not understand why he was not in the dock himself. But my approach has always been one of sticking to the law – I would wait for the judgment and act accordingly. If there were any reason for anyone else to be charged, then we would have to look at the evidence and analyse whether we would have a case strong enough for a conviction. I would apply the law and come to an appropriate decision.

With the benefit of hindsight, if I were NDPP at the time, I would have charged Zuma along with Shaik. They were inextricably linked to the allegations and the flow of money showed this close proximity. Shaik was sustaining Zuma, peddling his name and using his influence as a public official, and it was proven that money was paid.

I cannot guess what went on in the former NDPP's mind but perhaps it was simply too much of a political hot potato. I can only think that he succumbed to political pressure – and yet there is no evidence to show that. Perhaps he was hoping that if he secured a conviction against Shaik, the next logical step would be to charge Zuma.

In 2002, when I was still the DG of justice and he was NDPP, Ngcuka came to see me to seek guidance with this dilemma. Shaik had not yet been charged, and Ngcuka told me that the deputy president's name kept coming up in the investigation and the paper trail they were picking up could well implicate JZ. He didn't know what to do about charging him.

I was shocked. 'Bulelani, I don't know why you're coming to me. Why are you telling me this?' He said he didn't know how to deal with it. I told him that I couldn't tell him what to do.

I was not a politician so I don't think that could have been misconstrued as political interference. At times, prosecutors do consult outside counsel on matters they may find complex. But at the end of the day, they are the ones who must take the decision.

I think Ngcuka was beginning to feel the pressure and it was clearly weighing heavily on him, and the fact that he approached me illustrated that. If he had come to me, it was likely he might have taken others into his confidence.

I said to him, 'Do what is right, do what will make you sleep well at night.' I also told him that that this might have implications for the unity of the ANC. At the ANC's Stellenbosch conference that year, I bumped into Schabir Shaik's brother Mo. He said to me, 'Hey, bru, I don't mind about my brother, you know. He's old enough, he can look after himself. But when Bulelani starts chasing the old man, JZ, it's not acceptable.'

I listened to him but was careful not to engage because I suspected he was going to drag me into some kind of a discussion. I was DG of justice and I would not have been able to defend Ngcuka one way or the other, simply because I didn't have the facts of the case. The pressure on Ngcuka at the time must have been immense.

On a Saturday in August 2003, Ngcuka told reporters in Pretoria that Zuma would not be prosecuted in relation to the Arms Deal, despite a recommendation from the investigating team that a criminal prosecution be instituted. 'We have concluded that, whilst there is a prima facie case of corruption against the deputy president, our prospects of success are not strong enough. That means that we are not sure if we have a winnable case,' he said into the cameras as I watched on television. Justice Minister Penuell Maduna was sitting alongside him. Ngcuka did, however, announce that Shaik would be charged with corruption, fraud, theft of company assets, tax evasion and reckless trading and would appear in the Durban Magistrate's Court the following Monday.

As I watched the news bulletin, I felt that his decision would come back to burn Ngcuka. I was convinced that he must have met people at a higher political level before arriving at that decision. For him to have appeared at that press conference with a politician alongside him – the minister of justice, no less – told me that there may have been discussions at a higher level.

Most matters that are prosecuted are based on a prima facie case and the onus is then on the accused to rebut the adduced evidence but not necessarily to prove his or her innocence. It is for the prosecution to prove its case beyond any reasonable doubt and for the court to decide whether the state has been able to do so and then convict or acquit.

If you have insufficient evidence, then you don't go ahead and charge. You weigh up a reasonable prospect of a successful prosecution. If you say it is a prima facie case, that means you do have evidence against the accused and he does have a case to answer to. You put it to him; he answers; the court decides.

At the time, the matter was already in the public domain because details about the investigation had been leaked to the media, and Zuma was complaining that the leaks were designed to cast aspersions on his integrity. Perhaps Ngcuka and Maduna thought that by making the public announcement, they would lift the cloud over Zuma's head. In reality, however, it simply made things worse.

This matter would have been put to rest a long time ago with one trial, in which both Mr Schabir Shaik and Mr Jacob Zuma would have been charged in court. The case would have gone through all the processes of appeals up to the highest court in the land and it would have eventually arrived at a verdict. We would have gone through all the stages and the matter would have been settled. Instead, we have a president with a cloud over his head.

Following Ngcuka's public statement, the fallout led to the Hefer Commission and attempts to try to discredit him by accusing him of being an apartheid spy. I couldn't see how that would have helped Zuma in terms of the legal issue, because even if it were proven that Ngcuka was an enemy agent and his credibility was damaged, the charges would not have gone away.

With all this in mind, I took in Squires' judgment and thought about what my mother had said to me when I informed her about my position as

NDPP. She had had reservations about the nature of the job and was worried that what had happened to Ngcuka would also become my fate.

I felt differently. For me, the issue was that somebody had to do the job and in this case – as with any other – I had to be guided by the Constitution and the law. Of course, that would not protect me if someone put a scheme in place against me, if someone had spies or a devious plan. So that was always at the back of my mind. But I was resolute that I was simply going to do my job as it should be done and not be dragged into political games.

Perhaps some people thought I would be malleable when I was appointed or maybe it was a genuine case of thinking that I could do the job capably. When I accepted the position, it never occurred to me that I might be expected to do the bidding of politicians. It could have been that I was simply naïve or ignorant. However, when I started carrying out my functions, it did become clear that there were certain expectations and people started saying, 'Is this the right man for the job?'

A week after the judgment I called the Shaik prosecuting team to a meeting in my office and congratulated them. Advocates Billy Downer and Anton Steynberg were there, along with Scorpions senior investigators Johan du Plooy and Izak du Plooy. I had read through Squires' ruling and thought it was a good judgment. He had given it with the view of a possible appeal to the highest court in the country and not just the appellate division. He had to cover all his bases.

As a team we had to decide on the way forward and what we would do in the event of an appeal. At some stage, I altered the composition of the team by including two black prosecutors, one of whom was a woman from KwaZulu-Natal, Zuma's own province. We discussed the ruling, aspects with which we may struggle and how we would prepare for that eventuality. That was our priority. I believe there was a consensus in the room, although it was not spoken out loud, that it would be inevitable for Zuma to be charged, but a decision was not taken at that meeting.

In the week after Shaik was convicted, media reports broke that the NPA was 'preparing the ground' for Zuma to be charged. It was a time of intense speculation and swirling rumours. I was sensitive to the controversy that had dogged the NPA before my tenure, particularly the decision by Public Protector Lawrence Mushwana to uphold Zuma's complaint against the NPA and Ngcuka for the comments that he had made about a prima facie case. I was concerned that the leaking of confidential or incorrect information to the media was undermining the public's confidence in the prosecuting authority. I also realised the urgency of the matter, but still wanted to ensure that Zuma was treated with dignity and respect and not like a criminal.

After my meeting with the team, I received a call from the office of the justice minister asking me to go to Chile. It took me completely by surprise as nothing had been scheduled in my diary. The minister explained that the previous year, 2004, she had travelled to Chile with Ngcuka and they had discussed the signing of a memorandum of understanding between the two countries that would see mutual assistance on prosecutorial matters, exchange programmes and so on. The draft was in place and the agreement was to be signed when the South African president visited Chile to meet with his counterpart. President Mbeki was travelling to the country and I was to accompany him so that I could sign the agreement with the Chilean chief prosecutor during the president's visit.

My advisor, Kalyani Pillay, accompanied me on the trip. When we arrived at the airport in Johannesburg, I picked up the *Star* newspaper and read about my trip to Chile with the president and that it was likely I would discuss Zuma's case with him on the trip. The report speculated that once I returned, I would make my decision about whether or not to charge Zuma.

I was shocked. I couldn't understand how journalists could make such wild speculations. I had never even considered discussing the matter with the president.

Kalyani and I flew SAA and Mbeki travelled on his presidential jet. The same arrangement was followed on our return to South Africa. I had my own programme while I was there and Mbeki's was entirely separate to mine. He was delivering lectures and holding meetings and I was merely part of the delegation. The only time we were together was on the single occasion that the entire delegation met in his suite. Not once were we alone together; we didn't go and drink whisky in the bar and we absolutely did not discuss Zuma's case.

I have since heard stories about how we apparently flew home together and the two of us sat huddled on his jet talking quietly. The person who spread that rumour must have been on board the jet – but I was not. I don't know how many times I have had to field questions about the trip to Chile over the past few years. Perhaps people *wanted* me to be politically influenced, and that was an indirect way of putting pressure on me.

There was only one incident, shortly after my return from Chile, where there was an overt attempt to try to influence me. From time to time, I would meet with Police Commissioner Jackie Selebi and Billy Masetlha, who was the head of the South African Secret Service at the time. As members of the security cluster, we would be in touch to discuss relevant issues. Just days after my trip, the three of us met at Selebi's Waterkloof home. Selebi and Masetlha wanted to know what position I was going to take regarding Zuma. I shut them down immediately with, 'Guys, no, I can't tell you that.'

Masetlha was forthright, telling me that I could not possibly charge JZ. He had no legal reason why I should not; in my view it was purely a political sentiment that he was expressing. I wasn't angry about Masetlha's approach; I just said to him, 'Billy, you are out of order.' He was the only person who told me to my face that I could not charge Zuma. Selebi later confirmed this exchange when he was asked about it during his testimony at his corruption trial.

I had respect for Jackie Selebi in that meeting. He told Masetlha that no one has the right to tell prosecutors what to do in this matter and that it was for them to decide.

During those first weeks of June 2005, as I was contemplating charging the deputy president of the country, the president was grappling with his own dilemma. Mbeki had to decide whether or not to fire his friend and comrade of 30 years and, if so, how to go about doing so. Prior to our trip to Chile, he had put out a statement saying he would 'communicate to the public any decisions that he will have taken on the matter' when he returned. In Santiago, he quoted Chilean poet Pablo Neruda, saying, 'We go on loving love and in our blunt way, we bury the liars and live among the truth-tellers.'

Meanwhile, Zuma told attendees at a business breakfast in Zambia that his conscience was clear because he had not committed any crime. When Mbeki returned from South America, he met with his advisors, seeking counsel on what to do. He was hoping that Zuma would resign, but JZ dug in his heels and refused. Then, on 14 June, Mbeki stood up in parliament and relieved Zuma of his duties as deputy president.

The team and I took the decision to charge Zuma together and we were not influenced in any way by the political maelstrom that was playing itself out in the country. At a meeting on 20 June, a week after Mbeki's speech in parliament, we examined the evidence in its entirety and considered the strength of the case and came to the conclusion that there was no choice but to charge Zuma.

I said, 'We have to charge him, are we all agreed?' Once the unanimous decision had been taken, we called in NPA spokesperson Makhosini Nkosi to brief him. We advised him to hold back the press statement because I first had to inform the justice minister and the president. I met with the two on the same day before making the decision public.

Nobody told me that I should inform either the minister or the president, but I thought it was the proper thing to do. And I also felt it was proper and courteous to meet Zuma. It is unusual for an NDPP to personally inform an accused, but I had to take into account that this was no ordinary criminal matter. It was an unprecedented situation, to charge a former deputy president of a country, and there was no textbook to consult. I had to do things on my own and in my own way.

My first visit was to Justice Minister Brigitte Mabandla's home in Pretoria. It was not a difficult meeting – I was there simply to inform her of the decision.

'Are you sure, Vusi?' is all she said to me.

She was mildly flustered and I responded, 'Yes, we are charging him.'

As I left I said, 'From here, I am going to inform the president.'

My meeting with Mbeki at Mahlamba Ndlopfu was short and to the point. Again, I was simply informing him out of courtesy and we did not discuss the merits or demerits of the case. I simply said, 'Mr President, we have arrived at a decision to charge the deputy president and I'm going to inform him.'

We didn't engage on the matter. Mbeki didn't ask me, 'Are you sure you guys have looked at all the possibilities?' In my opinion, he was satisfied that at least we were handling the situation with dignity and respect by informing him personally.

Zuma was no longer the deputy president of the country, so, in a way, I was informing Mbeki – as president of the ANC – that his deputy was going to be charged.

As my driver steered my official car out of the gardens of the president's official residence in the Bryntirion estate in Pretoria and headed towards Luthuli House in the Johannesburg CBD, I was fully attuned to the gravity of the situation. You can't charge the former deputy president of the country and not expect political backlash. But perhaps it was my naïveté that led me to think that it was not really a big deal, and that it was merely a decision made in the course of doing my job.

When I walked through the entrance of the ANC headquarters, there was a buzz of expectation. It was the same atmosphere I encountered when I had to meet the president or a minister during a cabinet *lekgotla* and people's tongues wagged about what I was there to discuss.

There was this air of anticipation and when they saw me they knew: 'Ha! The decision must have been taken now – he's coming to see JZ.' In the lift, people looked at me and said searchingly, 'Hey, Comrade Vusi! What's up?'

I laughed and said, 'Hey, sharp … nothing.' Of course, they wanted to be the first to know what was happening.

When I walked into Zuma's office he was sitting at his desk. My heart was beating fast as he stood up to greet me and offered me a seat. He closed the door and it was just the two of us in the room. Our greetings were cordial, as we mixed isiZulu, isiXhosa and English.

'Ee, Baba, Kunjani.'

'Hayi, Baba, sikhona.'

'Undi phatheleni?' – 'What do you have for me?' he asked.

When I broke the news to him, it was in English. 'We have taken a decision to charge you,' I told Zuma.

If he was shocked, he did not show it immediately. He didn't ask me why we were charging him, and he didn't try to offer an explanation. All he said was, 'When you come to understand about these things, you'll be surprised how people plot and plan against other people and you get to know what has actually happened, the truth will finally surface.'

He was not putting it forward as a defence; he had no reason to try to explain that to me. It was as though he was suggesting that people had conspired against him, lies were being told and he was looking forward to revealing that as the matter unfolded.

It was an emotional experience for me, conveying my decision to Zuma. You know, sitting across from a person who is going to be charged, informing him that you are going to do so, is not easy. This is a man who had been my leader in exile for many years, in the liberation movement as well as in government. But I was not emotional about the matter. For me, it had to happen and if there were sufficient grounds to charge him, then it had to be done.

Zuma did not look shaken; he remained cool and calm. I think he must have braced himself for the moment. It was a polite meeting and we greeted one another as I left his office.

I returned to the NPA's offices in Silverton and briefed Makhosini Nkosi, who in turn called a press conference at 3 p.m. that afternoon. I chose not to address the briefing myself as I felt that a line had to be drawn. While everyone is equal before the law, certain circumstances require a different approach, but at the same time, if a person has been charged why should the national director make the announcement?

Nkosi told the cameras: 'This afternoon Advocate Pikoli informed Deputy President [*sic*] Zuma that he has decided to bring criminal charges against his person. Such charges will be constituted by, among others, two counts of corruption. Mr Zuma will in due course be informed of the date, time and place where he will have to avail himself at court to face these charges.'

An hour later, the presidency released a statement confirming that I had informed Mbeki about my decision to prefer charges against Zuma. I sat in my office, my phone didn't ring and, as far as I can recall, I didn't receive any messages from comrades responding to the decision.

When I got home that night, Girly and I didn't even discuss it immediately. My boys were teenagers and not really aware of what had happened. My daughter was at university in Cape Town and my eldest son lives far away in Fort Beaufort. As a family, we didn't feel the impact of my decisions as NDPP immediately; that would only happen over time and in the future.

Nine days after the decision to charge was announced, the ANC went into its National General Council (NGC) held at the University of Pretoria. The party's national working committee had initially granted a request from Zuma to withdraw from its structures until his corruption trial had concluded, but the NGC then did an about-turn. This meant Zuma was not excused from party duties and continued as deputy president of the ANC.

That led to internal strife within the organisation as it became clear that some members would not accept the decision of the top six. Some delegates became rowdy and called Mbeki names and, for the first time, you could actually see the tide shift against the president. There was a state of anarchy, with members reverting to rudeness and divisions emerging. At that time NGC General Secretary Kgalema Motlanthe spoke of the 'cancer of corruption' eating away at the party, while some delegates wore T-shirts with the words 'Innocent until proven guilty' and others chanted 'Zuma is the real president'. At the end of the NGC, Mbeki received a standing ovation during his speech in which he stated that it was imperative that Zuma be given an opportunity to defend himself against the charges. He added that the NGC had correctly expressed its support for Zuma during 'difficult and painful times', but he also spoke out against corruption. At its closing press conference, the party gave a reassurance that it was emerging 'much stronger and focused'.

As a member of any movement, you don't want to see your organisation being ruptured as a result of whatever you might have done or participated in. You don't want to be part of anything that pulls your movement apart. But, at the same time, I felt that I had taken a decision that was correct and that right-thinking members of the ANC should have been happy that we had state institutions that were able to carry out their functions without fear or favour or prejudice.

I had made a stand and was not having sleepless nights as a result of my decision – but I was nevertheless in turmoil because of what was happening within the organisation. I couldn't understand how there could be people who had no comprehension of how the law worked. We had always seen ourselves as a progressive movement and as an advance guard. It should have been easy to see that this decision was meant to strengthen the ANC, that the ANC was still occupying a moral high ground, that it does not matter who the personality was.

There was a sense of sadness within me, and that was exacerbated when I began to hear how people were insulting both the NPA and me personally. I was called a 'reactionary', amongst other things, and I was pained. This was an organisation I had served all my life, yet there were people who were supposed to be my comrades who regarded me as 'selling out' by charging JZ.

Call it ANC propaganda or what you will, but we were taught in the movement to always separate the organisation from its individual members. The party had not changed in terms of its values and principles or what it was seeking to achieve. But there were individual members who were acting contrary to those values and principles and were moving away from what the ANC stood for.

I wasn't resentful towards the ANC as an organisation. All political parties go through phases in their life cycle, through infancy, growth, maturity and degeneration, with old leadership being replaced by newly elected members. I believed that while I was being insulted and abused for deciding to charge Zuma, this period would pass and balance would be restored.

In the weeks after Zuma's first appearance in court, the team agreed that it was necessary for search-and-seizure operations to be carried out in order to gather further evidence. This was because a great deal might have taken place in the time between the Shaik trial and our decision to charge Zuma. There had also been restrictions on what we were able to do before he was charged.

The thinking was that the matter had not become static and the leads that emerged following Shaik's conviction needed to be followed up. The investigators felt that people don't generally destroy evidence overnight and that there are things that people might forget – a crumpled piece of paper in your office or a document that has not been properly shredded.

As a team, we discussed the matter at length and considered how we were going to go about it. Mine was more of an oversight role and I didn't get into the operational issues of knowing the names of people who were going to conduct the searches and whether or not they had received security clearance. At the time, I thought those issues were best left to the head of the Scorpions, Leonard McCarthy. I never requested to see a list of members and whether they had been vetted.

This would later emerge as a major criticism of my tenure as NDPP. In retrospect, I admit that perhaps I should have been more involved in this case simply because it was no ordinary matter. I certainly don't blame McCarthy for not checking if the members were properly vetted, but I did feel that it was an operational issue. I had sanctioned the operations and ultimately they were my responsibility. I accept that I failed on this score.

I was fully aware of the potential dangers the raids would pose and that they could provide serious security concerns. We had been granted warrants to search the seat of government, the Union Buildings in Pretoria, as well as the deputy president's offices in Cape Town, Tuynhuys. Zuma's Forest Town home and his Nkandla houses would also be searched, along with the offices of his lawyers Juleka Mahomed and Michael Hulley. My worst fear was that there could be a shoot-out because several of these locations were guarded by the SAPS and VIP-protection security members.

In fact, I was so concerned that I personally informed Minister Mabandla, the president and the new deputy president, Phumzile Mlambo-Ngcuka. It was a hard line to walk, especially as we didn't want anyone to know about the operations because that would defeat the purpose of the raids. At the same time, we couldn't just go ahead with them because these were government premises, a deputy president's office, that we would be searching.

We didn't just move in to those places without anybody knowing – the president, the minister, the deputy president and Frank Chikane all knew, because I told them personally.

And no one tried to dissuade me or to stop the raids from happening. We were also on sound legal ground as the judge president of the then Transvaal Provincial Division, Judge Bernard Ngoepe, had scrutinised the warrants carefully before granting them personally.

What was also not known at the time is that I took Jackie Selebi into my confidence prior to the raids being executed. I was worried about Scorpions members going to Zuma's homes, which were guarded by police officers. I went to Selebi the night before the raids took place, but I didn't tell my guys about it because they would never have agreed to it. I just wanted to make absolutely sure that there would be no shoot-out. Of course, you could argue there was the possibility that Selebi could have told his officers and they could have tipped Zuma off, but I had to make a calculated decision. I didn't want to have JZ convicted after 10 people had been killed in a shoot-out at his residence, so it was a risk I was prepared to take. I don't know how I would have felt if anything had gone wrong. Selebi agreed to ensure that his officers would cooperate with the DSO members.

At around 1 a.m. on the morning of 18 August 2005, I woke up, dressed quickly and was picked up from my home. I was driven to the Scorpions headquarters on the corners of Cresswell and Moreleta streets in Silverton to meet the team that would be conducting the operation. There would be raids across the country that morning, in Cape Town, Durban, Pretoria and Johannesburg, and I felt they may need a morale-boosting pep talk ahead of the operation. I knew it would be difficult conducting a search-and-seizure operation on a high-profile person, the deputy president of the ANC, and I wanted to reassure them that they had my full support. I did not want them to think that the senior officials were sleeping when they were hard at work.

I stressed the importance of the searches and warned them against any personal contact situation. I said, 'Look, guys, we are going to premises that might also be secured or guarded. I don't want any, any shoot-outs. I don't want anything that will lead to the use of firearms. You are equally armed, you have a right to be armed when you are conducting a search-and-seizure operation. You might get into a situation where you are provoked, but only use your arms in self-defence. Don't be the first ones to start.' I reminded them to honour the badge and to carry out their duties with dignity and to respect other people's property, but also to get the job done. I closed by telling the team to get to work.

I returned home but I couldn't sleep. Eventually, I gave up trying and went back to the office to monitor the operation. Gerrie Nel, the Gauteng head of the DSO, was coordinating proceedings. He sat down with Chikane at the Union Buildings to establish how the raids would be conducted.

It was not a haphazard operation where people simply pounced unexpectedly, guns in hand. The media were also never tipped off as far as I knew, and I was surprised when I heard on the radio that the Scorpions were at Zuma's Forest Town home.

And, despite my warning to Selebi, there was indeed an ugly stand-off at the house. While members of the Scorpions were inside searching for evidence, four police officers, armed with automatic weapons, screeched up to the house in a black jeep with blue lights flashing. They rapped on the gate and demanded to be let in before they ran inside waving their guns. The road outside was blocked off and journalists watched as the DSO members and the VIP-protection men argued and my guys urged them to calm down.

This was precisely what I had dreaded most and tried to avoid happening. The people who were being aggressive were the policemen, telling the Scorpions, 'You are not going to come in here,' and generally being obstructive.

As the day crept towards early evening, Selebi phoned me and told me to call my men off at the Union Buildings. He instructed me to tell them to go home. He said I had warned him about Zuma's home but not about the offices of the presidency.

'No, no, no. I'm not going to do that,' I told him.

That was a low point for me, but I still had no regrets that we had carried out the operation. I'm also not sure that things could have been done differently without risking the achievement of our objectives. I felt as though I had been thrown to the wolves and had to survive without knowing what to do. I didn't have the experience to plan such an operation and perhaps it could have been done in a different way.

The raids drew serious criticism from many quarters. Trade union federation COSATU reacted with venom. Zwelenzima Vavi called them 'a full-frontal attack on our revolution itself' and a 'brutal persecution' of Zuma. 'The political prosecution of Jacob Zuma risks plunging our new democracy into turmoil. It has already begun to divide our movement,' he went on.

The General Council of the Bar also condemned the raids and called on the Scorpions to return everything seized from Zuma's lawyers' offices as they believed the operation violated the principle of attorney-client privilege. We, of course, disagreed because the operations were perfectly legal and carried out on the strength of an order from the Pretoria High Court. We had discussed the issue of attorney-client privilege at length, and it was felt that if there is a suspicion that a lawyer is colluding in the commission of an offence, he or she should not enjoy a special privilege.

A couple of days after the operation, Minister Mabandla called me. She was angry with me about the Union Buildings raid. I reminded her that I had warned her about the operation and that she had agreed. I also had a meeting at my home with Selebi and Masetlha on the Saturday following the event, during which they came hard at me for what we had done. They were extremely unhappy, but still I stood my ground.

I still maintain it was the right thing to do and we have won almost every case in which there have been appeals against the raids, from the Supreme Court of Appeals to the Constitutional Court.

Shortly after the raids, Zuma and his lawyer, Michael Hulley, brought an application opposing the search and seizure operations in the Durban High Court, which ruled in their favour. We immediately took the decision on appeal and, in November 2007, the Supreme Court of Appeal ruling went the way of the NPA in three of the four appeals. In the fourth case the court ruled that documents taken from attorney Juleka Mahomed's office should be held by the South Gauteng High Court so that a trial court could later decide what to do with them.

Ultimately, the Constitutional Court ruled against Zuma, Hulley and the Thint companies in August 2008. The court found that the 93 000 documents seized in 2005 could be used in a potential trial.

In terms of the law, we did everything correctly. I had to ensure that people followed the proper procedures in the raids. But it was around that time that I began to feel I was losing the support of my colleagues in the justice cluster.

In September 2006, I watched the television in my office as the courtroom in Pietermaritzburg erupted. Some jumped up and shrieked with joy, obscuring Zuma's face from the cameras, as Judge Herbert Msimang told them to 'go outside, where people can do as they please'. Moments earlier, he had struck our case against the former deputy president off the roll, describing how it had 'limped from one disaster to another'.

Msimang found that 'it was inevitable that the State's evidence to prosecute in this matter would flounder' and that the state should have investigated further before charging Zuma as prosecutors had failed to take into account the legal challenges against the search-and-seizure raids. That same month our team had applied for a postponement to formulate a new charge sheet based on the additional material that had been seized in the August 2005 raids. We needed more time to deal with the legal challenges against the raids, which were winding their way through the courts. Msimang, however, refused to grant the postponement and kicked the case out.

Obviously, I was disappointed because our main argument was simply to ask for more time as we felt that the challenges related to crucial evidence in the matter and we couldn't proceed at the time. Msimang was not sympathetic, but it was not seen as a fatal blow to our case because we could still reinstate the charges in the future.

In 2010, in a speech to the Middle Temple conference, Advocate Billy Downer claimed I had acted against his advice that the legal challenges to the raids should be dealt with first, before going ahead with Zuma's prosecution. He said that by going ahead with the prosecution first, the state would not be able to use any of the materials seized in the raids as part of its KPMG forensic report on Zuma.

'The NDPP chose not to follow our advice, this time to delay Mr Zuma's prosecution until we had gathered all the new evidence that we had set about obtaining,' Downer said in his speech. Downer and I had differed on the timing of this matter. He needed more time, but I was in a hurry to get on with the case. He was ultimately proven correct – and I owe a delayed apology to the man I affectionately refer to as 'Billy the Kid'.

For the next year that I was in office, we continued with the matter, fighting the legal challenges to the raids. We had agreed we would reinstate the charges once that side issue had been resolved.

However, in September 2007, I was suspended before I was able to reinstate charges against Zuma. In November of that year, the Supreme Court of Appeal handed down its decision in favour of the NPA with regard to the validity of the search-and-seizure operations. Just days after the ANC's Polokwane conference, where Zuma was elected president of the movement, Acting NDPP Mokotedi Mpshe served an indictment on him. He was charged with racketeering, four counts of corruption, one of money laundering and twelve of fraud.

In 2008, Judge Chris Nicholson presided over Zuma's application to have the decision to prosecute him declared unlawful and, in September of that year, handed down a ruling that would rock the nation. He found that the charges were unlawful on procedural grounds. Nicholson went far, inferring that there had been political interference in the decision to prosecute Zuma and that Zuma should have been allowed to make representations to Mokotedi Mpshe before he was recharged. That judgment led to Thabo Mbeki being recalled as president, despite the Supreme Court of Appeal later overturning the ruling.

I was not happy that the NPA had lost the matter in court – again. I never expected that the NPA would lose. I was surprised, but I was also pleased that Judge Nicholson raised the question of the independence of both the NDPP and the NPA. However, I do think he was provocative.

Nicholson did not think it proper for the NDPP to have any interaction at all with the justice minister, which was in my opinion a wrong reading of the law. The NPA Act, as well as the Constitution, regards the justice minister as having final responsibility over the NPA, so there is no way that there could be no interaction at all between them. Fortunately, that judgment is not law in the sense that it was overturned on appeal at the Supreme Court of Appeal.

Nicholson also did not have any grounds to make the comments that he did about a political conspiracy against Zuma. He pointed to my suspension as grounds for political interference:

> *The suspension of the National Director [Vusi Pikoli] was a most ominous move that struck at the core of a crucial state institution. Of importance to the applicant was the fact that Pikoli's replacement, Mr Mpshe, who had to decide his fate, must have realised that to disobey the executive would in all probability ensure his own professional demise ... The timing of the indictment by Mr Mpshe on 28 December 2007, after the President suffered a political defeat at Polokwane, was most unfortunate. This factor, together with the suspension of Mr Pikoli, who was supposed to be independent and immune from executive interference, persuade me that the most plausible inference is that the baleful political influence was continuing.*

Nicholson concluded that he was not convinced that Zuma was incorrect in averring political meddling in his prosecution:

> *The court has gained the impression that all the machinations to which I have alluded form part of some great political contest or game. For years the applicant is under threat of prosecution for serious corruption and yet never brought to trial. There is a ring of the works of Kafka about this.*

There was nothing to justify that conclusion. Five years later, as I read those words again, I am convinced that Nicholson was completely wrong. I never conspired with anyone. The only people involved in that decision to charge were the prosecutors who were part of the matter. Nobody told us to charge Zuma or not to charge Zuma and no one came to say, 'So-and-so met so-and-so and this is what was discussed about charging Zuma.' I was the person who made that decision.

During the period of my suspension I was approached by several people who said that 'the man' wanted to talk to me. I refused, of course, because I did not know what I would say to him. I can only imagine that Zuma wanted to meet with me to discuss his own pending matter. He would hardly have been bothered by my suspension.

There were those within the ANC who wanted to get my views on what I would do if I were to be reinstated. 'Would you pursue charges against him?' they fished. I could never answer the question.

Those in the Zuma camp said, 'Look, man, if you can just give us a guarantee that on reinstatement you will not bring charges against the man, then the matter is straightforward.' They said that even if Ginwala were to recommend that I be fired and the matter went to parliament, they would simply instruct MPs not to follow that recommendation.

These were provincial leaders of the ANC. Once a businessman from KwaZulu-Natal requested a meeting with me to discuss the issue. On another occasion, a member of the Johannesburg Bar approached Kalyani Pillay on the same matter; he wanted to know whether I would be willing to meet Zuma and suggested that he would facilitate such a meeting. Of course, I rejected that – otherwise I would still be at the NPA. I was clear that I would not go back as a compromised person.

I watched at Twiggy Xiphu's as Mokotedi 'Corky' Mpshe addressed the country, from the same auditorium at the NPA's offices where I had been introduced to staff by the justice minister. It was 6 April 2009 and Mpshe had been acting in the position of NDPP for a year and eight months since I had been suspended. Mpshe and I have known each other since the days of the TRC when he was an evidence leader. I have always found him to be a capable and competent advocate and as my deputy I worked well with him.

It was then that Mpshe dropped the bombshell, paving the way for Jacob Zuma to become president of South Africa.

'I have come to the difficult conclusion that it is neither possible nor desirable for the NPA to continue with the prosecution,' said Mpshe, adding: 'It would be unfair as well as unjust to continue with the prosecution.'

Mpshe quoted from telephone recordings between Ngcuka and the former head of the DSO, Leonard McCarthy.

The so-called spy tapes had formed part of representations made to the NPA by Zuma's lawyers and had been declassified by the NIA to allow Mpshe to make them public. The origins and legality of the tapes have been the subject of much debate and speculation. For all intents and purposes, it is most likely that the recordings stemmed from an operation run by the SAPS Crime Intelligence unit during the height of the rivalry with the Scorpions. As part of Operation Destroy Lucifer, a campaign to gather information on DSO officials, McCarthy's phone calls were intercepted. A selection of those recordings was given to Zuma and formed part of Mpshe's justification for withdrawing charges against him.

In the conversations, taped just before the ANC's Polokwane conference in December 2007, Ngcuka and McCarthy discussed the timing of recharging Zuma and whether this would be done before or after the conference. At the time, Ngcuka had been out of the NPA for over three years, and yet McCarthy appeared to be consulting him on the matter. The transcripts also indicated apparent political allegiance to former president Thabo Mbeki.

The recordings released by Mpshe, taped between November 2007 and April 2008, covered the period after I was suspended. However, it is entirely likely that intercepts had been ongoing even during my tenure.

When I first heard about those recordings, I was annoyed because if they were indeed legitimate, I felt that it was a breach of professionalism on the part of McCarthy to have discussed the case with anyone not in the NPA. It doesn't matter whether it is a former boss of the NPA or not. It was wrong – but at the same time, I felt that it did not go to the heart of the case to the extent that it should kill the case itself.

The discussion they were having was about the timing of the charging. They were not conspiring to manufacture or fabricate evidence against JZ. I was irritated that they had been used at all. It was a bad decision in law. Yes, if the tapes are genuine and authentic, it was irregular and it was wrong. McCarthy should never have done that, but it was no fatal blow. All it did was strengthen the claims of a political conspiracy and suggestions that there was never a genuine case from the outset. And yet, we have a mountain of evidence to support the decision to prosecute.

While I was in office, there was never any indication that McCarthy was still consulting Ngcuka on any prosecutorial matters. Of course, I knew they were friends and that they visited one another, but I never thought their relationship involved anything that was improper. I never got the sense that Ngcuka was exerting influence over McCarthy or pulling strings behind the scenes. Personally, I never kept in contact with any of the Zuma team after I left office. I spoke to neither McCarthy nor Advocate Downer and I certainly didn't discuss the case with any of them.

I think it is important to establish the authenticity of the tapes and I do doubt the veracity of the recordings. The Democratic Alliance (DA) is still pursuing this matter in court, applying for a judicial review of Mpshe's decision, and the outcome of that will hopefully help us understand more of the facts. It is also important to establish how Zuma came to be in possession of these tapes. I can't understand how they would have landed with him because it would be a breach of the law for a state agency to hand over recordings to a private individual. At the time, Zuma was a private citizen and not a public office bearer, so the entire chain of events needs to be examined.

If the tapes are genuine, if they are authentic, then McCarthy would have been in breach of professional conduct. You would never expect a prosecutor to talk about the timing of a case to anyone because that could advance somebody else's cause or prejudice another person's agenda. They should not have been involved in these kinds of activities, especially considering the political context of the case itself.

It is my personal opinion that Corky Mpshe was put under political pressure. Zuma was on the verge of becoming the next president of the country and you could not have a president with such a matter hanging over him. This was a political solution using a legal decision to justify it. Mpshe also used a legal decision not really applicable to this case and which was overturned on appeal.

I felt sadness for the prosecutors and investigators who had worked for years on the case, who were sitting at the podium with Mpshe when he made the announcement. A man such as Billy Downer, who is an old prosecutor who believes in the hierarchy of the organisation, must have felt very angry, but he was never one to rock the boat. Even when Ngcuka decided not to charge Zuma along with Shaik, Downer disagreed, but accepted the decision of a higher authority. I suspect it must have been the same in this instance.

Corruption is a toxin in this country and it has to be taken seriously. I would have been happier if the matter was resolved either way – even if Zuma were to be acquitted, at least we would all know that he is innocent of corruption.

Very few people take Zuma seriously when he says, 'We are serious about corruption.' There was a time when he insisted that he wanted his day in court, but now he seems to be running away from court, doing everything in his power to avoid a trial and leaving the matter not fully addressed. He might not be facing charges now but we all know there is an elephant in the room.

How can you expect law-enforcement agencies to seriously engage in the fight against crime when they know that there are question marks around the man at the top? As a result, some cabinet ministers have question marks around them too. How do you lead a fight against crime and corruption when there are unanswered questions about you and your leadership? Who will take you seriously?

As an example, look at the controversy around the palace that is being built in Nkandla, in the midst of poverty. How do you justify that, morally and politically? That is arrogance of the highest order and Zuma is treating us like children with voices that do not matter.

In my opinion, this case places us firmly in the category of corrupt states in Africa. Once it is seen that there is corruption at the top, then the thinking and feeling is that organised crime syndicates are controlling those in government. There are indications that this is the case in many countries, particularly those in Latin America, such as Mexico and Colombia, where all-powerful drug cartels are able to infiltrate the highest levels of government. In Italy, there was a time when even the judiciary was infiltrated, along with the top levels of the police. The Zuma case made this prospect a reality for South Africa and it was happening right before our very eyes.

It was a betrayal of what we had fought for in terms of the values we had aspired to, as laid down in our Constitution. It pained me to see how others thought I had sold out. There seemed to be an expectation of me to protect corrupt comrades by virtue of us having fought alongside each other during the war of national liberation.

Even today, there are still people in the ANC who see me as a sell-out.

They can't believe that I, being a comrade, having been trained by the ANC, having worked for the ANC, would 'turn against' the ANC.

That is rubbish – and I'm not going to beg for their acceptance. I will stand my ground and do what I think is correct. If I had succumbed and agreed to protect Zuma in return for my reinstatement, I would have become part of the corrupt system.

I believe this issue will be with us for some time and will not disappear, no matter how much Zuma and others might like it to. If the DA's application for a legal review is successful and it becomes legally possible to recharge him, then he should be prosecuted and answer to the case in court.

I'm not suggesting that Zuma is guilty, but simply that he should respond to the charges against him. I know the strength of the case and I am confident about it. Speaking from the viewpoint of a prosecutor, who believes each time you take a person to court that the accused is guilty, I believe the state's case is winnable and, based on the evidence, that it is as strong as it could possibly be.

Zuma's rape case

'Ah, get away, Makhosini,' I told the NPA's spokesperson. I didn't believe him for a moment. It was Friday, 11 November 2005, two days before newspapers broke the story about a charge of rape against ANC Deputy President Jacob Zuma.

I hadn't been informed about the rape investigation because it was a police matter and at that stage it had not been brought to the attention of the NPA. When the papers hit the streets that Sunday, I was in the Seychelles signing a memorandum of understanding as part of an agreement with all countries affiliated with the Southern African Development Community (SADC).

The matter fell within the responsibility of Advocate Charin de Beer as director of public prosecutions (DPP) in Gauteng. I did not know much about her but was impressed with her commitment and dedication to her work. She ran a well-managed office in Gauteng and her reputation was an enviable one.

It was alleged that Zuma had raped a 31-year-old family friend, the daughter of a comrade, at his home in Forest Town. The woman came from a prominent ANC family and was HIV-positive and an AIDS activist. Zuma admitted to having consensual sex with the woman but denied the charge of rape against him.

The complainant had been dubbed 'Khwezi' by the media, but I was aware of her name because I knew her personally. Her parents and I were in exile together and we came to know each other as comrades. Her father was in Lesotho while I was there and I also got to know his daughter when I spent time in Lusaka.

The matter fell squarely within Advocate De Beer's competence and responsibility as DPP, so I didn't feel it necessary to study the docket or to take the decision on whether or not to charge Zuma. I also didn't see any reason why I should look at the evidence because Advocate De Beer had already examined the details. Rape is not a complicated charge in terms of the law and I had enough confidence in Advocate De Beer to deal with the matter.

For once, this was also not a matter involving the Scorpions because it was squarely in the domain of the SAPS. There was no way that I could ever have imagined somebody saying that the rape case was part of a broader political conspiracy. However, the claim was indeed raised when the woman testified that she had received advice and guidance from Intelligence Minister Ronnie Kasrils on how to proceed with the matter. Fikile Mbalula, who was the ANC Youth League president at the time, even alleged that the woman, who was referred to as 'Lucifer', had been bribed to lay a charge against Zuma. 'She has to explain to all South Africans, is it true that she's got all that particular money? The NPA in all its powers has got the right to probe that particular question. She could not have acted alone in that particular conspiracy,' he told the media.

On 8 May 2006, Judge Willem van der Merwe acquitted Zuma, much to the jubilation of thousands of his supporters gathered on Pritchard Street, outside the South Gauteng High Court. I was disappointed with the outcome. Some critics felt that Advocate De Beer may have been a bit rusty because she had not prosecuted for a long time and that she could have done a better job. Knowing her as a prosecutor, I think she did her best.

Others suggest that it was an unwinnable case because of the complainant and her history. Each case has its own dynamics and you can't say a woman wasn't raped just because, for example, she happens to be a prostitute or of low moral value. You have to look at the circumstances of each case. The issue with this particular matter was that the victim had a history of emotional instability.

For me, it was a clear case of comrades having rallied around Zuma and protecting him. There were female comrades who testified in Zuma's defence about the 'child' – as she was known to them – giving evidence about how she had been raped in Lusaka and other details. I felt that those issues did not need to be considered when looking at the circumstances of the case. People suggest that the case was weak because of her history. And yet that does not 'entitle' you to a woman or to take advantage of the unfortunate mental state of a child.

Having been in exile, I understand the nature of the relationship between Zuma and the victim. Given the difference in age and the fact that her father was a colleague and a friend of Zuma, the position could only have been that of parent and child. The culture in exile was that an older person was referred to as an uncle, *malume*, and the young girl would have seen him as a father. I can't imagine she ever would have fantasised about the man or why she would have been in his bed that night. I also don't see that it can be explained away as a cultural entitlement, or that he had a duty as a man to not leave her wanting, as he claimed.

I accept the decision of the court. I may not agree with it, I may not like it, but I've got to accept it. Regardless of the legalities, the strength of the criminal case and the fact that Zuma was acquitted, for me what is more important is the moral question that arose.

Here you have a leader of an organisation who is married and yet sleeps with the child of comrades he knows well. Even if the woman was being provocative, it cannot possibly be right – this is a child you saw grow up in front of your own eyes.

Furthermore, Zuma was the deputy president of the ANC and former deputy president of the country, responsible for the country's campaign against HIV, and yet by his own admission he did not use a condom. He couldn't be seen to be behaving in that way whilst we were dealing with the serious issues of rape and sexual assault in our country.

This was an illustration of the moral degeneration we face in this country and I couldn't understand why the ANC never charged the man internally for misconduct. I felt that he had brought the ANC into disrepute by admitting to having sexual intercourse with her without even using a condom. At a political level, that required decisive action on the part of the organisation.

And yet, instead of supporting the complainant, the ANC turned her into a pariah. I was disgusted by the behaviour of the ANC Women's League and of those women who went in large numbers to support Zuma outside court. You saw them outside the courthouse, participating in burning effigies of this child of the ANC. They're not saying, 'How dare Zuma sleep with a child of the party, even if there had been consent.' Nobody seems to have raised anything about this issue.

The complainant's mother was also harassed and had to leave her home in Durban. As far as I know, only one ANC woman came to her rescue and assisted her. The child was practically banished into exile and was granted asylum in Europe but has since returned to South Africa. And no one within the movement raised this issue. I was sickened by the behaviour and it really hurt me.

Again, I had to remind myself to distinguish between the organisation and the individuals within the party. However, when this type of conduct becomes an accepted way of doing things – even if it is by just a few individuals – then it becomes endemic and an organisational problem. If the party is not going to act or do anything about this behaviour, then you have got to blame the organisation.

When there are individuals who are so influential as to direct the course of the movement, then it is the organisation that is ultimately responsible. Otherwise somebody should stand up and say, 'Not in our name.'

I am saying that now.

Searching for Sizwe – Charity Kondile

Mandy Wiener

The thick, white mist sits heavily on the winding road, making it nearly impossible to navigate through the treacherous Kei Cuttings towards Butterworth. The persistent drizzle on the windscreen is whipped away by my overeager wipers and I can see little more than the alarming red brake lights of the truck ahead of me, leading me through the inclement weather across the Great Kei River towards Charity Kondile.

I know from experience that the hillsides here are dotted with pastel-coloured box houses, roaming cattle, women selling steaming heads of corn, and barefooted, uniformed schoolchildren, and when the cloud finally lifts, the images in my imagination are confirmed by reality. There is a sense of mystique and romance about this part of the Eastern Cape and the weather is playing its part in adding to the drama.

All I have is an SMS containing vague directions to the Kondiles' home near the Msobomvu Senior Secondary School and a warning to have a safe journey along the perilous pass towards Butterworth. Pedestrians point me in the direction of her house and I'm met in the street by her son, Teddy, his tall, imposing stature reflective of his professional rugby-playing prowess in his youth. I wonder if this is what Sizwe would have looked like.

The mustard-yellow and red ramshackle home appears worse for wear, with paint peeling off in chunks, exposing large swathes of its grey undercoat. The yard is sodden, the garden overgrown and the pavement outside the gates is littered with the detritus of passing schoolchildren. Charity

Kondile is at pains to stress to me that she is in the process of renovating the house and this explains why it is in a state of chaos. Inside the square structure, boxes and furniture cover the floor space and she struggles to manoeuvre around them, hampered also by a sore leg and the effects of old age.

I have seen photographs of her in articles and videos of the TRC hearings and now, 15 years on, she wears the passing of time well. Her beautifully soft skin negates the effect of her wrinkled eyes and she is dressed in a yellow-and-brown printed kaftan. She fusses about with coffee cups and kettles in the kitchen, disappears to dig up old photo albums and then talks me through the knick-knacks and trinkets on the bookshelf, which include faded portraits of her children, ceramic cups with their names engraved, trophies and pine cones.

Finally she settles down and we talk. We start at the beginning.

'They were fond of playing and kicking balls around, playing football, rugby and that sort of thing like township youngsters,' she says, reminiscing about what Sizwe and Vusi were like as little boys. 'They would chase insects, *springkaan:* it was a fashion for them to chase *springkaan*. Then one day Sizwe got very inquisitive and he asked me what those things were up there,' she says, pointing to the corrugated-iron roof, 'and I said they were stars. He wanted to know what they were for. I was kind of puzzled at first; why would he ask such a big question? I just said to him that they just gave us light, that they twinkled. Then I started understanding that this one is going to study further, he is very inquisitive.'

Sizwe grew up primarily in his grandparents' house in Port Elizabeth because that was the way things were done in those days, she tells me. He also spent most of his school-going years in Natal, and as a result, she doesn't remember much about Vusi as a youngster. At the time, she was still married to Sizwe's father, Dumile, and living in PE, but they would divorce while Sizwe was still a teenager. Charity recalls how the two boys clicked and went to their initiation ceremonies together, sharing the same *boma* on their journey into manhood.

'Sizwe was a very quiet somebody, he was a thinker. He would be a jovial person sometimes and he would be a changed person once he was studying, especially if he was with his peers and his brothers. But he was a loving somebody and he was highly principled. Sizwe would never swear. He was that type of a young man, who didn't like anything that was going astray, like drinking. He used to smoke a bit, but he hated people who were dealing with dagga. He was more interested in his rugby and schoolwork,' says his mother.

While New Brighton was a hotbed of political activism, Sizwe's mother insists her son only became political active when he went to Fort Hare University to join Vusi. It was then that they became 'mysterious and secretive' about what they were up to, hiding their activities from their parents.

'He was doing law at that time and as a law student, they were always querying everything that was going on in the country. I remember at one stage he was arrested and that was the time when he started thinking about skipping the country. They were very secretive to us; we did not know what was going on. I'm sure his brothers knew but we, as parents, didn't know. I remember at some stage he was sitting quietly, as if he was pondering. I think he was thinking, "Should I skip the country and leave my family?" but he would sit and think as if he was in a faraway country.'

As Vusi has recounted to me, Charity confirms that she and the other parents had very little, if any indication that the young men were going into exile. They were not consulted and they never asked their sons about their plans. She was shocked when she learned that he was in Lesotho, but she had no choice but to accept that Sizwe had left and that he was fighting for a free country.

Vusi has told me about his ANC-related activities before he went into exile, but as far as Charity is concerned, her son never went to Lesotho to join the organisation. She believes he and his friends went to Maseru to further their studies at Roma University. 'When they skipped to Maseru, they didn't go there with the intention of joining the ANC or of fighting, because the ANC was a banned organisation in South Africa. It's only when they got to Maseru that they got involved with the ANC. They went there to further their studies at the Roma University in Maseru. But unfortunately, they came across those people, like Thozamile Botha, and then they were recruited by Chris Hani and the others. That is what his father has always mourned about, that his son didn't go there to fight; he had gone there to further his studies but, unfortunately, he got himself involved in the ANC.'

During the Christmas of 1980, Charity, accompanied by Vusi's mother, went to visit their sons in Maseru.

'It was a lovely time,' she remembers, a smile stretching across her face. 'It was Christmas time and there was those people from the United Kingdom, Hugh Masekela and Miriam Makeba, and there were shows. I went there with Vusi's mother and other parents whose sons were there and we enjoyed it a lot. I met some of his colleagues and they told us that they were fighting for the country but they never allowed us to go and see where they were staying. They kept that secret. We were staying with friends in Maseru and that was a memorable visit for me because we were very happy together. He was driving us up the Maluti mountains and he was very happy.'

During that Christmas visit, Charity took her son aside and urged him to be careful and not to sacrifice himself unnecessarily. 'I said to him, "Sizwe, you must take caution, you mustn't be the one in front. You must try and avoid danger," and then he asked me, "Then, Mama, who is going to the front? We must go." The sad part of it, which I noticed when I was leaving, he had tears in his eyes and I didn't like those tears. I felt like, if I could, I would have asked him to come back home and abandon the whole thing. But I just prayed with him the last time. That was the last time that I saw him.'

Six months passed and in July 1981, the instincts of a mother set in. When Charity struggled endlessly to get hold of her son on the phone, she knew there was a problem.

'I used to phone Sizwe. He used to go to a friend's house and if I wanted to catch him on the phone then I would phone that house. I kept on phoning. They told me Sizwe had gone to Roma University. Each time I phoned they said he had gone somewhere and he would come again. Then I was surprised. Why is Sizwe not taking my calls now? Why is he not going to that house? I phoned his father and [said to] him: "Sizwe is not phoning, he is not taking his calls as usual." And then he told me that he is still investigating this chap's matter. I said, "What investigations?" and then he told me that Sizwe is missing from Maseru. I was shocked. I was shocked!'

Sizwe had been missing for a month and no one had had the courage to tell her. 'These friends never phoned to say that he was missing. Vusi's mother, for instance, knew, but I think they were too scared to tell us that such a thing had happened because they were still looking and trying to find out what had happened to him. We were very angry about that, that they didn't inform us. His father was informed.'

Sizwe's father, along with Silas Nkanunu, had been inquiring with the police about his whereabouts. They were told that the young man had been arrested and released but they could not track him down. Charity received a call from her ex-husband asking her to travel to Lesotho to go in search of their son and any answers she could find.

'I was very worried. I was about to study further, but I stopped everything. I was very sad.' The trip to Maseru was not what she expected – she was treated as a pariah and run out of town by her son's comrades in the ANC. 'When I got to [my friend's] house, she phoned the ANC people – the big guns – to say, "Sizwe's mother is here." They said, "She must leave Maseru immediately because Sizwe has stolen our car." She would not even allow me to stay. She said, "Please go to the hotel, I'm going to take you to the hotel." People told me that at that time hotels were being bombed in Maseru, so I should leave. I had to walk and find out where some Eastern Cape girls lived, and went to stay there and waited for the ANC.'

She also went to the UN refugee offices in Maseru in search of information about her son. She also wanted to reclaim his clothing and his belongings. There she was interrogated by officials who wanted to be sure she was indeed who she claimed to be. She had no success and was turned away. 'They said a man must come, not a woman. They wanted to be addressed by his father. So I had to leave. Sizwe was nowhere to be found. But I noticed his friends, some of the girls, were crying. I don't know what they were crying for. There was also a story that Sizwe might have crossed over and had become a spy.'

Her only flicker of hope was when Phaki Ximiya and his brother came to see her. Vusi, who was at Roma, chose not to join them. They explained to her why people were being so hostile – it was because they believed she may have information about her son, whom they thought had sold them out.

'They came to see me and they told me the ANC people are very angry because they want their car. We lived in fear because we were afraid they could come and they could kill me. But Phaki and his brother told them no, this is Sizwe's mother and Sizwe's mother did not take your car so you cannot harm her.'

Charity was adamant that there was no way that her son could have crossed over and become a spy. She couldn't believe that the same person who had insisted to her that he must go to 'the front' could have become a traitor. 'I didn't accept it. Even his friends, whom I had been happy with at Christmas, they wouldn't even greet me. They said Sizwe should have found a way to inform them that he had been arrested. And I said to them, "If the security was very tight or if he was being tortured, would you people be able to find ways of escaping from jail? Is it so easy?" They said, "Yes, he knows how to communicate with us inside jail".'

I tell Charity what Vusi has shared with me about the anguish and pain that he has carried with him over the past decades around his decision not to go and see her when she went to Maseru. It remains, for him, one of his life's greatest regrets. It remains a sore point for Charity too.

'This has been a stigma I have had against Vusi. Also my mother-in-law said Vusi's mother knew but she didn't come and tell us that Sizwe was missing. I don't know why he didn't come, but I was angry that he didn't come to see me because he was the closest to Sizwe. I thought maybe he was afraid of those ANC guys, that he didn't want to identify himself with me. He was afraid, he was a coward. He didn't have the courage because they were saying that they were being tortured. But the other guys were bold enough to come and see me.'

She says that it is for this reason that a question mark has always hung over her son's best friend, but the passage of time has softened her resolve. 'How can his best friend not come and explain to me what had happened to him? I felt very bad against Vusi at that time. But as time goes on, I am beginning to forgive him for that. But he has never come to explain why. This is one thing I didn't like about Vusi. I don't hate him, but I feel it was not right that up to now he has not come to the family, to Sizwe's parents, to explain.'

Despite her suggestion that Vusi has never been to see the Kondile family, I know this not to be his version of events. Vusi, Phaki and Thozi have all individually recounted, with much pain and anguish, how when they returned from exile, they tried to meet with Sizwe's father, Judge Dumile Kondile. Charity was not in Port Elizabeth at the time and likely never knew about the meeting. The attempts to meet were arranged by former Eastern Cape Judge President Cecil 'Doc' Somyalo.

Charity left Maseru feeling hollow and angry.

On the train ride back to Bloemfontein, she checked the face of every young man she saw, to see if she could recognise her son. 'It was a terrible experience,' she remembers, sadness etched on her face.

For nine long years, life went on.

'My daughters started having babies and I had to nurse those babies. I think that's what kept me busy. I had to go on with my life. But each time I was praying, praying, praying hard. I said, "Please, we must know what happened to Sizwe." Each time I was praying, praying. We were praying for his life or at least to know what happened to him. I even studied and finished a degree during that time. It tended to come back; I mean, we had lost all hope of seeing him again. Some people were saying that maybe he had crossed to the UK or whatever, and we kept on guessing and guessing and guessing ...'

She feels that her ex-husband failed to act swiftly enough when the car Sizwe had been driving was found abandoned and burnt out on the Swaziland border. 'They failed to trace that car with the number plates on because, as they said, the car was burnt. Then my husband and his lawyers were handling it. They were not fast enough to trace that car because I think that is where the clue lay.'

Then, on a Monday morning in 1990, at the crack of dawn, her sister arrived at her door in Butterworth with news. The *New Nation* newspaper that day was carrying a front-page report featuring the confessions of hit-squad leader Dirk Coetzee. In the article, it was revealed that Sizwe had been murdered.

'They came very early in the morning, I was still in my nighty. They had come to tell me that Sizwe had died through the *New Nation* information. I was shocked and I cried.'

The report came out shortly before Nelson Mandela was due to be released from prison and made note of the fact that while he would be returning home, others like Sizwe would not. Charity watched the release on television with fluctuating emotions. 'We sat here watching the Mandela release and it was beautiful, but I was crying when Mandela was released. I was crying. I was in tears as I was watching. I was wishing that my son also would be coming back. His younger brother, who was shot in 2004, also cried a lot, but he said, "Who should have died? If I say my brother shouldn't have died in the struggle, then who should have died?" That's how he comforted himself.'

Charity and the Kondile family kept a close watch on what emerged from Dirk Coetzee at the Harms Commission in London and clung to any information about how Sizwe had been killed. The lingering question she has is why the ANC never came to inform her about what had happened to her son – surely Coetzee had informed the organisation before going public? President Jacob Zuma has drawn her ire for this reason, amongst others.

'You remember that Dirk Coetzee joined the ANC in Lusaka at some stage and Dirk Coetzee told them about Sizwe's death and how they had killed Sizwe. But up to this stage, those people knew that Sizwe had been killed. Dirk Coetzee told them. But they didn't tell us. We are still wondering why they didn't tell us that Sizwe had died, that he had been killed. I think they should have informed the family. Chris Hani died and Alfred Nzo died, but Jacob Zuma is the one living who was told that our son had died and he never came.'

In 1996, Charity attended the TRC hearings of the four police officers who applied for amnesty for her son's murder and testified before the Commission. 'I was relieved to go and tell this story to the world about what had happened to him and thought now this is a time for the truth to be told,' she recollects. However, along with testifying came the torture and anguish of having to listen to the details of how her son was murdered.

'I don't know why Dirk Coetzee put it like that. That they were having a braai and the flesh was smelling good. That's where I said that it was an act of cannibalism, because only cannibals eat people's flesh.

'I was thinking since he had been arrested what was he wearing? My worry was, was he still wearing the same old clothes that he was wearing when they caught him? I was thinking of his state. What state was he in? How was he feeling? I mean, you could just feel it in your body as a mother; it was one of the most terrible things that had ever happened in my life. I could imagine how he was feeling when he was being tortured like that. It was a terrible, terrible time.' She believes the version that Sizwe was killed because he had suffered brain damage and that the police wanted to avoid another Steve Biko-type situation.

'The judge even said to Dirk Coetzee, "You thought you were God." And he said, "Yes, we thought we were God." "You were killing people as if you were God," and he said, "Yes, we were God."' At one point during the Commission, Coetzee turned to the Kondile family and asked for forgiveness, a request Charity shut down. 'I told my lawyer that he does not deserve to speak to me. I was sleeping in the same hotel as this one who killed … and sometimes I would be in the same lift as Dirk Coetzee and I would just jump out of the lift. I didn't want to meet him. I could see that he was keen to meet me and talk to me. I was avoiding him like anything.' However, now that Coetzee has died, she feels she can finally let go. 'Now that he is dead, we have forgiven him.'

Charity Kondile's position on the outcome of the TRC is reminiscent of that summed up by Vusi of how most families of victims feel – that the perpetrators benefited the most.

'I feel that justice was not done to the perpetrators. Even the lousy R30 000 that they are offering for the families is never a bad thing, but it's just that it will never bring back Sizwe. Sizwe's life was not worth R30 000. It was not worth any money,' she says, her demeanour shifting from sorrowful reminiscence to embittered anger. 'I didn't understand because it didn't become any justice. I didn't understand amnesty because if somebody has killed, they are sent to prison or tried or whatever. I didn't understand. They said that they only gave him R30 000 because he was young and had just joined the struggle. I was thinking of the people like Mandela and others and the spouses of the people who were in the struggle, whose husbands had died, they are still getting money today.'

Fundamental to her gripe is an issue in which Vusi played a central role: she did not receive the reparation payment; Sizwe's son Bantu did.

'Vusi Pikoli said I should not be given that money, it should be given to Sizwe's son. Sizwe's girlfriend came forward and she said that she had a son with Sizwe and she must be given that money for Sizwe's son. Vusi insulted me by saying that he didn't understand why in the first place *I* was the one who had testified at this Truth Commission.'

Vusi strongly disputes this version and insists that he never questioned why she testified at the TRC. However, he agrees that there was a dispute over who would receive a payout from the Commission, as Charity recalls.

'I didn't get the money, it was sent to Bantu, though I didn't mind. It was for Bantu, he was the son after all, and I had been given another lump sum. I fought for his pension and they gave me R30 000 of which I sent some of it to Bantu.'

She remains embittered that the ANC never acknowledged Sizwe, has held no memorial and has never been to see her to discuss her son. She tells me that her ex-husband is even more enraged than she. 'Up to this day, there was no ANC member who came to my house to pay any respects to Sizwe … I don't know why. They do things for other people but not for our son. They haven't even gone to his grave, like they do for other people. They erect tombstones. They haven't even had a memorial service for Sizwe, as an ANC.' The ANC also gave her an undertaking in writing that they would look after her health and Bantu's education, but she says neither promise ever materialised. 'The ANC and I are still on pause, because they have no answers for my son's death, they have not accounted for his clothes, they have not paid any respect to him, to us as a family. Why are they not holding a memorial service? Why are they skipping us? Our sons were just statistics. The ANC owes us a memorial service for our son whom they recruited into their organisation.'

I want to know from Charity, 30 years after her son was reduced to ashes on the banks of the Komati River, whether or not the anguish and the torment that she endured was worth it at all. Do the relatives of those who sacrificed so much for a free and democratic South Africa feel that their contributions have been in vain?

'I am staying in a poor-formed house, with a lot of rubbish in front of my house. And their people came back from exile to live in beautiful houses in Johannesburg. I feel they are not recognising us, they are not doing what they promised to do. I shouldn't be living like this, where I am staying. I don't know what is happening in South Africa now.

'At the beginning, when Mandela was president, at least you could feel that it was worthwhile what they fought for. But now, since this corruption and this greediness and all that, I feel now they fought in vain. The people in power are taking everything for themselves, the masses are not getting anything, so I don't think it's what they fought for.'

And if Sizwe were alive today, what role would he be playing?

'He would have been an advocate, like Vusi. He would be somebody opposing all this corruption and boldly speaking out as Barney Pityana is doing. He would be crushing everything that is corrupt. If he were alive, he would be acting like Vusi. If Sizwe was there, they would be strong enough and they would be fighting like hell for what is happening in the country every day.' Charity bursts into a hearty chuckle and adds, 'Sizwe would say the president is rioting! Because when they were rioting and the police were on top of them, he would say the police are rioting. So he would say that the president is rioting in South Africa. He is the one who is on strike!'

She drives home her criticism of the leadership of the country. 'If the person at the top of the country has a flaw then the whole country has a flaw. Can you see that the people are doing what he is doing? And nobody seems to understand what the president is doing is wrong. There are the masses who are not watching television, they are just voting for the shield and the spear. So the problem with South Africa is with the government, at the top.'

While Sizwe's mother wants some kind of formal acknowledgement from the ANC government and a tombstone or monument in his name, she is not concerned about reclaiming any of his remains. As far as she is concerned, there is nothing left to find. She repeatedly remarks about how she wanted his clothes, above all. I wonder whether her obsession with the material is because it is all that remains of him. 'We shall never know what happened to his belongings, certificates; his aunt had just sent him a lot of new clothes there and his certificates. All those clothes, we never have known what happened to them.'

Charity doesn't understand why the NPA's Missing Persons Task Team is trying to find the bones and doesn't hold much hope of success. After the TRC hearings, she was flown to the Komati River to a site pointed out by Dirk Coetzee for a memorial service arranged by a Japanese television crew. It was this process that she feels brought her closure. 'I scooped a lot of soil from that place and put it in a bag, hoping that at least one day when I am buried I know at least some of that soil has got my son's ashes.'

Clutching a grainy, weathered picture of Sizwe on his graduation day, there is a glimpse of how raw and painful her son's brutal death remains for her, more than 30 years after he was killed. 'I still have a feeling that maybe one day, he will come and meet me but it's just wishful thinking. My sisters were scolding me, "Look, Sizwe is dead. This is the truth. Your son died. You have got to accept that." But I still have that feeling at the back of my mind that at least maybe one day I will see him again.' Hers is a deep pain and I see on her face the same anguish Vusi wears on his each time he speaks of Sizwe. It is a loss that transcends blood.

Sizwe Kondile and I at a social function at the University of Fort Hare in Alice (1977).

Relaxing at home in Port Elizabeth during a holiday from Fort Hare (1978).

Girly and I at a music festival at the Maseru stadium (1981).

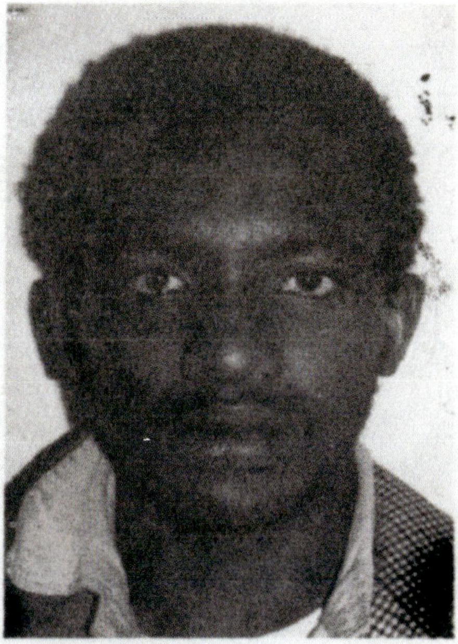

3173

3173 – My photo in the security police photo album of those who had left the country unlawfully and were declared as terrorists.

Our wedding day at the National University of Lesotho in Roma (13 February 1982).

At a social function in Lesotho while I was a student (1985).

My daughter's funeral, which we could not attend in Port Elizabeth. Zola Yeye and Thozami Xiphu are on the right (1986).

My two daughters (1986).

Thozi and I at a shooting range at a military camp in Uganda (1990).

Renewing our vows on our
21st wedding anniversary.
My daughter Zukiswa, my father
and mother, Girly and I (2003).

Girly and I on our first trip after my appointment as NDPP to a conference of heads of prosecuting authorities in Belfast and Dublin (2005).

With Cyril Ramaphosa at a celebratory party hosted by Sipho Pityana after my appointment as NDPP (2005).

During a speech in the Free State during my tenure as NDPP (2006).

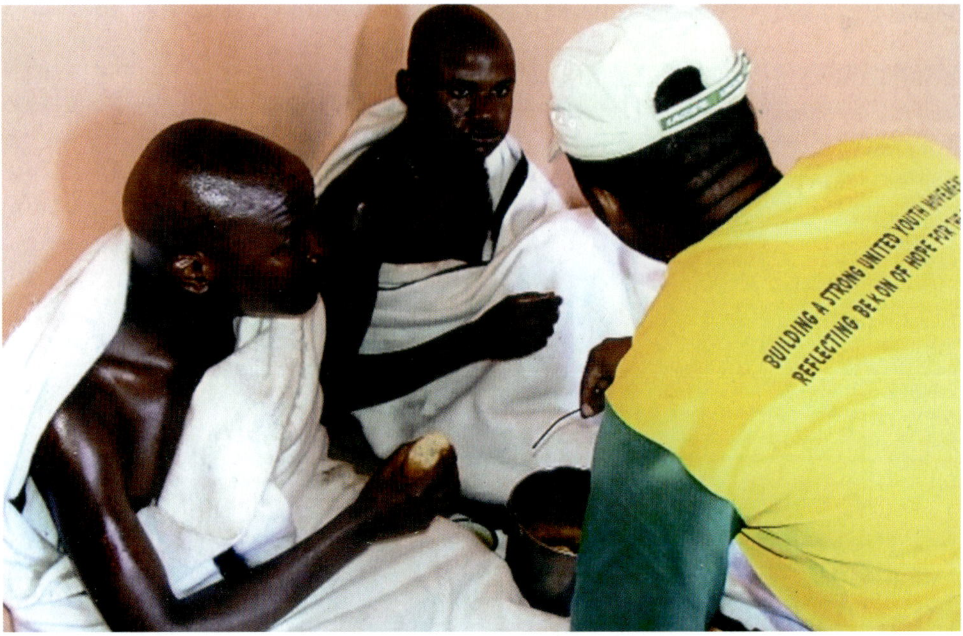

My two sons the day they returned from their initiation shortly after I was suspended as NDPP (December 2007).

Preparing a braai for my family during my suspension (2009).

Former Vlakplaas commander Dirk Coetzee at a potential site where Sizwe Kondile was killed (2009).

Charity Kondile, Sizwe's mother, holding a photograph of her son at his graduation ceremony (2013). Photo by Mandy Wiener.

Confronting former security policeman Hermanus du Plessis in Pretoria (2013).
Photo by Mandy Wiener.

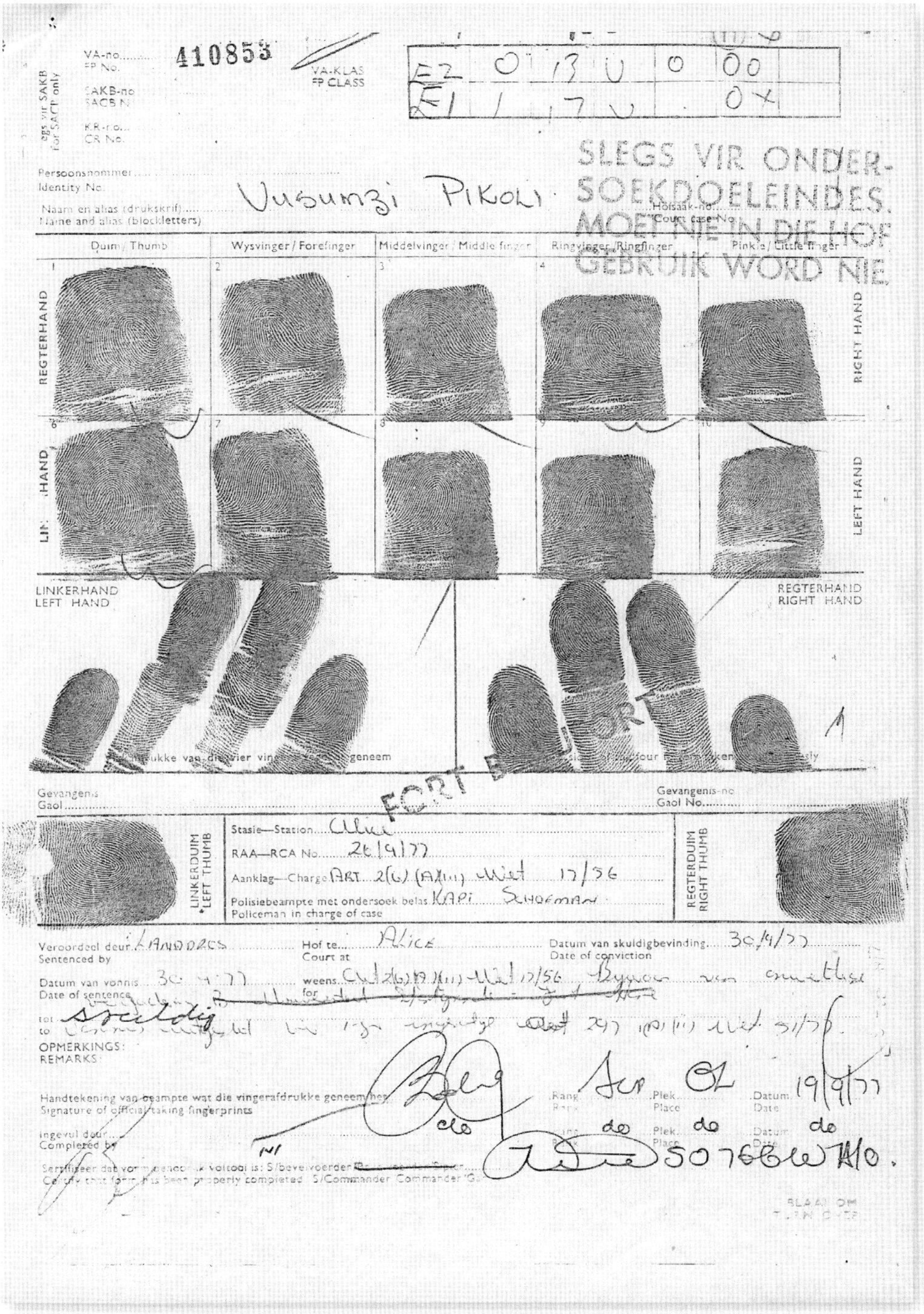

410853

VA-no. / FP No.

SAKB-no / SACB No.

KR-no. / CR No.

Slegs vir SAKB / For SACB only

VA-KLAS / FP CLASS

E2 O 13 U O OO
E1 1 17 U . OX

SLEGS VIR ONDERSOEKDOELEINDES. MOET NIE IN DIE HOF GEBRUIK WORD NIE.

Persoonsnommer / Identity No.

Naam en alias (drukskrif) / Name and alias (blockletters) Vusumzi Pikoli

Hofsaak-no. / Court case No.

Duim / Thumb | Wysvinger / Forefinger | Middelvinger / Middle finger | Ringvinger / Ringfinger | Pinkie / Little finger

REGTERHAND / RIGHT HAND

LINKERHAND / LEFT HAND

LINKERHAND / LEFT HAND

REGTERHAND / RIGHT HAND

FORT B... / FORT

Gevangenis / Gaol

Gevangenis-no / Gaol No.

LINKERDUIM / LEFT THUMB

Stasie—Station Alice

RAA—RCA No. 26/9/77

Aanklag—Charge ART 2(b)(A)(ii) Wet 17/56

Polisiebeampte met ondersoek belas / Policeman in charge of case KAPT SCHOEMAN

REGTERDUIM / RIGHT THUMB

Veroordeel deur / Sentenced by LANDDROS

Hof te / Court at ALICE

Datum van skuldigbevinding / Date of conviction 30/4/77

Datum van vonnis / Date of sentence 30-4-77

weens / for

tot / to

skuldig

OPMERKINGS: / REMARKS:

Handtekening van beampte wat die vingerafdrukke geneem het / Signature of official taking fingerprints

Rang / Rank

Plek / Place

Datum / Date 19/9/77

Ingevul deur / Completed by

do do do

Sertifiseer dat vorm behoorlik voltooi is: S/bevelvoerder / Certify that form has been properly completed S/Commander

507664 W/O.

BLAAI OM / TURN OVER

Fingerprints taken when I was arrested at Fort Hare University during a memorial service for Steve Biko (1977).

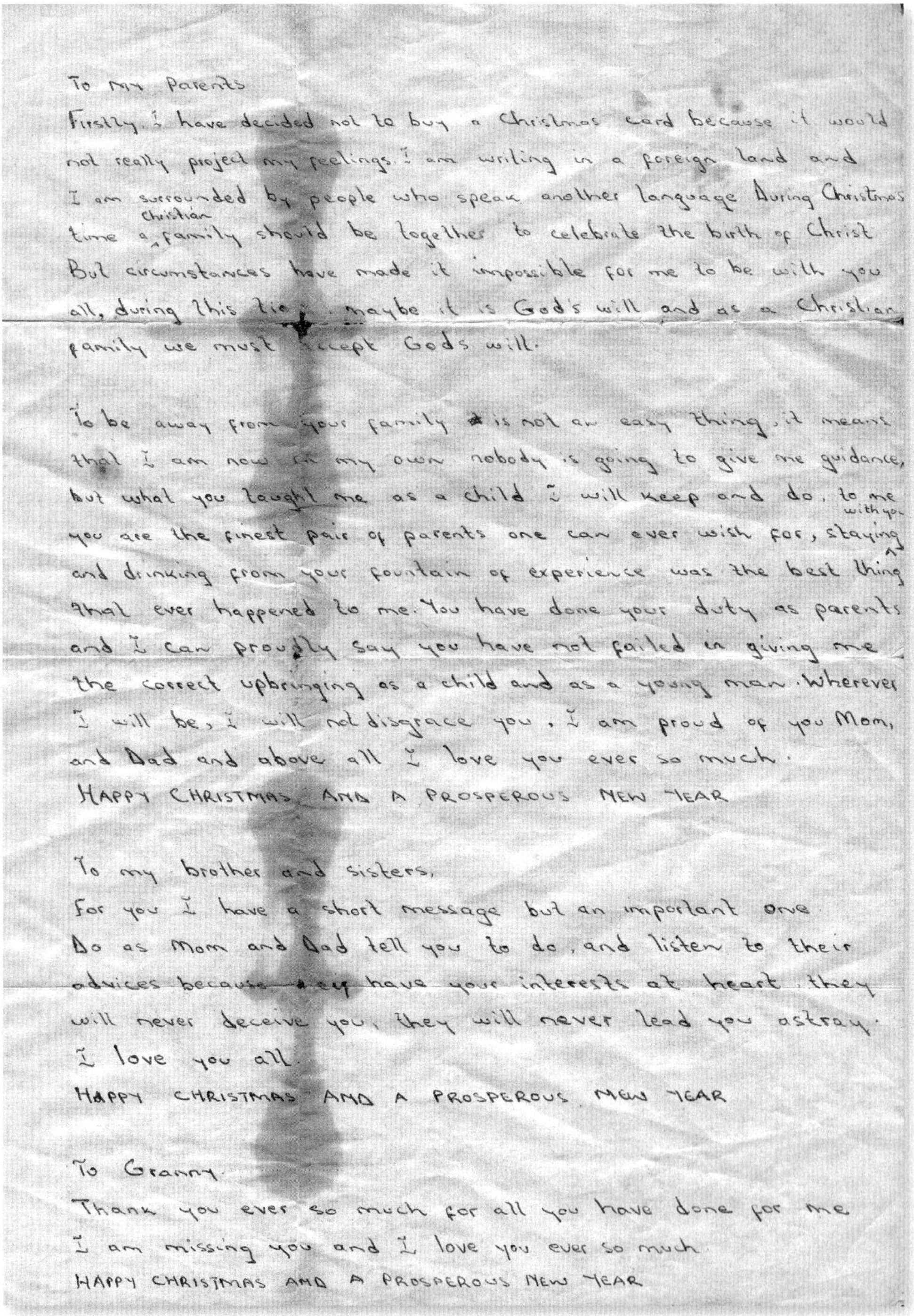

To my Parents

Firstly I have decided not to buy a Christmas card because it would not really project my feelings. I am writing in a foreign land and I am surrounded by people who speak another language During Christmas time a Christian family should be together to celebrate the birth of Christ But circumstances have made it impossible for me to be with you all, during this time, maybe it is God's will and as a Christian family we must accept Gods will.

To be away from your family is not an easy thing, it means that I am now on my own nobody is going to give me guidance, but what you taught me as a child I will keep and do, to me you are the finest pair of parents one can ever wish for, staying with you and drinking from your fountain of experience was the best thing that ever happened to me. You have done your duty as parents and I can proudly say you have not failed in giving me the correct upbringing as a child and as a young man. Wherever I will be, I will not disgrace you, I am proud of you Mom, and Dad and above all I love you ever so much.

HAPPY CHRISTMAS AND A PROSPEROUS NEW YEAR

To my brother and sisters,

For you I have a short message but an important one Do as Mom and Dad tell you to do, and listen to their advices because they have your interests at heart, they will never deceive you, they will never lead you astray.

I love you all.

HAPPY CHRISTMAS AND A PROSPEROUS NEW YEAR

To Granny

Thank you ever so much for all you have done for me

I am missing you and I love you ever so much

HAPPY CHRISTMAS AND A PROSPEROUS NEW YEAR

A letter smuggled into South Africa to my parents at the time of my first Christmas away from home in exile (1980).

TO OUR TWO DAUGHTERS

1. Zukiswa Lifakazi - 27 May 1982
2. Siyalithatha Sandina - 26 January 1986

The birth of you, filled our hearts with joy and pride. You were born at difficult times, - when our people were locked in a life and death struggle with the enemy. You were born at a time when the bright rays of the freedom sun were beginning to shine. You were born at a time when our people were prepared to lay down their lives so that you and those of your generation should not live like we, your parents and grand-parents, used to live, so that you live in a free Democratic and non-racial South Africa.

We as your parents have nothing to give you except love and to teach you to love your country and your people.

to love and value freedom.
to fight against all forms of oppression and exploitation
to fight against racism and tribalism
to fight against capitalism and imperialism
to wage a relentless struggle against poverty, ignorance and disease
to uphold the values and principles of the working class.

We as your parents have dedicated and committed ourselves to achieving the above. You must live to be true revolutionaries, - strive to transform society, strive for peace, progress and social justice.
Be prepared to die for the above, if needs be.
We have high hopes for you - our daughters.
We hope you will grow to be fine revolutionaries.
We hope you will grow to be fearless fighters for freedom.
We hope you will never, never betray the cause we stand for.
Never co-operate with the enemy.
You should be the first to battle and last to retreat !

Aluta Continua !!

Vusi and Girlie (20.02.1986)

I wrote this letter to my girls while I was inside South Africa on a mission (1986).
I knew the *boers* were looking for me.

VP1

PRESIDENT

REPUBLIC OF SOUTH AFRICA

23 September 2007

Dear Advocate Pikoli

As you are aware, the Prosecuting Authority forms an important part of our criminal justice machinery and, accordingly, our fight against crime.

This machinery to fight crime was further strengthened in 2000 when Parliament adopted legislation creating the Directorate of Special Operations (DSO), in the office of the National Director of Public Prosecutions.

In recognition of the particular threat posed by organised crime in the country, the DSO was specifically tasked to investigate and institute criminal proceedings relating to organised crime activities.

As a result of the importance of the Prosecuting Authority to the success of our fight against crime, I receive regular reports from government agencies and Ministries about the activities of the Authority.

Organised crime poses a serious threat to our national security. While I accept that the Prosecuting Authority has the discretion to enter into plea bargain and/or immunity arrangements with alleged offenders, the public interest must always be considered. Accordingly, in determining what is in the public interest, before exercising such discretion, the Prosecuting Authority must necessarily have regard to the totality of information available to the State.

Such plea bargaining and/or immunity arrangements cannot be done at the expense of our national security.

V.P.

My letter of suspension (2007). (PAGE 1 OF 3)

Clause 179(6) of the Constitution of the Republic of South Africa provides that the Cabinet member responsible for the administration of Justice must exercise final responsibility over the Prosecuting Authority. Accordingly, the Government, on whose behalf the Minister of Justice and Constitutional Affairs exercises this responsibility, must and does have an interest in ensuring that the Prosecuting Authority serves the public interest. In this regard, acting in terms of the dictates of the Constitution, the Minister of Justice and Constitutional Affairs informed me about some of the matters that the National Prosecution was seized with. Some government agencies also advised me of some of the activities relating to the same matters.

The information I have received shows that you have entertained the granting of immunity to members of organised crime syndicates in instances where the prosecution of such people would, in the Government's view, be in the public interest. In some of these matters there seems to be no reason why the Prosecuting Authority would not proceed against all persons implicated in the alleged offences.

I have evaluated the information at my disposal and have reached the conclusion that you, in your capacity as National Director of Public Prosecutions have failed to appreciate the nature and extent of the threat posed by members of organised crime syndicates to our national security. Such a lack of appreciation in itself amounts to a threat to our national security.

The Minister of Justice and Constitutional Affairs has also drawn my attention to the breakdown of relations between your office and hers due to several incidents, such as your testimony to the Khampepe Commission of Inquiry.

Accordingly, this letter serves to inform you that I, acting in terms of the provisions of section 12(6) of the National Prosecuting Authority Act (the Act), have decided to suspend you from office with immediate effect. You will continue to receive your full benefits during the period of suspension.

V.I.

Acting in terms of the same provisions of the Act, I have also decided to institute an enquiry into your fitness to hold the office of National Director of Public Prosecutions. The particulars relating to the enquiry will soon be communicated to you.

Yours sincerely

THABO MBEKI

Advocate V Pikoli
National Director of Public Prosecutions
Tshwane

V.P.

VP12

MINISTER
JUSTICE AND CONSTITUTIONAL DEVELOPMENT
REPUBLIC OF SOUTH AFRICA

Private Bag X276, Pretoria, 0001 Tel. (012) 315 1761/2/3 Fax (0120 315 1749
Private Bag X256, Cape Town, 800 Tel. (021) 4671700 Fax (021) 467 1730

Our Ref.:LNM: Lekgoro
Tel (021) 467 1700

Adv. V. Pikoli
National Director of Public Prosecutions
Silverton
Pretoria

BY HAND

Dear Adv. Pikoli

RE: INVESTIGATIONS INTO THE NATIONAL COMMISSIONER OF THE POLICE SERVICE.

The above matter refers.

I am advised that you have taken legal steps to effect the arrest of and the preference of charges against the National Commissioner of the police service. I presume that in making this decision, you have taken time to consider the seriousness and gravity of your intended course of action.

As you know, in terms of clause 179(6) of the Constitution, the Cabinet member responsible for the administration of justice must exercise final responsibility over the prosecuting authority. In addition, section 33(2) of the National Prosecuting Authority Act provides that the National Director of Public Prosecution shall at the request of the Minister of Justice, furnish the Minister with

V.P.

The controversial letter sent by the justice minister to my office (2007), instructing me not to proceed with the Selebi warrants. (PAGE 1 OF 2)

information with regard to any case, matter or subject dealt with by the National Director or a Director.

In light of the above and in order for me to exercise my responsibilities as required by the Constitution, I require all of the information on which you relied to take the legal steps to effect the arrest of and the preference of charges against the National Commissioner of the police service. This includes but is not limited to specific information or evidence indicating the direct involvement of the National Commissioner in any activity that constitutes a crime in terms of the laws of South Africa. In pursuing your intended course of action and any prosecution, the NPA must do so in the public interest notwithstanding a prima facie case. Such exercise of discretion requires that all factors be taken into account including the public interest. Therefore, I must be satisfied that indeed the public interest will be served should you go ahead with your intended course of action. Until I have satisfied myself that sufficient information and evidence does exist for the arrest of and preference of charges against the National Commissioner of the police service, you shall not pursue the route that you have taken steps to pursue. You should therefore and with extreme urgency cause for me to be briefed thoroughly in this regard.

Please advise me at your earliest convenience when you I should expect to receive the necessary documentation.

I trust that you find the above in order.

Yours sincerely

Ms. B.S. Mabandla, MP
Minister of Justice and Constitutional Development.
Date: 2007 – 09 - 18

(PAGE 2 OF 2)

PART THREE

Under pressure

The slippery slope

In among the files labelled 'Shaik', 'Zuma', 'Kebble', 'Yengeni' and 'Maharaj' was another high-profile matter to be dealt with: the Travelgate affair.

Dozens of members of parliament had been investigated by the Scorpions for abusing parliament's travel-voucher system. It had emerged that MPs had been colluding with travel agents to submit fraudulent travel claims in an elaborate scheme that saw the government being defrauded of millions of rand.

The MPs had claimed for false trips that never took place or had cancelled flights and still submitted crudely altered forms to parliament in order to be reimbursed. On occasions, they used the trips for personal use or allowed others to abuse their privileges and benefit from the flights.

As I had spent a considerable portion of my life within the ANC, I personally knew a number of the MPs implicated in the scandal, including such high-profile ministers as Siyabonga Cwele, Bathabile Dlamini, Maggie Sotyu, Lulu Xingwana, and Charles and Nosiviwe Nqakula, with whom I had been friends for some time. The former ANC Chief Whip Nyami Booi was also one of those implicated.

The fact that some of the Travelgate accused were my comrades and friends in no way influenced my decision on how to handle the cases. I would never have chosen not to prosecute somebody if the facts and the law were in our favour. I can proudly say that my membership of the ANC, and my continued allegiance to the party, never influenced any decision I took.

The prosecutor handling the matter was Jannie van Vuuren, a respected and capable advocate in Cape Town. Given the high-profile nature of the case, I flew down from Johannesburg for regular briefings, but I largely left Van Vuuren to handle it. I was satisfied with the way he was dealing with the case and it was his responsibility to take decisions.

The NPA was pursuing prosecutions against 30 MPs believed to have defrauded parliament in the scam. These cases were ultimately resolved through plea-bargain agreements that saw these lawmakers plead guilty, pay fines and continue with their jobs as MPs. Only Nyami Booi chose to fight his case and pursue a full-blown trial, but he ultimately also agreed to enter into a deal with the state.

While the matter was still pending and we were debating how to proceed, there was a series of meetings and confrontations during which pressure from the ANC, comrades and cabinet ministers was applied on me. As the case was being investigated by the Scorpions, the unit – unsurprisingly – also drew criticism.

Advocate Van Vuuren proceeded with the case and those who wanted to finalise plea bargains did so, while others – including some travel agencies and Nyami Booi – resisted. Those MPs who entered deals pleaded guilty, received suspended sentences and had to pay fines. As these were plea bargains and the sentences did not exceed 12 months and fines were paid, they could continue in their positions in parliament without being disqualified. While they would still have criminal records, they remained eligible to be MPs.

Parliament also bought the debtors' book of Bathong, one of the main travel agencies implicated, after the liquidators' estate ran out of funds, putting an end to the saga and writing off R12 million in debt. As Bathong was the largest creditor, it would have cost more to recover the funds than what they were worth. No fewer than 89 MPs were being pursued by the liquidators for amounts totalling over R5 million.

There was inevitably criticism of the NPA for entering into plea bargain deals. As NDPP, I was in a position to stop any of the negotiations, but I saw nothing wrong with the deals. I've always believed that if the NPA takes a wrong decision regarding plea bargains in terms of Section 105a of the Criminal Procedure Act, there is another checkpoint – the courts.

Each agreement must be sanctioned by a magistrate or a judge and he or she is empowered to refuse a plea bargain. There are also several contributing factors that need to be considered, such as what offence has been committed and the willingness of the accused to cooperate and confess, thereby saving time and money rather than trying to pursue a conviction even though the same conviction can be secured without going to full trial with all its attendant costs. Also, even if it is a conviction in terms of a plea bargain, the person will still have a criminal record and could pay a fine or receive a suspended or even a custodial sentence for that matter.

The fact that I personally knew many of the accused in the Travelgate affair added another layer to this case, but I was even more determined to pursue the matter because these were lawmakers who had broken the law. They had been entrusted with the weighty responsibility of representing the electorate as members of parliament in order to make the laws. And how do you make laws when you are a lawbreaker yourself? It means you have betrayed the trust of those who have voted for you.

I respected the position taken by Sindiso Mfenyana, secretary to parliament during that period, as well as Frene Ginwala, the speaker of parliament when the crimes were committed. The secretary was prepared to be a state witness for us and the speaker was honest and straightforward in her cooperation with the investigation. This indicated how seriously they took the charges against the MPs. I admired that greatly.

Looking back now, the interference and pressure I experienced was a sign of the rot beginning to set in. It went completely against the values of our struggle for national liberation, which is exactly why I could not compromise on the issue. You expect a particularly high standard from public representatives and there should be no exceptions to that.

Critics developed a habit of targeting prosecutors who had been prosecuting during the apartheid era because they perceived them to be conservative. However, the majority of them were simply doing their work, as was the case with Advocate Van Vuuren. He was unfairly criticised for his work on Travelgate, and yet I was satisfied with the way he handled the matter as a prosecutor.

I felt protective of my prosecutors because they were fulfilling an important role, and the institution they serve is crucial to the country. The potential of political interference in the NPA by the hands of those in power poses a depressing threat and a real reminder that the slope is a slippery one.

A scar to prove it

Acting on instinct, Ngoako Ramatlhodi threw out his hand to block the blade from piercing me in the chest. I hadn't seen one of the men flick open his pocketknife and come charging at me. Fortunately, Ngoako had noticed him pulling the weapon from his pocket and had reacted. The blade nicked me, leaving a scar on my chest that I would carry with me as a souvenir of that brawl on a Maseru street for the rest of my life. We *moered* those two boys there with almost the whole town watching as we beat them with a *baksteen*.

Ngoako and I had been visiting Maseru from Roma, where we were both students in the 1980s. He wanted to change his watchstrap and we were inside a store picking one out for him. The shop assistant laid out of several options on a cabinet and while we were looking through them, out of the corner of my eye I caught a glimpse of two other men in the shop. I saw one grab something and slip it into his pocket. The assistant was distracted but soon realised that one of the items was missing from the counter. I knew immediately who had taken it. I went over to confront him and to search him for the stolen property. His hands were in his pockets and he pulled out his knife so quickly that I didn't see it coming. Fortunately, Ngoako had my back and shouted before thrusting up his hand to defend me.

The first time I met Ngoako was when he came to Port Elizabeth as part of a delegation from the Transvaal in 1979. He was a founding member of AZASO, the Azanian Students' Organisation that later became known as

SASCO, and he was also a member of the team that formed COSAS, the Congress of South African Students, along with others such as Wandile Zulu. A group of five came to visit and we had to entertain them and hold political discussions.

Ngoako and I had similar easy-going personalities and we immediately hit it off. I remember he was wearing an ill-fitting woollen maroon jersey, hippie shoes with high heels and bell-bottom trousers. How I hated bell-bottoms and hippie shoes! They were just not my style.

We met again in exile in Lesotho when we were in charge of political classes, instructing new comrades coming to join the ANC in exile. Chris Hani didn't want either of us to go for military training at that time and I was occupied trying to strengthen underground structures in the Eastern Cape at the time. We were then both in the same class at Roma University. When Ngoako left the University of the North in Turfloop, he was doing his last year of his B.Juris and I had been doing my final B.Proc year at Fort Hare. We did our BA Law and LLB together and became increasingly close. Ngoako was the president of the SRC and was a member of the university council. At one stage, when we were both married, we even shared a house together. Ngoako married exactly a year after Girly and I, and chose the same weekend in February for the ceremony. We had babies at much the same time, lived together and I even used his law notes to write my final LLB exams after I missed an entire semester when I was on a mission inside South Africa.

When we left Lesotho, we both went to Harare, where Ngoako did his master's degree in international relations and I did mine in law. Ngoako was recalled to Zambia to become the political secretary and assistant to then ANC President O.R. Tambo and became his right-hand man and speech writer.

We stayed friends over the years after liberation and when he was the premier of Limpopo we regularly phoned one another. He came to my 21st wedding anniversary celebration in Port Elizabeth in 2003 and we saw one another from time to time.

When I was appointed NDPP in 2005, I had to deal with the Scorpions' investigation into allegations against Ngoako. The case was already in the public domain and had been reported on in the media. The investigation was ongoing and the team regularly briefed me. I encouraged them to continue with their probe until they felt they had a case to prosecute.

Although I hadn't thought much about the matter when I took office, I was also not looking forward to addressing the issue because I felt that some might think that any decision I would take would be influenced by the fact that Ngoako was my friend. In fact, Jackie Selebi had suggested to me that Ngoako's case was not getting anywhere because I was in charge of the NPA and I was protecting him.

The Scorpions first began looking into allegations of corruption against Ngoako sometime in 2003, under Bulelani Ngcuka. When Ngcuka resigned, Ngoako was tipped to take over as NDPP but the prospect of a criminal prosecution looming against him ruled him out. The corruption case related to kickbacks he allegedly received from a social grant tender awarded while he was still premier of Limpopo. In 2002, the contract was awarded to a company called Cash Paymaster Services and its empowerment partner Northern Corporate Investment Holdings, which was controlled by lawyer Solly Mohale, businessman Gideon Serote, cane furniture king Habakuk Shikwane and well-known Limpopo car dealer Haroon Moti. It was suggested that Ngoako had initiated the setting up of the company and had been secretly receiving a percentage of the profits, a claim he vehemently denied. There were also indications that Northern Corporate Investment Holdings may have channelled money to Ngoako through a third party, money that he used to buy a mansion nicknamed the 'Pumpkin Palace' outside Tzaneen. In 2006, I invited Ngoako to my house to talk about his case. Given that our relationship was well known, I wanted to play open cards with him. He sat in my home and I said to him, '*Broer*, you know that there is this matter that we are dealing with here and it's not just going to disappear. We've got to deal with it and you know that there is nothing personal.'

His reaction was reasonable and there was no bitterness towards me as he said, 'No, I understand, *broer*. Do what you've got to do.'

I told him we would send him a list of questions and his answers would determine the status of the case and whether or not we would prosecute.

Ngoako answered the questions, and we considered them and concluded that the investigation should continue. In some of my briefings with President Mbeki I had to explain why it was taking so long, because there were concerns that the case was being delayed and that this could be unfair.

Ngoako's advocate Seth Nthai, who was also the ANC's legal advisor, made representations to me but I rejected them and insisted that the matter should go ahead. Advocate Nthai is a flamboyant man with a penchant for colourful suits and garishly bright ties. He regularly represented the ruling party and its senior members and later also acted for the state against me in the Ginwala Inquiry. I had dealt with him extensively during the Travelgate affair.

In November 2006, the Scorpions executed a search-and-seizure operation at two of Ngoako's properties. The searches were made public by him the following day when he issued a furious statement attacking the Scorpions for prejudicing him professionally, politically and socially and for not acting with the principles of dignity and fair treatment enshrined in the Constitution.

'I stand firmly opposed to any form of corrupt or criminal activity. I respect and uphold the responsibility of the relevant organs of the state to thoroughly investigate all credible allegations of such activity,' he said. 'However, the conduct of this investigation and the surfacing of various allegations against me in the media over the past three years has been highly prejudicial.' He cited how he had attempted to be admitted to the Bar as an advocate in 2004 but had failed because the judge cited media reports of corruption against him and told him to produce a letter from the Scorpions. Despite a request for such a letter, Ngoako had not received one.

Ngoako shifted his political allegiance from Thabo Mbeki to Jacob Zuma, who was also being pursued by the Scorpions at that time. He formed part of the so-called Coalition of the Wounded who rallied around Zuma and led the attack on the Scorpions. In fact, in an article in the *Star* newspaper after the raids, Ngoako referred to a group of individuals inside the Scorpions who, he said, were on a witch-hunt to eliminate political threats.

'There is a group of people who have been probing for the past 10 years and are very interested in defending their positions. I won't mention names [but] they are now in charge, some of them are very new in the ANC and that's why they are killing children of the ANC, one after the other. It will not work in the long term. They are in for a very big shock. We can't afford a situation where the organisation is hijacked by anybody and we're sent to jail under false pretences,' he told the newspaper.

The case against him was being turned into a political issue despite the ongoing evidence that we were gathering. When I left office in September 2007 the case was still being pursued against Ngoako. In fact, in January 2008, there were reports in the media that Gauteng Scorpions head Gerrie Nel had prepared a report detailing a prosecutable corruption case against Ngoako, laying out the evidence and the intention to charge him for receiving kickbacks amounting to R785 000.

And then, out of nowhere, Acting NDPP Corky Mpshe announced through spokesperson Tlali Tlali: 'The intended prosecution by the Scorpions of the former Limpopo premier has been discontinued.' According to Tlali, 'the decision was informed by and based on a number of considerations, including the NPA guidelines on prosecutions as well as on the prosecution'.

I don't know what could have changed between the two sets of representations submitted by Ngoako's lawyers. I didn't see the second representations and I don't know what new evidence could have emerged, but when I heard that Mpshe had withdrawn charges, I was convinced that he must have come under political pressure. The prosecutors were so certain and so confident of the case against him that pressure must surely have been brought to bear.

I have not spoken to the prosecuting team about the case – neither have I spoken to Ngoako. Whenever I see him, the matter is never raised and it is not awkward in any way. I would be disappointed if he were to be found guilty but it would not mean that I would stop being his friend.

When I was to be replaced as NDPP, Ngoako's name emerged as a potential candidate and there was much talk that he would succeed me. With such a cloud hanging over him, I didn't think it would be right. I felt the matter had to be dealt with properly. It was much the same situation as the case with Zuma – he is the president of the country and of the ANC, yet he lacks credibility, despite being elected in a democratic, fair and open election. In my opinion, it is wrong on a moral level.

As much as Ngoako is my friend, I think that somehow he may have lost his way in the politics of power. This has been illustrated by his attacks on the judiciary, which are so out of character for him.

When he was elected chairperson of parliament's justice committee, Ngoako labelled Chief Justice Pius Langa 'an irritation' for comments he had made about Zuma's approach to the justice system and said Deputy Chief Justice Dikgang Moseneke 'should know his place' following utterances he made about the ANC at a private birthday party. Then, when delivering a memorial lecture in honour of the late ANC president A.B. Xuma in Upington in 2012, Ngoako claimed: 'I have seen now in our country the courts are being used to replace the executive. There is a tyranny, a minority tyranny, that is using state institutions to undermine democratic processes at this juncture in our country.' Ngoako had also written a newspaper article in which he stated that the Constitution was fatally flawed because it gave too much power to the judiciary.

In April 2012, I felt obligated to respond to what Ngoako had been saying about the judiciary and I wrote an article for the *Sunday Independent* newspaper entitled 'Ramatlhodi, you are dead wrong'. At issue was the question of the separation of powers between the executive and the judiciary, and I commented:

> *... Decisions such as those in the Glenister, Menzi Simelane and Mokotedi Mpshe cases have raised eyebrows in some quarters about the observance of judicial constraint by the judiciary. Herein lies the real concern and source of unhappiness – political unhappiness that is. How dare these unelected, learned gentlemen and ladies of the judiciary frustrate the political aspirations of the elected representatives of the people! This concern is dressed in a separation of powers robe.*
>
> *Before a constructive engagement, let me pause to momentarily reflect on legal basics. The doctrine of separation of powers is a theory varied by practice on application. There has never been a rigid compartmentalisation of the doctrine because the demands of governance make it impractical. In the South African context, members of the executive (except the president and ministers who are not MPs) are also members of Parliament.*
>
> *All judicial officers are legally required before assuming duties to take an oath or affirm that they will uphold and protect the Constitution. It therefore follows that those who are found to have acted in violation of this provision can be removed from office.*
>
> *This seems to take care of the serious concerns of Ramatlhodi about delinquent or errant judicial officers (my words) when they act in a man-*

ner not 'respecting' the Constitution. Section 177 outlines a process for dealing with such judicial officers. I hope this settles this notion that judicial officers seem to be a law unto themselves or are the untouchables and account to no one. They account to the law and the Constitution and Parliament has a key role to play in that process.

We should not forget that at the centre of the doctrine of separation of powers is the protection of liberty and the facilitation of good government by appropriate specialisation and that the independence of the judiciary is essential in a democracy. The segregation of these functions prevents overconcentration of power in one sphere of government and stops tyranny, arbitrary rule and other forms of undemocratic practices that detest criticism, accountability, responsiveness, transparency and so on ...

The Constitution has already been amended more than 16 or 17 times. The Constitution itself in section 74 as part of the national legislative process provides for such amendment. The Constitutional Court still has to decide on the constitutionality of any amendment to the Constitution.

There is nothing to fear because there is no matter that cannot be openly discussed, even if it might lead to the amendment of the Constitution. Anyway, we all want a living and vibrant document and not a dodo as Lwando Xhaso, a former clerk of the Constitutional Court, always challenges us to do.

We the people are the ultimate custodians of the Constitution.

I had begun to think that there was a concerted effort to discredit the judiciary – at around the same time ANC Secretary-General Gwede Mantashe had called judges counter-revolutionary. I felt compelled to respond and it did not sour my relationship with Ngoako. He called me up after reading the article and said, 'Hey, *broer*, what are you doing? This is rubbish!' It was good to have a public, intellectual debate on legal issues and to encourage others to respond and consider the merits of the arguments.

To this day, Ngoako and I remain friends. If we want to speak, I pick up the phone and I call him. We have had drinks together and seen one another at events. And he will remain a friend even if he were to be tried and convicted.

Perhaps therein lies my blind spot. I forgive easily and I am too trusting.

I expect people to do the right thing. But, of course, life is not always that simple. The prosecution of Zuma was not a pleasant experience but it had to be done. With Jackie, too, it was not pleasant but it had to be done. And it was the same with Ngoako. I bear no personal grudges against anybody, even those who have vilified me and put me through pain.

No political will

The Strategic Defence Procurement Package, more colloquially referred to as the Arms Deal in South Africa, has been the subject of repeated allegations of corruption. Towards the end of 1999, the government signed contracts to purchase weapons aimed at modernising its defence arsenal. The contracts to purchase corvettes, helicopters, submarines and fighter aircraft amounted to a total of R30 billion and was considered a cash cow for greedy politicians looking to grease their palms and line their pockets. Many allegations of corruption and wrongdoing have stemmed from this deal, several of which were investigated by the Scorpions. The most notable case, of course, has been that of President Jacob Zuma.

When I arrived in Silverton, several Arms Deal probes were already in full swing. Former ANC Chief Whip Tony Yengeni had already been convicted and the Schabir Shaik matter was being concluded. Investigators in France, Germany, Sweden and the United Kingdom were also conducting separate inquiries, looking at whether arms manufacturers in those countries had behaved inappropriately to benefit politicians in South Africa in any way.

In order to get a proper grasp of the investigations and of the outstanding issues, I met with AG Terence Nombembe and Public Protector Lawrence Mushwana in late 2007. Together with the NPA, these were the institutions tasked with the matter. There was no joint task team mandated to investigate so the Scorpions team continued to dig away on its own but the AG's office assisted where it could. If the investigators were unhappy with anything, the auditors would come in and take a look. Leading the Scorpions project was Johan du Plooy and Izak du Plooy.

I encouraged the Scorpions team to continue with its investigations into cases related to the Arms Deal. Some of the cases that were pursued, and which received a great deal of publicity, included the prosecution against Zuma and also cases involving Chippy Shaik and Fana Hlongwane. Shamin 'Chippy' Shaik, Schabir's brother, had been chief of acquisitions for the South African National Defence Force (SANDF) when the deal was struck. He was suspended from the position for giving his lawyer a classified document after being accused of having a conflict of interest – his brother's company was one of the bidders in the Arms Deal.

Hlongwane, an elusive businessman with a reputation as something of a 'playboy', was the advisor to Defence Minister Joe Modise during the Arms Deal negotiations. Britain's Serious Fraud Office (SFO) was running a separate investigation into allegations that Hlongwane had received kickbacks from arms company BAE Systems for his role in securing a R50 billion deal for Gripen fighter aircraft.

None of these cases was brought before the courts during my relatively short tenure as NDPP. There was always the possibility for more prosecutions other than that of Schabir Shaik because – given the magnitude of the programme and the variety of companies involved in France, Germany, Sweden and Britain – it was highly unlikely that he was the only guilty party. For me it was clear that there must have been people involved at the level of the defence force itself and beyond that to the political realm. A decision on such major contracts had to be taken at a much higher level.

My role as NDPP was to allow the team to continue digging and to fight the many legal battles in court, such as those over documents we were trying to acquire from Mauritius in relation to the Zuma case. I would then look at the evidence gathered and take a decision, with the team, on who should be prosecuted.

On the whole, I experienced no overt political pressure regarding the Arms Deal investigation, but there were incidents and interactions that raised question marks for me although I was never able to prove anything conclusively.

Towards the end of my tenure, the SFO in London made a request for mutual legal assistance regarding its investigation into BAE Systems and Fana Hlongwane. I was prepared and ready to give full assistance, but Selebi, together with Justice DG Menzi Simelane, tried to prevent our co-operation, and there was an exchange of letters between us over the heated issue.

The request had come through the appropriate channels and had been directed to the department of justice as the central authority. However, the British had anticipated a lack of cooperation so they had also sent the letter to the DSO and that letter was brought to my attention. In the letter, they listed names of individuals and companies, as well as bank account numbers and bank details. The information was all based on admissions made by senior executives of BAE Systems.

Simelane argued that the SAPS, and not the NPA, was the appropriate organ of state to assist the SFO. I said, 'Look, Menzi, the police have never been involved in the Arms Deal investigation; it has always fallen in the domain of the DSO, so I don't understand why all of a sudden now you're saying the police must assist the SFO.'

Selebi shared the same position as Simelane. Together with Advocate Billy Downer, we drafted a response to Simelane disputing all the positions he had put forward.

There was a suggestion from some quarters that this was a fishing expedition by the British but the letter listed names, account numbers, amounts and even the names of banks. The British wanted us to assist them to verify the information. So it was that I instructed my guys to help where they could and we cooperated with our colleagues in the UK. In my opinion, nobody who had read and understood the content of that letter from the British could come to a reasonable conclusion that it was a fishing expedition.

When I left office, the Arms Deal investigation was continuing. However, in September 2010 the head of the DPCI (the Hawks) pulled the plug on the probe and shut down the investigation.

Retrospectively, I'm satisfied with the way my team pursued the case. Based on the evidence to which I had access, I would have expected that by now there would have been further prosecutions – in my view, at the very least Zuma should have been charged and at least one person should have stood trial. The Swiss were willing to give us further assistance on bank accounts held there, including those held by Hlongwane. BAE executives had made certain admissions about money paid to South Africa and the bank accounts of individuals in this country would also tell a story.

I remain convinced that what we have now is an incomplete story. Any act or transaction involving corruption has to be investigated in terms of the law, and yet there is a degree of complicit silence within the ANC on the issue. I can appreciate that during the time we were fighting against apartheid and there were security considerations, there had to be a bond of silence. But that principle is now being abused.

Look at ANC MP Andrew Feinstein as an example. When he wrote *After the Party*, exposing details of the Arms Deal, he was branded a traitor and ostracised in parliament. He felt he was no longer welcome in the movement. My personal experience with Feinstein was a difficult one – when I became DG of justice and the books were still in a mess, he gave me a hard time until I sorted them out. He was always damn honest and wanted the ANC and the government to do the right thing. He wanted the parliamentary committee, SCOPA, to play an oversight role and enforce accountability. I think he was courageous and it was right for him to have spoken out in the way that he did.

Perhaps I am still wallowing in naïveté and idealism in terms of the revolutionary values instilled in us, such as being concerned with the poor and with eradicating poverty. The best thing the ANC could have done was to ensure that the process was transparent and that it was properly investigated. Those who have done wrong must be exposed and face the consequences.

Towards the end of 2011, President Jacob Zuma appointed a commission of inquiry into the Arms Deal under Judge Willie Seriti. I don't know what is to be achieved by such an inquiry when it is a straightforward criminal matter. As far as I'm concerned, such an inquiry is a compromise to a full criminal investigation and prosecution. I simply don't think the country will ever get to the bottom of the Arms Deal. There is no political will to do so.

Of spies, coup plots and smear campaigns

The head of a state body such as the National Prosecuting Authority is allowed a rare glimpse behind the curtain into a clandestine world of mystery and intrigue. It is where operatives plot, information is peddled and the sinister push their agendas. This shadowy world often spills over into the law-enforcement agencies of the state as opportunists seek out cracks in the system to abuse for their own benefit. The results are often detrimental. My experience of this was most evident in three instances: the Special Browse Mole Report, the Hoax E-mail Saga and the Malawian investigation.

Leonard McCarthy walked into my office at the NPA's headquarters and said, 'I've got something for you to read. Nothing urgent. You can think about it and we can talk about it later,' as he dropped a document on my desk.

It was March 2006 and we were up to our neck in high-profile cases and were all stressed out. I didn't study the document at length but merely flipped through it before filing it away. On the face of it, it appeared to contain a mixture of fact and fiction.

It was only when I read the final version of the document a few months later, in July 2006, that I realised the full implications of its explosive nature. Headed 'Special Consolidated Browse Mole', it was printed on plain paper with a cover sheet and there was no apparent author.

The report outlined evidence that foreign governments, including Angola under José Eduardo dos Santos and Libya under Muammar Gaddafi, were covertly planning to support Jacob Zuma in his bid for the presidency. It was alleged that those countries were channelling funds to Zuma in order to sponsor a street revolution. It also detailed a meeting of African leaders where possible military support was discussed and reference was made to a meeting of former Umkhonto we Sizwe veterans who were prepared to back a coup to sweep Zuma into power.

The author of the document was suggesting that there were grounds for Zuma to be investigated for crimes relating to money he was allegedly receiving in African countries and wasn't declaring locally. The DSO had been monitoring Zuma's bail conditions and had picked up that he had travelled to Libya, Angola and Mozambique during the course of 2005.

As soon as I laid my eyes on it, I knew this was one of those documents you wish you had never seen. I had a gut feeling that this report was going to cause trouble and I was angry.

I asked McCarthy to explain its origins. He told me he had received information that during the course of an inquiry in Switzerland, an investigating judge had come across a number of corrupt transactions involving Angolan government officials and it appeared that money had been laundered through South African banks. According to McCarthy, the DSO had established that Zuma received funds into his bank accounts that were unexplained. McCarthy then received two further reports from informants and raised the matter with a senior special investigator from the DSO and asked him to assess the information and provide him with a report.

I immediately told McCarthy that this Browse Mole document should enjoy no status in the DSO and that there should be no further work on the project. I believed it was clearly an intelligence report and did not fall within the mandate of the Scorpions, although some aspects did concern organised crime. At face value there was an element that might require criminal investigation but there was also the sensitivity of gathering political intelligence. It was also evident that it had been produced by a person who had contact with old apartheid structures of intelligence.

I told McCarthy I thought the document to be explosive and I wanted to know how it had come about. He couldn't say where it had come from and didn't name the person who had given it to him. He also appeared quite rattled when I told him that he should leave the matter alone. He suggested that he knew an individual within the Scorpions who was politically savvy and who could perhaps analyse the contents of the document, but I insisted it was not a matter we should get involved in. It was evident that McCarthy was pushing for me to declare an official full-scale probe based on the report, but I refused. And if there was ever a time when I thought McCarthy was going to leave the DSO, it was then.

My next step was to call the South African Secret Service (SASS) Director-General Tim Dennis to inform him that I had this document in my possession and request a meeting with him and National Intelligence Agency (NIA) head Manala Manzini. We met at the Sheraton Hotel in Pretoria, overlooking the lawns of the Union Building where they had just attended a cabinet *lekgotla*.

Over tea, I handed them the report and said, 'I don't think this document belongs to us. The Scorpions have no business being involved in this matter, but I will certainly have an interest if it involves a crime being committed or if you suspect a crime has been committed.'

I explained that it was for SASS to deal with and I would not authorise any investigation on what was contained in the report. We still had Zuma under investigation and anything related to him would, of course, pique our interest. Manzini told me that the information contained in the report was not new and they had already picked up on some of the intelligence.

At the Ginwala Inquiry into my suspension, Manzini homed in on my handling of the Browse Mole Report as it became evident the state would use this issue as a central pillar in its case. Manzini testified about how I arrived at the meeting excited and told him that I had 'a hot potato' in my hands:

> *When he met us he was very excited. In fact I will say it exactly in his words: 'I have a hot potato.' That's how he conveyed the message to us as he gave us the document. We perused it and for us it was not information that would have raised eyebrows. Some of the things we had already picked up and we advised him, 'What are you doing? Why are you engaging yourself in matters of political intelligence that you have no mandate of?'*

I dispute Manzini's account of my behaviour at this meeting, as well as his criticism that I had been 'sitting' on the draft report for four months. I believe I acted properly by passing the document on to Manzini and Dennis timeously.

Manzini went so far as to draw parallels between the Browse Mole Report and a document authored by former Defence Force Chief Georg Meiring in 1998. Meiring was forced to resign over that report, which implicated his successor Siphiwe Nyanda, Winnie Madikizela-Mandela and Robert McBride in an alleged plot to overthrow the government. Manzini said that when Meiring produced the report, he 'had to walk' and that I, similarly, had not been sensitive and responsible and had 'no clue' as to how to do my job.

On 7 May 2007, an 18-page draft of the Special Browse Mole Report, dated 7/12/2006 and marked 'Top Secret' was anonymously faxed and delivered by post to trade union federation COSATU. This was done against the backdrop of a fierce political feud between Jacob Zuma and Thabo Mbeki as the former continued to fight his prosecution in the courts. At the time, COSATU was a vocal supporter of Zuma and the document was hailed as further evidence of the political campaign against Zuma.

I received a letter regarding the report from lawyers representing COSATU General Secretary Zwelenzima Vavi. I sent a reply saying: 'I wish to thank you for bringing this matter to my attention, but advise, however, that I am not in a position to assist your client', which COSATU would later call 'short and unbelievably arrogant' in a press statement.

Before the report was made public, I felt it important to inform the president of its existence. I knew COSATU had a copy and that it would be only a matter of time before it hit the newspapers. The president had also been asking for a meeting alone with McCarthy and I couldn't understand why. I told McCarthy that under no circumstances should he meet Mbeki without me.

During a briefing with the president about the Selebi matter in May 2007, shortly before he went to Vietnam on an official trip, I told him about Browse Mole. McCarthy was in that meeting and so too was Frank Chikane, DG in the presidency. I explained to Mbeki that the document was in our possession and what it contained.

Mbeki told me he already knew about the report from his former spokesperson Smuts Ngonyama and from the DG of SASS. He also said that part of what was contained in the report was true and that a large portion of the information was accurate. He didn't say what was not true. The president suggested I meet with Minister of Intelligence Ronnie Kasrils and Minister of Safety and Security Charles Nqakula, and he then left on his visit to Vietnam.

That weekend I met with the ministers at Nqakula's home and told them that I had received a query from COSATU and that I had responded. Nqakula felt I should have taken Vavi into my confidence and not simply dismissed him outright. I explained that I did not feel that I had to discuss the matter with COSATU because they were a non-state grouping.

The matter came up again at a meeting of the National Security Council in Cape Town shortly thereafter. I was invited to talk to them about the Browse Mole document and briefed them on how I came to have it and what I had since done with it. A decision was taken to set up a task team to investigate the document. By that stage the newspapers were already full of speculation and concerns around possible infiltration by foreign intelligence services. The NIA publicly denied being the source of the document and the presidency embarked on a damage-control exercise, with Chikane stating that it was the work of 'information pedlars' and former apartheid agents intent on creating conflict within government. As DGs we prepared a press release and held a media conference clarifying that the report was the work of information pedlars.

At that stage I still had no idea who the author of the document was and whether the report had come from within the NPA, although all fingers were pointing at the Scorpions. Having worked with the intelligence and security structures both in exile and in government, I realised that there was always the possibility that the DSO had been infiltrated. That is why we had counter-intelligence to ensure that our people were not involved in counter-activities. That is also why, after the Khampepe Commission, we had worked closely with the NIA to ensure that all our members were properly vetted.

I wrote a letter to McCarthy telling him that there was a formal process that needed to be followed, that a task team had been set up to investigate and that he should cooperate with it. He reacted angrily but – angry or not – this is what had to be done.

My relationship with McCarthy was a solid one. From the time I met him when he was a state advocate and I a DG, he impressed me as being bright, conscientious and hard-working. He was also incredibly meticulous and kept notes of every single meeting we ever held – he was always there with a pen and paper. I also felt that I could trust him.

After briefing McCarthy, I called all the regional heads of the DSO to a meeting and told them about the investigation into Browse Mole and about the document's existence. I explained that I expected everyone to cooperate with the investigation.

Despite this, the NIA and in particular the agency's deputy director-general for operations, Arthur Fraser, slammed our cooperation during his testimony at the Ginwala Inquiry. He stated that the DSO had not provided the NIA with the name of the source of the document, but that they knew who was responsible for it. He blamed me for not instructing my subordinates to cooperate with the investigation. McCarthy did agree to provide the NIA with a database of the Scorpions' informers under strict conditions, but there was concern around one individual who would allow his name to be revealed to the president only if it was absolutely necessary. Fraser also took aim at McCarthy for attending the Rugby World Cup in France during the height of the investigation.

Once the task team began investigating, the name of Ivor Powell emerged. Powell was a senior special investigator based in Cape Town – and it eventually became apparent that he had authored Browse Mole.

The task team had been tasked with investigating the origins of the report, the sources of the contents, the contributors and their intentions, and to establish how the report was 'inserted into the public domain and the intentions thereof'. In July 2007 the task team made its findings public:

> *There is a considerable degree of clarity with respect to the role players involved in the leaks, their modus operandi and their intentions. Further, there is little doubt that the various leaks were deliberately orchestrated and timed.*
>
> *With respect to the contents of the 'Browse Report', it is quite clear that while some of the events cited actually occurred or are true, woven into them are provocative, deliberate and baseless allegations. For example, while former members of Umkhonto we Sizwe (MK), the former military*

> *wing of the ANC, actually met in Shaft 17, there is no truth to the allegation that the said meeting also conspired to violently and unconstitutionally remove the current government from office.*
>
> *At this point, it is appropriate to characterise some of the sources of the information that were used to compile the 'Browse Report'. They are predominantly former members of the present Intelligence agencies whose initial background was with the secret services of the apartheid government – the former Special Branch of the South African Police; Military Intelligence of the South African Defence Force and the National Intelligence Service. Others are people who had relations or associations with these entities.*
>
> *The investigation confirmed that some of the sources of the 'Browse Report' form part of wider networks of information peddlers [sic] who operate within our country as well as in other countries. In this regard they offer services to private businesses in the country and internationally as well as foreign intelligence entities.*
>
> *Within South Africa, there is evidence of concerted efforts to target the ANC and its Alliance partners, some organs of the State, government officials and departments. Their activities in the above regard have triggered considerable tensions, mistrust, anxieties, confusion and deductions about conspiracies affecting numerous people, both within Government and outside Government.*

In February 2008, parliament's Joint Standing Committee on Intelligence (JSCI), chaired by Siyabonga Cwele, released its own report on Browse Mole. The JSCI report described the document as 'extremely inflammatory' and containing 'numerous allegations and unsubstantiated statements about prominent political figures in South Africa and the African continent'. It also found that the DSO had 'fallen prey to dubious activities of information peddlers [*sic*]' and that the DSO was 'involved in intelligence collection activities for which they do not have the required competency neither the experience'.

The committee came to the conclusion that McCarthy had refused to cooperate with the task team and had denied them access to computers, particularly that of Ivor Powell. It also concluded that Powell had produced the final report and leaked it into the public domain.

By that time, I had already been suspended so do not know what action, if any, was ever taken against McCarthy or Powell. I knew from the outset that this report would cause trouble and it did.

In May 2009 Powell broke his silence on the matter with an article in the *Mail & Guardian* newspaper, emerging from two years in a 'wilderness of mirrors' in which he revealed his version of the role played by McCarthy in the production of the explosive document:

> *Special Browse 'Mole' was commissioned by the former head of the directorate of special operations (Scorpions), Leonard McCarthy – now vice-president responsible for integrity at the World Bank – in early 2006.*
>
> *I was sole author, subject to two caveats: that McCarthy passed certain pieces of (unsourced) information to me during my inquiry and he instructed that certain passages, written by himself, be inserted into the text.*

If what Powell is saying is correct, then McCarthy was less than honest with me. He never disclosed his role in the matter to me and I only got to know of Powell's involvement once the document had been investigated by the task team. I knew that there was suspicion because he told me that at one stage Powell's computer was hacked. If Powell is to be believed that McCarthy commissioned the report and that he was the 'combined' author supplying him with unsourced information, then McCarthy misled everybody, including me. And because I trusted him, that would be a disappointment to me. However, it would explain why he was so enraged when I told him the DSO would not be involved in the matter and I would not declare a full-blown investigation.

Again this exposed what is perhaps my most fatal flaw. I work on the basis that I can trust people to do the right thing because I believe that, until such time that they prove themselves otherwise, people are intrinsically good. Working on these cases, you know the power that you hold as a prosecutor and that you can determine an individual's freedom.

Who knows what McCarthy's agenda was, but read in conjunction with what emerged around the Zuma spy tapes, if true, perhaps he believed it would have strengthened Mbeki's fight against Zuma. However, this project boomeranged and it could well have hastened the demise of the DSO.

What stands out for me, though, is the fact that Mbeki told me he knew a portion of the contents of the document to be correct. When I told him about the document it was clear that this was not the first he had heard of it. It would be reasonable for critics of the Scorpions to suggest that there had been some collusion in the compilation of the Browse Mole document.

In hindsight I do believe that I handled the episode appropriately, but the report gave my detractors ammunition against me – criticism that I created the space for this to happen and that I 'sat' on the report for months. And Dr Ginwala also found that I should have disciplined McCarthy, despite the fact that he was appointed by the president and I did not have authority to do so:

> *It is my view that despite lacking the authority to formally discipline the head of the DSO, it was open to him to reprimand the head of the DSO for conducting the Browse investigation and preparing an intelligence report beyond the mandate of the DSO, as well as for failing to fully cooperate with the investigation by the Task Team. The head of the DSO would then have had an opportunity, if he had a defence for the conduct, to raise such a defence or justification.*

Ginwala also found that I should have acted sooner when I received the initial draft from McCarthy. She requested that I produce the initial draft to show how it differed from the later version that was sent to COSATU but, despite visiting my office at the VGM building, I could not locate the original document:

> *The evidence surrounding the Browse Mole Report strongly points to the DSO having conducted itself in a manner quite inconsistent with its obligations under the law and outside its legal mandate. It is a stark demonstration that national security may be seriously hampered if institutions act outside their legal framework. I am unable however to find that the intelligence gathering exercise done by the head of the DSO in the investigation and compilation of the Browse Mole Report was done through the instruction or with the acquiescence of Adv Pikoli. That said, however, Adv Pikoli was obliged to inform the Minister in March 2006 of the information gleaned as a result of the Browse Mole investigation, and to*

stop any further work on the report by the DSO. Had he taken this action he could have limited the damage caused by this intelligence gathering exercise.

Ginwala's findings on my response to Browse Mole played right into the hands of ANC members of parliament when the subject of my suspension came before the house. They used it as a primary argument to ratify then President Kgalema Motlanthe's decision to fire me.

Perhaps I should have made immediate contact with the other agencies when McCarthy brought me the first draft report, but he had assured me at the time that it was a work in progress and that it was not urgent. I had no idea that McCarthy was behind it, of course, if Ivor Powell is to be believed.

One could argue that I should have held a tighter rein on what was going on in my organisation but I believed I did. I was the one who had to take decisions about authorising official investigations and there were no official investigations running without my approval.

There was also criticism of the NPA for allowing foreign intelligence services to influence the DSO. I'm not aware of any alliances between the Scorpions and foreign intelligence services and at no stage did I liaise with the head of any foreign intelligence service. It is no secret that, from its inception, the DSO was trained by both the FBI and Scotland Yard. In 2004, when I was still the DG of justice, I went with ministers Maduna and Tshwete to the FBI headquarters in Quantico, Virginia, where we attended the graduation of DSO members. We shared an open relationship with the Americans, and also with the British through Scotland Yard. There was also a formal arrangement with 'Wall Street's Private Eye' Kroll International, a US-based investigations consultancy. But at no point did anyone in the NPA come to me to say that they were in touch with any other foreign intelligence service.

I do believe the Special Browse Mole Report, as suggested by some commentators, played a major role in tilting the balance of forces between the Scorpions and its foes in the Zuma camp. It fed into claims of a conspiracy against Zuma, and here was the DSO meddling in matters that were not within its domain by making allegations that JZ was conspiring against Mbeki and that there had been infiltration by foreign intelligence services. It was easy for COSATU and Zuma's supporters to milk that. I think McCarthy and Mbeki know more than what is in the public domain. Ginwala never made a finding on Manala Manzini's credibility, but in my opinion he has shown himself to have been an unadulterated liar whose credibility is in tatters, while Tim Dennis – former DG of SASS – proved to be honest and truthful at all times.

Of course, I must take the blame for the fact that the report originated from within the DSO, an outfit for which I was ultimately responsible. I didn't ask that this type of report be generated – it was simply brought to me and the person who handed it to me did not disclose that he was the one who had initiated it.

I would be interested to hear McCarthy's version of events. If he does not dispute Powell, then it would be a disappointment. He was reporting to me and so I must take responsibility and, morally, I must carry the blame.

On 24 May 2006, I received a letter from the director of public prosecutions (DPP) in Malawi, requesting assistance with an investigation into a conspiracy to overthrow the government of Malawi and assassinate President Bingu wa Mutharika. The vice-president of Malawi, Cassim 'Kaka' Chilumpha, had been arrested along with 12 other former ruling United Democratic Front politicians in connection with the plot. Chilumpha had allegedly hired 'expert assassins from South Africa' to kill Mutharika and the hit men had turned state witness against him.

I forwarded the request to the department of justice and the following month the DPP in Malawi called me to ask if we could meet. I agreed and invited Menzi Simelane, DG of justice, to attend. Then the Malawian DPP informed me that his minister of justice also wanted to attend. However, given that the minister was a politician, I felt that this request should be processed by the department of foreign affairs, although I could receive the DPP as my counterpart and colleague. I placed a call to the president's advisor Mojanku Gumbi and told her the minister wanted to come to see me. She gave me the go-ahead.

When we met, the Malawian DPP briefed me about the plot and explained that they wanted some investigations to be done in South Africa. I told him any request for assistance would have to come through the department of justice as the central authority and that it would be channelled through to us if we were the right institution to deal with the case. After that meeting, because I felt that the matter would require foreign intelligence assistance, I informed the DG of SASS. A formal request for mutual legal assistance from Malawi was sent and was processed by Simelane in terms of the International Co-operation in Criminal Matters Act and the approval of the minister was secured. It was then referred to the NPA and we were authorised to collate the information requested.

At the Ginwala Inquiry, Simelane claimed he had told me that the matter should be investigated by SASS before the request had even come through to us. He claimed I had told him that the DSO was already involved in the probe, but this was not true.

The state's main complaint against me at the inquiry was that my interaction with the Malawian authorities was not appropriate because it did not fall into my competence and that I should not have been dealing with a foreign intelligence operation. I had 'undertaken investigations into the conspiracy to assassinate the Malawian president', which 'amounted to an intelligence gathering exercise'.

The argument was that my failure to discharge my obligation to inform the minister of justice of the assassination plot when I first became aware of it yet again showed my lack of sensitivity in dealing with matters of national security. The state argued that I should have informed the minister because the conspiracy involved a South African citizen and was partially planned in the country. The NIA DG Manala Manzini also criticised me, during the evidence he gave at the Ginwala Inquiry saying that I never should have got involved. Manzini's affidavit was not publicly released at the inquiry because it was in itself considered to be a matter of national security.

In response to the state's case at the inquiry, my legal team and I pointed out that Minister Mabandla had not supported any claims that I had failed to inform her of a request for mutual legal assistance, which were made in the government's first submissions. I submitted that the only reason for this omission was that there was no truth to the contention. Her DG, Simelane, had joined me in the meeting with the Malawian DDP about the Chilumpha case. I also explained that the extent of the NPA's involvement in the investigation amounted to finding out whether a certain identified suspect had on specified dates stayed overnight at particular hotels in Johannesburg and Durban.

I presented a series of correspondence to the inquiry that included letters from the department of justice and constitutional development in which it is confirmed that the minister had been informed and had authorised the assistance. A further letter, dated 6 December 2006, thanks the NPA for its handling of the request.

Ginwala found that I had not been improperly meddling in foreign intelligence, but she felt that I – and Simelane – should have brought the plot to the minister's attention sooner:

> *The documents submitted before the Enquiry do not point to any investigation that Adv Pikoli would have undertaken nor the involvement by Adv Pikoli in matters of intelligence. On the contrary, the documents clearly show that the request from Malawi was indeed handled strictly in accordance with the provisions of the law and that the NPA merely collated the information requested by the Malawian DPP. And this they did at the request of the DG: Justice who is the central authority in terms of the International Co-operation in Criminal Matters Act. The DG: Justice also concedes that the Minister was informed when the formal request was processed by his officials. However there is no evidence that the DG: Justice specifically advised the Minister that there was a conspiracy in South Africa to assassinate the head of state of a neighbouring country, and there was a responsibility on the DG: Justice to bring this matter to the attention of the Minister. Similarly Adv Pikoli had such a responsibility to the Minister to alert her when he first became aware of this conspiracy, and he failed to do so. This constituted a failure to appreciate the responsibility of an NDPP to appraise the Minister on an issue that may impact on matters of national security.*
>
> *I cannot find that the Government has established that Adv Pikoli is guilty of investigating any intelligence matter or conspiracy or involved himself in an area outside his mandate. However, he ought, in my view, to have brought to the attention of the Minister that there was a plot to assassinate the Malawian President involving South African citizens and which was at least partially planned in South Africa. These are matters of national security which the executive is entitled to know in order to advise itself on what position to take in its global relations and international responsibilities.*

I was taken aback when the state focused on the Malawian investigation as one of the grounds for my suspension. As far as I was concerned, the matter had been appropriately dealt with by the Scorpions. The requests were set up through the proper channels and the minister even thanked us for the manner in which we had handled it. I had informed SASS timeously and the matter wasn't raised again at the time in 2006. Instead, it popped up again in 2008 when the state needed ammunition against me. An attack also came from Manala Manzini, who, it was established, was a close ally of Jackie Selebi and who was central to attempts to discredit the case against Selebi.

I felt it was clear that the charges were an afterthought and were trumped up to try to strengthen the case against me.

ANC Secretary-General Kgalema Motlanthe was handed a brown envelope outside his office in Luthuli House. Inside the envelope was a set of e-mails that named senior ANC members who were apparently conspiring against Jacob Zuma. According to an affidavit Motlanthe would later sign, he was 'shocked and disturbed' after reading the documents and immediately contacted Police Commissioner Jackie Selebi and NIA chief Billy Masetlha about the exchanges before tabling the documents at an ANC national executive committee (NEC) meeting.

These e-mails would become central to what is now known in South Africa as the 'Hoax E-mail Saga': 73 pages of fake e-mails and chat-room exchanges between senior ANC politicians, such as former Deputy President Phumzile Mlambo-Ngcuka, white media personalities, ex-DA leader Tony Leon and members of the NPA, including myself. The conversations were purported to contain claims of a political conspiracy led by a Xhosa faction within the ANC against Zuma and Motlanthe and any other political opponent who stood in the way of their political ambitions. This was in the midst of a succession battle within the ruling party as support for Zuma was growing against President Mbeki. The scandal would lead to a major political falling-out and the axing of Masetlha, the country's spy boss, who would also face criminal charges in court.

In October 2005, before the contents of the e-mails hit the media, Intelligence Minister Ronnie Kasrils issued a public statement warning against the 'sinister' and 'clearly fraudulent' e-mails doing the rounds and announced that Inspector-General of Intelligence Zolile Ngcakani was investigating their origins. He made it clear that they were 'crude, sinister and clearly fake'. Kasrils had already suspended three of his intelligence chiefs – Masetlha, Lizo Gisbon Njenje and Bob Mhlanga – for allegedly conducting unlawful surveillance on businessman Saki Macozoma, who was also central to the e-mail conspiracy.

Ngcakani's report later revealed that the saga started when the NIA began an operation named 'Project Avani', which looked at the political landscape within the ANC, without the knowledge of Kasrils. The e-mails were 'introduced' into the intelligence system and resulted in a climate of conspiracy – they had been artificially constructed and were made to appear as genuine electronic communication.

Masetlha was fired in March 2006 and was charged with withholding information and failing to cooperate with Ngcakani in his investigation into the saga. IT expert Muziwendoda Kunene and former NIA manager for electronic surveillance Funokwakhe Madlala were also charged for their roles in producing the e-mails. Kunene was allegedly paid R152 000 to intercept e-mails between certain individuals and hand over the information to Masetlha. Madlala allegedly made sure that Masetlha received the e-mails. All three denied any knowledge of the e-mails and were acquitted in 2009.

I first came to know that my name featured in the Hoax E-mail Saga in early 2006, when I was told by Selebi. He wanted to send Crime Intelligence officers to interview me at my office. I cooperated fully with them and I made available my laptop and my desktop computer for them to go through, and they also had access to the NPA's server, which on its own could have been a risky affair. Selebi also sent the e-mails through to me to have a look at.

When I saw the 'intercepted' correspondence I immediately realised they must be fake and was astounded that I was being smeared in such a way. I didn't even know what a chat room was at the time (I do now) – I was simply ignorant about these things. I also had never communicated with the people who were named in my so-called e-mails. I was amazed at how people could be so twisted to try to create these conspiracies. The following is an example of one exchange to which I was supposedly party, as replicated in the *Mail & Guardian* article on 15 December 2005, 'Spy-war e-mails: What they really say':

> *Macozoma to Vusi Pikoli, September 12*
> *SM: I had a chat with Bulelani regarding the issues at hand. I think we need to up the tempo on Masetla [sic] given the latest developments … We are fast getting into trouble that could stall all our plans. What are your boys finding on this guy? He needs to be replaced ASAP!!*
> *VP: As you know I had to take leave and relax a bit from all these pressures. You guys need to help me out here … [Bulelani Ngcuka] is offering me some shares in Amabubesi … Should I accept? For now my guys don't have anything on Masetla. However one of my guys, Nel, has a potential good friend in NIA, in the technology section … he may be able to assist. I agree that Masetla is becoming a problem. Only you can influence the decision of redeployment with the Chief.*
> *SM: I'm glad you have a potential ally on the inside. Let's use the* Boers *where we can.*

I had also supposedly e-mailed Frank Chikane:

> *As discussed, the final assault will take place. We have resolved to attack all Zuma's residences including his house in Nkandla [and] Johannesburg. We are also going after his lawyer and other friends of his to destroy this hope he is beginning to have. We'll use the 'A-team' from the old days and a few darkies to sprinkle on.*

The ANC NEC rejected the intelligence inspector-general's report that the e-mails were a hoax and Motlanthe appointed a task team to test the authenticity of the mails. I could not conceive how Motlanthe honestly believed that those e-mails were genuine and how he brushed off Chikane when he raised the matter with him. Included on the task team were stalwarts such as Hermanus Loot, Josiah Jele, 'Aunt Sophie' de Bruyn and Advocate Patric Mtshaulana. I was called to appear before that inquiry at Luthuli House.

It didn't take long before the e-mails were dismissed. I assured the inquiry that I had had no knowledge of the hoax e-mails and had not played any part in the production of them. My evidence lasted for less than five minutes. However, one of the team members grabbed the opportunity to raise his concerns about the case against Zuma and to tell me that it was all a conspiracy and no grounds for a credible prosecution. I, however, refused to be drawn on the matter and stated that we, as the NPA, act on the facts placed before us and decisions taken are purely prosecutorial.

In closing, Aunt Sophie de Bruyn, whom I deeply respect for the role she played in our past, asked, 'Comrade Vusi, can you please tell us why is the ANC in this mess? Why are we having all these problems?' It was a searching question and I believed it deserved an honest answer, especially as Aunt Sophie is one of the most honest and loyal members of the movement.

'Aunt Sophie, I strongly believe that the problems we have are because we might have thought that – as the ANC – we were ready to govern, politically, but we never gave serious thought to how the ANC would survive as a political party financially. The reason being that when we were in exile, we were dependent on donations as an organisation. We were dependent on the Anti-Apartheid Movement and Scandinavian countries for food, for clothes, for everything that we had. When we came back to South Africa, we had to participate as an ordinary political party in normal politics in a democracy and we had to establish 10 offices with full-time staff. Where were we going to get all the money from to pay these people competitive salaries? Nine provincial offices and a national office. And if we are to attract quality people, we have to pay well. Now, that's when we started thinking of establishing companies like Thebe, the investment arm of the ANC that would be able to contribute to the running of the organisation.

'We had to find ways of sustaining the ANC financially and we began having problems with fraud and corruption. Situations would arise where comrades would do fund-raising for the ANC, they would receive five million from one quarter, the comrades will perhaps just pass on three million to the ANC and take two million to put in their pockets. It was an entirely new environment for us. We were from the bush and now we were in government. I think this is the source of all evil.'

Aunt Sophie was not impressed. She said, 'No, Comrade Vusi, you are wrong. We had honest comrades in Lusaka and they looked after our monies well.'

I said, 'Well, it could well be, Aunt Sophie, but we are in South Africa now; things have changed.' I think my frankness on the origins of the problems we were facing really hurt her, but I still stand by what I said.

The ANC task team found that the e-mails were electronically genuine and put forward the names of those responsible, but the NEC rejected the report based on procedural flaws. Media reports at the time also suggested the NEC was concerned that a 'Mr X', an unidentified IT specialist, had hacked into the Scorpions investigators' computers to demonstrate that the e-mails were authentic.

I was not aware of the hacking into the NPA's system and we had the highest level of security on our computers. If someone had tried to hack us, it would have come to our attention immediately. During that period, late 2006 to early 2007, the Scorpions were investigating Jackie Selebi and it was clear to us that the SAPS was intercepting our e-mails because Selebi had referred to some of our intercepted mail, which he had in his possession, during an interview with him. We were fully awake to trying to secure our systems but the police had more capacity than us in that field.

As with Browse Mole and the Malawian investigation, the Hoax E-mail Saga was a painful example of how state institutions were manipulated to serve the personal interests of certain individuals.

This became evident again in August 2013, when the suspended general secretary of trade union federation COSATU released a rogue intelligence report that implicated me. Zwelinzima Vavi released the document as proof that his suspension was politically motivated and described it as a 'total fabrication'. It claimed that I had consulted with a US agency called the National Endowment for Democracy (NED) on President Jacob Zuma's corruption prosecution and that I had advised Dr Mamphela Ramphele's political party Agang. I didn't even know there was such a thing as the NED and I never played any role in Agang or had any discussions with Ramphele. I dismissed the report as rubbish. Unlike the Browse Mole and Hoax E-Mails, no one knows the origins of this document and I don't know who is responsible. This report was another example of personal agendas being driven and innocent people being damaged in the fallout.

State institutions are there to serve members of the public and not individuals. It is completely immoral for anyone in a position of power to abuse these institutions for personal interests because this undermines the tenets of our Constitution and erodes public confidence in these institutions. They become nothing more than a political playground, when they are meant to serve the interests of the public. It is morally wrong and I would not stand for it.

Untruths and half reconciliation

The National Unity and Reconciliation Act that established the Truth and Reconciliation Commission (TRC) provided for the prosecution of all those who had applied for but were refused amnesty. It also allowed for the prosecution of those who might not have applied for amnesty, but were subsequently implicated in gross human rights violations.

After the final TRC report was handed over to President Thabo Mbeki in 2003, he laid the grounds for the potential prosecution of those who may have been refused amnesty. In his speech to parliament, he announced that there would be no general amnesty:

> *Any such approach, whether applied to specific categories of people or regions of the country, would fly in the face of the TRC process and subtract from the principle of accountability which is vital not only in dealing with the past, but also in the creation of a new ethos within our society.*

Mbeki also left the door open for the security cluster to find a way of dealing with matters that needed to be prosecuted:

> *Government is of the firm conviction that we cannot resolve this matter by setting up yet another amnesty process, which in effect would mean suspending constitutional rights of those who were at the receiving end of gross human right violations. We have therefore left this matter in the*

hands of the National Directorate of Public Prosecutions, for it to pursue any cases that, as is normal practice, it believes deserve prosecution and can be prosecuted. This work is continuing.

However, as part of this process and in the national interest, the National Directorate of Public Prosecutions, working with our intelligence agencies, will leave its door open for those who are prepared to divulge information at their disposal and to co-operate in unearthing the truth, for them to enter into arrangements that are standard in the normal execution of justice, and which are accommodated in our legislation. This is not a desire for vengeance; nor would it compromise the rights of citizens who may wish to seek justice in our courts.

A unit was established within the NPA tasked with dealing with TRC prosecutions. It was headed by Special Director Advocate Anton Ackerman and its official title was the Priority Crimes Litigation Unit (PCLU). That unit had a working relationship with the police to carry out investigations that would assist in prosecutions.

After the president accepted the TRC recommendations, it soon became clear that there was a fear of potential prosecutions both within the police and within the ranks of the ANC.

I was still the DG of justice when we got wind of the fact the NPA was about to prosecute 34 members of the ANC's senior leadership. They had previously applied to the TRC for amnesty but were refused on the basis that they had done so as a collective. The TRC found that each person had to say what he or she had done and apply individually.

As the department of justice was responsible for the TRC and was central to the process, I had to discuss the matter with Bulelani Ngcuka. I was the de facto deputy chair of the justice crime-prevention cluster so it was my task to look into it.

I asked Ngcuka whether there was any truth to the rumour, and he explained that his team, led by Advocate Anton Ackerman, had probed the matter and had met with the police's Crime Intelligence unit to ask for its assistance in carrying out the investigation. Ackerman, who could be brash and abrasive, had some nasty things to say about the Scorpions in that meeting with the SAPS because he had his own frustrations when it came to the DSO.

Ackerman was looking at taking a balanced approach with the idea that if he was going to be objective and prosecute those from the ANC, he would then have to look at prosecuting the old-order police too.

Ngcuka explained that the investigators had looked at the TRC files and could find no grounds on which to prosecute the 34 ANC leaders and the docket had thus been closed. Ngcuka had also reported this to President Mbeki, but – for whatever reason – it was never really accepted. Perhaps the ministers of the cluster didn't trust Ngcuka.

National Police Commissioner Jackie Selebi was the one who seemed to be sowing this distrust, urging the ministers not to accept the decision. He felt that Ackerman was pushing for the prosecution and that there were counter-revolutionary or reactionary prosecutors that wanted to go after the ANC leaders. Selebi's open dislike of the Scorpions and his misplaced belief that the Scorpions had a hidden agenda made him vocal on this issue.

When I came into office as NDPP, the matter was still lurking in the background. It came to the fore again when the issue of prosecuting Adriaan Vlok and Johan van der Merwe arose. Vlok had been the law and order minister in the apartheid government, while Van der Merwe was the police chief.

Advocate Ackerman came to me in 2005 to say that he was considering prosecuting Vlok and Van der Merwe, along with three other policemen, for the 1989 attempted murder of Reverend Frank Chikane. They had conspired to place a substance called Paraoxon in Reverend Chikane's clothing, causing him to fall seriously ill as the poison attacked his nervous system, and he was admitted to hospital on several occasions. At the time, Chikane was secretary-general of the South African Council of Churches (SACC).

When Ackerman and I looked at the case, it seemed to be a clear matter. It was well known that the men had not applied for amnesty for the poisoning of Chikane and this was one of the obvious cases that flowed from the TRC. I told Ackerman to go ahead and do his job.

But because in some quarters, the justice security cluster included, the issue was being interpreted as the NPA gunning for ANC cadres, the subject was even tabled at the ANC's NEC meeting. They were convinced that we were simply opening up a way that would lead to the prosecution of

ANC people and that there was malicious intent on the part of the NPA. I don't know why I was not trusted, because the truth was that there were no matters involving the ANC on the table at the time.

Then, leading up to the court case, Chikane expressed concern that his matter was becoming part of a dispute over guidelines on how to handle sensitive post-TRC cases. Chikane was to be the complainant in the matter so he was in a difficult position. He couldn't stop the NPA from prosecuting, but he was nevertheless uncomfortable with the process.

Several NGOs, including the Khulumani Victims' Support Group, also challenged the process, saying the guidelines under which Vlok and Van der Merwe were to be prosecuted were too lenient and amounted to a rerun of the TRC. They were worried that new opportunities were being created for apartheid criminals to seek indemnity from prosecution with no benefits or opportunities being extended to victims and survivors of atrocities.

It was a remarkably tough time for me. At one stage, I was involved in serious discussions with Janet Love, the head of the Legal Resources Centre, which was challenging the TRC guidelines. She is an old comrade and friend, and we worked together in exile. We spent much time discussing the matter as we attempted to try to close the chapter so we could move on with our lives.

The way forward was something of a balancing act and a compromise, because the law said that people had to be prosecuted and the president had accepted that by stating there was not going to be a general amnesty. People had to face prosecution. But the ministers, the president's men and women, were reluctant to carry out what the president had instructed. The new Prosecutions Policy was intended to accommodate these concerns: people had a chance to come forward and disclose information, but the NPA would have to decide whether or not to prosecute.

It was an extremely difficult situation and nobody was entirely sure in which direction to move. We wanted to close the chapter, we wanted to move ahead with reconciliation, but there could be no general amnesty. So what do you do then? It was a half-hearted job, full of ambivalence, and we were walking on eggshells.

When Vlok and Van der Merwe made representations that they should not be prosecuted, I decided to set up a team to advise me internally, to look at the representations and to help me make a decision. I felt I should not accept the representations but I wanted another opinion too.

The issue for me was that the two men were implicated not only in the Chikane matter but in many other cases too. That is when the prospect of a plea bargain began to arise. Ackerman largely agreed and felt the deal would be a good move – as long as they undertook to tell us the entire truth about the Chikane poisoning.

Before agreeing on the deal, we of course also had to involve the victim. So, in order to get Chikane's viewpoint on the matter, Ackerman – together with his fellow prosecutor Mthunzi Mhaga – held meetings with Chikane prior to the plea bargain being agreed upon. We felt, though, that he was blowing hot and cold on the topic. He was cautious, saying he didn't want his case to be used in any internal battles that were taking place, but he also didn't want to stop the NPA from going ahead. Chikane never encouraged us to go for the full prosecution, but he did express reluctance about the plea bargains.

I even went to see him myself to be sure he was satisfied with the decision. He never said, 'Vusi, why don't you just prosecute these people?' His saying so would have been a major contributing factor because we couldn't have a key witness who was opposed to the deal.

When he testified for the state against me at the Ginwala Inquiry, Chikane complained that he never saw the final plea-bargain agreement before it was signed. I think that, out of courtesy, he should have been shown the agreement and I know that there was constant interaction between him, Mhaga and Ackerman.

In his testimony, Chikane described the experience as 'hostile, painful and degrading'. And, to this day, I don't understand what he means. I think his issue may have been with Ackerman because Chikane complained that Ackerman had been hostile towards him. I went to see Chikane to address that concern and I never got the impression that he felt so deeply about it. If he felt that his treatment at the hands of the NPA was so degrading and painful, I would certainly have addressed that concern and would have personally apologised to him.

In August 2007, Vlok and Van der Merwe pleaded guilty together with the three other officers, in exchange for suspended sentences as per Section 105A of the Criminal Procedure Act. The two men were sentenced to 10 years in prison, wholly suspended for five years. I would have preferred a full prosecution. Vlok and Van der Merwe had not disclosed everything and were only prepared to admit to what was already in the public domain regarding the poisoning. A full prosecution would have established the real truth.

The prosecution of Vlok and Van der Merwe was frustrating because the state, on whose behalf we were prosecuting, did not want us to prosecute them. On the other hand, the law required a prosecution. The plea and sentence bargain was thus a compromise. It resulted in their conviction and sentence – even though it was a suspended sentence. It was not what we wanted but it was the best we could achieve under those difficult circumstances where we did not even enjoy the support of the minister of justice.

I also would have been keener to go for a full prosecution if we had had a proper investigation and more evidence, but we simply couldn't rely on the police – and there was no point in going ahead if we didn't have the proof to back up the charges.

To the best of my knowledge, the Vlok/Van der Merwe case remains one of only two TRC cases to have been successfully prosecuted by the NPA. I can only speak for myself as to why this is the case – during my tenure as NDPP, there were many matters to which I attended. I had said to the team they should go ahead and investigate, and when matters were ready for decisions to be made, they should bring them to me. I have heard little about any TRC cases being followed up on in the past few years and Ackerman has since retired.

There have been other attempts at reconciliation – such as when Vlok requested to wash the feet of Reverend Chikane – and I have no problems with reconciliation, as long as it is has a genuine motive. Obviously we can't live in the past – we want to move forward and build a new country. For me, it has to be founded on justice and on the basis of people being genuine about true reconciliation. So the fact that there seems to be reluctance on the part of the state to go ahead with these cases means that there is almost a 'half reconciliation'.

Shortly after the plea bargains were agreed in court, the burning issue of the ANC prosecutions reared its ugly head again when a newspaper article claimed that the NPA was preparing to prosecute the ANC leaders. The article made reference to a letter written by Advocate Ackerman, so I immediately called Ackerman to ask him if there was any truth to the matter. He insisted he knew nothing about it so I contacted the police through Head of Detective Services Johan de Beer. He undertook to mail the letter to me, which he did.

Ackerman and I looked at the letter and came to the conclusion it had been fabricated and distorted. It was a letter written much earlier, during Ngcuka's tenure, but it had been tampered with to appear as though it was more recent. Someone within the police had changed the date on the document.

Fortunately, the person who had typed the original letter for Ackerman had included a reference on the document – but, she no longer worked with him. This was evidence that the letter could not have been recent. I had no idea as to how they were able to hack into Ackerman's computer and I immediately instituted a criminal investigation because I was holding what was essentially a fraudulent document.

This was all happening when we were about to arrest Selebi and he was understandably under significant pressure. It was also the height of the battle between the SAPS and the Scorpions. I suspect Selebi was doing whatever he could to discredit me and had planted the letter with the media. I was furious and rebuked the police and told them they would be investigated.

Following that threat, I was called to a meeting that was attended by several cabinet ministers, directors-general and Jackie Selebi. They wanted answers from me about the TRC prosecutions and my instituting an investigation into the police.

It was a bad, bad meeting and at the end of it I wanted to resign.

I explained that, by law, we were bound to continue with the prosecutions of those who did not apply for or who were refused amnesty. This is what we were in the process of doing and no one could stop us from doing that. In terms of the Prosecutions Policy, I explained that we had to amend it and, while we received a lot of criticism for the changes, we thought it was the best way of trying to deal with the matter under the circumstances. It would be up to the NDPP to decide on who was going to be charged and who wasn't. Those in the meeting then pushed me on the issue of investigating the police.

At one point I had a heated stand-off with Selebi. We very nearly came to blows. I stared him in the eyes and shouted, 'For once in your life, can you just tell the truth about this letter and shame the devil! This is a forged letter and this matter had been discussed previously – and you know what the correct position is about this letter.'

In response, he declared open war between the NPA and the police – right there, in a meeting where tensions were already on the brink of boiling over. We were sitting directly across from one another – fortunately, there was a boardroom table separating the two of us – and it was a fiery exchange. I kept saying, 'He's lying. Jackie, you are lying.' I was not willing to back down and I was incensed at the accusations Selebi was making against the NPA.

I couldn't understand the hold Selebi had over the ministers and why they were trying to protect him. I felt that I was fighting a lone battle and that I was no longer trusted. Nobody was prepared to listen.

I felt so low at that point that I went straight to my cousin's offices in Cape Town and told him I needed a new job. I was ready to resign and go work with him in business. I was ready to throw it all in.

It took some time before I calmed down and realised that the work of the NPA could not be defined by the disagreements between Selebi and me. I had taken an oath of office to carry out my duties and I simply had to do so. In that time of turmoil, I also remembered what was said to me by veteran advocate George Bizos in a seminar we had both attended. Prophetically, he had told me that when things got tough, I should never consider resigning.

Then Chief Justice Pius Langa also shared a similar message with me: if I was ever thinking of resigning from the position of NDPP, I should talk to him first. I had always enjoyed a good working relationship with Justice Langa and occasionally we would have lunch together or he would visit me at my home.

The words of both those legal giants echoed in my ears and I decided not to resign. That decision would be taken for me a month later, however.

The bones

Mandy Wiener

The Missing Persons Task Team (MPTT) deals in bones.

The unit was established in 2004 within the Priority Crimes Litigation Unit of the National Prosecuting Authority (NPA). It is tasked with conducting investigations into cases of missing persons who disappeared in political circumstances between 1 March 1960 and 10 May 1994. To date, the team has overseen over 80 exhumations and has investigated hundreds of cases of missing persons, having positively confirmed identities through elaborate forensic analysis and DNA testing. In some instances, remains have been handed to families and moving repatriation ceremonies have been held, bringing finality to decades of torturous grief.

They are a small team that operates on a budget of just a million rand a year for DNA testing, transport and excavations. This is minuscule in comparison to budgets of other governments around the world, such as Cuba, which has funded a team for 12 years to search for the remains of just one soldier in the Bolivian jungle. The Americans have an entire unit based in Hanoi dedicated to recovering the remains of pilots missing from the Vietnam War, the members of which sit in fields sieving soil, searching.

Included on the list of successes for Madeleine Fullard and her team at the MPTT are the closed cases of the Pebco Three – Sipho Hashe, Qaqawuli Godolozi and Champion Galela – who disappeared in 1985 near Cradock in the Eastern Cape, and the Cosas Two – Siphiwo Mthimkulu and Tobekile Topsya Madaka – who disappeared in 1982 in the same vicinity.

The apartheid-era Security Police had confessed to the TRC that all five had been shot and their bodies burned at an old, abandoned police station called Post Charmers near Cradock and then thrown into the Fish River.

Security policeman Gideon Niewoudt and others had described how they had removed the ashes and had thrown them in the river. Fullard and her team did not hold out much hope, but were determined to search for their remains regardless. In 2009, with the help of archaeologists, they were able to establish traces of a large fire and ultimately excavate a three-by-two-metre pit containing the remains of three adult men. They also discovered the site of a surface fire and just a few bone fragments and a tooth. A farmer had built a fence through the area and over time there had been a great deal of disturbance.

Fullard and her team established that the security policemen had pushed the remaining ash from the 1982 fire into a neighbouring septic tank. The MPTT set about draining the tank and what came pouring out, along with 20 000 litres of raw sewerage, were burnt bone fragments, bits of tyres, beer bottles and the charcoal from the original fires. More than 20 years after the Pebco Three and Cosas Two were killed, their partial remains were discovered and their families were able to find closure.

The success buoyed Fullard and her unit and, as a result, they began to take another look at some of the burnt-remains cases handed to them by the TRC. Amongst those they were keen to finalise was that of Sizwe Kondile.

'The story of Sizwe Kondile is actually one of the iconic cases that came out of the TRC that has stuck in people's memory. People have fragments of memory around different stories of the TRC, but almost anyone you talk to will remember Dirk Coetzee talking about how they burnt the body of Sizwe Kondile on one side and they braaied on the other and how they had to turn the meat and turn the body and so on,' says an NPA investigator with knowledge of the case. 'It's a very horrifying image that people won't know it's Sizwe Kondile, but they know that case. That image, it's the kind of heartlessness of cooking meat for eating on one side and burning the body on the other. That's the kind of remnant or fragment of the TRC that stays in people's memories. And that was really the power of the TRC to sort of embed those fragments, even if it's not connected to a coherent story of Sizwe Kondile. It's those fragments that people remember and are kind of very powerful.'

The MPTT needed to know a location. They were looking for something incredibly specific, such as traces of fire in the soil, but this was made difficult with the passage of time, vegetation growth and massive site disruptions. As Sizwe had been killed in a similar manner to the Pebco Three and Cosas Two, on a wood fire with diesel, the unit considered whether it might be possible to recover any remains in his case. The perpetrators had told the TRC that he was burnt in a surface fire that was lightly covered with soil and scattered. His burnt remains had been left uncovered on the site, which would have exposed them to greater deterioration and disintegration than those of the Pebco Three and Cosas Two. Nevertheless, Fullard was optimistic and felt it was necessary to locate the site. If her unit could do that, they might be able to narrow down an area for excavation and soil sieving. Two sorts of experts would be required – forensic archaeologists, who would be able to identify the markings of a large fire on the soil, and forensic anthropologists, specialists in the human skeleton, who could identify the small fragments of burnt bone.

In 2009, Advocate Anton Ackerman, who headed the Priority Crimes Litigation Unit and was the prosecutor in former Vlakplaas commander Dirk Coetzee's trial, approached Coetzee for assistance in the Kondile matter, amongst others. Coetzee was willing to help but all he could recall were the names of two farms they had visited near Komatipoort, Avondstond and Castilhopolis, and that the place where Sizwe was killed was the site from where the SADF had launched the Matola raid. In 1981, 12 people were killed in attacks on three ANC safe houses by SADF units who illegally crossed the border into Mozambique. Coetzee described the site as a 'farm off the Komatipoort to Border Gate road, where the road runs close to the Lebombo mountains and where there is a low crossing over the mountains to where a Mozambican road also runs close to the Lebombo mountains'. Advocate Ackerman took Coetzee out to do a preliminary search and they spent several days identifying possible locations. The former hit-squad commander could only remember that there were three cement bases that appeared to be the foundations of structures put there by the SADF for the raid.

During this visit in 2009, Coetzee identified a location as the site where Sizwe may have been killed in 1981. It was a vegetable patch on a private farm where labourers were growing produce. Fullard and her team brought in Candy, their mini excavator, and began to dig at the site, having had to negotiate with the workers whose veggie patch was being destroyed. Photographs of the dig show Coetzee standing amongst overgrown shrubbery staring blithely at a camera holding up a director's board with the date and location, like a criminal posing for a mugshot.

The site was trenched and examined by forensic archaeologists and anthropologists, both local and members of the Argentine Forensic Anthropology Team. By trenching in parallel lines, they hoped they would expose any major fire-site residue but were unsuccessful. The MPTT began to lose faith and realised that the site was geographically unlikely. The site thus lost credibility. The soil had never been disturbed and the farm workers, who had been on the land for decades, couldn't corroborate Coetzee's story. The area had changed dramatically – the roads, fencing and vegetation were all different. It was determined that while Dirk Coetzee's identification of the two farms was probably accurate, his specific site identification was incorrect. As a result, the investigation into the site was closed. Fullard gave up in despair and spent the next six months without much hope at all.

She and her team then decided to go back to Komatipoort and independently look for possible sites. They quizzed local police officers about areas that featured three cement bases and were surprised by just how many there were in the region. They pulled aerial strip photography of the area taken in 1979 and 1984 from the National Geo-Spatial Information Directorate but the resolution of the photographs was insufficient for small-scale study.

They drove up and down the border fence searching for potential locations. They searched mortuary books after it emerged that another detainee who died in 1988 during an interrogation had been disposed of in the river near a braai spot in the Komatipoort area. They approached the defence force for assistance in trying to verify the exact launch site of the Matola raid, but nothing really materialised.

Ultimately, the MPTT came up with two sites but forensic archaeologist Claudio Bisso determined that it was not viable to attempt excavation at either of them. The case went onto the back burner as other, more promising options were pursued. Fullard wanted Coetzee to assist with confirming which of the potential sites were most credible, but by then his health was deteriorating. Then, in March 2013, Coetzee died from kidney failure.

There was only one case in which he was still assisting the MPTT – that of Sizwe Kondile. He took with him to his grave the secret of the exact site where Sizwe was killed. Fullard had lost the only real lead she had.

Yet the MPTT has not given up hope. The only other real avenue to pursue now would be to track and trace the other security policemen who were at the scene of Sizwe's murder. Those who were not granted amnesty will almost certainly never speak of it. Failing a miracle, the MPTT will likely have to resort to organising a 'spiritual repatriation'. This has been done before in cases where a ceremony is arranged at a site, relatives are invited to attend and a ritual to take the spirit of the victim home is performed by a traditional healer.

Many relatives are desperate for bones. For others, as is the case of Charity Kondile, acknowledgement is all they truly want. They want those they have lost to be recognised as heroes and not to remain invisible for perpetuity.

The NPA has refused to comment officially on its ongoing investigation into Sizwe Kondile's death. It also declined numerous requests for Fullard to be interviewed for this book.

However, in June 2013, she travelled to Butterworth to meet Sizwe's mother, Charity Kondile, and his cousin Pat Kondile, to update them about the progress in the task team's search for her son's remains.

Fullard handed the Kondiles a report detailing the work her unit had done in searching for Sizwe's remains. According to that report, there is still a glimmer of possibility that the family can find closure:

> *It is our view that there is a fair chance that some remains can be recovered, even if very small and incomplete. Even in a formal crematorium where human remains are incinerated at much higher temperatures than those achieved in a wood and diesel fire, significant bone material exists at the end of the cremation. Even crematoriums then have to grind that material into ash. Although some of the perpetrators denied it, Dirk Coetzee stated that tyres were used in the fire. Tyres have an inner metal mesh that should be detectable by a metal detector.*
>
> *PROPOSAL:*
> *We propose that the MPTT take a metal detector to Site 3 and thoroughly*

> *scan the area for metal fragments. Through this we may be able to locate the fire site and thus a section of soil for sieving or closer examination for burnt bone fragments.*

On the final page of the report, Fullard offers the Kondiles the option of spiritual repatriation. She explains that several other MK members were killed and their remains disposed of in the Komatipoort area and have not been recovered. These include Selby Mavuso, who was abducted during the Matola raid of 1981 and killed the same year; a former ANC member who became a Vlakplaas *askari*, 'Peter'; and Stanza Bopape, an MK member from Mamelodi who was detained in 1988 and died in custody.

According to the report:

> *The first two were taken to the banks of the Komati River in 1981, drugged, shot and their bodies burnt. Their ashes were then pushed into the river. There is no possibility of recovering any remains. Stanza Bopape's body was reportedly thrown into the Komati River after he died in detention. No remains have been recovered.*
>
> *It is planned to take members of the abovementioned families to the site at the Komati River so that the families can conduct a spiritual repatriation. Spiritual repatriations are conducted in partnership with the TRC Unit in the Department of Justice and Constitutional Development (DoJ&CD) in cases where physical remains cannot be recovered.*

It is now up to the Kondile family to decide how to proceed and whether Fullard and her unit should continue to search for bones or if the repatriation of Sizwe's spirit will suffice.

PART FOUR

Suspended

Plea bargains and immunities

Brett Kebble regaled a story to a knot of enamoured senior government office bearers on the lawns of Gauteng Premier Tokyo Sexwale's lavish official residence in a forested suburb of Johannesburg. It was 1996 and a delegation of some provincial premiers, some members of the executive council, members of parliament, trade unionists and senior public servants, including Girly and me, were about to embark on a trip to Philadelphia in the USA. We were being sponsored to attend a business leadership course at the Wharton School of Business at the University of Pennsylvania. We would be trained on how to run successful economies and on the intricacies of the Industrial Development Zones. I was there in my capacity as special advisor to Justice Minister Dullah Omar. The entire trip was being funded and Kebble, a prolific ANC benefactor, had contributed funds through one of his companies.

It was the first time I had come across Kebble and my initial impression matched my expectations. I had always seen him as a progressive white businessman who was willing to help black people by empowering them economically and assisting them in their enterprises. He was a charming fellow, boisterous, gregarious and full of energy. He mixed easily with people and would laugh and talk politics and came across as genuinely progressive.

That meeting at Sexwale's residence was my first and only contact with Brett Kebble but it was the murderous end to his life that dramatically altered my own path.

We stumbled upon the Jackie Selebi investigation.

By the time I came into office the Scorpions' probe into Brett Kebble's financial affairs was well under way. Kebble had nothing but disdain for the DSO and he was insistent that the unit was being manipulated as part of a political feud between factions within the ANC. He accused Bulelani Ngcuka of using the organisation to suppress Zuma's growing power base and to prop up businessman Saki Macozoma's presidential ambitions. As a result, Kebble positioned himself close to the SAPS leadership and had a firm foothold within the ruling party. However, I wasn't aware of the complex criminal network linking the mining magnate to the national police commissioner that would be laid bare by the Scorpions' Operation Bad Guys.

When I was first told about Kebble's death on 27 September 2005, it came as a real shock. Little did I realise that the shots fired by hit-man Mikey Schultz into a Mercedes-Benz on that Melrose bridge would affect my own future, as well as that of the Scorpions, Selebi and the entire syndicate surrounding him.

I immediately suspected that Kebble had been murdered and the newspapers were full of rumours and stories about why he had been killed. It could have been simply a hijacking gone wrong, and those responsible had no idea who their victim was, or it could have been carefully planned and made to look like a robbery for more sinister reasons.

The SAPS immediately began investigating the shooting and we watched as newspaper columns were filled with reports about his car being removed and cleaned, how officers had compromised the crime scene and how his family had hired former Judge Willem Heath and forensic consultant David Klatzow to investigate. The Scorpions did not, however, get involved because this was viewed as a run-of-the-mill police matter, although there were clearly concerns about the progress of the investigation.

In January 2006, four months after Kebble was killed, Gerrie Nel – the head of the Scorpions in Gauteng – came to tell me that the director of public prosecutions in Gauteng, Advocate Charin de Beer, had written to the DSO requesting assistance with the murder investigation.

In the letter, De Beer made it clear that there was a very close relationship between Brett Kebble, National Commissioner Jackie Selebi, Kebble's head of security Clinton Nassif and businessman Glenn Agliotti. De Beer said that in order to verify these allegations, it was of the 'utmost importance' that their cellphone records be obtained and secured as evidence. However, the SAPS was experiencing extreme difficulties in acquiring these records and the five-month period for service providers to keep the records was about to lapse. This letter, coupled with information that was coming in from sources about the possible involvement of Mikey Schultz, Nigel McGurk and Fiazal 'Kappie' Smith, piqued Nel's interest.

Advocate De Beer came through to Pretoria to meet with us. Also in that meeting was the head of the DSO Leonard McCarthy, Chief Special Investigator and head of the Special National Projects Unit Andrew Leask, DSO Investigating Director Thanda Mngwengwe, my Special Director Kalyani Pillay, as well as Nel and De Beer's colleague Advocate Gerrit Roberts.

De Beer and Roberts informed us that they had been approached by Johan Diedericks, the investigating officer in the Kebble case, who had raised his concerns about the cellphone records. During his investigation, he had also come across the number of the national police commissioner and he wanted the detailed billing of Selebi's phone. Through careful cellphone technology and analysis, the police had established connections between phones belonging to Kebble, Agliotti and Selebi. De Beer recounted a story about how during a briefing with Selebi in which the phone numbers were discussed, the commissioner pulled out his phone and made a call to Agliotti. When the investigators had asked him for Agliotti's number, Selebi ignored them. During his corruption trial, he accused Chief Forensic Investigator Paula Roeland of lying about this version of events. The prosecutors had found Selebi's behaviour in the meeting peculiar and were worried that Selebi had inappropriately tipped Agliotti off. They wanted the NPA to assist with getting the detailed billing from the cellphone service providers.

Of course we were curious and the Scorpions began to scratch around. Two months after the meeting with De Beer and Roberts, the DSO hit pay dirt. Investigators were able to secure an explosive affidavit from Kebble's former head of security, Paul Stemmet, detailing his relationship with both Selebi and Agliotti. Stemmet, a former police reservist and karate expert, had met both Selebi and Agliotti during a Special Olympics promotion in Cape Town in 2001. In the affidavit, Stemmet revealed astonishing information about his security company, Palto, which emerged as Selebi's own dirty-tricks squad of vigilante freelancers who were using the SAPS and the commissioner as cover.

Further affidavits secured by the Scorpions from Palto employees revealed how cops moonlighting for the company carried out unlawful operations, such as planting Ecstasy in a man's home for retribution, making 'sushi' out of a debtor's koi fish on behalf of a businessman, and throwing explosive devices at a company's offices to encourage them to hire them as security.

Most alarming was a claim by Stemmet about how he had tipped Selebi off about Agliotti's involvement in a R105 million drug bust in Kya Sands in 2002, but the commissioner chose to ignore the warning. Instead, Selebi's photograph at the drug bust appeared on the front page of national newspapers. It would later emerge in court that Agliotti was, in fact, paid an informant's fee for the bust rather than having been arrested.

The Stemmet affidavit led to the official authorisation of Operation Bad Guys on 28 March 2006. The dominoes had begun to fall.

In a signed statement, McCarthy described the operation as follows:

> *It is an investigation into an organised crime network operating both in South Africa and abroad. I have been in the DSO for five years and I can confirm that this is one of the most extensive, complex and sensitive investigations that the DSO has ever undertaken. The investigation focuses on the offences of drug dealing, racketeering, money laundering, corruption and murder. Some of the allegations that are being investigated include: allegations of targeted corruption of senior law enforcement personnel; laundering of large amounts of local and foreign currency through at least seven destinations worldwide; smuggling of drugs from Europe through South Africa and on to other foreign destinations; the smuggling of large-scale contraband and counterfeit goods into South Africa; and the assassination of individuals who do not subscribe to the code of the criminal network.*

After I had viewed the Stemmet affidavit, I arranged a meeting with Justice Minister Brigitte Mabandla. I deliberately did so because I knew that individuals who were to be implicated in the investigation allegedly had close links with Selebi. I briefed the minister fully about the claims against the commissioner and how his name was cropping up but that there was nothing concrete connecting him to any crime. She was alarmed and we agreed I needed to meet with the president to inform him of these allegations.

I went to meet the president at his official residence, Mahlamba Ndlopfu. Mbeki and I were concerned about security issues, so he suggested we take a walk in the gardens so we could not be overheard. During our stroll on the lawns, I raised both the issue of the allegations against the cabinet minister and the concerns around Selebi.

Mbeki told me he would look into the matter regarding the minister and would report back to me. And he did come back to me to say that the person who had raised the issue was a disgruntled informant and the claims could not be taken seriously. I wasn't entirely happy with that response, but I had to be careful of picking too many battles at once and I didn't pursue it.

After I had relayed the gist of the allegations contained in Stemmet's statement as well as the concerns raised by De Beer, Mbeki instructed me to proceed with the investigation of the national commissioner. At that stage it appeared to us that Selebi was only protecting people whom he should not have been protecting. Of course, the president was shocked, but he also indicated he would not interfere in Operation Bad Guys. I knew he and Selebi were friends and had been close since Lusaka, but I felt that – irrespective of the president's relationship with Selebi – we had to do what was right. I also felt it would only be fair for Mbeki to know what was being alleged.

Those two meetings with Mabandla and Mbeki about Operation Bad Guys and Selebi were the first of many such briefings. Over the next two years I met Mabandla 13 times and Mbeki on 10 occasions to update them on our progress through both verbal and written reports. I continued to keep them informed at every step of the investigation and these briefings were always initiated by me when there was a new development.

In May 2006, the *Mail & Guardian* newspaper became aware that the DSO was investigating Agliotti. By virtue of the questions sent by the paper's journalists to spokesperson Makhosini Nkosi, it appeared as though the *Mail & Guardian* was going to report that Selebi was also the subject of a DSO investigation, which was not true at the time. He was yet to be identified as a formal suspect. I was annoyed the media had got wind of this investigation and had no idea how they had found out.

When I became NDPP I was sure that I was going to plug all the leaks and would take strong action against anyone who compromised the integrity of investigations. It was exactly what had happened between Zuma and Ngcuka that I was trying to avoid – much like the prima facie statement, Selebi's name would be put out there as a suspect without having been charged. It made me nervous and it had to be averted.

I asked McCarthy, Nkosi and the head of the Asset Forfeiture Unit Willie Hofmeyr to meet with Ferial Haffajee, the newspaper's editor at the time, to try to persuade the paper not to report that the DSO was investigating Selebi. A compromise was reached and there was appreciation for the sensitivity of the matter. The newspaper published a report on 26 May that made a vague statement that 'a wide-ranging fraud investigation by the Scorpions into Kebble's business appears to be probing the same links between Selebi, Nassif and Agliotti.'

We didn't want to dictate to the newspaper, but we were at such a sensitive point in the investigation. I believe that newspapers can play a role if they suspect a matter is not going to be fully investigated and the public has a right to know, but if it is a matter that is directed at a prosecution, there is a need for journalists to respect an investigation.

The next domino in Operation Bad Guys fell in July 2006. The DSO investigation led to a massive drug bust in Alberton, cracking an international smuggling syndicate. Steve Paparas and his father, Dimitrio, were amongst those who were taken into custody and the breakthrough became known as the 'Paparas Drug Bust'.

The tip-off had come from transport man and fixer Anthony Dormehl, who had been brought to the Scorpions by forensic investigator and self-appointed Selebi accuser Paul O'Sullivan. The Irishman had a long-running vendetta against the commissioner, stemming from an ugly dispute that had started when O'Sullivan was head of security at the Airports Company South Africa. As part of his crusade, he spent seven years dedicated to bringing down Selebi.

I didn't like O'Sullivan's involvement in the investigation and I didn't want it. I felt he would be more of a hindrance than a help to us because he came with baggage. I made myself very clear to both Leask and Nel that they should continue the investigation without involving any private eyes or anyone who might be seen to have personal gripes with the commissioner. I wanted a clean investigation that could not be clouded by personal motive or malice.

Following Dormehl's tip-off, the Scorpions began running Operation Coffee and an investigator infiltrated the drug syndicate. With the help of the Ekurhuleni Metro Police, the Scorpions cracked the network and swooped on a self-storage facility in Alberton where 672 kilograms of hashish and 1 114 kilograms of compressed cannabis, with a street value estimated at a quarter of a billion rand, were seized.

The Scorpions established that both Agliotti and Nassif had played a role in the logistics of moving the drugs and saw an opportunity to leverage complicity. Nassif, Agliotti and three other members of the syndicate entered into plea deals in exchange for their testimony against Steve Paparas, who, along with his father and driver Stanley Poonin, was ultimately acquitted. Robert Lottman – aka Bob the American – received a 10-year jail sentence, half of which was suspended as part of a plea bargain. Christiaan Alblas and Pedro Marques also entered into deals that saw them serve reduced prison time in exchange for their testimonies. Crucially, as part of their deals, Nassif and Agliotti agreed to testify for the state against Selebi in a possible corruption trial.

Just days after the Paparas bust, the *Mail & Guardian* came out linking the breakthrough to Agliotti and revealing his friendship with Selebi. Famously, Selebi was quoted as describing Agliotti as his 'friend, finish and *klaar*'.

I remember laughing when reading that quote and watching Selebi during a press conference demonstrating how clean his hands were. I thought, 'Well, he could be his friend, but what he is not saying is to what lengths he was prepared to go to save his friend.'

In light of Selebi's comments and information that had come to the fore, I believed it was again necessary to set up a meeting with the president. I called Mbeki and asked to see him, along with the ministers of justice, safety and security, and intelligence. The meeting was set up for early August 2006.

Only Mabandla and Mbeki were available to attend so I took them through the latest developments in the Bad Guys investigation, highlighting that Agliotti was part of an international drug syndicate and that Selebi had confirmed they were friends. I expressed the view that even though there were concerns about the link between the two, there was no evidence to show Selebi was involved in criminal activity. The meeting ended on the understanding that the investigations would continue.

In October 2006, the DSO arrested Clinton Nassif on a charge of insurance fraud related to damage he had inflicted on his own Mercedes-Benz. He was about to leave for the United States and was preparing to emigrate, but Leask succeeded in convincing Nassif to enter into a deal with the Scorpions.

Then, in a sworn statement, Nassif dropped the bombshell that Kebble had died as a result of a bizarre assisted suicide and revealed the names of Schultz, McGurk and Smith, confirming the identities of those who had killed the mining tycoon. Nassif also revealed in his affidavit that Kebble had channelled millions of rand to Selebi through bank accounts Spring Lights 6 and Misty Mountain Trading 18, which were both associated with Agliotti. The money was paid by Kebble via Agliotti in exchange for access to the commissioner. Nassif also claimed that Selebi had been protecting Agliotti by tipping him off about a Scotland Yard investigation into his drug involvement by showing him UK intelligence reports.

In return, Nassif wanted blanket indemnity for an array of crimes and a list of associates, including Agliotti, and as per Section 204 of the Criminal Procedure Act, a deal was struck with Nassif. He received indemnity from prosecution for his involvement in the murder and other crimes and in exchange undertook to testify for the state in the Kebble murder case and in Selebi's corruption trial.

I was so concerned about the contents of Nassif's affidavit that I felt it important to update Minister Mabandla, so I took a copy of the statement to my meeting with her and talked her through it in detail. I then did the same with President Mbeki in early November. The meeting with the president lasted for just over an hour and he closed it by recommending that I raise my concerns directly with Selebi. I considered this approach with my team and we finally concluded that I should meet with the commissioner.

I cried in that meeting. He cried in that meeting. Mine were tears of relief because I did not believe he could be facing accusations of that nature. I told him I believed him when he said he had never received the money.

I had called Selebi and asked to see him on an urgent matter. I didn't say what it was about, but I'm sure he must have suspected. We agreed to meet at my office at the VGM building on a Saturday morning, 11 November 2006.

At that meeting, I told Selebi his name kept coming up in our investigation Operation Bad Guys. I started off by broaching the subject of one of his official drivers who had been involved in suspicious activity, but a case against him had dubiously disappeared. It was really a test of Selebi's truthfulness. Then I asked him about the accounts and money that had been paid into them for his benefit, and about the UK intelligence reports implicating Agliotti in drug dealing, Palto and the protection of criminals. I laid it all out for him to respond to.

There I was, sitting with the national commissioner, whom I had known from my days in exile and with whom I had worked closely when I was DG of justice. Now I had to ask him difficult questions based on allegations against him.

During the meeting Selebi went off on a tangent. He started talking about the Scorpions and the vendetta they had against him because he wanted the unit to be shut down and incorporated into the SAPS. He raged about how he had never wanted the DSO to come into existence and because of this the unit had an agenda against him.

He revealed that he had seen Scorpions investigator Andrew Leask's performance appraisal and wanted to know why people like Leask were getting bonuses because of the work they were doing against the police.

I was surprised and asked, 'How did you get hold of Leask's performance appraisal?'

He refused to address the issue any further, but it fed into my suspicions that the police were intercepting our communications.

Some of the explanations he gave me about the accounts and the money being channelled through them were very convincing. On other aspects, however, he was less than convincing, so I felt we had to continue with the investigation. In a way, I was relieved by what he was telling me about the accounts and how convincing he was that he hadn't received any money. But then when I asked him about Agliotti and the UK reports, I suspected he was being less than truthful.

At that meeting I experienced a curious mix of emotions. At that stage I was still hoping Selebi was clean. I was hoping there had been some kind of a misunderstanding, that people were exaggerating things or lying about him. That was my allegiance to someone with whom I had worked closely, my comrade. Surely an ANC person could not be doing these things? It must all be a terrible mistake!

But at the same time, if there had been a mistake and he was indeed innocent, our investigation would have to be so thorough that his name would be cleared. This meeting was the only time I showed any weakness in dealing with Selebi. His arrogance as the investigation progressed hardened my attitude towards him. The more I began to believe that the man was guilty as charged, the more disappointed I became, because I had not expected him to be corrupt. I felt he would have to face the consequences of his actions. As the national commissioner of police and the president of international policing body Interpol, he should never have allowed himself to be compromised in that way.

We left the Saturday meeting with an understanding that on the Monday morning Selebi would check with his office about whether or not it had received the UK intelligence reports about Agliotti and report back to me. On the Monday, he did phone me but curiously he omitted any mention of the reports. Instead, he came back to me on the minor issue about the allegations against his driver.

I found his behaviour strange because I felt he should have been far more concerned about the serious allegation regarding the reports he had shown to Agliotti. It was at that point I began to believe that this man was lying to me.

I met with my team and briefed them on my meeting with Selebi. The next day I went to see the president and told him that even though I was of the view that the commissioner had not received payments, I remained concerned about the allegations. I felt that Leonard McCarthy should formally interview Selebi and the president offered no objection.

I then called Selebi and explained that there were some issues arising out of our meeting that we wanted to follow up on. He agreed to the interview with McCarthy, who went to see him armed with a tape recorder.

Meanwhile, Leask and his team were ready to move on Agliotti. On 14 November 2006, Mikey Schultz, Nigel McGurk and Fiazal 'Kappie' Smith signed affidavits confirming their status as '204' witnesses and, as per Section 204 of the Criminal Procedure Act, they were offered indemnity from prosecution for their role in the Kebble murder. In exchange, they undertook to testify truthfully against Agliotti. By doing so, and by again leveraging complicity, Agliotti would in turn be under pressure to testify against Selebi in his corruption trial.

After the affidavits were signed, the shooters had to go into hiding because there was a genuine concern that Selebi would send his guys after them. And, by all accounts, that is exactly what happened and the trio went on the run while the police hunted for them. Selebi knew that if they had turned against Agliotti, then his friend 'finish and *klaar*' would have to turn against him.

It was a bad night for me. I didn't sleep at all, worried about the safety of my men in the Scorpions' Bad Guys team. I was afraid the police would arrest them and throw everything into disarray. I kept checking with McCarthy, right into the early hours of the morning. The situation was hotting up and we believed the only thing that could diffuse it was the arrest of Agliotti.

Two days after the affidavits were signed, Agliotti was taken into custody at his home and arrested for the murder of Brett Kebble.

The greatest criticism of my tenure as NDPP remains focused on the decision to grant indemnity to criminals in exchange for their testimony as per Section 105A of the Criminal Procedure Act, which allows for plea bargains, and Section 204 of that same Act, which allows full immunity from prosecution.

Plea bargains have always been part and parcel of our law. Section 105A agreements happen almost on a daily basis throughout the country and are nothing new. Plea bargains are a device to ensure that prosecutors do not waste the court's time and save the costs of a trial where a matter can be settled.

At one stage during my term of office as the director-general in the department of justice and constitutional development, prosecutors from the bureau of justice assistance in New York came to encourage prosecutors to make use of plea-bargain arrangements. The benefit of this approach is to speed up matters and to ensure the cooperation of suspects in order to prosecute others who are guilty. It is important to note that plea bargains do not necessarily mean that suspects do not face jail time. Accomplice witnesses can give evidence in exchange for lesser sentences. The plea bargain, as a legal principle, has been used by prosecutors throughout the world.

Section 204 immunity arrangements are generally used in cases of organised crime where law-enforcement authorities are planning to bust crime syndicates. Immunity is international best practice in matters of organised crime, especially in cases involving corruption, which is often difficult to prove, because those who are involved in these crimes are seldom willing to talk. There is considerable reluctance to expose one another, simply because the one who corrupts is as guilty as the one who has been corrupted. Therefore it is very difficult to accumulate evidence, and at times the tactic of offering immunity must be implemented.

A prime example of this is the Selebi/Kebble matter.

When the Bad Guys team first came to me with the idea of offering 204 agreements to the shooters, Nassif and Agliotti, I didn't immediately buy into it and it took me some time to come around to the idea.

I said, 'Guys, whom then are we going to prosecute?' – because obviously it meant we were sacrificing a conviction in the Kebble murder trial in order to convict Selebi on corruption. A decision was ultimately taken to prosecute those who we suspected to be responsible for arranging the Kebble murder, Glenn Agliotti and John Stratton, whom we regarded as the kingpins at the top, and to enter into deals with the shooters – in other words, the runners. We never lost sight of the seriousness of the murder case but we were after the big guns.

I realised there would be a public outcry because most people would not understand the law, but I was prepared to face the fire. What most people see is a person who pulled a trigger roaming free. They don't realise that we have actually been able to bust a criminal syndicate right at the top. The 'button men', those who pull triggers for money, can be bought at any time. If they are sent to jail, others simply take their place. Much the same is true of runners in drug cartels, who can always be replaced. The only way to crack a syndicate is to kill it at the top.

I accept that the greatest criticism of my tenure is that I allowed Kebble's killers to go free, but what could possibly be worse than a national police commissioner who is a criminal himself: guilty of corruption and of protecting criminals? We would never have been able to solve the Kebble murder were it not for those deals. The police were in the dark and the case was stagnating, especially since the murder scene had been contaminated. The car had been washed and the evidence compromised, so the case was dead, dying, finished – until the Scorpions arrived.

Without the confessions of the shooters and them explaining the entire scenario, we would never have known what happened that night. We also ensured that the shooters remained on our radar in case they went on to commit other crimes. For me, criminals are criminals and we knew they had been involved in other crimes before.

I don't think it's fair to say we 'prioritised' the Selebi case over that of the Kebble murder. We had the confessions of the killers and we felt it was important to go after the people who had issued the instructions from the top rather than those who had pulled the trigger. We never envisaged that Glenn Agliotti would walk free. We also intended to prosecute Agliotti, along with John Stratton, and we believed both would have stood trial together for the death of Kebble.

It was then acting NDPP Menzi Simelane's decision to remove Gerrie Nel and the Bad Guys team from the case, replacing them at the last minute just as the case was going to trial. That original team was intimately involved with the case and knew everything about it. I can only speculate that this was done because the relationship between Simelane and the Bad Guys team had soured. I have also always believed that the move was an intentional act of sabotage so that the prosecution would fail and fingers could again be pointed at me for having entered into plea-bargain arrangements. In my view, Simelane was being spiteful and, as a result, he compromised the criminal justice system. They were experienced prosecutors and investigators and I believe that had they prosecuted Agliotti there would have been a far greater chance of securing a conviction. The team who replaced them was entirely at sea, and it was clear that this man was going to walk free. After I left the NPA, I also didn't see any enthusiasm in following through with the extradition of Stratton, who is still in Australia.

And, despite the continued criticism, I stand by my decisions in the Kebble/Selebi matter. This is not because I'm stubborn, but rather because I believe that those decisions were correct. The Kebble docket would be lying in a police office drawer, empty and abandoned, were it not for those deals. At least now the whole country knows how Brett Kebble died. The Scorpions should get some credit for that.

I know the public responds to these things on an emotional level but it is important for our democracy to allow institutions such as the NPA to make decisions without political interference. Even if you are wrong, and mistakes are made from time to time, it would be wrong to justify political interference based on these decisions. In fact, the independent panel appointed by Acting NDPP Mokotedi Mpshe to review these decisions found that we were correct and came to the same conclusion. You could not separate the prosecution of Jackie Selebi and all the 204 agreements and the plea-bargain deals we had managed to secure.

What the public sees are the killers, who don't appear remorseful, walking around as free men with the opportunity to commit crime again. From a legal point of view, the plea-bargain approach is sound and solid, but it remains difficult to argue against public sentiment.

On the same day that Agliotti appeared in court in Johannesburg, McCarthy and I flew to Cape Town hoping to meet with the president and the ministers of justice and safety and security. The president wasn't available so we met with Mabandla and Acting Minister of Safety and Security Ngconde Balfour. We briefed them on what had transpired with Agliotti and also on the ongoing battle we were having with the SAPS.

At the time, there was intense rivalry between the two organisations and, because we were both running parallel investigations into the Kebble murder, hostilities had increased, especially as the police knew we were busy with something and had been on the verge of making arrests. They simply refused point-blank to cooperate and hand over any documents to us. There was also intense disagreement over who should pursue the Kebble case.

Unfortunately, neither minister gave us any directive about who should follow the Kebble murder investigation through. A joint task team was set up to complete the investigation and two policemen were seconded onto the team, which continued to be led by Leask and Nel.

At a meeting in the following days, I asked the president to intervene by requesting that the SAPS hand over the Kebble murder docket to the

DSO. In my presence, Mbeki called Selebi's office to be told that the commissioner was on a flight from Cape Town to Wonderboom airport in Pretoria. The president was due to fly to Cape Town himself and duly delayed his own flight as he waited for Selebi to arrive in Pretoria. Two hours later Selebi burst into the room. There was no consideration for who was inside or what was being discussed. He was his usual abrasive self.

The president suggested I repeat my request to Selebi, which I did. I was very surprised by his response. I had expected resistance, but he promptly offered to hand the docket to me once the investigating officers had returned from overseas. And the docket was indeed handed over, but there was nothing of substance in it and I was not sure how the SAPS would have been able to justify any arrests based on such little evidence.

Over the following months, I continued to brief the president and the justice minister on developments in the Selebi investigation. Agliotti had agreed to testify against the commissioner and had signed affidavits detailing their corrupt relationship.

One of the allegations that had arisen was that Agliotti had paid for a pair of shoes during a shopping spree that Selebi had given to the president as a gift. Agliotti even recalled that the commissioner had told the shop assistant he wanted size seven, soft leather shoes because Mbeki had small, broad feet.

I didn't want any of the Scorpions investigators interrogating the president of the country about his shoes, so I asked him myself during one of our consultations. I said to President Mbeki, 'What size shoe do you wear?' and before he could even answer, I told him.

I said, 'Do you know how I know? It's because you got the shoes from Jackie.' He confirmed that Selebi had presented them as a gift from SAPS management. When I explained that Agliotti had paid for the shoes, he looked very surprised and asked if I was sure.

As a way of verifying Agliotti's affidavit, which he wrote in his cell, the investigators had gone to the Cradle of Humankind World Heritage Site to confirm the president's foot size. In 2002, Mbeki and former United Nations General Secretary Kofi Annan had visited the Sterkfontein Caves and casts of their foot imprints had been made and are on display there. The investigators measured the casts of Mbeki's feet to confirm the size of his shoes. It was ingenious investigative work.

During my meetings with the president and the minister, I also regularly raised my frustrations, and those of the DSO, with the lack of cooperation being afforded to us by the SAPS.

I was further angered by the lack of cooperation by the SAPS because in 2005, when the police had requested information from the NPA on a separate matter, I was extremely accommodating. Magistrate A.A.K. Singh had laid charges against the previous NDPP and several senior state advocates for defeating the ends of justice. The SAPS requested certain documents be made available by the NPA and when some of the files could not be located, I opened my office to them. Officers did a thorough search of the NPA's records. Similarly, in 2006, when the SAPS was investigating the DSO's alleged abuse of the 'C-Fund' used to pay informants, the NPA provided the SAPS with all relevant documents and files. And because highly confidential information was involved, I even gave them a secure boardroom to use so that the documents did not have to be removed from our premises. This investigation took almost three months and I obliged because I knew my cooperation was necessary to enable the police to conduct their investigation without any interference.

However, when we required similar assistance from the SAPS, they were being obstructive. Despite numerous requests and memos to the president, my minister and the minister of safety and security, the police still refused to hand over the documents we needed to complete the investigation. In my submissions to the Ginwala Inquiry, I detailed each and every one of these meetings: who was there and what was discussed, and produced reports written for the purposes of briefing the ministers and the president.

One such meeting was in March 2007, at Esselen Park in Ekurhuleni, where the ANC NEC had convened. Minister Mabandla had requested me to brief her, the minister of safety and security and the president. The president suggested that Selebi should also attend the briefing, but I expressed my reservations because the investigation had reached a new threshold and we were about to make the commissioner a formal suspect. Mbeki was annoyed by my response and indicated that the purpose of the meeting was not to discuss the investigation but to clear up issues of cooperation and to ensure that the NPA received documents that had been requested.

It was the first time I had witnessed Mbeki's impatience and irritability. I wasn't sure whether it was because of the NEC meeting or if it was because of what I had said. Regardless of my position, however, Selebi was indeed invited to attend and the president delegated the matter to his ministers so he wasn't in the room. Selebi was arrogant and refused to hand over the documents, stating that they were sensitive. He claimed he couldn't take the risk of the Scorpions leaking the contents and reasserted his claim that we had been infiltrated.

The ministers were powerless in the face of Selebi's arrogance. I got increasingly angry and stated, 'What is the purpose of going on with this meeting, ministers? Your commissioner is telling you that we are not going to get this information and you are not saying anything about it. You are not telling him that he must give us the information, so what is the purpose of this meeting?'

I concluded, 'There's no meeting, let's go.' I was furious.

The ministers had failed to call Selebi to order and I was thoroughly frustrated. By that stage the state attorney had become involved and all legal avenues were being closed to us. I was running out of options, so two days later, on 19 March 2007, out of sheer frustration, I wrote a memorandum to Mabandla.

In that six-page memorandum I placed on record all our attempts to deal with the matter 'in a manner that is expected of an institution of State and to perform our mandate without embarrassment to our Government and country.' I stated that it was clear from the Esselen Park meeting that the SAPS was not willing to cooperate with us and that the national commissioner refused to make the documents available. We had requested five UK activity reports, videos that had been recorded with Agliotti and Paul Stemmet, as well as the police informer or source files of Stemmet and Agliotti, but none were forthcoming. I also listed the examples of instances when the SAPS had requested assistance from the NPA and we had willingly obliged.

In the report I also told the minister: 'It is the investigating team's view that we should formally apply for a search warrant to gain access to the information. Such an application will inevitably bring the dispute into the public domain which of course is highly undesirable but the only legal option available to us if this matter is not resolved soon.'

I undertook not to take any further action until three days later – Thursday, 22 March – but after that we would be forced to approach a judge. 'In the circumstances, we will have no alternative but to seek the assistance of the courts to obtain the relief we require.'

The following day the DSO converted the initial preparatory Bad Guys investigation into a full-blown probe in terms of Section 28(1) of the NPA Act. That same day the minister informed me by SMS that the SAPS had agreed to hand over all the information we had requested. A week later the police handed over the five UK activity reports, but withheld the remainder of the information we had requested.

At an NPA Stakeholders' Conference towards the end of March, I advised the minister that the SAPS was still refusing to hand over the remainder of the documents. She was surprised, and during the course of that conversation also raised her concerns about the DSO relying on the evidence of accomplice witnesses. I reminded her about Section 204 of the Criminal Procedure Act, which allowed us to rely on the evidence of accomplice witnesses.

In April, we again repeated our request to the SAPS and when this was ignored, the investigating team – together with the four national deputy directors of public prosecutions – agreed we should proceed with an application for a search warrant for the SAPS headquarters, Wachthuis.

By mid-May we were still waiting and nothing was produced. I prepared a memorandum to the president in which I recorded that a deadlock had been reached and efforts to resolve this by engaging the ministers accountable had failed:

> *I am addressing this letter to you as a last resort. As you know, in the course of last year, information was brought to my attention which incriminated the National Commissioner. Some of the revelations came as a painful experience but had to be looked into properly. The DSO's approach has been not to react to some of the questionable allegations, unless they were backed up by independent reliable corroboration.*

I informed the president that the DSO intended seeking a search warrant to obtain the information relevant to the investigation into the allegations against Selebi. While the warrant would be wider than the initial request for information, I felt that was justified but the DSO remained willing to execute a 'friendly search' so as not to cause embarrassment. I also stated:

'The DSO will be amenable to enter the premises of the SAPS in a way not to draw any attention, and is willing to effect the search in a way and at a time not to cause embarrassment to, or affect SAPS operations.'

I appealed for the president's intervention, otherwise the DSO would have no option but to proceed with the drastic step of applying for a warrant. The letter was sent on 7 May 2007. I told the president that time was of the essence and that the investigating team would like to take whatever steps necessary to gain access to the documents by 8 May.

Obviously I was concerned about having to conduct a raid at the police headquarters and the potential dangers involved with that. We were, however, engaged in a legitimate investigation as a state institution. South Africa is a stable, constitutional democracy and I had already informed the relevant minister, who was not coming to the party. My minister was of no assistance either. The president was well aware of the information we wanted and that there had been no breakthrough. What were our options? Either we had to abandon the operation or we had to seek out other legally available means open to us.

I don't think the ministers and the president were deliberately trying to block us. I simply think they were powerless against Selebi. They couldn't impose themselves on him and they appeared to be afraid of him. It was simple: Minister of Safety and Security Charles Nqakula should have instructed Selebi to cooperate with the Scorpions. He should have said, 'Let them see those documents, let them take notes.' He didn't do that. This meant we were forced to take a step we did not want to take, and even at this late hour we were willing to ask the president to intervene.

Our office manager hand-delivered the letter to the president's office. Late that evening, Mbeki called me on my cellphone to say he had received my letter and I was not giving him enough time to act. Unwittingly, I had made an error of dates in my letter that had given rise to concern. The letter had been drafted sometime earlier but I had not changed the deadline date of 8 May, which gave the impression we were going to apply for warrants the very next day. I assured him that we would hold back on the applications in order to give him some time to intervene.

The following day I met with Mabandla and Minister of Defence Mosioua Lekota. They wanted to know how convinced I was of the case against Selebi. I spent two hours taking them through the allegations and the evidence. At the end of it, they felt there was a case to answer to. They raised concerns about the use of accomplice evidence and I explained that this was sanctioned by the law and was common practice.

The president subsequently arranged a meeting between McCarthy and me and the leadership of the SAPS in order to facilitate cooperation between us. I was reluctant to attend because I didn't want to be dragged into a situation in which I was dealing with a suspect in an ongoing investigation. I was also worried the president was putting himself in a position where he may have to be called as a witness. I had hoped he would simply instruct the national commissioner to give us the documents. I don't think that was an unreasonable request. In the end, however, I decided to attend because I couldn't send McCarthy to a meeting on his own with the president and the entire leadership of the SAPS. The meeting was held at the SAPS Crime Intelligence office and was chaired by Mbeki.

At that meeting, Selebi suggested that the SAPS had fully cooperated and that it was the DSO that was moving the goalposts. He accused the Scorpions of having an ulterior motive of trying to discredit him. Mbeki said that if the evidence revealed Selebi was corrupt, he would also want to know whether or not any other senior SAPS officials were corrupt too.

The president tasked Deputy Commissioner Rayman Lalla with liaising with McCarthy to facilitate the production of the information required. Lalla would later claim the president had directed we would not be allowed to make any copies or remove any of the material. This was simply not true.

The following week the Scorpions went to the offices of the police's Crime Intelligence Division. While they were allowed to view some information, they were not allowed to remove any documents and were not provided with all the information requested. The police were creating the impression they were cooperating but they really weren't. It was a farce.

Over the months of May, June, July and August a series of meetings was held about the police's continued failure to hand over the documents. McCarthy met with the president and his DG Frank Chikane, then McCarthy, Leask and Nel met with the SAPS management. The Bad Guys investigating team and I also briefed the justice minister and emphasised the urgency of the issue. We informed her that we were on the verge of arresting and charging Selebi. Mabandla viewed the situation as a crisis, indicating that it would shake the foundation of the country, and urged us not to have a long drawn-out trial but to resolve the matter as quickly as possible. I could tell she was nervous and she urged me to brief the president before I took the next step.

Towards the middle of July, just as the Selebi investigation was reaching a crescendo, my mother took ill and passed away.

I had recently returned from a trip overseas and called home to speak to my mother. It was a Saturday. I could hear she was breathing heavily but she was trying to hide it. I asked, 'Ma, are you okay?'

She said, 'Yes, I'm fine.'

But I could tell she was not, so I urged her to call a doctor. My mom had undergone a heart operation in 2005 so I thought perhaps this was a re-emergence of the problem. I'm told that when she was taken to hospital, she looked quite bright and in high spirits. She was admitted to High Care and all of a sudden things took a turn for the worse. When my family saw her again her skin appeared very dark and she did not look well. She fell into a coma. I went to visit her in hospital, and spent a few days with her. Two days after leaving Port Elizabeth for Pretoria I got a call from my sister that she had passed on.

It was such a difficult time for me. I had not shared all my work frustrations with my mother because I knew she had always had reservations about the job. I also felt, though, that the upbringing I received from my mother – in terms of teaching us proper values and a good work ethic – had assisted me in doing my job as well as I could. My mother always taught me: 'Brighten the corner where you are, always be that spark that brings hope and do the right thing.'

When she died, I felt the only way of honouring the memory of my mother was to do the right thing and to do my job well.

But while I was mourning the death of my mother and making important preparations for her funeral, there were other national challenges facing me in my office. This was made even more difficult when I received a message from the office that the justice minister was making inquiries about the Vlok/Van der Merwe matter. In my absence, I had mandated McCarthy to meet with the president about the SAPS issue. He was not able to do so but had met with Chikane instead. McCarthy compiled a memo to me in which he said: 'Rev Chikane has advised that they will brief you when you are back. The whole matter is rather overwhelming, but it is better that you make your own judgment. I can only hope that things will settle down and that maturity will prevail.'

Throughout the month of August, there were numerous attempts by my office to arrange a meeting with the president in order to report to him. Unfortunately, he was not available and these requests were not met. Meanwhile, the Bad Guys team was ready to move and the investigation had been completed. We felt that there was a solid prima facie case and we had lined up witnesses who would testify. We concluded that arrest and search warrants should be secured.

Together with my deputies McCarthy, Hofmeyr, Ramaite, Mpshe and my special advisor Pillay we concluded that we should proceed. We consulted a senior counsel, Alfred Cockrell, for one last opinion in order to be sure. Another source of comfort was that when we apply for warrants, it would be yet another opportunity to test the strength of our case because the judicial officers would have to go through our application and look at the affidavits in order to justify the warrants. It was an additional safety net to ensure we were not being frivolous about the matter and that we had given it careful thought and consideration.

The Bad Guys team was called in and I confirmed to them that they could go ahead with the applications. I told them that they should inform me once they had obtained the warrants so I could brief the president before those warrants were executed.

On 10 September 2007 an arrest warrant for South Africa's national police commissioner was issued by the chief magistrate of Randburg, Professor Cheryl Loots, for the crimes of defeating the ends of justice, corruption, fraud, theft and contraventions of the Police Act. Four days later, search warrants were issued by Deputy Judge President Phineas Mojapelo of the Johannesburg High Court.

Skating on thin ice

My pursuance of Jackie Selebi was not driven by any sinister motive. It was never an attempt by the Scorpions to target the SAPS in order to keep the unit alive. I also never saw it as a personal battle between Selebi and myself – as Presidency DG Frank Chikane seeks to portray in his book *The Things that Could Not be Said*:

> *To me, they began to see each other as enemies or adversaries although they would deny this. Some attributed this to their locations and roles within government, but this is simplistic. In time the relationship deteriorated, unfortunately, to the point where the battles were carried out through the state agencies they led, including the intelligence and investigating arms of the entities under their command.*

I felt that this was an investigation that the Scorpions unit was compelled to pursue in terms of its lawful mandate. It had nothing to do with the survival of the unit or my personal relationship with Selebi – and this was borne out by the fact that Selebi was ultimately charged and convicted. I knew it was such a sensitive matter that those who didn't want the Scorpions to exist would use it as the final nail in the coffin of the organisation, but it still remained a matter that had to be pursued. There was no personal agenda, no personal motive, and it was certainly not driven by politics.

Once the arrest and search warrants had been obtained, I went to see

President Mbeki and Chikane. It was a Saturday afternoon, 15 September, and we met at Mahlamba Ndlopfu. The president was surprised that the warrants had been applied for and issued and also said he was unaware that the SAPS had refused to cooperate and hand over copies of documents. I, in turn, was astonished that this came as a surprise to the president, especially considering my memorandum to him in May. McCarthy had also informed Chikane that cooperation had not been forthcoming.

Time was of the essence because the investigation was nearing an end and it was becoming increasingly possible for information to be hidden and evidence to be destroyed. There was also pressure on us in terms of other cases that had to be tied up, such as the Paparas Drug Bust and the Kebble murder.

Mbeki looked a little annoyed and asked whether I was sure of this case.

'We are certain,' I said.

Chikane then requested I prepare a written report for the president that would enable him to apply his mind as to what he needed to do about Selebi, and I consequently undertook to do so.

I went home that Saturday and called the investigating team to assist me with preparing the status report outlining the nature of our case. We had to prepare it in such a way as to explain broadly the strengths of the case without giving away too much in terms of the evidence we had gathered. The report laid out who would testify, what corroborating evidence there was and the urgency of the matter:

> *We are bound by ethics to inform the defence team in the Paparas matter and the court in the Kebble matter, that Agliotti and others have brokered a deal with the State. Because this takes place in open court, it will cause media frenzy and a lot of speculation that cannot be afforded.*
>
> *This will lead to what could be termed a 'trial by media' of a senior government official based on speculation and removed from the facts. We have to approach members of SAPS for witness statements and will have difficulty to get versions with Mr Selebi still the head of SAPS.*
>
> *We reiterate that the investigation is not an investigation of the SAPS as an institution but of Mr Selebi as an individual. The allegations we have and are investigating are serious in themselves but more serious if one takes into account that the target of the investigation is the head of SAPS.*

> *I hereby inform the President that the execution of both the search and arrest warrants is imminent and that the merits of this case have been thoroughly considered, before taking this decision.*

The following day I handed the report to the president. He said, 'Vusi, do you realise that the police are angry? They are prepared to do anything to defy you.'

I replied, 'Mr President, I don't understand why the police should be angry because this is aimed at the national commissioner – it is not aimed at SAPS. I don't understand why the police should be angry.'

Then Mbeki asked for a two-week grace period and I said, 'No, Mr President, two weeks is too long, I am prepared to wait a week.'

Mbeki didn't explain why he needed two weeks, but Chikane claims it was 'to interact with the national command of the police and the commissioner himself, and take specific actions to ensure that if and when the commissioner was charged, there would be no instability created within the criminal justice system'.

I felt that a week would be a fair compromise and was more than reasonable because we had already had the warrants for a week. I didn't go to Mbeki and brazenly announce, 'We have the warrant, we're going in!' as Chikane has attempted to portray. I went to Mbeki as a matter of courtesy so that he didn't have to hear about it through the media. I had briefed him and the justice minister over a long period of time and the ministers of the security justice cluster also knew about the investigation. They knew an arrest was imminent.

As the commander-in-chief of the country, of all the security forces, how long does it take to convene an urgent meeting of your security chiefs? How long could it possibly take to pick up the phone and speak to the head of the defence force, the head of NIA, and the others to say, 'Guys, we are faced with this situation. Can you come up with a plan of doing things?'

I was in no rush – and nobody can accuse me of having been rash, given all the steps I had taken. In fact, I had been more than patient. I bent over backwards to accommodate the situation because I appreciated the implications of what was about to happen. I was fully cognisant of what the potential repercussions would be.

Why should the president think more of defiance of the law than of enforcing the law? Why should the president be more sympathetic to the plight of the police than the fact that there was ample prima facie evidence indicating that the national police commissioner had committed a crime?

This was the national police commissioner, the president of Interpol and an embarrassment to our country, and all President Mbeki was concerned about was that the police were angry. I couldn't understand it then and I still do not understand it to this day. Did the fact that the police were angry mean we couldn't act against Selebi? I had already explained we would not go and handcuff the commissioner and make a spectacle of it.

It was also evident that the president's attempted intervention to get the SAPS to hand over the source-file documents had failed. The only action to put it on track was to obtain the warrants that would allow us to lawfully enter the offices of Crime Intelligence and still hope for their cooperation. We could have conducted the searches in a non-hostile environment. The president still had the opportunity to call in all the security chiefs, including high-ranking police officers with the exclusion of the commissioner, and create an enabling environment. He also could have decided to suspend the national commissioner to ensure he was no longer in charge of the SAPS. I put that option on the table and stressed yet again that it was not necessary for the search to be hostile. All that was required was the co-operation on the part of Crime Intelligence. We never said we would go in there, guns blazing – despite the position taken by Chikane in *The Things that Could Not be Said*:

> *The reality dawned on us that with the warrants in the hands of the NDPP and the DSO (Scorpions) and given the irrational way the NDPP was arguing the matter, a raid on the intelligence headquarters was possible without notice. In fact, there was a concern that some of the elements within the DSO were ready to act without any consideration of the consequences of their actions. Some were clearly ready to create a crisis for interests other than those of justice and that is why the presidency had to intervene to avoid the unimaginable – a bloodbath amongst national security agencies, a massacre that might have been far worse than the Marikana tragedy. Questions would have been asked about how the president could not have foreseen the incident and why he did not act*

> *to avoid it – just as people are asking now about Marikana. The world would have called us a 'banana republic', incapable of governing itself.*

This is absolute rubbish.

The reason I did not immediately order the execution of those warrants was because I was trying to create an enabling environment to conduct the search. I could have decided not to inform the president. The reason I did so was for the president to prepare the necessary grounds and environment in which we could then conduct the search-and-seizure operation.

If we go back to the time when the Scorpions had obtained search warrants for Zuma's offices and residence, I didn't approach the president before that application, but I did inform him after we had obtained the warrants so that we could create an enabling environment for their execution, and out of courtesy as well – just as I did with Selebi. It was never an issue. He never asked, 'Why did you first apply for a search warrant and come to me when you have already accomplished that?' I also took the risk of informing Selebi beforehand about the Zuma searches and gave clear instructions to my officers not to use any weapons or to risk any violence. I did this all simply because I am not a bloodthirsty person. I am a responsible citizen who is mature and old enough to appreciate security considerations. Why should I want to cause mayhem in this country and all the embarrassment that would follow suit?

When it came to the Selebi warrants, my approach had been exactly the same. I did not have to ask for anybody's permission to apply for the warrants and I had gone to the president to request him to make sure that the environment was not hostile. Raising the issue of the Marikana police shooting is out of all proportions of rationality.

In my opinion, Chikane is being sensationalist. He is suggesting that they were faced with this madman (me!) who had no consideration for anyone's safety. That is the picture Chikane is trying to portray in his book – and the same portrait he attempted to present at the Ginwala Inquiry.

At that meeting on Sunday, 16 September, Mbeki asked me if I would be prepared to attend a meeting of the National Security Council (NSC). I agreed but stressed that while I was prepared to brief the NSC, the council must understand I was not requesting permission from them to proceed with the execution of the warrants. Mbeki asked Chikane to organise that meeting – the NSC met that week, but I was not invited to attend.

Two days later, on the Tuesday, I met with Minister Mabandla. I had, in the previous week, already informed her of the arrest warrant and she had not asked me why I did not inform her before applying for such a warrant.

The minister told me she had received a letter from the president about the warrants and that she wanted information from me. She had prepared a letter for me and handed over a sealed envelope. She had to rush off to the airport and the meeting was cut short but it wasn't an unpleasant meeting at all.

When I returned to my office, I opened the envelope and read the letter:

> *RE: INVESTIGATIONS INTO THE NATIONAL COMMISSIONER OF THE POLICE SERVICE*
>
> *The above matter refers.*
>
> *I am advised that you have taken legal steps to effect the arrest of and the preference of charges against the National Commissioner of the police service. I presume that in making this decision you have taken time to consider the seriousness and gravity of your intended course of action.*
>
> *As you know, in terms of clause 179(6) of the Constitution, the Cabinet member responsible for the administration of justice must exercise final responsibility over the prosecuting authority. In addition, section 33(2) of the National Prosecuting Authority Act provides that the National Director of Public Prosecution shall at the request of the Minister of Justice, furnish the Minister with information with regard to any case, matter or subject dealt with by the National Director or a Director.*
>
> *In light of the above and in order for me to exercise my responsibilities as required by the Constitution, I require all of the information on which you relied to take the legal steps to effect the arrest of and the preference of charges against the National Commissioner of the police service. This includes but is not limited to specific information or evidence indicating the direct involvement of the National Commissioner in any activity that constitutes a crime in terms of the laws of South Africa. In pursuing your intended course of action and any prosecution, the NPA must do so in the public interest not withstanding a prima facie case. Such exercise of dis-*

cretion requires that all factors be taken into account including the public interest. Therefore, I must be satisfied that indeed the public interest will be served should you go ahead with your intended course of action. ***Until I have satisfied myself that sufficient information and evidence does exist for the arrest of and preference of charges against the National Commissioner of the police service, you shall not pursue the route that you have taken steps to pursue. You should therefore and with extreme urgency cause for me to be briefed thoroughly in this regard [emphasis added].***

Please advise me at your earliest convenience when I should expect to receive the necessary documentation.

I trust that you find the above in order.

Yours sincerely
Ms B.S. Mabandla, MP
Minister of Justice and Constitutional Development
2007-09-18

I was completely shocked. This astonishing letter was completely out of keeping with the long history of interaction between the minister and me about the Selebi investigation. It was also completely at odds with the friendly tone the minister had adopted with me at our earlier meeting. It immediately made me wonder whether Minister Mabandla had actually read the letter at all, and I was convinced she had not written it.

The essence of the letter, indicated by the paragraph highlighted above, was to stop the investigation and the intended prosecution of the national commissioner of the police until such time that the minister was satisfied that it would be in the public interest to do so. That is unlawful, constituting political interference in the work of prosecutors. She was entitled to ask for reports and for reasons for certain decisions, but she could not instruct me to halt a prosecution. And I could not, in all honesty, obey an unlawful instruction.

This letter was the turning point. I later realised that my refusal to submit to the minister's order culminated in my suspension a mere five days later.

During the Ginwala Inquiry we battled to gain access to the initial letter written by President Mbeki to Minister Mabandla on Monday, 17 September, which caused her to write to me. The state claimed that the communication between the president and his minister was privileged, but Ginwala did an about-turn and agreed that the letter should be released. This was the letter presented by the state:

September 17, 2007

Dear Minister

I have been informed that the National Director of Public Prosecutions has taken legal steps to effect the arrest of and the preference of charges against the National Commissioner of the police service.

As you are aware, our constitutional and legal framework recognises that the prosecution of offenders is pursued by the prosecuting authority on behalf of the State, represented by our duly elected government.

Accordingly, clause 179(6) of our Constitution provides that the Cabinet member responsible for the administration of justice must exercise final responsibility over the prosecuting authority.

Section 33(1) of the National Prosecuting Authority Act repeats this constitutional directive. This Act goes further, in section 33(2), to provide, among others, that the National Director of Public Prosecutions shall, at the request of the Minister of Justice, furnish the Minister with information with regard to any case, matter or subject dealt with by the National Director or a Director.

The National Commissioner is appointed by and accountable to the President of South Africa.

In view of the constitutional responsibilities of the President with regard to the Office of the National Commissioner of the police service, I deem it appropriate that you obtain the necessary information from the National Director of Public Prosecutions regarding the intended arrest and prosecution of the National Commissioner. This would enable me to take such informed decisions as may be necessary with regard to the National Commissioner.

Kindly keep me informed of progress in this regard. Needless to say, this matter is urgent.

There was nothing to this letter at all. Like me, my advocate Wim Trengove SC is dubious about the veracity of this letter. Trengove comments:

> *We called on the other side to produce that letter and there was a lot of to-ing and fro-ing. They lied about it initially and [offered] a lot of resistance and eventually produced the letter. And when they produced the letter, it was this innocuous, inane letter. Possibly, what went from the presidency to the minister was a letter that said something like, 'Stop him from prosecuting Selebi'. The letter that they produced was a funny, inane letter which said something like, 'Please ask Pikoli what his time frame is in which he intends to act,' some innocuous question. Written on the face of it, after Mbeki and Chikane had two long meetings with Pikoli and his plans had been discussed at length on the Saturday and Sunday and it's just not the kind of letter you then write to the minister saying, 'Please ask him what his time frame is.' So the letter just didn't make sense in the context of the events before and after the letter. Secondly, the letter was so innocuous that it was inexplicable that they resisted so vehemently before they gave it to us, and in the third place, it was clear that on the Wednesday, when the minister then tried to stop him, that she was acting on the president's letter. I wondered if it was not more likely that there was a letter from the presidency instructing the minister to stop him. Ginwala ordered them to give us the letter and then they produced this innocuous document. So I think that it is possible that we never saw the real document and I think that the real document could have been the smoking gun. We could do nothing about it. We knew that at the time but in the face of just a denial from the presidency, you can't prove that the letter is forged.*

I stared at the letter from the minister for a few moments and asked myself if I was hallucinating. I just couldn't believe it. I then called in McCarthy and Hofmeyr and showed it to them. I was emotional and felt that I could inflame the situation, so it was important to have my colleagues assist me in framing an appropriate response.

Together we wrote a six-page response in which I told Mabandla that if her letter constituted an instruction, I would be acting in breach of the oath of office I had taken and my duties under the NPA Act. I reminded her she had been briefed on at least 10 occasions and that the president had also been regularly updated.

My response was clear in that I was not going to do what she was asking me to do. I also suggested that perhaps she did not fully appreciate what she was asking me to do because she was putting me in a terrible, untenable situation. I did not even consider acceding to her request, because it was clearly an unlawful instruction. For me it was so inconceivable that I didn't even think twice about it. I had to find a way to be courteous without being downright rude. While I was duty-bound to uphold the independence of my office, I also sought to avoid a showdown with the minister.

That same day I received a response from Mabandla advising that she did not agree with all the points I had made and that my briefings only constituted progress reports on the investigation and she still urgently required all the evidence that informed my decision to apply for warrants. She ended by asking me to provide a full report by close of business that day.

I was in Cape Town and called my team together in order to prepare a full report for the minister containing as much detail as possible, falling short of complying with everything she wanted. I was due to attend a function that evening, but skipped it so that we could stay in the hotel room to draw up the document. All my deputies were there, barring Corky Mpshe, who was in Hong Kong at the time.

I was sitting at a table in the hotel room when my cellphone rang after 10 p.m. It was the minister. She burst into a tirade, screaming at me. She asked me whether I thought she was 'a moron'. She said she was 'tired of this rubbish' and referred to our communication as an 'unproductive discourse'. She also accused me of being disrespectful and contemptuous for sending her 'an ugly letter' and for telling others that she loses documents.

Naturally, I was not a passive listener – I felt abused and responded angrily, denying the accusations she was levelling against me. I stood my ground and dismissed her, but don't feel that I was disrespectful or rude. Mabandla told me she did not want to see me the following day and that I should just send her my report. Before hanging up, she apologised and told me that she does not usually shout in this way at younger people.

I was so shocked by the outburst that I immediately scribbled down notes about what had transpired during the conversation. It was the first time she had spoken to me in this way, and I had no idea where this was coming from. It was as though she was preparing the ground for the excuse of a 'breakdown in the relationship'. The National Security Council had also met and I suspect a decision had been taken there for me to be suspended, and that Mabandla had called me thereafter. It was a provocation from nowhere.

I was so furious that the following day I instructed McCarthy to take the report to the minister because I also did not want to see her.

The confrontation had hurt me deeply as it had gone against everything that had been instilled in me by my mother as I was growing up. It had not been long since I had buried my mother and the minister's words had left me emotionally abused – and extremely angry.

I flew back from Cape Town on that Thursday morning and called Chief Justice Pius Langa. He had told me when I was appointed that if ever I was considering resigning, I should speak to him first.

I shared with the chief justice the immense pressure I was feeling and that I wanted to quit. We had a long discussion and he urged me not to resign. He insisted that quitting would not be the solution. It was extremely helpful to talk to someone about issues that were close to my heart and to have a supportive, listening ear. I had always regarded Pius as something of an older sibling and it was brotherly advice he was imparting. I don't think our meeting compromised either his integrity or mine. I also recalled the words of Advocate George Bizos, who had urged me not to walk away when the job got too difficult.

I was in such mental turmoil at that time that when my deputies walked into my office on the Friday afternoon, they found me writing a letter of resignation. They sat down and dissuaded me from quitting. They reminded me that we were all in this together, and I felt compelled to listen to them. I didn't want to be a coward and abandon a sinking ship and leave all the sailors on board. As the captain, I should be the last to leave.

So it was that I agreed not to resign. I took a deep breath and said, 'Well I'm going ahead, let's see where this will all end up.'

I am pleased I didn't resign then, because I would have felt that I had failed the prosecutors. The fight for the independence of prosecutors had to be taken forward and I would have compromised that if I had resigned.

It was an extremely emotional and difficult time for me, as my wife recalls all too well:

I had spent the five years before Vusi's appointment working for the National Intelligence Agency as a deputy director-general, corporate services, so I understood the environment he was in. I had my own fears. As soon as I could tell he was full of tension and he wasn't speaking, I knew something was not right. When he began to have heated exchanges with his minister, it absolutely confirmed that all was not well. He would say very little.

Of course, at the time when he took up this appointment at the NPA, he withdrew from many things, but he was still the Vusumzi that I know, the father that we know. But as the tensions grew, I could pick up that he was withholding something, that something big was definitely happening. I had to prod him and prod him and eventually he told me that he was having problems with his minister and the president.

The only time that I got to know the nature of the issues was one evening when he had attended a meeting with the president. He called me and he was so angry he was crying. He said, 'Look, things have deteriorated so much, I'm being made out as a liar here. But I'm going to stick to what I know best, which is the truth, because that's how things are. I'm being called a liar by my own minister.'

I don't know who else was in that meeting. All I knew was that he was crying and because Vusi has had problems with his temper, when he is absolutely angry, he cries. It was upsetting. All I could say was, 'Please, take a deep breath, take a deep breath. Just don't allow anybody to run over you. Allow no one to walk over you, but please keep that temper down.' That was the best I could say – keep that temper down – because people would take advantage of it.

On that Friday, Reverend Chikane called me to advise that the president would meet me at 7.45 p.m. that Sunday evening and that I should meet with the minister beforehand. Mabandla also wrote to me again, confirming she had read my report and that there was nothing substantially different to the information I had already provided. She undertook to make herself available to meet with me that Sunday at 5 p.m. before my meeting with the president.

The weekend passed with me waiting for Sunday evening to come.

On the Saturday I attended a wedding in Pretoria. Barney Pityana's daughter was getting married and the guest list proved interesting because amongst those invited was Minister Mabandla. We greeted each other politely and were cordial to one another, but didn't really engage in conversation. Bulelani Ngcuka was also there, along with the deputy president, his wife Phumzile. The following day I received a number of calls from others who had attended to tell me that I had been the topic of conversation amongst some of the guests. They were discussing the issue of Selebi and tensions between Mabandla, Mbeki and me. I'm not certain if they knew what was coming my way or if the minister was party to those discussions.

Over the weekend I received a phone call from Sibongile Sigodi (née Ngam) in the legal division in the presidency. She was looking for the National Prosecuting Authority Act and I could guess what was going on at the Union Buildings. I wasn't anxious or worried – in fact, I was prepared for any eventuality. In my mind I had resolved to continue to fight for the independence of prosecutors and I was not going to allow any political interference in our decision-making processes. That was clear.

I had been involved in the struggle and I knew the type of enemy we were facing, but that never deterred me from joining the struggle for the liberation of our country. I was clear that this was yet another phase of the struggle I had reached. I believed that whatever plan they were going to put in place, I would be able to respond.

On the Sunday I also received a call from Mpshe, who told me that the president's legal advisor Mojanku Gumbi wanted him to go and see her. He was checking to see if I minded, which I didn't. I suspect that meeting was to confirm he would be willing to act in the position of NDPP.

That Sunday had been a week since I last met with the president and our now infamous 'one week, two week' conversation had taken place. The week was drawing to a close and the president must have felt urgency to avoid the Scorpions acting on the warrants. He and Chikane thought we would execute on the Monday and they could not trust me not to go ahead. In reality, that was not the case, as at that point I was not even considering executing the warrants the following day. There was no real threat.

As 5 p.m. neared, I made my way to The Meat Company restaurant in Brooklyn that Minister Mabandla had selected as her venue of choice. Coincidentally, it was the same restaurant she had taken me to for a celebratory lunch when I was appointed NDPP two years previously. There was poetic irony in her choice.

During my tenure, I had an official driver and a VIP protector, but to avoid any leaks I always went alone and drove myself when I went to see the minister or the president. As per usual, I drove myself to the meeting and was, typically, early, and when Mabandla walked in we greeted one another politely. The tension was so thick you could cut it with a knife. There was none of our usual banter we had shared over the years and we were both cagey.

Mabandla and I had a long, shared history and we had known each other for decades. In 1986, when we were deported from Lesotho – the time of 'Total Onslaught' by P.W. Botha – Girly was in a transit camp in Lusaka. Mabandla's husband was there with their young children and Girly took to them immediately and looked after the little ones. I also have photographs from 1988 of Mabandla and me in Sweden together when we were sent there on an educational trip to study the legal system. We worked together in the legal department in Lusaka and enjoyed braais and parties together, and she and Girly worked together in the ANC Women's League. We were old comrades and friends.

She sat across from me in the restaurant and said, 'Vusi, look there are problems that we need to talk about but mostly I think there's a breakdown of trust between the two of us.' The accusation shocked me.

'Really? A breakdown of trust, Minister? You know, as you are sitting there, that there is no breakdown of trust,' I responded. I had always enjoyed a cordial relationship with her and at no stage prior to this meeting had she ever suggested she could not trust me.

Mabandla then asked me to resign. I refused, stating that I had no reason to do so and that my resignation would not be in the interest of the rule of law and prosecutorial independence. I was also clear that if I resigned, I would be lying to the nation.

The minister looked at me across our cups of tea and said, 'Vusi, this is all about integrity and one day I will talk.'

To this day I am puzzled by what she meant by that. I have seen her since and we have chatted about Girly and the kids, but we have never broached this subject again. I am still waiting for that day. I'm looking forward to it because it is my impression that we always worked well together and had a good relationship. One of Girly's greatest disappointments with the entire issue was how Minister Mabandla handled it:

> *When they were about to appoint Vusi to this job, I immediately knew that I would get out of the NIA because I knew the security environment, I knew how things were and I had many questions. And then the minister – Sis' Brigitte – came over to see us on a Sunday and she spent three-quarters of the day with us. It was partly to convince me. She said, 'Girly, we know each other with Vusi, we've worked in the ANC department of justice.'*
>
> *I knew that she got on well with people and that Vusi always got on well with people on the whole, and also that many people were supporting his appointment. I said, 'Sis' Brigitte, I just want to know that it won't turn against him,' and she said, 'No, believe me.'*
>
> *All I'm coming to is that she ditched him and she never even said, 'You know, Girly, things are not right.' We had been friends – not intimate, but we had been friends – from exile days and the struggle. We've always been activists together because government at the senior level has always been like that, but she really disappointed me. I think she came not necessarily to convince me, but to assure us as a family that she would be there, but when things were crumbling, she didn't even lift a phone and say, 'Girly ...' because in my opinion there was more to it than just being minister and a national director.*

The minister mentioned she was uncomfortable about having been in office at a time when she had to ask both my predecessor Ngcuka and me to resign. She also again apologised for her abusive tirade on the phone earlier in the week.

The meeting was over. It ended cordially but the atmosphere remained frosty. I had refused to resign.

I had a couple of hours to spare before my meeting with the president, so I returned home to reflect on the minister's request. Once the sun had set and my resolve was steeled, I drove towards Mahlamba Ndlopfu and the president.

I parked my car and took the walkway to the imposing building a short distance away and made my way up the stairs, through the main entrance.

An immaculately dressed butler opened the door and informed me that the president was expecting me.

The president's residence was unusually busy and there was a buzz of activity. Mahlamba Ndlopfu was normally eerily quiet. It is a big house with two large lounges – you would ordinarily wait in one of the rooms, depending on where your meeting with the president was scheduled to be held.

As usual, the butler came to ask me what I would like to drink. I usually asked for green tea or rooibos – as a rule I never ordered whisky despite being very fond of it. On occasion when I went with McCarthy to see Mbeki, he would order alcohol but I would not. The president would usually be drinking whisky.

That evening I sat in a lounge drinking tea watching the activity around me. There was a lot of movement in the corridors and out of the corner of my eye I caught sight of Mojanku Gumbi. Then Reverend Chikane arrived and we made small talk while we waited for the president to come in. Mbeki arrived dressed in casual attire: khaki pants, a golf shirt and a lumber jacket. He appeared relaxed and sat across from me. We exchanged pleasantries but I knew this would be serious, considering the minister's request for me to resign and my refusal to acquiesce.

Mbeki said he was aware of the minister's request and I informed him I was not prepared to resign. He advised me that if I did not, he would have to suspend me. He then asked whether I would reconsider and pushed me on why I would not resign. I told him what I had told the minister – that it was for the sake of the independence of prosecutors, for the rule of law, and that I would be lying to the country and to myself if I claimed to have resigned voluntarily. I told him to go ahead and suspend me if he felt he should.

Mbeki asked Reverend Chikane to go and prepare the letter of suspension, and I made the connection as to why Gumbi was there at that late hour on a Sunday. Chikane left the room and I remained with the president.

I turned to Mbeki and asked him a question, 'Mr President, can you tell me why you are suspending me?'

He suggested that what had influenced his decision was the question of plea bargains and immunities. He told me it was all about 'interpretation' and that I did not fully appreciate the nature and extent of the threat posed by such criminals to national security.

'Oh, is that so, Mr President?' I paused and looked him in the eye. 'I think you are skating on thin ice on this matter, because this area is the sole domain of prosecutors. I don't think it's your domain.'

The president made no reference at all to the breakdown in my relationship with the minister, which would be the reason given to the country for my suspension.

When Chikane returned with the letter, the president signed it and then handed it to me in an envelope. I didn't open it and placed it on the table next to me before asking Mbeki whether he had thought of appointing an acting NDPP. He assured me he had attended to it.

I stood up and he walked me to the door before shaking my hand. As I was about to leave, the president turned to me and said, 'Vusi, you must remember there is life after the NPA. We'll talk.'

I said, 'Thank you, Mr President.'

I walked out of the door, with the envelope containing my letter of suspension in my hand. Before I reached my car, I passed the president's spokesperson Themba Maseko. We greeted one another and I noticed he was dressed in shorts. He said, 'I was sitting at home when I got the call to come. I don't know what it's all about.'

I said, 'Oh, okay, sharp,' and left it at that. I knew that the media machinery was being kicked into action.

In *The Things that Could Not be Said*, Reverend Chikane has his own version of how events unfolded that Sunday evening and of the difficulty with which Mbeki took the decision:

> *I remember the pain with which Mbeki took the decision to suspend Pikoli. He talked to him like a comrade or a member of the family and expressed a concern that Pikoli was forcing him to contemplate action that he did not want to take, action that might jeopardise his future and his career. Mbeki even asked him how he thought he should act on this matter. Pikoli's response was that the president could act in whatever way he saw fit but he was not going to delay his action as contemplated notwithstanding the risk of a possible bloodbath at the intelligence headquarters.*
>
> *At this stage I remember Mbeki retreating to his office to give Pikoli time to think about this matter and perhaps to find an amicable way of*

dealing with it. However, on his return there was no change in Pikoli's position. Reluctantly, the president had to act by suspending him. If my memory serves me correctly, this interaction with Pikoli took place over two to three days. I could not open the heart of Mbeki to determine how deep the hurt was but from his demeanour and external expressions I can say that he acted as if it was bleeding. It was not the action he wished for, as the public discourse suggests; he was forced to do it.

I still maintain that Reverend Chikane's version and recollection of what transpired is incorrect.

When I arrived home I told Girly what had happened. To her credit, while she was shocked, she showed no panic at all. I retreated to my office and opened the envelope to read the president's letter:

Dear Advocate Pikoli

As you are aware, the Prosecuting Authority forms an important part of our criminal justice machinery and, accordingly, our fight against crime.

This machinery to fight crime was further strengthened in 2000 when Parliament adopted legislation creating the Directorate of Special Operations (DSO), in the office of the National Director of Public Prosecutions.

In recognition of the particular threat posed by organised crime in the country, the DSO was specifically tasked to investigate and institute criminal proceedings relating to organised crime activities.

As a result of the importance of the Prosecuting Authority to the success of our fight against crime, I receive regular reports from government agencies and Ministries about the activities of the Authority.

Organised crime poses a serious threat to our national security. While I accept that the prosecuting Authority has the discretion to enter into plea bargain and/or immunity arrangements with alleged offenders, the public interest must always be considered. Accordingly, in determining what is in the public interest, before exercising such discretion, the Prosecuting Authority must necessarily have regard to the totality of information available to the State.

Such plea bargaining and/or immunity arrangements cannot be done at the expense of our national security.

Clause 179(6) of the Constitution of the Republic of South Africa provides that the Cabinet member responsible for the administration of Justice must exercise final responsibility over the Prosecuting Authority. Accordingly, the Government, on whose behalf the Minister of Justice and Constitutional Affairs exercises this responsibility, must and does have an interest in ensuring that the Prosecuting Authority serves the public interest. In this regard, acting in terms of the dictates of the Constitution, the Minister of Justice and Constitutional Affairs informed me about some of the matters that the National Prosecution was seized with. Some government agencies also advised me of some of the activities relating to the same matters.

The information I have received shows that you have entertained the granting of immunity to members of organised crime syndicates in instances where the prosecution of such people would, in the Government's view, be in the public interest. In some of these matters there seems to be no reason why the Prosecuting Authority would not proceed against all persons implicated in the alleged offences.

I have evaluated the information at my disposal and have reached the conclusion that you, in your capacity as National Director of Public Prosecutions, have failed to appreciate the nature and extent of the threat posed by members of organised crime syndicates to our national security. Such a lack of appreciation in itself amounts to a threat to our national security.

The Minister of Justice and Constitutional Affairs has also drawn my attention to the breakdown of relations between your office and hers due to several incidents, such as your testimony to the Khampepe Commission of Inquiry.

Accordingly, this letter serves to inform you that I, acting in terms of the provisions of section 12(6) of the National Prosecuting Authority Act (the Act), have decided to suspend you from office with immediate effect. You will continue to receive your full benefits during the period of suspension.

Acting in terms of the same provisions of the Act, I have also decided to institute an enquiry into your fitness to hold the office of National Director of Public Prosecutions. The particulars relating to the enquiry will soon be communicated to you.

Yours sincerely
Thabo Mbeki

The following morning, Themba Maseko issued a statement announcing my suspension in which no mention whatsoever was made of the indemnity agreements:

> *24 September 2007*
>
> *President Thabo Mbeki has with immediate effect suspended the National Director of Public Prosecutions (NDPP), Advocate Vusi Pikoli, in terms of section 12(6)(a) of the National Prosecution Act 32 of 1988. This decision was taken on the basis of an irretrievable breakdown in the working relationship between the Minister of Justice and Constitutional Development and the NDPP.*
>
> *The President considers the relationship between the Minister and the NDPP central to the effective administration of justice and the smooth functioning of the National Prosecuting Authority. The relationship breakdown had adverse implications for the NPA and the functioning of the criminal justice system.*
>
> *An enquiry will be instituted in terms of the NPA Act to investigate all matters pertaining to the functioning and role of the NDPP, and make recommendations to the President.*
>
> *The President has appointed Deputy National Director Adv. Mokotedi Mpshe as Acting National Director of Public Prosecutions to ensure that the work of the NPA continues unhindered.*
>
> *Government would like to reassure all South Africans that the functioning of the justice system will not be compromised, especially within the context of the collective challenge to fight crime.*

I believed then – and still believe today – that my suspension was for none of the reasons offered, but rather in order to stop me from prosecuting Jackie Selebi. This belief is supported not only by the contradictory reasons given by Mbeki and Mabandla, but also by events after my suspension that demonstrate government interference in the Selebi case.

Girly shares my view that the sole reason for my suspension was because of my insistence on prosecuting Selebi:

> *It's happened to all liberation movements. We come from a culture of*

when qabane has done something, when a comrade has done something, you cover up, you don't expose each other, you stick together. That is the mantra, basically. You don't expose him, you cover up, you stick together. And the pressure becomes very strong on you, even from your superiors. It was about covering up for Jackie. I hear the part about the fact that Vusi defied the president. But it had to do with the fact that the president was covering up for Jackie.

In my opinion, Jackie's shenanigans started as far back as Shell House, when he was working in the department of social welfare. Those vibes were strong when you met him, this guy, he has a tsotsi angle about him. But it was just the talk. Those were the days when they covered up, kept it quiet.

I'm not entirely certain why Mbeki was so anxious to protect Selebi, but the position of national commissioner is a powerful one. At the time Mbeki was an isolated president. The ANC no longer trusted him and there was this groundswell anti-Mbeki movement following the dismissal of Zuma as deputy president of the country.

I found Mbeki to be a lonely man and this came through when our meetings would go on unnecessarily – he simply wanted to talk politics and there were few people he could talk to. Also, given his long friendship with Selebi, he must have seen in Selebi an ally that could assist him in his political fights within the ANC. Selebi was in control of the VIP protectors and of Crime Intelligence and that gave them control over the instruments they needed. Selebi was an ally Mbeki needed in place in the run-up to the ANC conference in Polokwane.

The next morning, I held a meeting with my deputies to inform them all of my suspension. My special advisor, Kalyani Pillay, recounts what transpired:

It was a Sunday night towards the end of September when Vusi called to say that he was suspended, and of course I was absolutely shocked. I never thought that that would happen and when I realised that he was serious about it, it was disappointing and really shocking purely because I know the kind of person that he is and I knew what he stood for and how

> *true he was to his own beliefs. He never acted contrary to how he spoke and what he believed in and one of the things that he asked was the next day – it was Monday and a public holiday – and he had asked that we come; he asked for a meeting with the deputy national directors of public prosecution and myself, so it was Advocate Mpshe, Leonard McCarthy, Willie Hofmeyr, Silas Ramaite and myself. Leonard and Willie were neighbours of Vusi because they lived on the property of the DSO. And he said to us that he called us in just to tell us that he was suspended. It wasn't a very long meeting; we were all of course disappointed and upset about it and he handed over the office keys to us because he felt that he would rather not keep the office keys because he didn't want to be seen to come onto the NPA property or to go into his office because he didn't want to have allegations made about him interfering or removing anything. I think I was almost in a state of shock. I didn't think that that would happen purely because for me there was no wrongdoing. We dealt with the matters in terms of the law. We dealt with the matters based on the facts before us, the information had been put in front of us by the investigating team and the prosecuting team, decisions were made based on what was there, and so it comes as a little bit of a shock that you suddenly find that he was suspended. So the mood was quite sombre, everyone was a little bit down.*

Mpshe mentioned to us at this meeting that the president and the minister were upset that the DSO had applied for warrants against Selebi, without reverting to the president. It was clear to me that this was the main reason for my suspension, although – in view of the numerous reports and briefings to both the minister and the president – I could not understand the complaint.

The day after that Reverend Chikane spoke out following a briefing to opposition parties. Chikane is reported to have told representatives that the breakdown between the minister and myself was not personal but rather that 'something had gone wrong' in the exercise of reporting to the minister in terms of the Constitution. On the same day, Mpshe, who was by now acting NDPP, held back a media statement prepared and agreed to by the deputies and himself. The reason given for holding back the media statement was that the minister was unhappy with its contents, particularly the part stating that management of the NPA supported me. Mpshe was also asked to review my decision on the same day that he was appointed acting NDPP.

A few days later Mpshe announced he was appointing an independent panel to review the case against Selebi. Even though Mpshe insisted at the time that it was his decision to do this, I believe it was a decision imposed on him by government. Why would Mpshe see the need to appoint an independent panel when he was party to the decision to prosecute Selebi and on more than one occasion indicated that he believed Selebi had a case to meet? Curiously, the day before Mpshe had apparently made this decision, the president – speaking from New York – was quoted on SABC making reference not only to the enquiry into my fitness to hold office but also a 'second enquiry', which could only be a reference to the independent panel reviewing the Selebi case.

Advocate Gumbi then requested that Mpshe apply for the cancellation of the Selebi warrants. It emerged during the Ginwala Inquiry that Menzi Simelane, the DG of justice, had prepared a draft affidavit in support of the application to cancel the warrants. This is a clear indication that government interfered in the prosecution of Selebi and led the decision to apply for the cancellation of the arrest and search warrants. A magistrate in Randburg cancelled the arrest warrant five days after I was suspended, but Mpshe was unsuccessful in trying to cancel the search warrants. Both Gumbi and Simelane attempted to conceal their involvement in the decision to apply for the cancellation of the warrants, as this amounted to overt interference.

Kalyani Pillay remained at the NPA for a short while after my suspension. She remembers that time well:

> *Advocate Mpshe was appointed as the acting head and we said we would do a press statement and we sat down as an executive on the Tuesday and we prepared a short press statement. It was not controversial. It was just stating the fact that he had been suspended and that he – Vusi, personally – was happy to go through the process of having a fair opportunity to have the matter investigated and for him to have the opportunity to give his side of it and that we would support the process. But it was … I was told, being the special advisor to the national director, I was obvi-*

ously seen as a 'Vusi person' and I fully accepted that. I think when you are a special advisor you go with the person, so I was not invited to the further meeting except that I was informed there was a decision by the minister of justice at the time who said that there was no need for a press statement to be released. It was disappointing. I didn't see why not; it was just letting the public know, Mr Pikoli was a public figure. The head of the National Prosecuting Authority and to be suspended, there was nothing wrong with showing some solidarity towards him because we honestly believed that there was no wrongdoing and, of course, it was proved there was no wrongdoing. I was notified telephonically by Advocate Mpshe that the warrants had been withdrawn. I was really surprised. I was very disappointed actually, because I didn't believe that it was the right decision. And it was one of the things that made me realise that, as advisor, I probably had no role to play any further and so I made the decision that that was the time that I should leave the NPA. If I had no value to add, then it was pointless being there.

Over the next two months my lawyers addressed faxes and e-mails to Simelane and Gumbi requesting all documents relating to the investigation and prosecution of Selebi. Eventually, in early November, Simelane responded: 'We are not aware of any prosecution processes that may have been initiated against the National Commissioner.'

This response was remarkable, bearing in mind that Gumbi had requested Mpshe to apply for the cancellation of the warrants and therefore must have been aware of the NPA's decision to prosecute Selebi. Similarly, Simelane must have been aware of the NPA's decision to prosecute Selebi, as he had prepared a draft affidavit for the application to cancel the warrants.

The chronology of the events that took place after I was removed from office demonstrates to me that my suspension was not the result of the many complaints pressed by government in its submissions to the Ginwala Inquiry. Rather, it was the direct result of the fact that the NPA under my direction had obtained arrest and search warrants against Selebi. It shows a pattern of lies.

Those in government and the ANC leadership didn't expect me to refuse to resign and my refusal caught them napping. They had not expected that from a loyal cadre of the ANC. But they confused two important issues: my political allegiance to the party and my oath of office. To me, the Constitution and the law come first.

PART FIVE

Life after the NPA

The Ginwala Inquiry

When news of my suspension hit the radio and newspapers, I began to get messages from friends and colleagues voicing their concern, outrage and support. To this day some people even joke that they remember where they were when they heard about it. Throughout that period I received many calls from people and I was regularly stopped in the street or in shopping malls, from Pretoria to Queenstown, by people expressing their support.

I am not so naïve as to believe that everybody supported me. There were many who may not have, but they certainly did not confront me. I remain extremely grateful to those who genuinely came to my defence, from all corners of South Africa; ordinary people who told me they believed the truth would come out in the end. All of a sudden, my face was recognised in shopping malls and even car guards would say, 'I know you! I know you! *Hayi*, Mr Pikoli, man, I've read about you. Keep it up, Mr Pikoli, keep it up. I like what you are doing.' So I would be buoyed and that also strengthened my conviction.

Soon after my suspension all the directors of the High Court divisions at the NPA came to see me at home. They were very concerned and wanted to know how they could mobilise the prosecutors behind me. I insisted that I did not want marches and I did not want demonstrations. I wanted everybody at their desks doing their jobs. I felt that was the honourable way of supporting me, by getting on with the job. I knew the fight was not about me, that it was about the institution, so I didn't want to disrupt the service.

I did not feel bitter or even betrayed about my suspension. I accepted it as something I simply needed to work through. In the days after the announcement, a delegation of pastors and priests from my church came to see me at my home in Port Elizabeth. They asked how I felt about what had happened, and I explained that I regarded my suspension as my second initiation into manhood.

When you go to the mountain or to the bush to be prepared for manhood, you face all sorts of difficulties and pain and it is not an easy process. Firstly, it requires courage to go through that but it is also an untravelled path you are walking for the first time. It is only once you arrive that you get to know the pain you will go through, the difficulties you will experience and the challenges with which you will be faced.

You learn how to stand up to challenges in life and not buckle. You begin to understand that there will be times when you will fall. You have to pick yourself up and continue along the path. You go through that training and you absorb the wisdom of the elderly.

This experience reminded me of that time.

It was painful, but I had to endure the pain in order to get through it. There were many challenges I had to weather. I turned to the elders in my community and in my church for their wisdom and their guidance.

Sizwe was not with me but this time I had my wife and my family and my genuine friends at my side. I was also getting support from the broader community and that strengthened my resolve to get through it. I had to endure a second initiation in order to become a man again.

I had dedicated myself to government and to doing my job properly – and my reward was a suspension. I accepted it, of course, but I also acknowledged that it was not personal. I was not suspended because I was Vusi Pikoli, but rather because I was an incumbent in an official position in government and I just happened to be occupying the post at that time. I harboured no bitterness.

I was, however, puzzled as to why I was sitting at home. What wrong had I done? I felt I had done my job to the best of my abilities and I was not being defiant. I also believed I had made the right decision by refusing to resign and that the inquiry would be the correct forum for me to tell the country what I had done and why.

I spent many long months waiting for the inquiry to start. Girly took strain emotionally over that period, but also believes that it may have been a blessing in disguise:

Those were terrible, difficult, hard months. I felt real pain. We certainly found ourselves with very, very few friends. People were afraid to be seen with us, or even to visit us, or even to pick up a phone to us. One of the saddest, most malicious things was that they often would not pay Vusi. For several months we didn't have a cent and we had to live off friends, relatives and strangers, who were touched by Vusi's case. Nangomso, maz'ethole! And may God bless all those who supported my husband during that period.

Lawyers would then raise the salary issue formally with the department and only then would the situation be attended to. I will always ask the question as to who issued the instruction not to pay and on what grounds as I considered this malicious. Time heals but it's difficult to forget. This is one of the incidents that made me grow up in leaps and bound emotionally. In life even in the midst of pain there will always be good lessons; we just have to stop focusing on the pain and look deeper.

We kept ourselves busy. Vusi wasn't prepared to find himself loitering and he had to keep himself occupied. We are both into gym, into going for long walks, that kind of thing, so we went into that in a big way. It was a rule, you don't sleep beyond seven o'clock. Go to the gym, go for a walk, read, get in touch with what's happening at home.

Also, it was a chance to reconnect with our families. At the end of the day, we had neglected them. We were children who went from university into exile, from exile into building our careers and, at the same time, continuing with the struggle in terms of the ANC and raising children.

We had time now to have a relationship with our parents. And it also gave us a chance to find ourselves. I got in touch with who I am and where I come from. I suddenly was just Girly Majola Pikoli, and he was suddenly just Vusumzi Pikoli. Just walking and being amongst your family and knowing how to make do.

I always tell people that one thing is for sure: if Vusi had still been national director of the NPA, he wouldn't have been able to connect with his children in the way that he did. It was the year my children went into the bush, both of them, and most of the time, the father figure tends to be very close, to spend more time with the boys and make sure that everything is in order. It gave him time with the boys he wouldn't have had if he had been the NDPP, so it was a real benefit in one sense.

I used that time to reconnect with my family. I had been involved in government work ever since I had come back from exile and had been so immersed in my jobs that I had little to no time to spend with my relatives. Now I had the time to go home to Port Elizabeth to be with my father, who was sickly. I also spent time with my wife and my children, watching sport on television with my kids, on the golf course and doing what I love to do – cook. I can't say that my handicap improved significantly over this time though, despite playing as regularly as I could. But my cooking certainly improved. I have always admired my mother's cooking, so this gave me an opportunity to spend more time in the kitchen cooking my favourite dishes: oxtail and pig trotters. Regardless of my wife's many attempts to get me to eat vegetables, I still spent more time cooking meat.

There was also an opportunity for reflection and introspection. I was able to reflect on why I had joined the struggle and what had happened to me subsequently. I considered whether I had missed something in terms of not doing what comrades expect of people deployed to government positions. I reflected on what Ngcuka had been through and recalled my mother's warning about the position of NDPP. And yet, although it was a tough time, I never regretted taking the job.

It was also a time of spiritual growth for me. I met a chap in the gym who happened to be a pastor and he would come to my house to pray for me. I've always been spiritual and even while I was deeply involved in the struggle for national liberation, religion remained a constant in my life. My faith strengthened my resolve because I knew God would not forsake me as I was fighting for the truth and that would emerge victorious. I knew it didn't matter how long it would take because the truth would not change and liars would have to have good memories to remember what they had said.

During periods when I am going through bouts of depression for whatever reason, be it financial trouble or a death in the family, what strengthens me is my determination to abstain from my favourite whisky. I do not drink when I am down, simply because I believe that this is a time for reflection. By indulging in alcohol, your problems will not disappear; they will only be made worse. You wake up and the problem is still there. Life ebbs and flows and is never linear, and during periods when I feel I am not in control then I must remain alert and vigilant. During tough times drinking becomes a luxury I can ill afford.

During this difficult time, I also cast my mind back to my first initiation and the support I had received from Sizwe. At the initiation school, we gave each other support. He was not with me this time to help me through the experience, but I have no doubt he would have encouraged me in my moments of despair and turmoil. Fortunately, Phaki and Thozi and other loyal friends were indeed at my side and over that time I was truly able to establish who my friends were.

Of course, I also lost friends. Some felt I was being defiant and disrespectful to the president, that a cadre of the ANC should not behave in such a manner. Those accusations didn't worry me as I felt that those people were not able to draw a distinction between the state and the party. I never suspended my ANC membership, but I did not attend branch meetings because I did not want to be the cause of any tension. I felt I needed space.

But at no point was I ever deflated – instead, I was determined for the truth to emerge because I sincerely believed my suspension had everything to do with trying to protect Jackie Selebi.

I had my first meeting with Advocate Wim Trengove in Grahamstown shortly after my suspension. I had met Trengove before when he had done work for the Scorpions and when we had both addressed the same conferences. I have always held him in high regard as he is a brilliant lawyer with a sharp mind. He is also progressive, very sincere, warm and meticulous. He never misses a thing.

Trengove was doing work at Rhodes University at the time so we met at my cousin Zimasa's house in Grahamstown. Trengove recalls how he first heard about my suspension and why he agreed to take the case:

> *I had been advising the state on their planned search and seizure of Selebi's offices and home and for some months I had given them some advice in relation to their plan to arrest, search and prosecute Selebi. So I had been involved in that saga and I also knew of Pikoli's role in it and I had also read papers that they had provided me with from time to time. I was at the first 20/20 World Championship cricket at the Wanderers when I received an SMS from Willie Hofmeyr to say that Mbeki had suspended Pikoli, and in those days Willie was as outraged as the rest of us were. It*

was obvious to me that Mbeki was just stopping him from prosecuting Selebi and I was really shaken, and Willie too. I had no doubt from the beginning that that was the reason.

I first approached law firm Bowman Gilfillan to represent me as my attorneys. They were initially eager to take the case and I had a consultation with Tim Gordon-Grant, but the firm's board was reluctant and cited a 'commercial conflict of interest' because they were doing work for the department of safety and security and SAPS at the time.

I then went to Deneys Reitz, which is now Norton Rose Fulbright, and met with the chairman Michael Hart. He asked attorney Aslam Moosajee to represent me. Moosajee is an absolute workaholic and incredibly efficient and capable. Coincidentally, his article clerk at the time was my daughter's best friend, Lwando Xhaso, whom I regard as my own daughter. That gave me comfort – she is a brilliant young lady. She once served as Justice Edwin Cameron's clerk at the Constitutional Court and then went on to study at Notre Dame University and has just obtained her second LLM *magna cum laude*.

That legal team took the case on as its own and it became personal for them. They realised that it was bigger than me – it was about our democracy, about the legal profession and about the independence of prosecutors. It was an investment in our democracy.

I spent a considerable amount of time in chambers with Trengove and at Moosajee's offices in Sandton preparing for the case and drawing up legal papers. I had to be nudged on dates and needed to scrutinise my memory bank. There were preliminary hearings for which we had to submit papers and the process was intensive. Moosajee was methodical in preparing documents but he also had to overcome unusual difficulties, as he recalls:

It was lots of hard work. It was also not the conventional way that we were used to doing things because fairly early on we got told that you've got to be careful about how you disseminate information. You've got to be careful that people may be intercepting e-mails, they may intercepting telephone calls. And I just thought that it's pie in the sky. But because the client – what I thought was paranoia at the time – because the client wanted me to be careful and those were his instructions, I had to be a little more careful. So it was often a case of not simply preparing a draft statement and e-mailing that to counsel, but having that saved onto a memory stick or disk and then having that delivered to counsel's secretary and getting them to download it onto their computer to try to protect the information.

It turned out that Vusi's concerns were not at all entirely misplaced because there was some guy that had intercepted communications between myself and Vusi that then tried to sell stuff to eTV but they chose not to pay that particular person. I didn't know exactly who the individual was but we had received the threat that unless we pay a sum of money, he is going to be releasing information. We said we are not going to respond to blackmail and we immediately notified Dr Ginwala that the threat had occurred. It was, in fact, a very stressful time for all of us because we were all working really, really hard and eventually I decided that I am taking a three-or-four-day break to go down to the coast, and while I was at the coast with my family, the story broke and there were lots of journalists phoning and wanting interviews.

The day before the inquiry was scheduled to begin, I received a pleasant surprise. A friendly conspiracy had taken place among my wife, my eldest sister and my aunts. All five of my aunts and two of my sisters had travelled all the way from Port Elizabeth and from Itsoseng in the North West province to be with me. I was so emotional, I almost cried. I had not expected anyone from home to be there and they had travelled 15 hours on a bus to be with me.

We prayed together that evening for the truth and for justice to prevail. It reminded me of my younger days when there were all these people around at home. The house was full and warm and my resolve was strengthened.

On the morning of 7 May 2008, before I left home, I said my own private prayer to ask the Lord's guidance and for help to remain cool and not get worked up. I knew people would be there to lie in order to ensure I lost my job and I would need strength to make sure that I didn't hold them personally responsible.

We made our way to the council chamber in the Metropolitan Building in Braamfontein, the designated venue for the commission's hearings. It is a monolithic, grey building perched on Braamfontein Hill and the chamber is buried deep within. Plush, green high-backed chairs form an auditorium-like setting with microphones, their red lights announcing your intention to speak, on the polished wooden desks before you.

I have never been photographed so much as when I walked into the chamber and took my seat alongside Trengove, Advocate Tim Bruinders and Moosajee.

Shortly after my suspension, the president announced that former Speaker of Parliament Dr Frene Ginwala would be chairing the inquiry into my fitness to hold office. I knew her well from my time as NDPP and at one stage she had even asked me to be her legal advisor in parliament. We had met occasionally at legal conferences in the days of exile and were together in Lusaka for a short period.

I had always known Dr Ginwala to be a person of integrity, one with a reputation as a strict taskmaster who sometimes annoyed even the ANC benches in parliament. Although I did have some apprehension – because I knew she was close to the president at the time – I was also certain she would remain professional as a lawyer in pursuit of the truth.

I greeted Ginwala and the rest of her commission, which included Advocate Ishmael Semenya SC, Dines Gihwala and Kasper Hahndiek as well as the inquiry secretary Lawson Naidoo. I also knew the state's team – Advocate Kgomotso Moroka SC, Advocate Seth Nthai SC, Advocate Horace Shozi and Advocate Mahlape Sello. On my team was Trengove, Moosajee, Bruinders and Advocate Benny Makola.

Ginwala opened proceedings by outlining her terms of reference:

> *This is an inquiry that is contemplated in legislation, namely the National Prosecuting Authority Act. The inquiry is required to report to the president. It is akin to an internal inquiry to review and to advise the president on the fitness of Adv Pikoli to hold the office of National Director.*
>
> *After I have submitted my report to the president he may, should he wish to remove Adv Pikoli from office, table a report to parliament with this recommendation. Parliament will then discuss the recommendation from the president and may concur with it or reject the recommendation. If it is rejected the president will have to reinstate Adv Pikoli. If on receipt of the report of the inquiry the president decides to reverse the provisional suspension he will simply reinstate Adv Pikoli as the National Director of*

Public Prosecutions.

I want to emphasise that this process is not a judicial one. It is not a commission of inquiry governed by the Commissions Act and the president has not issued any regulations with directives about the rules. Indeed the terms of reference specifically delegate to me the power to formulate the rules of the inquiry. It is an information-gathering exercise and one that must assist me in reporting on the matters raised in the terms of reference. It is an inquisitorial as opposed to an accusatorial process.

The terms of reference identify the issues that have to be determined as: The fitness of Adv Pikoli to hold the office of National Director, in particular whether he in exercising his discretion to prosecute offenders had sufficient regard to the nature and extent of the threat posed by organised crime to the national security of the Republic. Whether he in taking decisions to grant immunity from prosecution to, or entering in plea bargaining arrangements with, persons who are allegedly involved in illegal activities which constitute organised crime as contemplated in the Act, took due regard to the public interest and the national security interests of the Republic as contemplated in Section 198 of the Constitution, as well as the Prosecution policy. Whether the relationship between the National Director and the Minister has irretrievably broken down. In particular whether he failed to appreciate the nature and extent of the constitutional and legal oversight powers of the minister over the prosecuting authority and such other matters as may relate to the fitness and propriety of the National Director to hold office.

As I have already said the process will be an inquisitorial as opposed to an accusatorial process. However, we need to provide structure and clarity to the process bearing in mind that we do not have precedents. With this inquiry we are charting new territory and must be guided by the principles enshrined in the Constitution and specifically ensure that it is a process that adheres to the tenets of natural justice, embodies fairness and follows due process.

The state's advocate Kgomotso Moroka had an opportunity to make opening remarks, which concluded with the nub of her argument:

We will show at the end of this inquiry that the oral evidence tendered

> *by government, together with the affidavits filed and as a totality of the evidence, that there are no disputes of fact that directly impact on the decision this inquiry is called upon to make arising from the terms of reference. We will therefore ask at the end that this inquiry find and recommend that having regard to this evidence and the circumstances that Mr Pikoli is not fit and proper to hold that office and that having regard to the nature and constitutional responsibilities of the minister, the relationship between the minister and Mr Pikoli has indeed irretrievably broken down.*

The public hearings lasted for 11 days, between 7 May 2008 and 1 August 2008. In total, evidence was tendered by seven witnesses. These included, for government, Deputy Minister of Justice and Constitutional Development Johnny de Lange; DG in the Presidency Reverend Frank Chikane; DG of the Department of Justice and Constitutional Development Menzi Simelane; DG of the National Intelligence Agency Manala Manzini; and Deputy DG of the National Intelligence Agency Arthur Fraser.

I testified in my own defence and also called Gerrie Nel. This evidence was supplemented by written affidavits from colleagues Thanda Mngwengwe, Silas Ramaite, Charin de Beer, Kalyani Pillay and criminal attorney Ian Small-Smith.

All the witnesses called by the state, with the exception of Deputy Minister De Lange, wanted me to be fired. De Lange was the first to take the stand and was there to testify about his understanding of the relationship between the NDPP and the jstice minister and the issue of independence.

Chikane took the stand after him. He mentions in his book *The Things that Could Not be Said* how difficult it was for him to sit opposite me in the inquiry and to testify against me.

For my part, I saw no pain in his face and heard no pain in his voice. I was puzzled by his evidence and, to be honest, I could not believe what he was saying. He painted a distorted picture and tried to create an impression that I was callous and reckless to the extreme, that I refused to listen to the president and was disrespectful to him. He claimed I knew little about state security – even though I 'grew up' in that environment – and tried to convince the commissioners I was not fit for the job. Chikane and I had always worked well together; I respected him and still do, so I'm not sure what caused the shift but he clearly felt I had to go. He presented this picture of a madman who had to be stopped, failing which the whole country would go up in flames. In my opinion, it was a deliberate distortion, a lie, and I suspect he was trying to cover up his own failure in handling the process.

My team and I were hopeful that Minister Mabandla would come to the inquiry and testify, but we suspected that she would not because she knew her testimony would not have withstood the rigours of cross-examination. I was disappointed because one of the reasons cited for my not being fit and proper for office was because of the so-called breakdown in our relationship. The minister was the best person to testify on that because no one else can testify to the relationship between two people. Under oath, she would have been forced to tell the truth. Unfortunately, Dr Ginwala also seems, in my opinion, to have protected Mabandla because she could have called her to testify and yet she did not. I believe Dr Ginwala should have called Mabandla – I reported to the minister and she took final responsibility over the NPA.

Lawson Naidoo was the secretary of the Ginwala Inquiry. As he explains, Dr Ginwala felt that she did not have the power to subpoena the minister:

> *There was no manual available in terms of what sort of inquiry this was. One thing that was clear is that it wasn't a Commission of Inquiry governed by the Commissions Act and therefore we had to sort of make it up as we went along. There were certain discussions that we had. Whether we had the right to subpoena witnesses was an issue that was in doubt because we weren't a formal Commission of Inquiry, so we were not clear that we necessarily had the right to subpoena witnesses. But Dr Ginwala felt, on the basis of the affidavits that were presented and the other witnesses that were presented by the government, that sufficient opportunity had been given for the government allegations to be made and for people to be cross-examined on the basis of those allegations and, obviously, specifically Simelane.*

Instead, DG Menzi Simelane was called as the state's main witness. His evidence before the inquiry received considerable attention and ultimately proved to be the indelible stain against his character that saw him lose his job as my successor at the NPA.

I have never been Simelane's friend, and as I sat there listening to him testify I felt anger welling up inside me. From his demeanour to the language he used and the way he talked down to me, his attitude reflected only disdain and dislike for me. I would have expected him to be more professional, and I was appalled.

One of the most contentious issues he covered was around the independence of the NDPP and the oversight of the justice ministry and who the accounting officer was. Simelane disputed that the Constitution guarantees the independence of the NPA and that the justice minister could determine whether or not it was in the public interest for someone to be prosecuted. He felt that I should have reported to him as DG and, prior to my suspension, I had heard talk that he felt there was not space for both him and me in the department.

When he was appointed DG, I believe I tried to create a platform for us to meet and to discuss matters of mutual interest between the department and the NPA, because I had enjoyed a fairly good relationship with Ngcuka when I was DG. Simelane, however, kept dismissing me and we never actually met. Then he began to interfere in NPA matters, on personnel issues, such as who should be appointed, and I felt he was overstepping the mark. I told him as much. Eventually, in January 2006, I took the extraordinary step of writing a letter to the justice minister out of frustration:

> *Unfortunately, an impression is being created that there are two Heads of the NPA or there is co-management. This manifests itself in members of the NPA engaged in core business being called by the DG without me being requested or informed. I find this untenable and am not going to allow it to continue any longer.*
>
> *I have always favoured partnership and cooperation and I still do but an impression must never be created that the DG is my manager or I account to him. It is the Minister of Justice and Constitutional Development who in law and fact exercises final responsibility over the NPA in terms of s33 of the NPA Act and the NPA in turn accounts to Parliament in terms of s35(1) of the NPA Act. If I am to succeed in my job, I cannot be told by the DG as to what a scarce resource is and the competency profile of staff in my office. I find it annoying, undermining and totally unacceptable.*

During his testimony, Simelane attempted to mislead the commission about the fact that he had sought legal advice on this issue:

> <u>ADV TRENGOVE</u>: *You said you took no legal advice on this issue, correct?*
> <u>ADV SIMELANE</u>: *No, I don't remember really getting counsel opinion on it. No in fact, yes I think you are quite right, we actually did, we got the opinion of Adv Maleka, yes now I recall and Adv Khoza, yes we did.*
> <u>ADV TRENGOVE</u>: *Mr Simelane, you said you took no advice. You repeated that same answer and then when you saw me turning up a document you changed your mind.*
> <u>ADV SIMELANE</u>: *No you are quite wrong. What I was trying to recall was what the opinion was and it actually covered quite a lot of issues, more than this one specific issue. So I am quite correcting myself that we did actually get an opinion on a whole range of issues about the role of the NDPP. If I recall that was our opinion yes.*
> <u>ADV TRENGOVE</u>: *And from whom did you take the opinion?*
> <u>ADV SIMELANE</u>: *I remember from Adv Maleka and Adv Khoza.*
> <u>ADV TRENGOVE</u>: *Adv Maleka, one of the most senior practitioners at the Johannesburg Bar and an advocate of high standing, correct?*
> <u>ADV SIMELANE</u>: *Yes he is regarded as such.*
> <u>ADV TRENGOVE</u>: *Now in fact he provided you with an opinion and a supplementary opinion, is that correct?*
> <u>ADV SIMELANE</u>: *Yes I think there was a sup, yes.*
> <u>ADV TRENGOVE</u>: *I would – they are quoted in our heads of argument, do you have a copy of our heads of argument?*
> <u>ADV SIMELANE</u>: *No not here.*
> <u>ADV TRENGOVE</u>: *Can I present you with a copy? Madam Chair I am referring to page 48 of our heads of argument, paragraph 85. Mr Simelane, we quote in that paragraph from the main opinion of Advocates Maleka and Nobanda of 16 January 2007 and they say the following in paragraph 50:*
>
> *'Our view is that the director general has no authority at all over the exercise of powers, functions and duties by functionaries of the National Prosecuting Authority. All that the director general is entitled to do is*

> *to exercise financial responsibility on the financial requirements of the National Prosecuting Authority. His powers in that regard are set out in Section 36 of the NPA Act, read together with the relevant provisions of the Public Finance Management Act.'*
>
> *Is that correct?*
> *ADV SIMELANE: Yes, that is correct, the opinion, yes.*

He was obviously wrong – both in law and in fact. Simelane ignored the legal advice and I think the department still ignores that advice today. It is as if the NPA is a division of the department of justice, even though it cannot be because the NDPP must be responsible for setting targets and therefore setting budgets. He should determine the type and quality of skills he needs in order to be able to achieve that. You can't have two people competing over that; it is important for the independence of the NPA.

Under cross-examination at the Ginwala Inquiry, Simelane also confirmed that he was the author of the letter that Minister Mabandla had handed to me instructing me not to arrest Jackie Selebi. I had suspected at the time that she had not read or written it and my suspicions were finally confirmed by Simelane.

In her findings, Dr Ginwala was highly critical of Simelane's evidence and labelled him arrogant and condescending. She found that Simelane could have misled the inquiry by hiding the legal opinion on the relationship between the DG and the NDPP:

> *The DG: Justice had an incorrect understanding of his accounting responsibilities under the PFMA [Public Finance Management Act], despite being in possession of legal opinions from senior counsel explaining the ambit of his responsibilities. He allowed the Minister to continue with an incorrect understanding of the responsibilities of the NDPP.*

Ginwala also slammed Simelane for drafting the 18 September letter from Minister Mabandla to me, in which she instructed me not to proceed with the arrest of Selebi and which amounted to political interference:

> *The conduct of the DG: Justice in drafting the document in the manner*

> *it reads was reckless to say the least. The DG: Justice should have been acutely aware of the constitutional protection afforded to the NPA to conduct its work without fear, favour or prejudice. The contents of the letter were tantamount to executive interference with the prosecutorial independence of the NPA, which is recognised as a serious offence in the Act.*

Ultimately Ginwala found Simelane to be dishonest:

> *I must express my displeasure at the conduct of the DG: Justice in the preparation of Government's submissions and in his oral testimony which I found in many respects to be inaccurate or without any basis in fact and law. He was forced to concede during cross-examination that the allegations he made against Adv Pikoli were without foundation.*

After her report was released, new Justice Minister Enver Surty asked the Public Service Commission (PSC) to investigate Ginwala's findings. The PSC recommended disciplinary action be taken against Simelane, but Surty's successor, Jeff Radebe, ignored the recommendation. Instead, Simelane was appointed as the national director of public prosecutions as my successor.

The Democratic Alliance (DA) went to court to challenge the appointment on the basis that the president did not properly apply his mind and that Simelane was not fit and proper to hold the office of NDPP. The DA based its application largely on Ginwala's findings and Simelane's testimony at the inquiry.

In October 2012 the Constitutional Court, in a hard-hitting judgment, set aside Zuma's decision to appoint Simelane. The court found that Simelane's testimony at the inquiry was 'contradictory and, on its face, indicative of Mr Simelane's dishonesty and raised serious questions about Mr Simelane's conscientiousness, integrity and credibility'.

During his testimony at the inquiry, Simelane clearly showed that he lacked integrity and was not fit to be the head of the NPA. He got what he deserved, but I refuse to rejoice in someone else's misery.

Advocate Trengove succinctly sums up Simelane's experience on the stand:

It's no doubt that Simelane was the mastermind behind all of it. So I suspect that it was Mbeki who wanted Pikoli out of the way, but Simelane who then did all the dirty work to do whatever is necessary. Simelane also confirmed under cross-examination that he was the architect of the case against Pikoli. He scraped together all the charges and he formulated most of it and so on. Fortunately, his dishonesty showed up in evidence. He was just thoroughly dishonest. He's a clever man, but tragically flawed. I'm glad that he got his comeuppance at the end of the day and in fact, Ginwala criticised him. I just remember that from time to time in the course of his evidence, how affronted Ginwala was, and even sympathetic people like Ish Semenya, whom you must know was an Mbeki-ite, he was very close to Mbeki so there was no impartiality lost there, but he was from time to time offended and outraged by Simelane's arrogance and dishonesty.

My wife was sitting in the public gallery during the inquiry and, with her background in the ANC and the National Intelligence Agency, she had a shared history with many of those who came to give evidence. As she recalls, it was sometimes difficult to keep her emotions in check:

I had always admired Frene Ginwala and, maybe she didn't know, but going into parliament as a member of parliament, she was my mentor. I had always admired this woman who was so forthright. She didn't need friends to concoct her profile because she knew her work in her own right and worked so hard. So she would take me aside, like this little girl, or daughter she never had, and she would say, 'Girly ...'

But at the same time, she must be the chairperson of the commission and I said, 'No, no, no, Frennie, don't worry, just do your job.' I must admit, it was difficult to manage that relationship, but I think Vusi handled it well.

And I tried, but I will not lie, there is one person I couldn't handle at the Ginwala Inquiry and that was Menzi Simelane.

Once all government's witnesses had been called, it was finally my turn to give evidence. I considered this my opportunity to tell the country what had actually happened and to tell the world the truth. I spent two days giving evidence-in-chief and under cross-examination.

I was relaxed and at peace with myself, grateful to have the opportunity. I had always known my time would come to take the stand and people would finally know what had happened. This was my moment to take the country into my confidence.

Probably the most explosive interchange under cross-examination was when Advocate Moroka pushed me on the 'two week, one week' conversation with Mbeki. I had disputed Chikane's version of what had happened. He had presented me as eager to execute the warrants irrespective of the consequences and I vehemently disagreed. In fact, I got quite worked up and emotional:

> ADV MOROKA: *Rev Chikane gave a version of events in this enquiry, is that correct?*
> ADV PIKOLI: *That is correct.*
> ADV MOROKA: *That version was not disputed under cross-examination, is that correct?*
> ADV PIKOLI: *Now which particular version was not ... [intervenes]*
> ADV MOROKA: *The version that says this is what happened, this is what Mr Pikoli said and this is our response or understanding of what Mr Pikoli said. That's the version that he gave or the account that he gave.*
> ADV PIKOLI: *I am not sure. You know ... [intervenes]*
> ADV MOROKA: *No I am not saying whether ... [intervenes]*
> ADV PIKOLI: *May I? You know I gave my evidence-in-chief which clearly contradicts what Rev Chikane said in his evidence-in-chief and there is no dispute that Rev Chikane did not make any reference to two weeks or one week, or one week for that matter, that is correct, it is not in dispute. And it's not in dispute that I said to the president: A week Mr President would be enough and I have got my reasons for having said that.*
> ADV MOROKA: *Oh no Mr Pikoli we are saying there was no mention of two weeks or one week in that conversation, that's the dispute. And we are saying to you this is a recent fabrication that surfaced when you started giving your evidence-in-chief.*
> ADV PIKOLI: *That's a very serious dispute. If Rev Chikane is to say that there was no mention of time frames. If Rev Chikane is to say there was never any talk of two weeks and a week in my meeting with the president*

and Rev Chikane and the following with Adv McCarthy, going back to that issue, this is very serious. Perhaps counsel might want to rephrase that question.

ADV MOROKA: *Counsel has no intention of rephrasing the question Mr Pikoli, because we are saying it's a contrived version.*

ADV PIKOLI: *I have taken an oath to speak the truth and nothing else but the truth.*

ADV MOROKA: *So did Rev Chikane.*

ADV PIKOLI: *I am sitting here having taken that oath. What would make me want to invent two weeks and a week? This is very serious. The president asked, asked for two weeks. I said: Mr President, I can't afford that. This matter has already unduly delayed the other matters that are in court tied up with this matter. I will be prepared to concede to a week which I thought will give the president as the commander-in-chief sufficient time to call all the security chiefs and command them to create that conducive atmosphere. I said to the president: Mr President, a week. I don't know why we should keep on talking about this. I said it myself and the president said it himself.*

ADV MOROKA: *Mr Pikoli you also had an option … [intervenes]*

ADV PIKOLI: *What did I contrive counsel? What did I contrive counsel?*

ADV MOROKA: *You see Mr Pikoli you are asked, we are asked as the government's legal team in examining Mr Manzini to reflect on a number of issues and one of those issues is the enabling environment. Mr Manzini is asked to set out the enabling environment – let me go to the question itself. The question is to Mr Manzini: What is the nature of the environmental assessment that needs to be conducted in respect of the arrest and/or search of high-profile persons? Mr Manzini speaks to this question. You then contrive an answer, having taken account of what Rev Chikane has said and Mr Manzini about your own concerns about an enabling environment. You had no such concerns before you deposed to your affidavit.*

ADV PIKOLI: *I don't know how to respond Chairperson. I am basically being told by counsel that I am lying. That the president never asked for two weeks, that I never said to the president one week. I don't know how to proceed because I stand by what I said.*

CHAIRPERSON: *I would suggest, Advocate, without directing with how you proceed, that we move on from that because we have got two versions now. So please proceed.*

Watching from the bank of seats alongside me was my legal team of Moosajee, Trengove and Bruinders. Moosajee has one stand-out memory from my time on the witness stand:

> *I remember one particular afternoon when Seth Nthai was cross-examining him and it was just a dreadful afternoon and I was concerned about the image that was being created by that. It was related to the plea-bargain arrangements and cross-examination about that. It was just the way he was being cross-examined and the licking of the lips and the licking of the tie by Nthai [a curious mannerism occasionally displayed by Nthai]. I was quite disgusted by it and I don't know what was going through Seth's mind at the time. It was an uncomfortable afternoon. By the next morning Vusi had gathered his thoughts and was back on track.*

Trengove reflects on how I did under cross-examination:

> *Pikoli is a man of not only high integrity, but integrity comes to him innately, intuitively. He doesn't have to intellectualise about it and he doesn't have to think things through to determine what the proper way is of doing things. It just comes naturally and intuitively. He talks too much, he's too naïve and spontaneous in the way that he discusses these things and gave evidence, so from that perspective he was not an ideal witness, but at the same time, those very characteristics made it very obvious that he was an honest, a naïvely honest witness. So I didn't think he gave evidence particularly strategically well, but his honesty and his integrity and sincerity and naïveté shone through and that won the day.*

When I stepped off the stand I was satisfied with the way I had told my story. The only witness my team called was Advocate Gerrie Nel to give evidence about the plea bargains and indemnity agreements. He put this issue into perspective and explained the basis in law and strategy.

The public hearings were closed and then it was left to Ginwala and the rest of the commission to come to a conclusion based on the facts presented. I felt the whole country had been afforded the opportunity to judge who was right and who was wrong. I was prepared to accept the outcome, whatever it was.

During the time we spent waiting for the findings to be released, I was given an award by the International Association of Prosecutors (IAP) for the stand I had taken in the Selebi matter. The award was made at the 13th annual conference and general meeting of the IAP in Singapore.

The IAP said in a statement that the matter was important not only to South Africa, but also to the international community: 'By defending the principle of independence on behalf of all prosecutors, Mr Pikoli deserves acclamation and recognition from his fellow prosecutors and the community of prosecutors worldwide.'

In receiving the award I stated, 'I am taking a stand for the dignity, credibility and honour of all prosecutors.' Privately I could not help but reflect on the irony of the timing of the award given the inquiry I had just lived through.

The Ginwala Report and what followed

Dr Ginwala completed her report and signed it on 4 November 2008. By that time, the country had a new president. Thabo Mbeki had been recalled – a year to the day after my own suspension – and Kgalema Motlanthe was the president of South Africa.

I was saddened by what happened to Mbeki and felt he conducted himself in a dignified fashion. In my opinion, the ANC treated him badly. All he had was six months to finish his term and it was not as if he had done something so unconstitutional or committed such a heinous crime or gross act of misconduct that would have led to his recall. And, in fact, it turned out that the ANC had based its decision on a judgment that was later overturned on appeal. I think it was simply a matter of dirty politics.

Minister Mabandla resigned along with Mbeki and was replaced as justice minister by Enver Surty. It would now be up to Motlanthe to decide on what action to take regarding my future. In the week after President Motlanthe received the findings, he tabled them before a cabinet meeting and then sent a copy of the report to my lawyers and me, giving us a week in which to express our views.

In short, Ginwala found that the government had failed to prove many of the allegations against me and did not show that I was not a fit and proper person to hold the office of NDPP. Ginwala found that while I impressed her as a man of 'unquestionable integrity, with passion to execute his constitutional responsibilities without fear, favour or prejudice', my suspicion that I had been suspended in order to frustrate the investigation and prosecution of the national commissioner of police was incorrect.

She was also heavily critical of my understanding of issues pertaining to national security and my apparent lack of appreciation of the sensitivities of the political environment in which the NPA operated. Her most serious concern was around the 'one week, two week' conversation with the president and the warrants for Crime Intelligence. Ginwala found that had this been put forward as a reason for my suspension, she would not have hesitated to find the reason to be legitimate.

I was generally happy with the outcome, but I was not pleased with some aspects of her findings. It would not be right to use the word 'vindicated' – at times I get lost in the meaning of 'feeling vindicated' because it becomes a personal triumph. I've always tried to be dispassionate on this matter. However, I was particularly happy with the finding that I am a person of integrity who is fit and proper to hold a position such as that of the NDPP.

In her executive summary, Ginwala detailed the background to the inquiry and began with an explanation of the allegations levelled against me. She said 'some of these allegations are quite tangential to the terms of reference' and are 'often far removed in time from the date of the suspension' while the 'nature and content of the allegations against Adv Pikoli also changed during the course of the Enquiry'.

She then went through each of the allegations and her findings:

> *11 Government's allegations with regard to Adv Pikoli's conduct and the findings that have been made are as follows:*
>
> *11.1 Government alleged that the relationship between the Minister and Adv Pikoli had broken down irretrievably.*
>
> ***This allegation has not been proven.***
>
> *11.2 It was alleged that Adv Pikoli should not have authorised plea and sentence agreements with the persons implicated in the alleged murder of Mr Brett Kebble and should rather have prosecuted all suspects.*
>
> ***Government did not show that Adv Pikoli, in exercising his discretion of whether or not to prosecute, did not take heed of the threat posed by organised crime to national security.***
>
> *11.3 Government alleged that Adv Pikoli should not have concluded*

plea and sentence agreements with some of the alleged Equatorial Guinea mercenaries, and should not have authorised the prosecution of the other alleged Equatorial Guinea mercenaries. It was alleged that the plea and sentence agreements with Mr Agliotti and Mr Nassif did not take due account of the prosecution policy and particularly the public interest and the national security interests of the Republic.

Government failed to produce evidence to show that the cases of plea and sentence agreements it cited had contravened the prosecution policy.

11.4 Government alleged that Adv Pikoli sought to pursue the listing of the DSO as a public entity under the Public Finance Management Act ('PFMA') despite the Minister's concerns that it was a policy matter that required discussion by Cabinet.

Adv Pikoli was legally obliged to inform Treasury that the DSO was not listed as a public entity, but he should have informed the Minister before doing so.

11.5 Government complained that Adv Pikoli failed to account to the Director General of the Department of Justice and Constitutional Development, and thereby prevented the latter from executing his accounting responsibilities.

Adv Pikoli was not obliged to account to the DG: Justice in the manner alleged by Government.

11.6 Government alleged that Adv Pikoli failed to inform the Minister of the information that came into the possession of the DSO and led to the preparation of the Browse Mole Report, and also that he failed to stop the DSO from pursuing a matter that was outside its mandate.

Adv Pikoli was obliged to inform the Minister of the information that emerged from the Browse Mole investigation in March 2006, and he should have ordered the DSO to stop any further involvement in the matter.

11.7 Government complained that Adv Pikoli failed to inform the Minister of the alleged conspiracy to assassinate the Malawian President, and that the involvement of the DSO in the Malawian investigation constituted intelligence gathering and fell outside its mandate.

Adv Pikoli was obliged to inform the Minister of the plot to assassinate the Malawian President as soon as he became aware of it. The

NPA dealt with the matter in terms of the law, and did not investigate an intelligence matter outside its mandate.

11.8 Government alleged that Adv Pikoli did not prevent a member of the DSO from engaging in unregulated contact with foreign intelligence services.

Adv Pikoli could not be held responsible for interaction by members of the DSO with foreign intelligence services that occurred before he took office or of which he was unaware through no fault on his part.

11.9 Government alleged that Adv Pikoli should have informed the Minister before applying for search and seizure warrants at the Union Buildings and Tuynhuys, and should have ensured that adequate measures were in place to prevent any security breaches during the execution of the warrants.

Adv Pikoli failed to inform the Minister and the President prior to applying for the search and seizure warrants at the Union Buildings and Tuynhuys in August 2005, and failed to ensure that proper security measures were followed during this operation.

11.10 Government complained that Adv Pikoli failed to inform the Minister and the President prior to applying for the warrants of arrest and search and seizure against the National Commissioner of Police, and that he failed to exhaust the options for accessing information from the SAPS put in place by the Presidency, which information was required by the DSO for its investigation of Operation 'Bad Guys'.

Adv Pikoli should have informed the Minister before applying for arrest and search and seizure warrants against the National Commissioner of Police. He also failed to exhaust all the options available through the facilitation of the Presidency to access information held by SAPS.

12 Adv Pikoli asserted that the reason for his suspension was to stop the prosecution of the National Commissioner of Police.

This view could not be sustained on the evidence before the Enquiry.

13 I have found that Government has failed to prove many of these allegations and has not demonstrated that Adv Pikoli is no longer fit and proper to hold office as the NDPP. The grounds advanced by Government for the suspension of Adv Pikoli have not been established before the Enquiry.

14 I am not of the opinion that there has been an irretrievable breakdown in the relationship between the Minister and Adv Pikoli. However, their interaction has been marred by differences in understanding of the respective duties and responsibilities of each office with regard to the prosecuting authority. These differences can be overcome though collegial discussion and the establishment of formal channels of communication on operational and policy matters. Moreover, I find it probable that the differences in their respective understandings were precipitated by the DG: Justice's misconception of his authority over the NPA, which influenced his reports to the Minister.

15 I need to draw attention to the conduct of the DG: Justice in this Enquiry. In general his conduct left much to be desired. His testimony was contradictory and without basis in fact or in law. The DG: Justice was responsible for preparing Government's original submission to the Enquiry in which the allegations against Adv Pikoli's fitness to hold office were first amplified. Several of the allegations levelled against Adv Pikoli were shown to be baseless, and the DG: Justice was forced to retract several allegations against Adv Pikoli during his cross-examination.

16 I have also found issues of concern in the capacity and understanding of Adv Pikoli to carry out the responsibilities of the office of NDPP. These relate primarily to his understanding of issues pertaining to national security and his lack of appreciation of the sensitivities of the political environment in which the NPA needs to operate, which sensitivity would not be incompatible with his prosecutorial independence.

17 My most serious concerns arise from the evidence of the discussions between the President and Adv Pikoli at their meetings just prior to Adv Pikoli's suspension. Adv Pikoli also did not give due consideration to the actions the President might need to take in order to defuse a potential security crisis and instability and to preserve the country's international reputation. He did not take seriously the President's concerns about the mood of the SAPS and their possible reaction to the arrest of the National Commissioner; and even challenged the President's assessment of the time he would require to manage the situation. Had this been presented

> *as a reason for the suspension, when his conduct would have held a real risk of undermining national security, I would not have hesitated to find the reason to be legitimate. However, these were not among the reasons put forward by Government before this Enquiry.*
>
> *18 The recommendations that I make are aimed at facilitating a more co-operative approach between the NDPP and the Minister of Justice and Constitutional Development as the political head with final responsibility over the National Prosecuting Authority. It is to be hoped that the implementation of these measures will create a more harmonious relationship between the offices of the NDPP and that of the Minister, and enhance the capacity of the prosecuting authority to execute its functions.*

Naturally, I take issue with some of Ginwala's findings and feel that, at times, she may not have properly applied her mind.

In terms of the conclusions listed above, the first finding against me is with regard to Browse Mole. Ginwala failed to take into account that I did report the matter, although it may not have been immediate because I was told it was still a work in progress at the time. As soon as I was given the second report, I approached the DG of SASS and the DG of NIA. She also ignored the fact I even told the president about it.

On the Malawi investigation, she criticises me for failing to inform the minister, yet the minister wrote a letter to the NPA thanking it for the role it played in that investigation.

Ginwala lashed me for not informing the minister or the president prior to obtaining warrants. There is no legal requirement anywhere that I first had to seek permission or inform either the minister or the president when it came to search warrants. I don't know the legal basis for arriving at such a conclusion and she certainly didn't quote the relevant authority. We had given the minister an extensive briefing in her boardroom and I believe that constituted 'keeping her informed'.

On the question of the search and seizures, we employed a company previously used by SAPS itself to carry out the mirror imaging of computers. I accept I was not aware that not everybody was vetted, but I had put a mechanism in place that Nel and Chikane were to work out how the search was going to be conducted. However, I don't want to come across that, in my opinion, I am faultless or without blame. Perhaps I should have thoroughly checked that the people involved were properly vetted. I accept that.

Ginwala's finding that I failed to exhaust the process established by the president regarding access to SAPS information is simply incorrect. I don't know what else I could have done, and I brought all the relevant information to her at the commission. I listed all the attempts we had made to get the police to cooperate with us.

Ginwala concluded that she could find no substance to my assertion that the reason I was suspended was to stop the prosecution of Selebi. I believe it is at this point that Ginwala's closeness to the president might have influenced her judgment. I don't see how she could have had regard to all the evidence placed before her and still arrive at the conclusion that my suspension had nothing to do with the Selebi case.

Look at all those charges that were brought against me, many of which pre-date my suspension. They could have been brought against me long before Selebi's case. Why were they only levelled when Selebi was about to be arrested? The timeline tells a story.

I think some of Dr Ginwala's findings were to 'save face', especially considering the fact that Mbeki and Mabandla were never called to give evidence. They were the major complainants in the case and, in the normal course of events, the complainant is the main witness, and yet they left it to the officials to do the dirty work – and Ginwala appears to have ignored a number of negative findings against Mabandla and Mbeki. In my opinion, her judgment was clouded by her closeness to the president and she seems to have been torn between doing a professional job and protecting the president. Had Mabandla and Mbeki been called to give evidence and be cross-examined, I'm sure a lot would have come out.

Trengove is perhaps slightly more eloquent on what he made of Ginwala's conclusions:

> *I thought that if we got a fair report we'd be absolved and we got more or less what I expected we would. Although Ginwala did her job with honesty and integrity and I don't accuse her of anything else, she was obviously sympathetic to the president and the party and the establishment and that would be her inclination. Despite that inclination, she still wrote*

a pretty damning report of Simelane and the prosecution of Pikoli and mostly exonerated Pikoli. So it wasn't as unambiguous a vindication as I would have liked, but I thought it had, in the circumstances, gone well.

Lawson Naidoo, the secretary of the inquiry, explains Ginwala's thinking on her findings:

The thing that struck me, and I know it struck other members of the inquiry team, was the absolute integrity of the man. His integrity could not be doubted and I think the character of the man came through, that he was someone that may make mistakes, but he makes honest mistakes and certainly his integrity shone through. When somebody is under the spotlight like that, one is going to find some mistakes that were made. The issue that Vusi is probably referring to is the issue around the one week/two week issue in relation to the implementation of the warrants against Selebi. Dr Ginwala's view was really, this was a call that the president was in a far better position than Vusi to make; as the commander-in-chief, he would have had much greater knowledge of the security threats that were there and if he was to say that he needed two weeks in order to create the conditions, then Vusi was in no position to second-guess him and he had to respect the decision of the commander-in-chief. Yes, it may have left the door open, but from her perspective, that was something that came through and that was the view of that set of circumstances and she felt that she needed to make that point. When you shine a spotlight like that on someone for that length of time in as much detail, you are going to find some flaws. No one is going to come through that kind of a process totally unscathed. And the fact that he came through so relatively unscathed is, I think, testimony to his character.

Some may say that I emerged from the inquiry as defiant and arrogant and far too strong-willed. I believe it was about remaining true to my conscience and my principles. As Thozi explains, that is how I was taught to behave as a young man by Chris Hani:

We believe in our independence, nobody must control us. If you ask me to do something, ask me to do it and I will do it. I don't want to be used by nobody. I'll do a thing that I'm conscious is correct. That's how Chris groomed us up from Lesotho. He said, 'All I'm going to do is to help you theoretically, in terms of doing things, but the things are going to be done by you.' That's the confidence Chris gave us from the word go. And Chris gave us this independence that we must respect him, but guys, let's argue. Don't take things for granted. And we grew up in that culture within the ANC and with Chris. And that is where I think Vusi, that's how Vusi is and that's how we are.

President Motlanthe had to decide what to do with Ginwala's findings and I felt that she had left him a convenient hook that would justify him relieving me of my duties. So it was that at a press conference at the Union Buildings on 8 December 2008, Motlanthe announced I would be removed, despite Dr Ginwala's recommendation that I be reinstated. He cited Ginwala's criticisms that I was not sensitive to matters of national security as his reasoning:

Mindful of all these factors, it became clear to me that I could not come to a decision without taking into account the entirety of the findings of the Enquiry, including in particular the observation that the suspension would have been found valid if the totality of the evidence given by the State had been the basis for the suspension. In the end, I was required as President of the Republic to make a final decision in terms of section 12(6)(a) of the NPA Act on whether or not Advocate Pikoli was fit and proper to continue to hold the office of the National Director of Public Prosecutions. Adv Pikoli's professional competence is not in question. However, it should be noted that the requisite skills would, necessarily, include professional competence as well as those outlined by the enquiry, in particular, appreciation for and sensitivity to matters of national security. Furthermore I have had regard to the provisions of the Constitution. In this regard, acting in terms of sections 12(6)(a)(iv) of the National Prosecuting Authority Act, I have come to the determination that Advocate Pikoli should be relieved of his responsibility as the country's National Director of Public Prosecutions.

I was surprised and disappointed by Motlanthe's decision, mostly because on the basis of Ginwala's recommendations I had expected to be reinstated. What was the point of setting up the commission in the first place? I think it was a political decision that was more about Zuma than anything else at that stage. They could see I would not be pliable.

In accordance with the NPA Act, Motlanthe undertook to communicate his decision to parliament within 30 days. Parliament could then either confirm or reject his decision, but I expected the house to vote along party lines and for the process to be a mere rubber-stamping of Motlanthe's view. In January 2009, a 22-member joint ad hoc committee was set up to consider the president's decision and thereafter advise parliament on whether or not I should be restored to office.

While I was waiting to appear before that committee, I was approached by a number of people concerned about Jacob Zuma's future. They wanted to know whether if I was reinstated, would I still pursue the case against Zuma? I sincerely believe that had I given anybody an assurance that I would not charge Zuma, I would have been reinstated.

During the course of the inquiry I received many requests to meet people. In fact, on one occasion I even had a senior counsel from the Johannesburg Bar who was prepared to facilitate some of these meetings, who approached Kalyani to request a meeting with me.

In February, the special parliamentary committee endorsed my dismissal in a vote that went 11–5. Chairperson Oupa Monareng said that the panel had concluded I had 'messed up' as NDPP and had compromised national security.

'We supported the president's decision because Pikoli had messed up in his duties as National Director of Public Prosecutions. He was clumsy and very unprofessional in his handling of especially the Browse Mole report,' Monareng was quoted as saying. Opposition MPs were fiercely opposed to the decision, but Monareng had refused a request by them to table a minority report on the matter.

Monareng was a former MK comrade and I bumped into him at one of the MK meetings after I had been removed from office. He said to me, 'Hey, Mfetu, you know, I was given instructions that there's no way in which you could come back.'

I told him, '*Ek verstaan*, it's all right.' I knew the ANC MPs were told which way to vote. That much was clear. I felt betrayed and sad, but it came as no surprise because they had to protect Zuma this time.

During the debate in the National Assembly, Freedom Front Plus MP Pieter Groenewald caused a stir when he accused former President Mbeki of 'acting like the three little monkeys. I hear, I see and I say nothing!' – alluding to the proverbial primates who fail to see, hear or speak evil of a situation they know to be wrong.

Girly accompanied me to parliament and best articulates the betrayal we felt:

> *When we went into parliament, our comrades could not look us in the eye. We had prepared ourselves for that but still it was difficult to accept what was happening. For some reason, on that day, I had admiration for Patricia de Lille. Not because I wanted her to support my husband, but because I had a deeper understanding of how she could have been in the struggle and now she was in the opposition. Remember the people who were in the liberation struggle were now in power and they were the ones doing the opposite of what the ANC as an organisation had championed all these years in the struggle.*
>
> *I lived that episode of betrayal until they called Vusi for that last hearing. I really felt betrayed and pained. Because remember, many of those ministers were people who were friends to us – sleeping in the same place and bringing up kids together and all that. But now, when the moment came to do the right thing, they couldn't honour the word. These were people I held in high esteem; some we regarded as intimate friends. But now we had to part ways. That's how life is. At that moment it dawned on me that people will always make decisions that are about the self and one's survival. I calmly accepted this reality of life. The time had come for us to part ways with some of our dear comrades, friends and colleagues.*

In February 2009, both the National Council of Provinces and the National Assembly ratified Motlanthe's decision and voted in favour of my dismissal. The vote in the National Assembly was 233–60. I was under no illusion that this was anything other than a rubber-stamping of the executive decision in parliament. They didn't really consider the points I had put forward, and even Ginwala herself had recommended I be reinstated. The process made a mockery of the role of parliament in terms of the executive truly being held accountable.

Moosajee also had experiences that suggested that the parliamentary process was a *fait accompli*:

> *What disappointed me the most was that there were various politicians – some of them I didn't know – that would bump into me and there was a time during all of this that my dad was in the clinic and I even remember bumping into somebody in the corridors of the clinic who said to me, 'Aren't you Vusi Pikoli's lawyer?' and I said, 'Yes.' He said to me, 'You are doing a great service to the country and thank you.' But when you then look at the list of MPs who all voted to approve, it included those sorts of people. I remember going to a cricket function one day and meeting an MP again saying those sorts of things, and the few people that said those things to me toed the party line and voted in favour of Vusi's removal from office which was also quite disappointing for me. But we knew that we were going to take it further. We knew this was a 15-round bout, it was never going to be a quick in and out, so we were in it for the long haul.*

Within minutes of the vote, we moved to challenge the decision in court and petitioned the Pretoria High Court to set aside the dismissal on the grounds that it was not rational and violated the constitutional principle of prosecutorial independence and the principles of legality. I wanted an independent court to decide on the weight of the evidence because that would have helped establish legal certainty on the nature of the relationship between the minister of justice and the national director of public prosecutions. Judge Chris Nicholson had made reference to this in his Zuma decision, but he missed some critical issues. Nicholson went to the extreme of saying that there should be no interaction between the NDPP and the minister and that my suspension was an ominous sign of some kind of interference. A formal judgment would clear up all this confusion.

While I was waiting for a court date for my matter to be heard, the presidency informed me that a permanent successor would be appointed despite the fact that I was challenging my dismissal in court. Moosajee wrote to the state attorney requesting a date for the appointment.

It was July 2009, four months since the National Assembly decision, and Mokotedi Mpshe was still acting NDPP. Zuma had been elected president of the country in April 2009 and wanted to appoint a permanent head of the prosecuting authority. I applied for an urgent interim order to stop him from making a permanent appointment, pending the outcome of my application to set aside my dismissal.

Judge Ben du Plessis found we had presented a prima facie case and interdicted the president from appointing a successor until the full application could be heard in November that year.

Selebi and settling

Six weeks before my matter was due to be heard in court, Jackie Selebi finally went on trial for corruption in the Johannesburg High Court. In his opening statement to the court, he took a swipe at Bulelani Ngcuka and me.

Selebi claimed he was being maliciously prosecuted because he supported the dissolution of the Scorpions and because he had discovered alleged wrongdoing by both Ngcuka and me. In a plea explanation, he accused me of 'obtaining a material gratification through his wife from the late Brett Kebble/JCI Group in an improper way'. The 'gratification' consisted of shares in mining company Simmer & Jack. He claimed that after he confronted me about this I 'became very emotional' and allegedly confessed to him that my wife was my 'Achilles heel'.

My attorney immediately issued a statement denying Girly and I had received any gratification from Kebble or the JCI Group:

> *Ms [Nozuko] Pikoli does not own any shares and did not previously own any shares in Simmer & Jack Limited and Jaganda (Pty) Limited. Ms Pikoli owns 2% of the shares in Vulisango (Pty) Limited, in which she became a shareholder, after Mr [Lizo] Njenje (a close friend of hers) invited her to take up a shareholding in Vulisango (Pty) Limited. Ms Pikoli had no business dealings with Mr Kebble. Mr Selebi did not meet with Mr Pikoli in that regard. The directorate [of] crime intelligence has never*

approached Mr and Ms Pikoli in regard to the matter. It is clear that Mr Selebi's latest allegations are an attempt to deflect attention away from the very serious charges he is facing and a ruse designed to create the impression that Mr Selebi is a victim.

I always felt that Selebi's claim was an act of desperation and a continuation of a litany of lies he had always told. It was a distraction from his own charges and if there was any criminal wrongdoing on my part or by my wife, why did he not simply investigate and charge us instead of waiting until he was charged himself?

A couple of weeks later I was called to testify for the state against Selebi and I was asked about his allegation. I told the court that Selebi had never confronted me about the shares and that 'it is only the work of an evil and cruel mind that can concoct such things'. I also testified in defence of the decisions to grant indemnities to the Kebble killers and explained that we knew it was a gamble, but one worth taking.

To me Selebi was just another accused who had to answer to the charges against him. My attitude was hardened by his lies and malice. I did not feel sorry for him, because he was still arrogant and showed no remorse. He cut a pathetic figure in the dock and looked ill and much older than his real age, and at one stage I thought he had begun to lose his marbles.

A week after I testified against Selebi, I was preparing to return to court to challenge my removal from office. I had been offered a settlement of around R10 million in damages after I was fired, but had decided to forgo the money in order to challenge my dismissal. There had been numerous approaches after I was suspended, and even during the inquiry there had been suggestions of a settlement. The state's advocates Kgomotso Moroka and Seth Nthai made overtures. Moroka even spoke directly to me, saying she was uncomfortable with the hearings going ahead. Before Motlanthe became president, he had also spoken to me about a possible settlement.

Once parliament had ratified the decision to remove me, it was decided government would no longer pay my legal fees. My salary was also stopped. This meant that in order to continue the fight, I had to fund my own way. It was a worry, of course, but my legal team had met and had come to the decision that they would continue regardless.

There was a gentleman from Stellenbosch who had been following my case closely and, out of the blue, he called Wim Trengove. He was appreciative of the stance I was taking and wanted to be of assistance. He offered to contribute towards my legal fees and also offered to pay me the same salary I had been earning. This benefactor, Michiel le Roux, was extremely generous, but I paid him back everything once I had settled with government. I have met him and he's a progressive, thinking man who simply had concerns about the Constitution and the effectiveness of institutions of state.

My application was due to be heard in the High Court in Pretoria on Monday, 23 November 2009. On the Thursday prior to that, Moosajee received a phone call from John Brand, a partner at Bowman Gilfillan. He wanted to know whether we had considered the possibility of mediation. Moosajee picks up what happened:

> *I was in Durban that afternoon when I got a call from John Brand and he said, 'Aslam, you have seen the benefits that mediation can bring and shouldn't we consider mediating this particular dispute?' So I said, 'Well, I'm not sure that this matter is capable of an amicable resolution and in any event, this matter is due to be in court on Monday.' He said to me, 'Just be careful that you are not prejudging the outcome of a mediation and part of a mediation is for people to be creative and leave that in my hands and I'll be assisted by another very experienced mediator, but just give the process a chance.' So I then said, 'All I can do is put it to Vusi and see what he says,' and I phoned Vusi and he said, 'We're in court on Monday. We must have the fight.' He kept saying it's not about the money for him and so when I suggested the thing about mediation to him, he said it's a pointless exercise.*

It so happened that Moosajee and I would be at the airport at around the same time on the Friday morning and we agreed to meet to discuss the possibility of a mediation over the weekend:

> *So I had the discussion with him at the airport at the Mugg & Bean. He obviously was under strain and the fact that his dad was quite ill at the time must have exacerbated the strain that he was going through. I said to him, 'You know, Vusi, this is an incredible investment that you have*

> *made and you say that this is an investment in our democracy, but you've got to understand that even if we go to court on Monday and we win, I predict that government will apply for leave to appeal to the Supreme Court of Appeal. It's a matter of national importance, so I anticipate that leave to appeal to the Supreme Court of Appeal will be granted. Even if we win there, I anticipate that that will then go to the Constitutional Court. So it's not like this thing is going to end next week, or as soon as the judgment is delivered after the matter is heard next week. I still think there's probably two or three years in this dispute and I can see the strain you are taking.' I said, 'Just let's give the process a chance. I'm not saying that you must settle a particular matter, but let's see what comes out of the process.'*

I had to be in Port Elizabeth that weekend as my father was ill and there were traditional ceremonies I had to attend. That posed a logistical challenge because I couldn't attend the negotiations. I agreed Moosajee would attend the discussions at Bowman Gilfillan and he would be accompanied by his chairman, Michael Hart, and Advocate Tim Bruinders. They would use speakerphones to communicate with me in PE. Meanwhile, Trengove continued to prepare for court on Monday morning, as we were not confident the mediation process would produce a satisfactory result.

Moosajee phoned me regularly while I was driving around PE, picking up relatives and attending the ceremonies:

> *We sat in completely separate rooms with John Brand and Charles Nupen moving from room to room. We didn't know who was there as part of government's delegation throughout the day but we suspected that there were people coming in and out. By the time the matter had settled, it was in the evening already and by then, when we went across to the next room just to shake hands and it was a room with lots of glasses and empty drink cans or plastic water bottles, so you could see there were certainly lots of people in there at the time. We started off on the basis that Vusi wants his job back. I think John and Charles through their incredible skills understood immediately that this was a case of Vusi wanting government to acknowledge the importance of the principle of prosecutorial*

> *independence, which is a constitutionally guaranteed principle, it was that and it was a vindication of his name. And if that was going to fall in place, the other issues were going to be minor issues.*

As the day progressed, I began to think more seriously about the possibility of settling. At the time, I was mentally exhausted and struggling emotionally. It all felt like a drain on my resources and I had to consider the toll it was taking on my family. I was tired.

I phoned Trengove to ask him what he thought:

> *I got a call from Vusi and he said to me, well knowing that I was opposed to a settlement, he said to me, 'Listen, I want to settle.' I can't remember the language he used but the message was, 'I have had enough, I just can't live with this any longer.' And they had offered him a substantial financial package and I think the part of it that was even more attractive to Vusi was that they intimated that they want him back in government and they had various things in mind for him. I remember when he justified the deal to me, he spoke about not only the money but also the prospect of being accepted back in the fold and it was clear. At that point, I said to him, 'Sure, absolutely, go ahead.' I wasn't disingenuous because that was the point where we all stood up for the principle, but he was the man who was bearing the brunt of it all, paying the price for it. What he was saying to me is not that he thought it was strategically wise or good, but simply that he has come to the end of his tether and he now wanted to settle. So it was clear to me that he wanted to and I don't think that I had the moral right to hold him back, so rather than argue with him, I thought it better to give it my blessing and okay it and make him feel that it's fine. I'm sorry today that he settled but I certainly don't blame him because he did pay a heavy price and it was a heavy thing for him to do.*

Late on the Saturday afternoon we finally reached an agreement.

The deal-maker for me was an undertaking by the government's team to include in the settlement its commitment to the principle of prosecutorial independence and a line that it recognised I was professionally competent, sufficiently experienced and conscientious, and had the requisite integrity to hold a senior public position. The team also agreed to offer me a position in government and that I would consider such an offer.

As part of the settlement, there was an acknowledgement there had been a breakdown in our relationship, but that we wanted to restore it to one of mutual trust and respect. Government agreed I would be paid the sum of R7.5 million in a full and final settlement of all claims, including a claim for pension payments. The state also agreed to pay my legal costs, including the cost of the court application and of the mediation.

At 8.20 p.m. on the Saturday night, the government issued a statement announcing there had been an out-of-court settlement. Unfortunately, as Moosajee recalls, the statement was not exactly what was agreed upon as it did not include the references I had specifically requested for inclusion in the agreement:

> *I immediately started getting calls from journalists to say the matter has settled and Vusi Pikoli is abandoning his court case and he's been paid a substantial sum of money, which again was very, very disappointing for me. By the next morning then, the settlement agreement had been released but by then the newspapers were already reporting and so the critical things that we would have liked reported, like government's commitment to prosecutorial independence and the acknowledgement that Vusi was a man of integrity and qualified to hold public office, didn't find their way into the initial reports that appeared on the Sunday.*

Girly had told me to do what I thought was right and what I wanted to do, and she supported my decision completely. The pressure was really beginning to tell and this entire saga had changed my life and my environment. The activist in me still wanted to carry on, but the reality was different.

Once I was initiated, I had to move on. When you go to the mountain you are taught not to look back at your hut on fire, not to look back at your childhood, but to look forward. I had moved on, I had been through all the hardships. I was pained, it healed, and to take myself back to the same environment would not have benefited anyone, least of all me. I had to move on.

A lot of people came to talk to me, even the bishop at my church, Malusi Mpumlwana, to say, 'Look, you have made your point,' long before there was a settlement. After the commission's findings, people felt I should simply leave it because I had been vindicated, but I felt that the struggle had only just started and I didn't see any sincerity on the part of government about the independence of prosecutors.

Most people said things along the lines of, 'Look, Vusi, there's a time when you need to be selfish and just think about you and your family and forget about the higher notions and ideals. Why should it always be you who is this sacrificial lamb? Think about yourself. Think about your family now. Think about what you have already gone through and what you are still going through.'

On one hand, I was relieved that the battle had been set aside, but at the same time I was concerned that I was selling out my principles to some degree. I had resisted all along – even when there was a higher offer on the table I had rejected it – because I wanted government to be sincere when it came to upholding the independence of prosecutors. I wanted more than just lip service.

I also felt I had missed out on an opportunity to have the matter decided in court once and for all, for posterity, in terms of establishing certainty around this issue. I'm still not happy with the way the DG of justice, the politicians and the NPA interact. By settling out of court, I felt I had betrayed the struggle for the independence of prosecutors.

You don't know how much I have thought about that settlement over the years. I'm still not sure whether I did the right thing or whether I betrayed the cause. People tend to say, '*Ja*, this guy got R7.5 million,' and they think it's a lot of money. The taxman takes almost half of that, and the rest went to settling expenses, and in the end I was left with very little.

I do believe I emerged with my integrity intact and that is a value I still retain, but knowing what I know now and what has happened, I regret not finishing what I started. I should have fought to the end.

Had I known that Menzi Simelane would be appointed to succeed me, I would have resisted even further. Given his remarks at the inquiry, his appointment was an indication that the government is not serious about the independence of prosecutors. When I heard the news I immediately phoned Moosajee, as he recalls:

> *I must tell you that if Vusi knew that Menzi was going to be appointed his successor, the matter would never have been settled – no matter what*

sum of money had been put on the table. I remember that on the day that the announcement was made, I got a call from a journalist to say that Menzi Simelane is due to be appointed as the national director of public prosecutions today; do you want to comment?' and I said, 'That's such a bad joke, I'm not going to comment, I don't believe that that is true. Not after Frene Ginwala's findings.' Probably about two hours later, I got a call from Vusi, who was irate. Vusi obviously took lots of strain through all of this, but I very seldom heard him express a vulgar word through all of this. But in that moment, he said something like, 'You can't believe what these bastards have done.' Then he said to me, 'We shouldn't have settled this thing.' That was a difficult moment for me and it was a disappointing moment for me because obviously, in the settlement agreement, we had some pretty strong messages about prosecutorial independence, whereas Menzi tried to argue that the prosecutors were still subject to the direction of the minister and the minister had a greater role to play in relation to prosecutorial decisions. Vusi was livid.

Trengove is also of the view that Simelane's appointment was a political one:

However much debate you might have about Motlanthe's dismissal of Pikoli, the same party then a few months later appointed Simelane. Now if you dismiss Pikoli for the mild criticism in Ginwala, how can you honestly at the same time – virtually the same time – appoint Simelane, who was the villain of the piece? I don't accept it in good faith, it was a bad-faith scheme to get him out of the way and to get Simelane there. I suppose not only to protect Selebi, but ultimately to protect Zuma. They had to have somebody there.

When Simelane was first appointed to the NPA as a deputy national director, it was reported in the media that he had given a speech to say he was there to implement the ANC's vision for the NPA. He was clearly there to serve the interests of the ruling party. Call me arrogant, but Menzi Simelane can't be more ANC than I am. Yet I never uttered those words, because I knew the responsibilities of the national director – you have to be above party politics if you are occupying that position, even if you are a party member. You don't play politics there.

If I had played politics in that position I would have failed dismally in my task as the national director. Of course, politicians would have applauded me and I would still be there because my term was only due to expire in 2015. I would still be the NDPP.

Wobbling like jellyfish

On the evening he suspended me President Mbeki told me that there was life after the NPA. Now I had to go and find out for myself. After I settled with government, I spent some time thinking about what I wanted to do. For the first time since I went into exile as a young man, I had no mission.

I received a number of requests for public speaking so I addressed several conferences about fraud and corruption. I also addressed the Law Society in Johannesburg and spoke at universities across the country. I even did a stint lecturing at the International Law Enforcement Academy (ILEA) in Botswana, where I taught human rights.

On the public-speaking circuit I mostly discussed the independence of prosecutors or corruption, but invariably people were more interested in how I had been fired and in the details of what had happened, which I never really spoke about publicly.

I didn't want to put anyone down. The experience was still too fresh and I refused to become emotional about the issue and perhaps regret what I said. I wanted a cooling-off period, time to think things through, so that I could reflect on what had happened. What happened to me could have happened to anyone, but the outcome would depend on how the individual reacted and faced those pressures. I had to think about the implications for our fledgling democracy, for our future and for the future of our children. I resisted being dragged into a public debate about what had transpired.

I never really went looking for a job. In 2008, I was approached by Tokyo Sexwale's Mvelaphanda Holdings and offered a position as internal legal counsel. I considered the post, but I felt uncomfortable because I was reluctant to become embroiled in politics, and I suspected that somehow the whole thing would become political at some point.

I was then asked by the University of South Africa (UNISA) to develop a faculty on good governance and corruption. I started talking to the dean, but again nothing really materialised out of that. I had discussions with PricewaterhouseCoopers, but those also fizzled out. I was beginning to get the sense that though these organisations would like to hire me, I was too much of a risk in terms of securing government business at the time.

I considered the possibility of starting my own legal consultancy and was looking into that quite seriously when I received an offer from auditing firm Gobodo Incorporated. The audit and advisory practice was led by Nonkululeko Gobodo, the first black female chartered accountant in the country, and the company worked with parastatals and government departments.

The offer came through a friend, Moss Sindane, whom I often met at the gym. He asked me what I was doing and said, 'Why don't you come and join us?' So I went to meet with Nonkululeko Gobodo, the chairperson of the firm.

She told me that they had done a 'political audit' before taking the decision to hire me. I understood that to mean they had made contact with some senior ANC people to check whether the party or government would have a problem with me coming on board. I understood where they were coming from because most of their business emanated from government as the auditor-general could not do all the work alone. It was also before Gobodo merged with SizweNtsaluba VSP in 2011 so she had to be mindful of the risk involved.

And so I was hired and my task was to set up a forensic investigations division within Gobodo. I felt confident I was well qualified for the job because I had been a senior administrator in government as an accounting officer in the justice department and had faced challenges before, such as the amalgamation of the 11 departments into one in 1994. However, when I arrived at work, there was only one person in my division and he was only working 50 per cent of the time, so I essentially started off with half a person.

The first few months were all about branding this new division, doing interviews with the media and raising its profile. I was invited to a number of fraud conferences and busied myself trying to bring in work by approaching private sector companies and banks. It was going very well and the company seemed excited to have me there.

It was, however, a shift for me to step into a corporate environment as all my life I had been in the service of the public, trying to improve the general living standards of citizens. I had been brought up on a diet of Marxism and Leninism, and while in exile I had worked for the South African Congress of Trade Unions (SACTU) pontificating against profits and the exploitation of workers.

And here I was in an environment motivated by profit. I experienced a sense of discomfort, particularly around the way of doing things. On occasion I was told, 'Look, Vusi, at times in our business, you might not think that we are doing the right thing but it's for the sake of the business.' Other people in the company would suggest that the client is always right and I would respond by saying that I wanted to retain our impartiality, our independence, our objectivity and integrity as forensic auditors. With some clients, there was the view that because they were paying us they could predetermine the outcome of the investigation – even though that could be at the expense of our own integrity.

I don't think the issues I outline here were specific to Gobodo; it's the general practice in the sector. I had to get used to the way they did business and perhaps I was a little slow on the uptake. It's not that they engaged in any unethical business conduct, but I did learn that if a client wanted a particular result then I should probably not get too involved. I was also taken aback by the aggression and vigorous 'marketing' in the pursuit of new clients or in trying to retain existing ones.

In 2011 we went through a merger with SizweNtsaluba VSP, which resulted in SizweNtsalubaGobodo (SNG) being the largest black-owned and -managed accounting firm and the fifth-largest accounting firm in the country. However, in terms of revenue, we were still far behind the top four firms and needed to keep up. Since we had reached the top five, we needed to remain there and to do so we had to make sure we increased our revenue.

There were three major audit contracts in our sights: Transnet, Eskom and Denel. If the company were to get one of those contracts, or perhaps all of them, we would truly be playing in the big league.

Towards the end of 2011, in the midst of the tender-bidding process, Nonkululeko Gobodo called me at home to say, 'Hey Vusi, *Le nto yakho*' – 'This matter of yours is coming up again.' She told me that there were some people in the ANC who were not happy with me and she suggested I 'check with my people'. She did not tell me who those people would be.

Around that time, I was a founder member of the Council for the Advancement of the South African Constitution (CASAC) with other like-minded individuals such as Dr Frene Ginwala, Sipho Pityana and Advocate Wim Trengove. CASAC is an initiative led by progressive people who want to advance the Constitution as a platform for democratic politics and who believe in the advancement of a society whose values are based on the core principles of the Constitution. Of course I was interested because I am concerned with anything to do with the Constitution. It was an opportunity no patriot would want to miss.

CASAC is not a trouble-seeking or troublemaking organisation. It is about ensuring that as a country we live by the values of our Constitution – openness, responsiveness and accountability, with a particular focus on socio-economic rights. While we were not confrontational in outlook, we knew that if government needed to be challenged on any matter, then that is what we would do, and we did.

It is likely that my involvement with CASAC is what led to Gobodo's warning that I should check with my people. Immediately after her call, I spoke to Dr Khulu Mbatha, an advisor to the deputy president. I said, 'Khulu, I understand there's some unhappiness about me working at Gobodo from the side of the ANC; can you check?'

He said, 'I'll check, Vusi, but I haven't heard anything.' He came back to me and confirmed that there was nothing.

I called Gobodo the following day and relayed to her that I had checked with my people and there were no concerns. She admitted then she regretted having told me about it because she should have handled the matter herself and should have stood up for me when the issue arose.

In mid-December 2011, I stopped in at Gobodo's office. We had maintained a good rapport and she had become chairperson of SNG, while the

CEO of SizweNtsaluba retained his position as the CEO. I often popped into her office to chat and see how things were going. At one stage our offices were next to each another and she would come into mine if she needed something.

On this occasion, I walked in and I could tell she was not in a very good mood. I asked her, 'What's up?'

She replied, 'No, it's nothing, it's nothing.'

Having been in the thick of things previously, I was now very sensitive to the work environment and I immediately sensed that things might not be right.

In January 2012, after SNG had been awarded the Transnet contract, Gobodo came to me again to say, 'This thing of yours is not going away.' She told me the Transnet contract had been sitting on Minister of Public Enterprises Malusi Gigaba's desk and he had not signed it because I was involved with Gobodo. She explained she was going to find it difficult to explain to other directors why the company was not getting contracts. She also told me she had to think about those who were employed by the company and had to take responsibility for the hundreds of workers who were being paid. She was implying that one person could not hold things up.

Gobodo never explicitly asked me to resign – it was more a suggestion that I should decide what I wanted to do. I was puzzled by the situation and wasn't quite sure what she expected. I got the message that she would struggle to defend the loss of the contract to her board and her employees if it affected the bottom line.

I felt that if I was going to leave the company, I would not lie about why I was leaving. The entire thing was reawakening old, bad memories. If I was pushed into resigning, I could not go out and tell the media and the public I was resigning to go in search of 'greener pastures'.

So when Gobodo later came to my office and raised the issue again, I told her I wanted to discuss it with my lawyers. She asked that I not do that and suggested we meet with Victor Sekese, the CEO. The following day, we met with Sekese at his offices in Woodmead, and it was clear they wanted me to resign as a director. Sekese explained that according to the terms of the memorandum of partners, a partner can leave with three months' notice and they were willing to offer me six months to look for another job.

I was deeply angry and annoyed by what was unfolding before me and I became very emotional in that meeting. The memory of how I had left the NPA had resurfaced and now a similar nightmare was playing itself out at a black firm where I had felt I could really contribute to their success.

I was overwhelmed and I cried, uncontrollably.

I was not just going to allow this to happen and I was angry, and said as much. They insisted that theirs was not a political decision, but for them to take their cue from politicians about whom they wanted to employ was hypocritical. They couldn't plead ignorance of politics when they were succumbing to political pressure. If they were going to give in to government on this, then how would they stop government from telling them what they wanted in the results of an audit? Who would believe them?

I agreed to resign. I don't know why. I suppose it was because I was not thinking properly at the time. In retrospect it was a stupid decision.

I was confronted by the possibility of once again working in an environment in which people would question my involvement; they would look at me and blame me for having lost this contract. I could have challenged them legally and, in fact, I called Aslam Moosajee to arrange to see him, but then cancelled the appointment. It was too soon for me to be back in the newspapers, challenging and fighting. I decided not to involve the lawyers. I just couldn't go there again.

Here I was at this black company, which I had chosen to work at because I felt I had a contribution to make, regardless of my reservations about being involved in the private sector. The company's profile was already higher than it was when I had arrived and I felt I had made a positive impact on the business. And now I was being dumped! They couldn't stand up for themselves. When they wobbled like jellyfish, I felt my whole life crumbling under me.

When I left the NPA, I was not as enraged as I was when I was booted out of SNG. They couldn't tell me who in the ANC was putting them under pressure and to this day I don't know.

I called ANC Secretary-General Gwede Mantashe and he told me he knew nothing about the matter. I also raised it with Cyril Ramaphosa, now the deputy president of the ANC. Ramaphosa told me during a meeting at his office that he was shocked at this development and undertook to follow it up within the ANC, but he never came back to me. Public Enterprises

Minister Malusi Gigaba also publicly denied Gobodo's claim that the contract had remained unsigned on his desk.

The thing is, the ANC is a big organisation and it wouldn't table a resolution to say, 'Vusi Pikoli should never get a job anywhere.' That would be neither morally nor politically correct. But there will always be individuals who have a problem with me, who will apply pressure and use their influence to ingratiate themselves in order to make their way up the ladder or abuse their power. The same thing has happened to Reverend Frank Chikane. If you disagree with the ANC or government on certain matters, then you'll find yourself out in the cold.

This is not the end of the story for me and I have resolved to dig deeper.

CASAC laid a complaint with the Independent Regulatory Board for Auditors (IRBA) and I subsequently heard that some directors at SNG were giving poor performance as an explanation for my leaving. I invite them to raise that issue of performance at any time on any platform and I'm prepared to have a public engagement with them because not once did this issue ever come up. No one ever raised a concern about my performance.

I was paid out for six months of employment and SNG was awarded the Transnet contract.

I never went to the newspapers about the matter and a report only came out two months after I resigned. I was clear I was not going to lie if I was asked about it and I had already told my friends about what had happened.

Most people didn't want to believe I could have been forced to resign because of the ANC. Others stated that this was exactly what had happened to Chikane and others after Mbeki lost at Polokwane. People's lives were being made very difficult, and many began to speak about their experiences of being sidelined and targeted.

The scourge has, however, persisted and I can recount several instances where I have been interviewed for jobs and, when it came to the crunch, I was not hired, for reasons I would characterise as dubious.

I was, for example, headhunted by an employment company for the post of CEO of Business Against Crime. They asked me to send my CV; I was shortlisted and then interviewed for the post. I thought I had a really good interview, but they never came back to me. I did, however, hear that there had been an appointment and, a week or so later, the person who had initially contacted me called. He was embarrassed by what had happened. He revealed that I had indeed been the best man for the job but that politics had intervened. The job involved working with ministers in the justice cluster and they didn't want to place the government in an embarrassing situation.

I have since busied myself doing consultancy work and forensic investigations, including a contract for the Nelson Mandela Metro. Today I am an independent board member of Cricket South Africa and am serving on the Khayelitsha Commission set up by the premier of the Western Cape to look into policing in the township.

I find myself living hand to mouth now as I depend on whatever contract work comes my way and I have no sense of permanency in terms of job security. I did not foresee this, but I doubt anyone ever does. It has not weakened my resolve to try to do the right thing – I would rather live this life than sell my soul for money.

Confronting Du Plessis

Mandy Wiener

Throughout the months of interviews I had done with Vusi, one lingering question remained: What happened to the four police officers who had been granted amnesty for Sizwe's death? Vusi was adamant that he wanted to track them down and meet them face to face in order to get closure and answers. Most importantly, he wanted to face his own personal tormentor, Captain Hermanus Barend du Plessis.

It had been over 30 years since Du Plessis confronted Vusi outside a meeting of students at St Steven's Hall in New Brighton and threatened he would ensure Vusi would never work as a lawyer in his hometown. And it was nearly 15 years since Du Plessis was granted amnesty for Sizwe's murder.

I set about trying to track down the former Eastern Cape security policeman. All I had was his date of birth from his TRC application but just one phone call produced Du Plessis's current home address and cellphone number, amongst other details. As fate would have it, Vusi's arch-nemesis lived less than five kilometres away from him in Pretoria and just a kilometre from where his office used to be at the NPA.

One morning in May 2013, I gave Vusi the phone number. '*Jis*, I must call this guy. I have been looking for him all my life,' he exclaimed excitedly and immediately picked up his cellphone and dialled the number:

> Hello. How are you?

> I'm fine, thanks.
> My name is Vusi Pikoli.
> Yes, sir.
> Does the name ring a bell?
> (Pause.)
> Um … not really.
> Originally I am from PE, but I am now in Pretoria.
> *Ja*?
> I would like to set up a meeting with you because I am in the process of writing my memoir.

Du Plessis agreed to meet Vusi and me the following week.

Vusi saw this as an opportunity to cement closed the gaping holes in Sizwe's story, primarily the mystery of what happened between Maseru and Bloemfontein – how Sizwe came to be in the custody of the Security Police in the Free State. 'An impression is created that they caught him inside the country driving the car, so I really want to know what actually happened,' he explained hopefully.

Du Plessis picked the venue – a bustling butchery and coffee shop in Silverton, frequented by ex-cops. We arrive to find him sitting at a wooden bench on the stoep overlooking the parking lot, watching the trolleys rattle across the cobbled street. Vusi spots him first, despite having seen him last three decades ago. I recognise him from the TRC videos of his testimony to the Commission. I am immediately struck by how he has aged, his droopy hangdog face creased by a criss-crossed spider web of wrinkle and his eyes narrowed by crow's feet. Although his hair is still thick, it is whiter than it appeared in the video. Du Plessis stands to shake Vusi's hand, exposing the full extent of his bulky frame. The two men, enemies at war once intent on killing one another, sit down on the wooden bench alongside one another, to talk over cups of freshly brewed coffee.

The two exchange formalities and feel one another out. They dance around fragments of history as Vusi tries to establish just how much Du Plessis remembers about their interaction and attempts to put the ex-policeman at ease. His call had come as a bolt from the blue and Du Plessis is clearly apprehensive about the purpose of the meeting. Vusi spends some time putting forward his recollections as a student activist, his arrest while at Fort Hare University, the confrontation outside St Steven's Hall and how the pamphlet-distribution mission led to his unit going into exile. Du Plessis listens intently and interjects occasionally with questions about names of people mentioned, his memory a little fuzzy. '*Ja*, I was thinking the other day, I can't even remember that you people were detained,' remarks the ex-cop, his hand shaking considerably as he sips from his coffee cup. Nerves? Signs of an early-onset illness perhaps?

A metre away from the table, a long-haired, khaki-clad security guard repeatedly hacks into a handkerchief and swigs from a water bottle in a packet, loitering just close enough to listen in on the conversation. He lingers throughout the meeting, constantly distracting Vusi, who is suspicious of his motives. Afterwards, Vusi would admit that he suspected the man was positioned there by Du Plessis as protection. Just in case.

Du Plessis calls Vusi by his first name. Vusi makes a point of calling him 'Captain'. 'Excuse me, I call you "Captain". I know you are a retired colonel but I know you as Captain Du Plessis,' Vusi explains. 'That's how you feature in my life. As Captain Du Plessis, not as the retired colonel.'

Finally, Vusi gets to the point of the meeting.

'But really, what I really want to find out is about Sizwe.'

Du Plessis turns to look at Vusi. 'How did you get hold of Sizwe?' Vusi asks. The elderly ex-cop takes a deep breath, holds it for several seconds and finally answers. 'I don't know,' he says quietly, before adding, 'I can find out for you, Vusi. I can't remember anything.' He nods his head with apparent sincerity.

Vusi tries a different tack. 'When did you first see him in 1981 in Port Elizabeth?'

'Date-wise? I don't know when I met him, I can't remember where I met him.'

'Do you still remember anything about Sizwe, then?' Vusi probes further.

Du Plessis's response is consistent and firm. 'No.'

'Come, Captain … you can't …' pleads Vusi, desperate for any fragment of detail.

'No, really; I can still remember his dad,' he ponders absently. 'What worries you about Kondile?'

'All along, we didn't know what happened to Sizwe. Sizwe was a very close friend of mine, we were very close.'

'Is it?'

'We were very, very close with Sizwe. We grew up together, we did almost everything together. And now, when he just disappeared, in 1981, it hurt me, it hurt a lot of us. It hurt Phaki, it hurt Thozi. So please, try to think.'

Du Plessis stares ahead, deep in thought, his coffee cup trembling as it makes its way towards his lips.

'Can I think about that stuff and make another appointment with you?' he finally asks.

'For me the real issue here is going to be to find out what happened to Sizwe. I've read your story, I've read your testimony in the TRC. But there are gaps. How you guys got amnesty, I don't understand, with those gaps in between, because you didn't tell the full story. But that's not the issue now – you got amnesty, that cannot be reversed. I think the least you can do is just talk about it. For your own therapy as well. For my own therapy, for Sizwe's son's therapy,' Vusi pleads.

'No, you are right,' admits the old man. There is a glimmer of hope in Vusi's eyes, behind his shaded glasses, under his tweed paddy cap. He has waited so long for this. For extra impetus, he tells Du Plessis about Bantu, Sizwe's son, and how he too is in need of closure.

'But, Vusi, can I, well, first of all, can I just read my statement again and more or less enlighten myself?' he says, fidgeting with his hands on his face. 'I can't remember exactly what was testified and then if you've got anything that you say there are gaps … possibly we don't know between those gaps what happened. I don't know. Then I can check for you.'

I realise that this is a futile exercise and Du Plessis is giving nothing away. Perhaps he simply doesn't remember, maybe he has blocked it out; alternatively he's terrified of being prosecuted and doesn't want to admit a thing. Vusi persists and explains again about 'the gap' between Maseru and Bloemfontein. Du Plessis insists he does not remember how Sizwe came to be in their custody but undertakes again to 'try and find out'.

Vusi is becoming increasingly frustrated. 'I find it incredible that you can't remember. I think you need to take out the old SAPS culture. You have got that conspiracy of silence,' Vusi says, using his hands for extra emphasis. 'You guys are known for not talking.'

'No. No,' Du Plessis insists. He sees Vusi becoming increasingly emotional and decides to share a piece of himself. He reaches over and puts his hand on Vusi's shoulder.

'Vusi, can I tell you what changed my life? I lost my son three months ago,' Du Plessis says, revealing his own personal human tragedy. 'And that's still a hell of a battle in my own life. I lost him on the Ben Schoeman Highway. I was with my daughter in the UK when it happened, when the accident happened. That's why I say, I don't mind to talk to you about it if it can help us because it doesn't matter what happened, the history.'

Vusi hopes to prise open the opportunity that has presented itself. The atmosphere is thick and heavy. Nearby, the security guard wheezes and stares.

'If we talk about this thing, you will be doing yourself a big favour, you will be relieving yourself of a big burden. The war is over. The war is over now. There's no way in which we can go back and have the war we had. We are not going to have the new government on a witch-hunt,' Vusi implores, his tone measured and reassuring. 'I could have decided, after reading Sizwe's story, after reading your own testimony, I could have decided to carry out my own individual and private mission to hunt you guys down, those who were involved, I could have done that.' There's a poignancy to his statement.

'I know,' Du Plessis acknowledges, 'I know.' Yet, he guides the conversation away, to names and individuals and trivialities. Vusi tries to shepherd the discussion back to Sizwe, but it's a roundabout journey to get back to the destination. They talk about Vlok and Van der Merwe and how Vusi refused their representations, choosing to prosecute instead. They speak about the whereabouts of other police officers, particularly 'Roely', and the others who received amnesty.

Vusi points out the symbolism of their meeting in Silverton in light of the 'Silverton Three'. In 1980, three Umkhonto we Sizwe members were on a mission to attack a petrol depot in Pretoria, when they realised they were being followed and took refuge in a bank. They held 25 people hostage and made several demands, including the release of Nelson Mandela from prison. The police stormed the bank after a six-hour siege and killed them.

Finally, Vusi gets back to his subject.

'So what I am saying to you is, the fact that I am sitting with you here today, 32 years down the line. You would not have expected that when you were speaking to me in St Steven's and then later arrested me for my role, that 32 years later, the two of us both from the Eastern Cape, would be sitting in Pretoria, in Silverton. This is an opportunity that we have in life to talk about these things so that future generations will know what happened. We can't move on and pretend as if there is full reconciliation; we have to discuss these things honestly and truthfully.'

He tries again.

'Can you just talk to me now about when you came across Sizwe the first time? Tell me about your discussions, tell me how you handled him?'

'With respect, that I can tell you. That I had a lot of respect for him too.'

'What made you have respect for this young terrorist who wanted to overthrow the government that you were loyal to? That you had taken an oath to defend? And now here is a young, black guy, a terrorist who wanted to overthrow the regime?'

'He was a wonderful person as far as I can remember. Soft-spoken, intelligent, and I think he was honest too. Well, that's what I thought. Sizwe was ultimately another thing altogether,' Du Plessis says, the haze of time lifting ever so slightly. He takes a moment before continuing. '*Ja*, things went wrong there, Vusi, but I don't think I want to talk about that really. I know you want to, but you must also respect that. That's a piece of my life that, first of all, I didn't kill Kondile. I possibly was instructed to do so or gave instructions, but I myself didn't do it. So I don't want to talk about that if possible, please.'

The security guard packs away his box of cigarettes and steps closer, within reaching distance of Du Plessis. Vusi composes himself and leans forward.

'You know, Captain, when Solomon Mahlangu was executed, he was found guilty and sentenced to death and he didn't kill anybody,' says Vusi.

'No, neither did I.'

'South African law coined a term at the time called "common purpose". It was on that basis that he was found guilty and sentenced to death. At an early age he was hanged. Now, you can't say that you didn't kill Kondile. You took a decision that the man has got to be killed. You can't later turn around and say you didn't kill him. You were there when he was killed.'

'No. I understand that.'

'You agreed that you wanted him killed, therefore you were part and parcel of that decision.'

'I understand that.'

'Please then do not say that you did not kill him.'

'What I mean is that I don't want to talk about that, Vusi, please.'

'It will help you. When you are about to die and meet with your maker, you would want to come clean. You are old now.'

'I'm pleased that I'm still alive, that's one reason. But let us think about this stuff. I didn't know what you wanted to talk about. Now I know. Don't pressurise me now as you say we pressurised you years ago. You were a youngster those days, you could handle it. And we didn't pressurise you. I think we handled you with respect.'

'How did you handle me with respect?'

'I think so, I can't remember anyone that I was not handling with respect. You were a sharp youngster in those days also.'

'You harassed us.'

'*Ja*, but we were also doing our jobs.'

Vusi speaks with an urgency born of frustration. He displays remarkable control over his emotions.

'We took a conscious decision to be involved in the struggle for liberation. We felt that we had to take it upon ourselves to liberate us. That's why we abandoned some of our studies, because we said we must join the fight for the national liberation of our country. It was a war situation. When I decided to leave Fort Hare and abandon my studies, I knew what I was doing. When I left the country for Lesotho, I knew what I was doing. When I went fighting in Angola, I knew what I was doing.

'But it was not just about us. The pain you caused and the harm you caused was also felt by our parents. No parent would want to have his child or her child being detained by you guys so early in the morning. And when you knocked on those doors, those windows, it was not with respect. You were kicking doors open, you were just waking up everybody around, so please, don't say that you handled us with respect. I know it was a war situation, we didn't expect that, we didn't ask for respect, we didn't ask for any favours because we didn't expect any favours from anybody.'

Vusi slams his hands repeatedly on the wooden bench for emphasis. Du Plessis responds by changing the subject to what Vusi is doing these days and whether there's money in private consulting. I fear Vusi may explode.

'Now just tell me how you felt when driving from Jeffrey's Bay. You were going to the Eastern Transvaal with the man who you knew was going to die. It's a hell of a distance, travelling with a man that you know you were going to kill?'

'But you *mos* know how it will feel.'

'I don't know.'

'It can't be easy, *broer*. And as you say, war is never easy. But I suppose the decisions must be made. Nothing you can do about it. It's hard today and that's why we, in the TRC, say we're sorry. I know sorry can do nothing, but what else can we do?'

Vusi wants to know if Du Plessis tried to meet with the Kondile family to apologise personally.

'No. We were advised those days with the TRC not to do it and if you ask me now why, I can't remember the reasons why.'

'You are retired now, you are independent. Take your own decisions.'

'Vusi, there are *maar* certain things that a person must do.'

Du Plessis is adamant that he wants to consult with 'others' before he speaks further. Vusi cannot comprehend that there is still a command structure in place, a network hangover from the apartheid era in which the former policeman is still operating.

Vusi turns to Du Plessis and with a sneer remarks, 'You know what they say, "The truth will set you free."'

'That's why, honestly, before my God, I said everything in the TRC. That's the truth,' Du Plessis insists.

I cast my mind back to a paragraph in the book *In the Heart of the Whore*, by journalist Jacques Pauw. In it he reveals Du Plessis's involvement in Kondile's disappearance and how he 'faked' his release, based on the testimony of Vlakplaas commander Dirk Coetzee:

> *On 10 August 1981 Captain Hermanus 'Doep' du Plessis of the security police in Port Elizabeth had sent a message to Security Branch headquarters in Pretoria informing them that the interrogation of the 'subject' was completed, that there was no case against him but that he was willing to become a police informer. According to the message, he was then released.*

Sizwe's father, Port Elizabeth attorney Dumile Kondile, was told by Du Plessis that on 10 August he personally took the detainee back to Bloemfontein where his car was standing. His son was allowed to proceed to wherever he wanted to go and he was not seen again by any member of the South African Police. However, nine years later a police document would show that more than a month after Kondile's official release, he was still in police custody in the Eastern Cape.

Both men sit in silence and stare directly ahead, each contemplating their next move, when all of a sudden, with the fumbling strategy of a Keystone Cop, Du Plessis blurts out a partial secret.

'There's one thing that I want to tell you later on. Only one small thing. But not now.'

'Not now?' Vusi asks, incredulous.

'No, because, honestly, you're not going to believe me.'

'Say it. I will tell you whether I believe it or not.'

'I'll tell you later.'

Du Plessis recounts an innocuous anecdote about the TRC but doesn't get away with it for long before Vusi pushes him again. He wants to know the full secret.

'In that same thing about Kondile, I told a small lie, but that I'll tell you later why,' says Du Plessis, his fingers indicating the tiny size of the lie he says he told. 'It does change nothing, or I think that's so in some people's mind, but we didn't lie, honestly. I mean, that's why we decided to go there. We decided in my house to go and testify in the TRC. And the people looked after us, the TRC people. That's why we were honestly telling them everything. Shit, you can just tell what you know.'

Du Plessis refuses to reveal what the lie was.

Instead he tells me how good it feels to see Vusi, how much he respects him as a man and how he will absolutely try to help him by reading through his files and trying to recollect what happened to Sizwe. Out of the corner of my eye, I can see Vusi shifting uncomfortably and the grimace on his face. Finally, he has had enough of the chumminess.

'Let's cut it out,' he says straight to Du Plessis. 'At that time, we were enemies. I was on the other side, you were on the other side. I don't blame you for that. You had to defend apartheid and you did. I had to fight against apartheid and I did. For me the thing is, now that the war is over, let us sit down, former adversaries, people who were on different sides of the battle lines, and have this decent chat that we're having, because if you had any chance you would have killed me. Had I had a chance, I would have killed you. Let's respect each other and not try to say, "He was a nice guy." It was not a nice war.'

'No, it wasn't,' the old cop concedes.

'I want sincerity, I want to discuss with honesty the situation at the time. I knew what you were doing. It was war. Now the war is over. We can have a drink together. But at least we need to know the stories that happened. You are an old man now, you are independent, you've got your own thinking.'

'Let me just sort that out and go back to my records and talk to you openly.'

Du Plessis admits that he is still concerned about being prosecuted for the crimes he committed under apartheid and that he even considered going to see Vusi when he was still the NDPP. Vusi gives him an assurance that he is not interested in his prosecution or conviction. He simply wants to establish the truth.

I ask him if, in his quiet reflective moments, he regrets what he did during his time as a policeman?

'Well, we can never say it was a good thing. There was a war and we had to do what we were supposed to do. But still, I don't know how to tell you, it's difficult.' He shrugs his shoulders and gives me a half-hearted smile. He is struggling to verbalise how he's feeling, desperate to remain politically correct. 'If I can get my life over again, I would rather listen to my mom when she told me to become a teacher. But still we had good times also.'

Vusi interjects, 'I would do exactly the same thing that I did. And, Captain, you should be able to say you would not have lasted in the police services if you did not believe what you were doing was right. You should be man enough and a soldier enough to say it.'

'While we were there, there was nothing else you could do. We tried to do it as best you can. We're sorry that some people had to die. We knew that if you're in a war, somebody can die. But I don't like it. I'm not a soldier, I was a police officer.'

Vusi has reached boiling point.

'No, no.' He wags his finger at the old man. 'You're not going to get away with this.' The scrawny, haggard security guard puts down his bottle in the plastic packet and turns to face our table. 'Don't say you were not a soldier. You were a policeman. We were killed by policemen from 1976 onwards. You were part of that machinery.'

'No, I wasn't.'

'You guys were in the security branch and you were dealing with political issues. You were part and parcel of that machinery. You can't separate the two.'

Du Plessis concedes and Vusi simmers. The two break the awkward tension by giggling in disagreement. Vusi calls for the bill. There is no point continuing. Du Plessis again gives Vusi an undertaking that he will come back to him with answers but that never happens. The security guard watches as the crumpled old man walks away and Vusi heads off to his car, which he's parked a distance away from the venue, an old underground operative instinct – 'Just in case', he says.

In the quiet serenity of Vusi's home office in Faerie Glen, we 'debrief' about the meeting. How does he feel it went? He's still frustrated and annoyed by Du Plessis's reluctance to speak freely.

'He reminds me of the old apartheid policemen. He's suffering from selective amnesia and I think it's part of police training in terms of the conspiracy of silence. You heard him saying that he would think about it, he would get in touch with some people and he would come back to me. He is retired, he is independent, he is getting old, he should be able to just come out openly. He's still sharp mentally. It's just that he does not want to remember about Sizwe. He does not want to give more details about it. So it's a deliberate amnesia. He was cagey. I could tell that he's afraid of a possible prosecution. I think he has got this overriding fear at the back of his mind that he might still be prosecuted for not having disclosed everything.'

Vusi is particularly irritated by Du Plessis's *boetie-boetie* attitude towards him.

'Had I met him outside South Africa or even inside the country when I was on one of my missions, I would not have hesitated to shoot him. I think the same with him. We need to be honest about it and talk about it and not make out as if we were friends or that it just happened to be like that. It was war. And many people died in the process. Many families were broken up. People suffered. It was not a picnic. I didn't like the sort of patronising attitude that he was having. I felt that he was not being genuine about it.

'It annoyed me when he said that he didn't kill Sizwe. Of course, he might not have been the one who gave him the poison, who shot him in the head and even responsible for burning him. But he was part of the group. He played a role in deciding that Sizwe needed to be killed. And he left with Sizwe from Jeffrey's Bay all the way to Komatipoort. You have got a man that you know you are going to kill. You drive all the way from the Eastern Cape to the Eastern Transvaal at the time. There's no way he could have said that. Why did he go to the TRC if he didn't kill Sizwe? What was he applying for in terms of amnesty?

'So I suppose it's the first meeting, perhaps it is just a feeling-out meeting. I'm not sure whether … I'm not sure whether … or perhaps I am still angry. I'm not sure.'

What does Vusi make of the 'little lie' that Du Plessis hinted at?

'There's no way in which Sizwe's story can start from Bloemfontein. I'm interested in finding out what that little lie is. As people who were on different sides of the war for national liberation, I'm not moved by any vengeance. I knew what I was doing when I joined the struggle for national liberation. I just want him to be honest and own up. And just be truthful about what happened.'

Even though his questions were not answered, Vusi feels at least some sense of catharsis and is relieved that he has finally been able to sit across from his nemesis and meet him face to face.

Despite Du Plessis's assurance that there will be further meetings, Vusi does not hold out much hope. In reality, no further meetings ever take place and Vusi never hears from the old cop again. He also does not try to call him. However, Vusi still maintains that there is scope for discussion and he envisages a forum for erstwhile adversaries who were involved in opposing sides of the war for national liberation to sit down and talk.

'I still think it was good that I met him. To sit down man to man, eyeball to eyeball. I hope that we will be big enough and man enough to own up. I hope that many of us who fought this war on different sides will be courageous enough to meet and talk as erstwhile enemies. And bury the past and say, "Let us move forward".'

Keeping the faith

I love the ANC. To some, it might seem inexplicable that I still maintain such loyalty to the organisation after what I have been through over the past decade, but I remain a paid-up member of the party. I still regularly attend branch meetings and participate in policy discussions in my branch. When I meet old friends, we talk ANC. When Phaki and I sit down together in Port Elizabeth, we talk politics; when Thozi is in town, we talk politics. It is what affects us on a daily basis.

I know the ANC does not always do the right thing and I get incredibly frustrated by this, but it would take a lot for me to abandon the party because I still believe it will come right. We are going through a necessary stage in the evolution of a liberation organisation and all such organisations go through dips and rises, ebbs and flows.

I genuinely remain optimistic about the ANC, even though when I look at the state of the ANC today, it is not good. There will always be denials about weaknesses in the unity of the party but the truth of the matter is we are not a united, solid organisation. Due to the conduct of some members, we don't see things in the same way we used to when we were fighting for our liberation. We wouldn't be killing one another in the North West, Mpumalanga and KwaZulu-Natal if all were fine and going smoothly. We would not have the spat between the trade unions NUM and NUMSA, the public outbursts and the sudden falling-out with COSATU and Zwelinzima Vavi. What is happening within COSATU is a reflection of what is occurring internally within the ANC. We need to be honest about the problems we are currently experiencing – and we need good leadership that is honest and strong enough to tackle these problems.

I have no doubt that my critics will use this statement to claim I am not loyal to the organisation and I am looking to start a fight. But I am not going behind anyone's back; I am prepared to stand up and say this anywhere – let us not lie to our people and say we are a united party, because that is simply not true. We need to stop pretending we do not have problems; we need to solve them.

These problems include issues of corruption, of cronyism, of promoting self-interest.

We see people in positions for which they are ill-suited, and cadre deployment is resulting in people being appointed to support principals when they are not qualified to do so. They are put into positions because it is known they can approve certain tenders that will benefit comrades. That is a fact of life. They use revolutionary-sounding phrases and appear militant, yet they act in a way that is counter-revolutionary.

The ANC needs to renew itself and that is only possible with new leadership. We need a new cadre. We talked about this idea of a 'new cadre' as far back as 2000, at the ANC's midterm National General Council, held between elective conferences, in Port Elizabeth when we came up with 'Through the eye of the needle' – a new type of cadre that this organisation requires to take the struggle forward to consolidate the gains of our revolution. We need a committed cadre who is selfless.

I don't believe we can blame any one person for the state of the organisation and it is not helpful to point a finger at someone such as Julius Malema, who was misguided and misled by people who have been able to get away with things.

Malema did a lot of damage, but he enjoyed the backing of party leadership at the time, so why should responsibility lie with him alone? Why should we individualise the issues? Where was the leadership? At one stage, it was even suggested that Malema was set to become president of the ANC and eventually the country. He should not be the only one in the dock – when you speak of the damage done to the ANC there are several co-accused. I have no doubt that if Malema was still in political favour, he would not be facing criminal charges today.

And still I believe that the future of the ANC is bright. I am hopeful a new generation of leaders will rise out of the organisation. Individuals are produced by the conditions of the time and I am convinced sound leaders will emerge. Within the party there has always been some sense of the collective, and that identity politics is not at play. The truth of the matter is that you can speak of collective leadership, but as a president of the ANC, you must possess certain qualities, qualities that actually help define the organisation. As the leader, you should be able to influence and change the direction when and if necessary.

Many may not have liked Thabo Mbeki's style of doing things, but there was no uncertainty while he was at the helm. He had views on the economy, he had views on African renewal, he had views on HIV – whether you agreed with him or not – but he could stand up and argue his point and try to persuade or influence you on why you should follow his point of view. At the time of Mandela, we knew we had a leader. At the time of Tambo, at the time of Albert Luthuli, we knew we had a leader.

As the ANC, we should move away from the concept that people should not contest elections and they should wait until they are nominated by branches. By fostering that position we are contributing to the lie. People do campaign for positions, they mobilise support, and in some instances they even pay for positions. Why should we perpetuate this lie, this false modesty? It is rubbish.

The impact of slate politics is that you lose leadership. If a person is seen to be falling in with one group, regardless of how good he or she is as an individual, that person will not make it onto the NEC of the party.

People should be free to mobilise and campaign for the leaders they want and there's nothing wrong with that. If people think they are ready to lead, then they should avail themselves. They should tell us what they are going to do for the organisation and for the country.

In the run-up to the elective conference in Mangaung in 2012, we heard stories about money being used to influence people to vote in a particular direction. Even in my own branch, when we were about to begin nominations, all of a sudden we had food and drinks and a member had taken it upon herself to organise this, which we never had before.

The constitution of the ANC states very clearly that anybody can contest an election in any position. Nowhere in the constitution does it say that if you want to stand for a position, you must be nominated by a certain number of branches to be in the NEC. That's why, at a conference, there's an opportunity for people to be nominated from the floor.

And yet, despite all the problems evident in the organisation, it remains my organisation. I get angry and frustrated with it, but it was the first political organisation I belonged to and I see no reason why I should leave it.

Many of my friends and comrades, including my wife, left the ANC to join the Congress of the People (COPE) when it first started. Girly was on the first national executive of COPE that was appointed in Bloemfontein. We didn't argue about her decision to leave the ANC. She was simply fed up with the party and felt that the ANC no longer stood for the same principles and COPE offered her another avenue to pursue:

> *We have very different personalities. Vusi has to be convinced about something. I'm a pragmatist. For me, something has to make sense. It has to be practical. It must have logic. It must have values.*
>
> *We discuss the ANC and I respect his views. He feels that what the ANC stands for is exactly what is documented and what is there and is the way we always grew up. I agree with that.*
>
> *But the truth is that the organisation now is not what is written, is not what you find in those good documents. I still am proud of those documents. But that's not what the leadership in power is about.*
>
> *Vusi has a big heart, he has an ability to appreciate that people make mistakes and one day they will find themselves. And he thinks, he really believes, that this organisation will rise again.*
>
> *I believe more in doing good for my community than in sacrificing everything for the sake of the few who are actually advantaged. When I went to COPE, I was doing exactly that. I can't benefit people who are already rich or who already have full stomachs.*
>
> *And I've seen with my own eyes how people steal, how they take from those they are meant to be protecting. Long before I resigned, I saw it. That's why I'm saying the disappointment started happening while I was still working there. So this was more like a crystallisation of things.*
>
> *There was a period in which I was in mourning. I was sad and upset about Vusi's suspension, but I was never as sad as when I saw what was happening when they started the process of evicting Thabo out of office.*

> *I'm crying – sometimes, actually, physically crying – for what is happening to the country. This is the start of all our values crumbling because it's about our short-term pleasures. Is this what I wasted my time for? This absolute nonsense?*
>
> *It was also the sheer impact of being disappointed by many of those comrades who could not bring themselves to stand up and say, 'This, I'm not going to be party to.' I would think of Chris, think of Comrade O.R. – a gentleman and a father figure – who sacrificed so much. For this? Where are we now? Where are we now?*
>
> *But then I saw some of our comrades say, 'I'm getting out.' That's what brought me out of mourning. I said, 'I want to make a statement as an individual and I am an individual separate from Vusi.'*

When she drove to Bloemfontein to explore what COPE was all about, I didn't see any reason why I should go with her. I had no problem with the formation of another political party and with COPE arriving on the scene. Our Constitution calls for a multiparty democracy. If people want to leave the ANC then they should not be held back. No one should be a prisoner of any organisation.

Girly has since left COPE and politics altogether. She remains angry with the ANC but I think at heart she is still ANC.

My kids often tease me that I exhibit all the symptoms of a battered wife and that by insisting on remaining loyal to the ANC I am suffering from 'battered-wife syndrome'. I laugh and take it on the chin because I know that I am loyal.

When I joined the ANC, it was the only vehicle I felt was adequate to take us to our liberation. Close friends and comrades argue with me and say the time has come, the organisation has expired, we need a new cadre, we need new skills. I often agree with them, but the time has not yet come for me actually to leave the organisation.

Many thought I would be amongst the first to join COPE and they did in fact try to win me over. Some comrades I never thought would leave the ANC decided to go. It was a natural development because there is no liberation movement that has fought a war for national liberation and not had its splits.

Dr Mamphela Ramphele's Agang initiative is another example of how people feel that our current political organisations are not going to achieve what the majority wants. They are frustrated with corruption, with the lack of foresight, with ongoing poverty, with a lack of vision, with being stuck in the past.

The ANC will never rule 'until Jesus comes'. By way of an example, ZANU came into power in 1980 and has ruled for 33 years. Signs of cracking began to appear around 2000, which was natural, and the strength of ZANU has deteriorated since despite being declared victors of the 2013 elections. History has shown that the life cycle of any national liberation movement is not linear but rather cyclical. Usually, after about 20 years, they experience splits, divisions and splinters – this happened to ZANU and it is now happening to the ANC.

The day I leave the ANC will be the day it begins to brutalise or terrorise opponents and kill political adversaries publicly, which is what has happened in Zimbabwe. That will be the point at which I pack my bags and go. But it would take an extreme situation for me to leave the party. At times I ask myself, 'Is it still worth it to remain in this organisation?' but I have not yet reached the threshold that will see me walk.

Crooks protecting crooks

The current state of the National Prosecuting Authority, one of the most crucial institutions in South Africa, is shameful. Some of the appointments that have been made are simply shocking.

Prosecutors are powerful people. They can ruin innocent lives if their work is not done with integrity, objectivity and impartiality – all of which are compromised if there is political or other interference. By interference, I do not only mean by the executive, but also the influence of friends, family and business people.

It is a power that must be carefully exercised. I would rather be seen as rigid than as politically flexible. If you act in the interests of today's politicians and they lose power, you will have to dance according to the tune of the new power. We should not be ruled by the whims of those who govern us; we should be ruled according to the law. It is the rule of law and not the rule of mere mortals that underpins our work.

Certain things that happened after I left the NPA have contributed to my concerns about the state of the organisation and its commitment to the independence of prosecutors. The first of these was when a press statement was drawn up by the NPA regarding my suspension – it had to be vetted by the minister and permission for it to be released was refused. Collectively, the prosecutors had made a decision and then someone at a political level gave them an instruction. They did not exercise their independence on the issue and they showed that if they could be subject to such influence, they were also vulnerable on more important matters. That was immediately an indicator to me that things were going downhill.

The second source of serious concern for me was when Mpshe was told by politicians to review my decision on Selebi and appoint an independent panel, even though he had been party to the decision that had been taken.

Then there was Menzi Simelane's appointment as a deputy national director. During his very first remarks to the employees at the NPA, he indicated that he was there to do the ANC's bidding. Simelane then overturned Willie Hofmeyr's decision on the freezing of Arms Deal suspect Fana Hlongwane's bank accounts in Switzerland, which was another indicator of what was to come. Never mind that Minister Jeff Radebe had ignored the Public Service Commission's recommendation to act against Simelane following his comments at the Ginwala Inquiry.

Perhaps the most obvious cause for concern about the slackening of prosecutorial independence was the decision by Mpshe to withdraw charges against Jacob Zuma. It was clear to me then that the leaders of the organisation were not performing according to their oath of office.

This is most evident in the appointments that have been made at the institution. The fact that Nomgcobo Jiba was acting as national director of public prosecutions for over a year and a half, Lawrence Mrwebi is head of the Specialised Commercial Crimes Unit (SCCU) and Prince Mokotedi is in charge of the Integrity Management Unit is astonishing.

These are the people who acted against the NPA (by testifying for Selebi in his trial) and were behind the arrest of Selebi prosecutor Gerrie Nel – an act of intimidation to show they were still powerful. The role played by Jiba, and her subsequent elevation, is simply baffling. If you look at how her husband was given a presidential pardon, it leaves you with the impression that people are rewarded for what they do for the powers that be, irrespective of their competence. It also gives the impression that they are there to do as expected of them by those who put them there.

I would not have expected Mrwebi to be appointed as head of the SCCU, because when he was in charge of the Scorpions in KwaZulu-Natal, his weaknesses meant that we had to take steps to discipline him. Minister Mabandla and Simelane actually intervened to stop me from taking action against Mrwebi, which was one of the things that led to my memorandum of complaint to the minister in 2006.

What kind of appointments are these?

The fact that prosecutor Glynnis Breytenbach was suspended for her determination to prosecute former Crime Intelligence head Richard Mdluli is an example of what I am talking about. It smacks of political interference by the leadership of the NPA to protect a friend.

I have a lot of respect and admiration for Breytenbach. I know her as a tough prosecutor who takes no nonsense and who is straightforward. She will do her job the way she sees fit and is always guided by the law. I've never known her to be at anybody's beck and call. As a result, I am inclined to believe her version of things rather than to accept what is being put forward by the NPA.

Advocate Wim Trengove, who acted for me in my own challenge, is also representing Advocate Breytenbach in her fight against the NPA. He sums up the scenario:

> *You can look at recent affairs as a good example. It was necessary for Zuma to get pliant crooks at the NPA. Today you sit there with crooks, advised by crooks, abusing the NPA. The NPA with the Scorpions was an extraordinary institution. Very few countries in the world have crime-fighting units that actually have the balls to go for the deputy president and for the commissioner of police. The fact that we had institutions with the guts to do it was an unbelievable compliment for our society but we now, from being one of the stars in the world, we have now deteriorated to being one of the lesser lights.*
>
> *It's a double tragedy because the people who have been in charge of the NPA are firstly corrupt and they use the power for corrupt purposes. But it's a double tragedy because they have been put in charge of the NPA for that quality of being pliant and not for their skill, so the organisation is also inefficiently run. Nobody is looking after the shop and the quality of leadership and administration and management is disintegrating and that is why you get J. Arthur Brown getting away and these spectacular failures like Andries Tatane and Anene Booysen. And they are merely the ones that make the headlines. In the courts, at ground level, the quality of prosecution is appalling. Crooks are getting away with it because the organisation is being run for its political purposes rather than to be an effective crime-fighting machine.*

> *Unless you have a very strong principal insulating those who exercise the power to prosecute from improper influence and you allow the political elite to exercise that powerful tool for their own expedient purposes, then you deteriorate into a society where people get prosecuted because they are out of political favour and they get protected when they enjoy political protection. The credibility of the justice system then completely disintegrates.*

The NPA was without a permanent, legitimately appointed head from when I was removed from office in 2007 until the end of August 2013. This was an issue of great concern to constitutional organisation CASAC, as its spokesperson Lawson Naidoo explains:

> *Since the time of Vusi's suspension, the NPA if not quite in free fall has been in a downward spiral ever since. We haven't had a credible leader of the NPA since Vusi and I think that was the start of the undermining of the institution and it seems that what is happening now seems to be a deliberate undermining of the credibility of the NPA and I think the NPA is in dire need of someone of the ilk of a Vusi to be back at the helm.*

We see the failures in high-profile cases and the quality of decisions being taken at a higher level, all of which affect public perceptions of the effectiveness of the NPA. I know those perceptions start with the issue of plea bargains and the feeling that those who are rich can always bargain their way out of jail. One of the things I tried to do when I came into office was to clarify that a plea-bargain sentence does not necessarily mean a non-custodial sentence and that granting a deal does not mean there cannot be jail time served. However, I know there is a perception out there that if you have money, you will get off, and this concept is exacerbated by the fact that poorer people only have access to legal aid and can't afford high-priced attorneys. There is always the danger of a miscarriage of justice.

Of course, an accused should be represented in court, but that does not always happen because of the cost of litigation and the price of lawyers. If you conduct a survey of prisons, you will find the majority of convicts are from a disadvantaged background. Because of the corruption within the system, it can happen that if you are rich, you can make it work for you. Naturally, this isn't always the case and we should be careful to avoid generalisations, but at the same time, of course, officials can be bribed. It is important to base the discussion in fact and to treat each case individually.

A sharp 'celebrity' lawyer can take advantage of technicalities in the system and in a criminal matter the burden of proof must be beyond a reasonable doubt. Therefore, the accused does not have to do much in terms of proving his or her innocence. Often, it's a matter of waiting to see how the investigation was conducted and uncovering flaws in the case – did they break any rules and procedures, and were you properly warned when they took your statement? An astute lawyer looks at all those legal requirements in the law and smart criminals who belong to organised crime syndicates always keep the best criminal lawyers on retainer. It becomes a mismatch if you don't have properly trained investigators and prosecutors who are not skilful or experienced – poorly trained and inexperienced prosecutors and investigators are no match for skilled and experienced litigating lawyers.

A debate on the effectiveness of the criminal justice system in fighting crime needs to consider other factors too, such as the work of law enforcement and the police.

I've always referred to the National Crime Prevention Strategy adopted by cabinet in 1996, which seems to have been abandoned. The emphasis there was on coming up with ways and means of preventing crime and not only dealing with crime after it has occurred. That is a strategy that must be put in place at a national level. What do we do to prevent crime? Once a crime has occurred, how do you then come up with sentences that also act as a deterrent to those who continue to commit crime? We need to consider a combination of factors.

It is important for criminals to be deterred by an effective criminal justice system rather than simply laugh at the efficacy of the courts. A person who has planned a crime has done so with confidence that he or she is not going to be arrested. And if he or she is arrested, then the criminal is equally confident about how to go about beating the system.

From empirical studies and my own experience, only about 10 per cent of people can be considered inherently 'bad'. Another 10 per cent are genuinely good and wouldn't even consider committing a crime. Around 80 per cent of us fall somewhere in the middle. So it doesn't matter how good the criminal justice system is; there will always be that 10 per cent criminal element. The issue is to look at the 80 per cent and how to deter them from committing a crime.

As citizens of South Africa, we shouldn't blindly trust the criminal justice system – that system must earn the trust of the people. But this depends on what measures are put in place and who is appointed to do this. It starts at the top with the leadership of the organisation.

At the end of August 2013, President Jacob Zuma finally relented and appointed a new NDPP. KwaZulu-Natal attorney Mxolisi Nxasana was named as the new director. Little was known about him at the time of his appointment and his ability to handle the position will be watched closely. The NPA needs a new head to restore the dignity of an organisation that is faced with a lack of leadership – and the influence of political pressure is glaring. As Trengove articulates, the NDPP must be fiercely independent and impartial, and must not buckle under undue political pressure:

> *The organisation can only be as independent as the NDPP is because the rest of the organisation has very little independence. They depend to a large extent for their independence on the protection of their boss, and if their boss doesn't protect them and their boss connives with those who want to corrupt the organisation, then there's very little left.*
>
> *What I think is perhaps the most devastating impact of the Pikoli story is not only that a great injustice happened to him, but that it will leave a lasting message to all his successors that you dare not stand up to the powerful elite because they will destroy you. I think the impact of what they did to him will far outlive him and the time that he should have been there as NDPP. That is why I think, for instance, resistance by small fry like Breytenbach is important because it might help to stem the tide. If she were to go down, it will simply reinforce the message broadcast by the Pikoli saga that as prosecutors you should not trust this fanciful idea that the Constitution protects you or your independence. Ultimately, if you come up against the powerful elite, you'll be squashed. That for me is the worst part of the Pikoli story – the message that it sent to Pikoli and other constitutional office bearers like him who are told that ultimately the elite will have their way.*

The political dice

When I cast my mind back to the night I went into exile and my unit and I were scrambling through darkness over that mountain into freedom, our mission was to fight a system we believed to be unjust. I knew that when I left the country, anything could happen. I could have died in exile as Sizwe did. But it was a risk I was prepared to take rather than staying behind in South Africa, graduating from Fort Hare and working as a lawyer at home. I made that choice and embraced the sacrifices that came with it.

I look now at what I have been through and where I am today, and my own situation pales into insignificance compared to fellow ex-combatants whose position is far, far worse. There are people who sacrificed everything, who went to the camps, who left school at an early age, who came back and fought in this country. They risked life and limb and their living conditions today are terrible, and I think they are worse off than they were when they left the country. My friend Thozi feels much the same way:

> *Everybody is thinking about his stomach now, not about the country and about the people. We always say we are fighting for the poorest of the poor, but are we really doing that? People are still starving. You know they still cry. They meet me in the street, they still call me their commissar and I feel so bad when I see them. 'Commissar? You left us now.' And the last words O.R. Tambo said to me, the last words on the 10th of April 1993 in*

> *my camp in Uganda. He called me next to the chopper when he was there and he said, 'You take care of these kids. Take care of these kids.' Those words are still vivid and fresh in my mind. Everybody is asking me, why are you not?*

So I can still sit here, in my comfortable home, and I can have nice food and I can talk about so many things. I can be philosophical; I can use highfalutin language and have intellectual debates. But many people face real, grinding poverty and desperation is part of their everyday lives.

No one thought we would come into power and all of a sudden millions of our people would live a better life. No one was that naïve, but what is both annoying and frustrating is to witness the daylight looting of our resources that could have gone towards uplifting the living standards of our people.

Citizens would be willing to wait their turn for improvements in service delivery to come to their villages or townships if there was a clear indication that the government does not tolerate corruption. People would be prepared to hold out if they could see a principled leadership that is able to allocate resources appropriately and to ensure there is no misappropriation. They would be patient if we did not have politicians who occupy senior positions with their fingers in the cookie jar. People are being killed for exposing corruption.

Of course, no nation has been able to solve all its problems overnight and even countries that achieved democracy a long time ago still experience high levels of unemployment and poverty. But in a country like South Africa, endowed with so many resources, you still sit in Sandton and look across and see poverty in Alexandra, you stand in Dainfern and you look across at the misery in Diepsloot. And these inequalities are widening by the day.

As a democratically elected government that has committed itself to uplifting and bettering the lives of our people, you would expect it to do more than any other government in rooting out corruption. You can't have ministers being accused of corruption day in and day out; you can't have the president being accused of corruption.

I am mindful of the fact the charges against Zuma were withdrawn, but that doesn't take away from the fact that Zuma once faced those charges and the matter never went to court. That is what people will always remember.

I've always seen the driving forces behind the corruption currently ravaging the country as a combination of three bad factors: a corrupt civil servant, a corrupt politician and a corrupt business person.

From personal experience, the genesis of this corruption dates back to when we were in exile. People operated in underground conditions, in secrecy, and the things that suffered were transparency and accountability. If there is no transparency and accountability, then whom do you hold liable?

At a basic level, it came down to the command structures. During the time of the liberation struggle, when you needed to infiltrate inside the country, a report would note that a unit had been given *X* amount of money. Who would dispute that? The unit would be inside the country and you would not write a report to Lusaka to say, 'We were given *Y* and not *X*.' Receipts were not signed and the lowest levels of command answered to the highest.

This may be something of an oversimplification, but the same scenario applies to grand corruption at the level of the state. It is important to speak to low-level corruption in order to understand the problem.

The majority of our people spent years in exile fighting, not governing. People spent years on Robben Island, imprisoned and not governing. Then, in 1994, we had to take over. We had all these brilliant ideas. We had a framework of what needed to be done. But, of course, the apartheid system itself was intrinsically corrupt. The public service has always been corrupt. We had people coming back from exile who had nothing and had never worked in a government office. Now they were occupying senior positions, were politically powerful and had access to political and economic control of state resources.

They came back to find their homesteads destroyed and their people looking at them as if to say, 'Now that you are free, what is in it for us?' They were put under so much pressure. Then, of course, there were corrupt business people who knew how to make their money. They would step in and say, 'No, no, we can get you a flat, we can rent it for you, don't worry. I've got three cars, I can give you one. We'll take care of your kids,' and people fell for those promises.

I remember how excited I was when I was given a monthly salary of R4 000 when I returned from exile. But within two years somebody else approached me and offered me a job for R12 000 a month. I turned it down because I was still shocked by the idea of earning R4 000 a month. How many comrades would have jumped at that? Some comrades lost their way, but others, the majority, were able to stay true to their course.

That's the roll of the political dice.

I still believe the ANC counts among its numbers many, many sincere individuals who are in the majority. But if those people don't play ball then they are out of the game. The only way to fix it is to act against it. But the fixing must start at the top and filter down, from the president to whoever is next in line. People will always look to those at the top and every day the leaders talk about fighting corruption and setting up structures and strengthening laws. But what happens when people are compelled to act? What happens when investigators have to act against them? What happens to prosecutors when they want to prosecute?

What happens? You see curious appointments being made. Important cases are withdrawn.

We must have a true commitment, in real terms and at a practical level, not at a level of talking. This government must act against corruption and not select who should be charged with corruption while others are allowed to get away with murder. It seems as though only once people fall out of political favour are they charged. That's the reality we are faced with – and it's not right. When you have a government remote-controlled by criminals and people are so entrenched in corrupt practices and have been bankrolled by corrupt business people, they can't escape it. Billions of rand have been lost to corruption as a result.

When I cast my ballot for the very first time in 1994, I was so absorbed by the magnitude of the moment that I didn't think about where we would be as a country 20 years into democracy. We had all these grand ideas and had engaged in so many consultative meetings and seminars and conferences. We knew what had to be changed, we were clear in our minds about it and we didn't underestimate the size of the problem and of the challenge. But somehow we have managed to create an overwhelming dependence on the state, a perception that government will be able to provide everything to everyone.

Apartheid is a fact of our past and of our present, but how do you blame poor service delivery on apartheid? How do you blame apartheid when there is a budget and it is meant to last? How do you explain a lack of textbooks at schools other than the tenders were corruptly awarded? How do you blame apartheid for poor transport for pupils? How do you blame apartheid for the fact that children are not receiving food from a feeding scheme when a tender has been awarded for it?

Who is responsible for these failures?

We are! We must admit our own shortcomings because only then will we be able to address them. If we don't, we will go on blindly for the next 20 or even 40 years. And the patience of people is not endless. South Africans are not stupid and they expect delivery.

We cannot look past the fact that we are in charge now and we have a democratically elected government. All we have fought for simply cannot be in vain.

I have lost many comrades along this journey and several have paid the ultimate price, none more so than Sizwe, who died at the hands of the security policemen in a most brutal and cruel way. The murder of my best friend could not have been for nothing. It is important for his story to be told as a testament to those who have given so much for our freedom and democracy, and to remind us how deeply we should value where we are today.

Those comrades we lost along the way would be devastated, disappointed and frustrated by where the country is today. I don't think they would be pleased with what we have become, given the fact that we are an increasingly unequal society, the fact that we are still struggling with issues of poverty and a high rate of unemployment, and the fact that we have rampant corruption in our country. I fear the impending demise of our hard-won democracy if corruption is not limited soon. But I don't think comrades like Sizwe would have simply folded their hands, watched and kept quiet. They would have continued to play a role that would save us from total collapse.

It has been a difficult journey, both personally for me and for the country, but overall there have been more ups than downs. I have not lost faith in humankind. I still believe in the goodness of humanity until proven otherwise. It has been tough, but my faith in God has never been shaken. I feel at peace with myself for doing what I did, even though I encountered extreme challenges along the way.

During the difficult stretches I have always maintained that the sun would rise again and I have been hopeful that things would change for the better. I have had moments of weakness in which I failed to listen to my heart and have succumbed to pressure. But for me, it is about what makes me sleep comfortably at night and doing what I believe in. I always want to be able to look my interviewer in the eye and have a clear conscience about what I am saying.

In Memoriam: Sizwe Kondile

They yanked him from the phone
With the skill of wolves
Bundled and brought nearer home
To bare his soul.
His cries filled the motherland
And we gasped appalled,
'Are they still at it?
When will they stop?'
He was so close
Yet we didn't know.

With needles of death
They punctured his life,
At Nkomati signed for the soul.
A gun salute
Sealed the deal with the devil.

They were laughing
When they set him ablaze
Making an offering to gods.
They were dancing
While they braaied alongside
Starting the fire from his ashes
Eating and drinking with joy
A satanic communion
To dare God.
They ate him and left no bone
That we may bury
That we may bury.

Winston Mzikayise Mahola

Acknowledgements

I would like to thank the following people who have played an important role in my life and in the completion of this book:

- my wife Girly for standing by me through thick and thin and for insisting that I complete my LLB and LLM;
- my children for their understanding and accepting that we could not send them to private schools because we had to share the little we had with the extended family;
- my sisters and brothers for all their support during the hard times;
- my uncles and aunts for their visits and prayers;
- Sandile and Baby Nogxina; Twiggs and Brenda Xiphu; Lizo Njenje; Baba Mkangisa; Hlubi and Nolitha Radebe; Bada Pharasi; Bishop Malusi and Sis Thoko Mpumlwana; Sipho and Nkuli Pityana; Kalyani Pillay; Danie Schmidt; Blendyn William;
- the legal team at Webber Wentzel, especially Dario Milo, Greg Palmer and Okyerebea Ampofo-Anti; as well as Wim Trengrove and Faizel Ismail;
- the team at Pan Macmillan publishers, in particular, Andrea Nattrass and Terry Morris; and
- my co-author Mandy Wiener for her scrupulous attention to detail, her integrity and for her care in crafting my story.

All mistakes and errors remain my own.

Vusumzi Pikoli
September 2013

Index